P9-BJK-363

Books by George Thayer

THE WAR BUSINESS
THE FARTHER SHORES OF POLITICS
THE BRITISH POLITICAL FRINGE

The War Business

THE INTERNATIONAL TRADE IN ARMAMENTS

by

George Thayer

A CLARION BOOK

Published by Simon and Schuster

A Clarion Book
Published by Simon and Schuster
Rockefeller Center, 630 Fifth Avenue
New York, New York 10020

First paperback printing 1970

SBN 671-20705-9
Library of Congress Catalog Card Number: 74-75868
Manufactured in the United States of America

To

Fergus and Anne Reid

Contents

Foreword

This is a book about the international trade, or traffic, in armaments, with special emphasis on developments since 1945.

By *international,* I mean that I am concerned here more with the fact that the U.S. government exports tanks to foreign nations than I am with the fact that the Chrysler Corporation makes tanks for the U.S. government. Likewise, I am concerned more with the fact that Lee Harvey Oswald's assassination rifle was imported into the United States from Italy rather than I am with the fact that the weapon was purchased by mail order from Klein's.

By *trade,* or *traffic,* I mean the sale rather than the grant aid (or giveaway) of arms. Grant aid still plays a part in today's arms trade, and it is commented upon in the following volume wherever appropriate; but the primary thrust in recent years has been to sell arms, and it is this aspect on which I wish to concentrate.

By *armaments,* I mean the actual instruments used to kill people in battle: rifles, pistols, tanks, artillery, fighter and bomber aircraft, missiles, warships and explosives. Occasionally, where it seems appropriate, I have strayed from this path to include such items as engines, electronic equipment and other "nonlethal" goods. The words arms, armaments, weapons, weapons systems, hardware and ordnance are all used interchangeably even though each has a slightly different meaning.

Lest there be any misunderstanding, this is not a book about America's, or any other country's, domestic gun trade; nor does it concern itself with military-industrial complexes except insofar as they are involved in the international arms trade.

The major purpose of this book is to examine exactly how and why the post-World War II international arms trade works and to what extent the presence or acquisition of arms encourages the outbreak or the continuation of hostilities. Also of concern is the effect weapons have on a particular situation, the forces at play, and how both donor and recipient countries are influenced by the trade in arms. No true understanding of the subject is possible, nor can any corrective steps be taken, unless this is done.

The nature of the arms trade militates against the full story ever being told. There is too much at stake for the subject to become one of general conversation for those intimately connected with its operations. However, background material was made available to me from a number of well-informed individuals with the understanding that the sources remain confidential. To all of them who put their trust in me I wish to record my debt and gratitude. Their information has been extremely valuable.

Equally as valuable has been the help I received from public sources. I wish to acknowledge my gratitude to them here in detail. Almost without exception they bring to the study of this subject an enthusiasm and doggedness that I envy. My research was made infinitely more rewarding by their assistance and cooperation.

I would first like to thank Senators Clark, Dodd, Fulbright and McCarthy, and Congressmen Farbstein, Gross and Widnall for all the material they sent me. I am also most grateful for the material sent me by the late Senator Robert F. Kennedy. I am particularly indebted to Miss Amelia Leiss, Mr. Uri Ra'anan and Mr. Bart Whaley of the Center for International Studies at the Massachusetts Institute of Technology; Mr. John H. Hoagland and Mr. Erastus Corning, III, of the Browne & Shaw Research Corporation in Waltham, Massachusetts; the Honorable Alastair Buchan and Mr. Geoffrey Kemp of the Institute for Strategic Studies in London; and Mr. Kenneth M. Glazier, librarian at the Hoover Institution on War, Revolution and Peace at Stanford University, who permitted me access to their research material. I am also indebted to the (London) *Sun* and the Washington *Post* newspapers for allowing me access to their clippings, and to Herr Hans Klatte of *Der Spiegel,* Miss Jeanne Kuebler formerly with *Editorial Re-*

search Reports, Mr. George Franklin of the Council on Foreign Relations, Mr. Joe H. Wagner of *Military Export Reporter,* and Miss Johanna J. Bosch of the Fellowship of Reconciliation, who helped me find special source material. To the staff of the Senate Subcommittee to Investigate Juvenile Delinquency, to Miss Alma Kieny, Special Assistant to Mr. Henry Kuss, and to Colonel Grover Heiman, Jr., and Lieutenant Colonel C. W. Burtyk of the Defense Department's Book and Magazine Division, I wish to express my appreciation for all the courtesies they extended.

I also wish to express my gratitude to Mr. Henry C. Armstrong, Mr. Stephen C. Barber of the London *Sunday Telegraph,* Mr. Oliver Carruthers of Gemini News Service, Miss Kay Halle, Mr. Richard Kershaw, former editor of *Africa Confidential,* Mrs. Elizabeth K. MacAfee, Mr. Charles Burton Marshall of Johns Hopkins University's Washington Center of Foreign Policy Research, Mr. Spencer T. Olin, Mr. George R. Packard, III, Mr. Fergus Reid, III, Mr. Andrew St. George, Mr. Neil Sheehan of *The New York Times,* Mr. and Mrs. D. Thomas Stern, Mr. William H. Tantum, IV, of the National Shooting Sports Foundation, Mr. Charles W. Thayer, and Mr. John S. Tompkins, formerly of *Business Week*. Their expertise in various aspects of the arms trade was invaluable to me.

To Miss Susanna Schroder I am most grateful for the help she gave in translating foreign language source material; to Mr. Landon Thomas, Jr., for both help in translations and financial analyses; to Mr. Michael V. Korda, my editor, and Mr. Val J. Forgett for technical assistance; and to Miss Lucy G. Carlborg and Miss Susan T. Koelle who helped me with the paperwork.

I am especially indebted to all those who offered many valuable comments and suggestions on parts of the manuscript.

G.T.

Washington, D.C.
March 1, 1970

Aloof with hermit-eye I scan
The present work of present man—
A wild and dream-like trade of blood and guile,
Too foolish for a tear, too wicked for a smile.

FROM *Ode to Tranquillity,* Samuel Taylor Coleridge

PART ONE

PROLOGUE

I

The Age of Arms

"The Angel of Death has been abroad throughout the land; you may almost hear the beating of his wings."

—JOHN BRIGHT

1

In the twenty-five years since 1945, there have been fifty-six wars of significant size, duration and intensity throughout the world.[1] This means that mankind faces a new and violent conflict somewhere in the world slightly more often than once every five months, any one of which is capable of provoking a holocaust. If one adds to this total all the coups, large-scale riots and clashes of unorganized, low-order violence,[2] then the total of postwar cases of armed conflicts that have had significant impact on the course of history would number in exess of fifteen score—more than one per month.

We have been inclined to view these many wars as relatively small ones, since none have involved the use of nuclear weapons; in truth, the advent of The Bomb has simply upgraded our definition of what is small. Today we are far along the way to losing our sense of proportion, for by any definition many of these wars have been quite large. For instance, bombing tonnage in the Korean War exceeded all the tonnage dropped by the Allies in the Pacific Theatre of World War II. In the "small" six-day Sinai War of 1967, more tanks were committed to battle than by the Germans,

Italians and Allies together at the crucial twelve-day battle of El Alamein in 1942. And from July 1965 to December 1967, more bomb tonnage was dropped on Vietnam than was dropped by the Allies on Europe during *all* of World War II.[3]

One knowledgeable source estimates that today there are some 750 million operable military rifles and pistols extant in the world. In other words, there is one small arm for every adult male on earth. To this inventory of conventional weapons, one must add hundreds of billions of rounds of ammunition and other explosives; tens of millions of machine guns, mortars and antitank weapons; millions of field artillery pieces and armored tanks; a hundred thousand fighter and bomber aircraft; and tens of thousands of missiles and offensive naval craft. In the twenty-five years of the "Atomic Age," it has been these weapons that have done all the killing in the "small" wars we have experienced.

We live in an age of weapons. Never before in the history of mankind have the weapons of war been so dominant a concern as they have been since 1945. Armaments now have enough destructive power to destroy most life on earth. Their acquisition or presence determines, in large part, the makeup of governments, the course of foreign policy, the thrust of economic effort, the social climate in which man lives. No significant act of contemporary history is free of their influence. Few other concerns in the world demand so much effort, time and money.

Armaments can be used to balance international accounts and create prosperity. They are capable of cementing international relationships more effectively than any other human endeavor. They can—and do—provide work that challenges all the skills that man possesses; they create wealth for the manufacturer, the seller, the nation; they stimulate economic and social stability by the maintenance of a high and continuing level of production; and they can create an atmosphere of security and a sense of national unity, purpose and pride that is often reflected at every level of a nation's experience. In one sense, armaments are mankind's most continuing good business.

On the other hand, however useful in trade and diplomacy they may be, armaments cannot be divorced from their function of killing. They can—and do—provoke wars, ruin treasuries, bankrupt nations, destroy property and create panic. Thus, in another sense, armaments are also the world's most unsettling influence.

Man's anxiety about war and its effects has taken on a desperate quality since 1945. We have become obsessed with the question of armaments. At the highest level, this obsession begins with our concern about nuclear weapons. Millions of words have been written on test-ban treaties, space treaties, nonproliferation agreements, the establishment of nuclear-free zones; on questions of strategy, defense, the prevention of misunderstandings and accidents, and the elimination of atmospheric pollution.

Yet, once past these levels of major concern, man has displayed little interest in what is, in many ways, the most crucial postwar political fact of life: *the proliferation of conventional weapons of war.*

One of the major postwar phenomena connected with conventional weapons is the large trade in these items. The yearly volume is estimated to be currently $5 billion. This is more money than the entire world spent annually on defense in the early 1930's. Since 1945 the amount of military aid, whether extended as grant aid or sales, provided by non-communist countries has totaled an estimated $61 billion. Of this, the United States has given away or sold nearly $52 billion in military equipment and services, the United Kingdom has provided an estimated $5 billion, and France approximately $3 billion. The Soviet Union and Red China, and their respective allies, have delivered an additional $8 billion in arms to non-communist nations in the same period of time.[4]*

If we were to plot a graph of the volume of conventional armaments given away or sold since 1945 by the great industrial powers or by private merchants, one would find that the upward curve would closely parallel the curve on the incidence of violence since

* Soviet and Red Chinese arms sales to their own communist allies are considered here as internal transactions and thus, with the exception of Soviet and Red Chinese aid to North Vietnam, which is treated separately in Chapter VIII, are not examined in this volume.

1945. At least one obvious conclusion can be drawn from this—namely, that an increase in the availability of weapons is concomitant with an increase in their use.

The upward curve of violence shows no sign of leveling off. In a speech to the American Society of Newspaper Editors in Montreal on May 18, 1966, Robert S. McNamara, then the United States Secretary of Defense, and a man who should know, said, "The planet is becoming a more dangerous place to live on—not merely because of a potential nuclear holocaust but also because of the large number of *de facto* conflicts and because the trend of such conflicts is growing rather than diminishing."[5]

Consider some of the political consequences that today's arms trade has produced:

The fall of Germany's Erhard government in 1966 can be blamed in large part on Bonn's purchases of American military equipment which it could not afford and did not need.

The cancellation of the *Skybolt* missile by the United States in 1962 was one of the contributing factors that led to Prime Minister Macmillan's resignation in 1963.

The Pakistan-India War of 1965, in which American equipment was used on both sides, produced two results adverse to United States interests: it forced Pakistan to take a more neutral position in world affairs, and it forced India to consider manufacturing nuclear weapons. Had there been no large infusion of American weapons into the area (ostensibly as a defense against communism), the war would not have taken place.

Taiwan, to cite another example, maintains a huge U.S.-equipped military establishment, the total strength of which is too large for internal defense purposes and too small for the purpose of reconquering mainland China. No one yet has explained satisfactorily why Chiang Kai-shek must maintain (mostly at U.S. expense) such a large military force.

Great Britain, by merely selling an obsolete aircraft carrier to Brazil, can precipitate a minor interservice civil war in that large South American country simply over the question of which service is to run the ship.

West Germany can exacerbate world sensibilities by permitting its rocket experts to work for the Egyptian government on missiles obviously designed to destroy Israel. It can further goad public opinion by offering to send gas masks to the Israelis during the six-day Sinai War of 1967.

France and Italy, with equal disdain for public opinion, sell military equipment for political and balance-of-payment reasons to the South African government.

Nor is the Soviet Union free from the consequences of arms sales. It has, for instance, witnessed pro-Soviet governments in Indonesia, Ghana and Algeria ousted by dissidents armed with Soviet weapons. It has seen approximately one billion dollars worth of its equipment either destroyed or captured by the Israelis within six days; it has then been forced to replace the equipment in order to save face and influence in the Arab world.

Consider the ironies of the arms trade today: the United States, perhaps the world's most vocal proponent of disarmament, is also the world's largest seller of arms; emerging nations, needing all the financial resources they can for capital improvements, spend their money on armaments for show; the West German government, overloaded with arms it does not need, is urged to buy more by the United States; the Soviet Union, claiming to champion the equality of all peoples, sells military equipment to South Africa; Red China, barely able to control itself internally, sends arms to rebel groups in Africa; Czechoslovakia, a communist state, sells arms to Western and nonaligned nations with old-fashioned capitalistic fervor; Sweden and Switzerland, both "neutral" nations with long histories of peace, are two of the world's most aggressive arms exporters.

2

The trade, or traffic, in the weapons and accessories of war, as we know it today, can be traced back to the Middle Ages. Undoubtedly instances of this trade predate this era by many centuries, but as modern man understands the term, it began with the introduction of gunpowder into Europe in the fourteenth century.

The market for powder-charged weapons grew quickly. Kings

and knights demanded cannons—primitive devices called "bombards"—in order to demolish hitherto impregnable battlements. Farsighted warriors began arming their troops with portable weapons, called "arquebuses," which proved highly effective in breaking up squares of pikemen and archers, and ranks of mounted knights in armor.

Such was the demand for these and other weapons that a thriving industry soon sprang up in Europe. Armorers and smithies, previously concerned with the shaping of doublets, corselets, halberds and edged weapons, began turning their attention to the manufacturing of firearms. Most weapons were made for local consumption; however, several entrepreneurs sold their wares throughout Europe, to whoever had the money to pay.

The arms industry first developed in Belgium, in the Liège area. Iron and coal were in plentiful supply, and the roads and rivers provided excellent transportation facilities. The industry soon spread up the Rhine to Solingen, through the Black Forest, over to Bohemia around Prague; then into Italy at Turin, Milan, Florence, Brescia and Pistoia; then to St. Étienne and Bayonne in France; to London and Birmingham in England; and to Seville and Toledo in Spain. These same towns and areas are still today the centers of the European arms industry.

The weaponsmakers of Liège hold a special place in the history of the arms trade, for from the very beginning they have been and continue to be the most aggressive salesmen in the world. They were so dynamic in the pursuit of profits from arms, for instance, that Charles the Bold of Burgundy, in the fifteenth century, issued an edict forbidding the Liègeois to manufacture arms. The ban was defied and Charles promptly besieged the city, captured it, burned it to the ground and slaughtered all the inhabitants who did not escape. But the arms industry there somehow survived and has thrived ever since. By the middle of the eighteenth century Liège was producing 100,000 pieces a year and was one of the largest and best-known arms centers in Europe. Today, Liège is the home of perhaps the most efficient, inventive and aggressive arms manufacturing company in the world: Fabrique Nationale d'Armes de Guerre.

Liège was also the city that produced the first known instance of the antinational traffic in arms—that is, the sale of arms to a known enemy. In 1576 the Duke of Alva and his army invaded the Low Countries. The Dutch and Flemish defenders were armed with weapons manufactured in Liège. So were the Duke's Spanish legions.[6]

The beginning of the nineteenth century marks a major watershed in the history of the arms trade. Three developments at the time were to have a profound effect on the weapons business, and their influences are still very much felt today.

Prior to the French Revolution, wars were essentially private affairs in which the public at large did not participate. By current standards the armies were minuscule: only 82,000 men were involved in the Battle of Crécy in 1346; only 9,000 Americans and 8,000 French fought against 7,000 English troops at Yorktown; and Cromwell's New Model Army numbered only 20,000. The weapons used were limited essentially to six items: rifle, pistol, saber, mortar, cannon and grenade. Because the first three items were often the personal property of the individual soldier, it was possible for a wealthy man to underwrite the cost of such units.

All this changed with the rise of national armies, first created under Napoleon Bonaparte. Napoleon's legions were of a size hitherto unknown to Europeans. Troops under his command at the beginning of the 1812 Russian offensive, for instance, numbered half a million men. In 1813 over one million men were wearing the uniform of France. So large were his armies that Napoleon could declare to Prince Metternich that he lost 30,000 men a month in his campaigns, a figure nearly seven times greater than the total number of American dead in the entire Revolutionary War. What took place was, in Walter Millis' words, "the democratization of war."[7]

The second development was the coming of the Industrial Revolution. Actually the phenomena of national armies and the Industrial Revolution arrived concurrently on the world stage, for indeed the former could not have occurred without the latter. The machine was coming to the aid of war, and war was subsidizing the growth of the machine age. Large citizen armies created a heavy and instant demand for weapons and the armsmakers of Liège, St. Étienne, Birmingham, Solingen, Turin and Toledo responded to the need. Thus developed an industry that in wartime was capable of supplying quickly large quantities of weapons to large armies fighting large battles; but, at the same time, there also developed an arms industry that never had a large enough market for its wares in peacetime (until recently). The stage was set at this point for the bitter peacetime competition among armsmakers and dealers that was to last for nearly a century and a half.

The third development to have a profound effect on the arms trade has been the fragmentation of the world. For all intents and purposes it began at the Congress of Vienna in 1815 and, ever since, has steadily increased in tempo until today there are some 130 nations, all of which buy weapons of one sort or another.

Other changes were wrought by the Industrial Revolution. One was that the increasing number of technological advances in industry as a whole vastly stimulated weapons development. Before the Age of Mechanics, for instance, improvements on a particular weapon—say, a rifle—took years, even centuries, to develop. Over one hundred years were to pass before the matchlock rifle gave way to the wheel-lock, over two hundred before the wheel-lock gave way to the flintlock and over a hundred before the flintlock gave way to the percussion-cap rifle. With the advent of the Industrial Revolution, however, innovations and improvements upon existing armaments have come about so quickly and in such volume that armies of powerful nations hardly have had time to get used to their weapons before the equipment was being discarded in favor of something newer and more up-to-date.

The British "Brown Bess" rifle, for instance, was standard infantry equipment from 1690 to 1807, perhaps a modern-day record for longevity. In the twentieth century, weapons become obsolete far more quickly. The model 1903 Springfield rifle was standard issue to United States forces for only thirty-three years; the M-1 Garand for only twenty-one. Since the end of World War II technological improvements have become so numerous that the rate of obsolescence has increased even faster. The United States Army, for instance, has had two new infantry rifles since 1957, or one every six years, and there is no sign that the latest one—the M-16 Armalite—will be kept any appreciable amount of time. In fact, so rapid are technological innovations coming onto the market today that often a new weapon is obsolescent before it leaves the blueprint stage.

Another development influencing the arms trade was the concept of the interchangeability of parts. Pioneered first by Eli Whitney and later by Samuel Colt, this practice vastly prolonged the life of a weapon. Thus an "obsolete" or "obsolescent" weapon was still very much a usable item. The 1903 Springfield, for instance, still has a practical life, if properly maintained, of at least an additional one hundred years.

One of the greatest changes wrought by the Industrial Revolution was the proliferation of new forms of armaments, a direct result of the scientific and managerial revolutions. Not only were improvements being made along the way to the rifle, pistol, saber, mortar, cannon and hand grenade, but entirely new weapons were being invented: the rocket, submarine, machine gun, tank, airplane, bazooka, recoilless rifle, flamethrower, proximity fuse, the defensive and offensive missile and the nuclear bomb. All these weapons, in turn, have experienced continuing improvements, and many of them eventually have joined old rifles, pistols, sabers, mortars, cannons and hand grenades as surplus items.

By the middle of the nineteenth century, all these developments were in an embryonic state. There was, to be sure, a lively international trade in the weapons of war, but nothing on today's scale. There was also a spirited trade in secondhand, obsolescent weapons, but again it was relatively small in volume; the problem of obsolescence usually solved itself because the unwanted equipment was absorbed by the world's growing population and by the demands of the colonies and the smaller nations. Technology was not yet so sophisticated that it forced large quantities of older equipment onto the surplus market. Competition among manufacturers was also muted somewhat because the arms industry was not yet so large that it could not readjust to civilian demands when necessary.

A number of individuals and industrial firms were active in the arms trade during this period. For instance, John Pierpont Morgan, Sr., spent part of his time during the Civil War selling arms to Union forces. One of his most celebrated transactions was in 1861 when he bought 5,000 defective Hall's carbines for $3.50 each and then sold them to General John C. Frémont for $22 apiece. So many of Frémont's men had their thumbs shot off as the result of their carbine malfunctioning that the government refused to pay the bill. Morgan sued and eventually won his case, receiving the full amount for his wares.[8]

Around the same period of time, the Winchester Repeating Arms Company contracted to supply 1,000 rifles and half a million rounds of ammunition to Don Benito Juárez, a former President of Mexico who was in rebellion against Napoleon III's puppet monarch Maximilian. Juárez hesitated to pay the sum agreed upon, and the Winchester salesman, "Colonel" Tom Addis, let it be known that unless full payment in silver was received immediately the arms were to be sold to Maximilian. Juárez capitulated to this blackmail; he paid his money and secured the arms and ammunition, and eventually ousted Maximilian.[9]

The Remington Arms Company, in the years immediately following the Civil War, carried on a spirited trade in arms; it sold 85,000 rifles to Spain in 1867; the following year it sold 30,000 rifles to Sweden and 50,000 to Egypt. France was to buy 145,000 Remingtons, Puerto Rico 10,000, Cuba 89,000, Spain another 130,000, Mexico 50,000, and Chile 12,000 rifles in the decade ahead. In 1879 Remington made handsome profits by selling to both sides in the Russo-Turkish War.[10]

The Du Pont Company was also involved in the arms trade. Most of its wares, principally black powder, were purchased by the U.S. government, but on occasion it sold its products on the international market. In the Crimean War of 1854, for instance, the Wilmington-based company supplied powder to England, France and Turkey on one side and to Russia on the other.[11]

The two most famous arms salesmen during this period, and extending well into the twentieth century, were Sir Basil Zaharoff of Vickers-Maxim and Francis Bannerman of New York City.

Zaharoff was the single most powerful private arms merchant

the nineteenth and twentieth centuries have seen. He began life as a brothel tout in Constantinople and reportedly acquired his first stake by stealing 7,000 pounds' worth of securities from a Greek merchant. From there he soon became an agent in the Balkans and Near East for the Anglo-Swedish firm of Nordenfeldt. Between the time he first began selling weapons in the 1870's as a young man until his death in 1936, Zaharoff amassed an immense fortune in the arms trade and was reportedly the wealthiest man in Europe of his time.

He was a chameleonlike character who could appear to be more French than the French, more Russian than the Russians, and more English than the English. He not only spoke eight languages fluently but was a Greek with a Russian surname who ended up becoming a French citizen and an English knight. He was also a brilliant but cold, cruel, secretive and sinister figure who had the power—which he never hesitated to use—to bring down governments, to promote arms races, to make or break kings and statesmen, to start wars. He was a friend and confidant of Lloyd George, of Clemenceau, of Greek Prime Minister Eleutherios Venizelos, of Sir Hiram Maxim, of Sir Charles Craven of Vickers, and in later years of Spanish millionaire Juan March, the Krupps and Hitler.

He was completely corrupt and unscrupulous in his business affairs. He lied, he cheated, he bribed, he stole, he broke laws. He was once able to prevent the Allies from shelling a town in German hands on the Western Front during World War I where, it was revealed later, a factory existed in which he had a financial interest.[12]

Zaharoff's big break came in the 1880's when a test was held in Vienna between the Nordenfeldt machine gun and the new machine gun invented by Hiram Maxim, an American. The Emperor Franz Josef was in attendance, and Maxim impressed him and the assembled crowd by spelling out the monarch's initials on a target with his gun. It was clear that the Maxim was the better weapon. But Maxim did not reckon with the guile of Zaharoff, who circulated among the press claiming that it was actually the Nordenfeldt gun that had proved superior and so versatile. Although Maxim won the day, Zaharoff won the orders.

Maxim was impressed with Zaharoff, and in 1888 he and the Nordenfeldt company merged their interests. This amalgamation in turn was bought by Vickers in 1897. For the next twenty years Vickers had a virtual monopoly on machine guns and sold them throughout the world.

Zaharoff, as Vickers' chief salesman, was not above selling to both sides in a war; in fact, he raised this tactic to the level of a fine art. For instance, during World War I the Turkish guns served by German crews at the Dardanelles were of British manufacture and had been delivered by Zaharoff. During the Boer War, Zaharoff sold weapons to both the British and the rebels. His arms for the Boers were packed in piano cases and marked "ironmongery."[13]

Throughout his life he played one Balkan country against another. On one occasion he supported Greece against Turkey, Turkey against Serbia, and Serbia against Austria. On another occasion he sold one submarine to Greece and then proceeded to frighten Turkey into buying two. Soon thereafter he convinced the Czar that all this activity on his southern flank warranted his buying four.[14]

By current standards his methods of bribery were crude. He once secured an arms order from the reluctant Russians, for instance, by leaving his wallet with a large check in it on a minister's desk. On other occasions he dispensed with a check and simply filled the wallet with money.[15]

At the height of his powers Zaharoff held 300 directorates and had large financial interests in arms firms, banks, railroads, hotels, oil and mining concessions, and assorted factories and shipyards. At his death he held 298 decorations from 31 countries. But in spite of his wealth and honors, Zaharoff was so much the personification of human evil in the eyes of so many people that he acquired the sobriquet of "merchant of death."

Most arms merchants during the Zaharoff era were also from Europe, for that was where the business was. Friedrich and Alfried Krupp, Eugène Schneider of Schneider-Creusot and Skoda, and many other individuals were active peddling their wares around the Continent to eager buyers. World War I is full of examples of one nation finding its own weapons being used by its enemies. For instance, when Germany invaded Belgium, its soldiers were met by Belgians armed with German guns; when the Germans invaded Russia they were met by Russians armed with Krupp cannons; French troops in Bulgaria were bombarded by Bulgarians firing French 75's; Austria-Hungary, with its Skoda factory, faced Skoda guns in the hands of Russians. Even Switzerland, a neutral, helped this process: it sold electricity to both sides and allowed French material for the Germans and German material for the Allies to be exchanged through its territory.[16]

America had only one arms merchant of any note at this time: Francis Bannerman of New York. He differed from all the other arms merchants in that he only sold secondhand and surplus weapons. His firm, Francis Bannerman & Sons, got its start in 1865 when it bought at auction (and subsequently sold for handsome profits) huge quantities of surplus military equipment left over from the Civil War. The company maintained a large arsenal, built like a Scottish castle, on an island in the Hudson River not far from West Point. Bannerman furnished antiques to museums and collectors, and costumes to theatrical groups, but his primary business was to sell surplus arms to governments or interested individuals.

Bannerman sold his wares with missionary zeal and larded his sales pitch with a heavy dose of Christianity. He promoted military preparedness by noting in his catalogue that there were two swords in the company of the twelve apostles which, he added, "makes rather a good percentage in favor of weapons." The firm also stoutly defended the idea of the "Christian soldier" and claimed that when peace shall reign on earth Bannerman's Military Museum, located on Broadway in New York City, would be known as "The Museum of Lost Arts." Its catalogue once even went so far as to state: "The Good Book says that in the millennium days, swords shall be turned into plowshares and spears into pruning hooks. We are helping to hasten along the glad time by selling cannon balls to heal the sick."[17]

Bannerman openly advertised his wares in his annual catalogues—many of which today are collector's items—which often ran to more than 360 pages with 5,000 illustrations. Some 25,000 copies were sold each year. Perhaps the most famous catalogue was the one published in 1903 in which Bannerman outlined the scope of his operations. Speaking of purchases in 1900, he wrote:[18]

> Readers can judge the magnitude of these sales when we inform them that our purchases . . . amounted to over 160,000 guns, 30,000 revolvers, 10,000 saddles, 15,000 swords, 16,000 canteens, 60,000 belts, 50,000 cartridge boxes, 20,000,000 cartridges, 50,000 stirrups, 150,000 gun stocks, with hundreds of tons of gun barrels, gun parts, equipments, Gatling guns, etc., etc. Naturally, as we make this business our specialty, with thirty-six years' experience, and with the whole world for our market, we availed ourselves of this opportunity to purchase, and when other small dealers and speculators hesitated as to what could be done with such large quantities of obsolete arms, we went in and purchased nearly all the [U.S.] government offered, thus placing ourselves in position to give our customers the benefit of large assortments at lowest rates.

As will be shown later, there is a striking similarity between Bannerman's activities and the current crop of arms traders.

Another famous Bannerman catalogue, published in 1933, noted that the U.S. government depended on Bannerman "to purchase at their sales the large quantities of obsolete and discarded goods." Of the 21,154 rifles and carbines captured in Cuba and Puerto Rico during the Spanish-American War, for instance, 20,220 were sold at auction, of which the New York company bought 18,200. Many of these weapons were subsequently sold to the Panamanians, who were in the process of winning their freedom from Colombia.[19]

"On short notice we can deliver promptly from our stock 100 high power rapid-fire guns at bargain prices," declared the same catalogue. Evidently the ability to be quick on its feet was highly prized by Bannerman. The catalogue went on:[20]

> Recently, a shipping firm in Europe gave us an order to convert a large ocean passenger steamship into a warship for a South

American government. In one week the peaceful passenger ship sailed, altered by us into a man-of-war, fully armed and equipped: a record for quickness that could scarcely be beaten today in any up-to-date government establishment.

The following passage, from the 1903 catalogue, could just as easily have been written by one of today's arms merchants:[21]

> Our customers include many of the South and Central American Governments. . . . For years we have supplied the Dominican and Haitian governments. Our largest customers are governments who, having limited financial resources, must necessarily purchase army guns and supplies at low prices, and who are not averse to adopting a good serviceable gun which has been cast aside by a richer and stronger government.
>
> We purchase large quantities of arms, which we hold in our island storehouse, for times of emergency, when arms are in demand, when even obsolete serviceable guns are purchased by first-class governments. . . .

Bannerman's company still exists today, but it no longer trades in large quantities of surplus items. It limits its activities to producing catalogues of antique firearms and to finding rare military items for collectors. The firm's heyday ended with the arms it purchased after the Spanish-American War. Its activities increased somewhat after World War I, but by the outbreak of World War II it had lapsed into relative obscurity.

The two decades between World Wars I and II were a period of transition for the arms trade. It was a period that saw the impetus for arms trading shift from the private manufacturers to national governments. The shift was due in part to the belief held by many people that men like Zaharoff had been responsible for the Great War. The arms merchants were now on the defensive; a cry went up in political circles demanding more control over them. The League of Nations Union in 1936, for instance, put forward a ballot in the League itself asking for a vote on the abolition of the private manufacture of arms. It received overwhelming support;

however, nothing concrete followed. There even was a resolution, put forth seriously by a U.S. congressman, that if passed would have required the wealthiest men in the United States, particularly those in the arms trade, to serve first at the danger points in a war.[22]

The League also kept two sets of statistics on armaments in the belief that with public exposure the trade would diminish. One set, compiled from 1924 to 1940, dealt with the level of armaments and details of armed forces. The other set, compiled from 1924 to 1938, was called "The Statistical Yearbook of the Trade in Arms and Ammunition" and purportedly was an effort to record and correlate all incidences of arms trading. Both were valiant efforts, but no one was impressed by them, nor did the trade wither away.

There were two major investigations of the arms industry in this period. One was the U.S. Senate Munitions Inquiry, known as the "Nye Committee," of 1934–36; the other was the Royal Commission on the Private Manufacture of and Trading in Arms, held in London in 1936. Both investigations unearthed an enormous number of unsavory practices: bribery, collusive bidding, profiteering, the violation of arms embargoes, illegal financial transactions, the production of shoddy equipment, and even sales to the enemy.

A number of businessmen involved in the trade faced interrogation by these two committees: in the United States men such as J. Pierpont Morgan, Jr., E. I. Du Pont, arms lobbyist William B. Shearer, Henry R. Carse of the Electric Boat Company, and various officials of steelmaking and shipbuilding firms; in Great Britain, Sir Herbert Lawrence and Sir Charles Craven of Vickers, among others. None of these people offered any cooperation or assistance to the committees. In fact, Sir Charles Craven deemed it wise to be flip: to a novelist member of the Royal Commission who asked him whether he thought his wares were "no more dangerous, or noxious than, we will say, boxes of chocolates or sugar candy," Craven replied, ". . . Or novels? No."[23] Perhaps the most fatuous statement to come out of both investigations was the one made by Admiral Sir Reginald Bacon, Britain's Naval Director of Ordnance in World War I. Said he: "I have seen it stated that British ammunition was used against our troops at Gallipoli.

That is very likely—why should it not be? I think at that particular moment German ammunition was probably a little better than ours, but the main point is that, if they had not used English ammunition, they would have used German, which would have been to the disadvantage of our troops."[24]

These two investigations sparked several other countries into holding their own inquiries, specifically Chile, Brazil, Argentina and Peru. None were to cause much of a stir. They also led to an increased interest in legislation as a means of curbing arms sales.[25] In 1933 Great Britain placed—but failed to enforce—an arms embargo on the belligerents in the Manchurian War; France, in 1935, began regulating arms exports from France to Algeria; and in the same year the Dutch and the Swedes enacted arms control measures.

The United States, in 1934, placed an arms embargo against Bolivia and Paraguay, belligerents in the Gran Chaco War. The following year, as the result of numerous congressional efforts to throttle the trade by American firms, and in keeping with the country's desire to withdraw from world affairs, a Neutrality Act was passed. Its two major provisions prohibited the sale of arms to belligerents and set up a licensing system subjecting export sales to government scrutiny. In 1936 the act was renewed, and was revised three years later when hostilities broke out between Germany and Poland.

In spite of these efforts, the trade continued to prosper, though at a level far reduced from pre-World War I days. British, Czech and French companies sold arms to either the Chinese or the Japanese, or both, in the Manchurian War; Italy exported arms to Turkey, Rumania, Finland and several South American countries; American firms succeeded in outflanking the embargo against Bolivia and Paraguay. Vickers (at this point called Vickers-Armstrong) held a financial interest in several foreign subsidiaries of German arms manufacturers; it was also a partner with Schneider-Creusot in Rumanian and Polish arms companies. Most surprising of all, Germany, prohibited by the Treaty of Versailles from manufacturing arms, was reported to be the chief source of arms for thirteen countries by 1929, twenty-two countries by 1930. The

Czechoslovakian arms industry was to experience boom times in the 1930's as the result of large orders from Germany, then in the process of rearming under Hitler.[26]

Private entrepreneurs still had considerable freedom of action between the wars. Colonel George Burling Jarrett, perhaps the world's leading authority on armaments,* tells the story of an Englishman who made a fortune in the 1930's selling miscellaneous equipment in the Orient. On one occasion this intrepid individual—"a first-class crook," according to Jarrett—sold the Chinese some German 7.92 mm rifles he had acquired from the Poles, plus seven million rounds of Russian 7.62 mm ammunition, neither of which, even to a novice, are complementary. He then bought a batch of old British uniforms, replaced the brass buttons with wooden ones, and sold them to the same customer. The brass buttons, sold elsewhere, brought in more profits than all the uniforms were worth.

3

Whatever may have been the condition of the arms trade between the two great wars—on the defensive, struggling to survive, carrying on with more subtlety—it changed forever in 1940 when

* Colonel Jarrett is a legend in his own lifetime. He began collecting arms in 1915 and by 1945 had amassed 9,000 pieces—everything from Sopwith Camels to a complete set of German rifles manufactured between 1865 and 1945. The collection, which would be worth over a million dollars today, was broken up in 1950, much of the priceless material ending up as scrap. Jarrett's greatest moment came in 1941–42 when he was the ammunition adviser to the British in North Africa. The British were short of 75 mm tank ammunition, and they turned to Jarrett for help. He heard that there was some superior quality German 75 mm ammunition that had been captured at Tobruk; but, he was informed, the shells would not fit the Allies' guns because the rotating band was too large. Undaunted, Jarrett set up a mobile machine shop on the banks of the Suez Canal; each shell was mounted on a lathe and the rotating band was turned down by Royal Ordnance Corps technicians. He knew that the German 75 mm ammunition became fully armed when rotated at 1,500 rpm, so he kept the lathes turning no faster than 400 rpm. There were no accidents but, he told me, "It scared the life out of a lot of people." These shells, some 17,000 pieces, were to play a vital part in later battles of the North African campaign.

President Franklin D. Roosevelt, fearing a Nazi conquest of Europe, approved the transfer of fifty American destroyers to Great Britain in return for rights to build military bases on British territory in the Western Hemisphere. The United States, after abstaining for years from the arms trade, now opened the doors of its arsenals. In March 1941 the doors were flung wide open with the passage of the Lend-Lease Act. This piece of legislation empowered the President "to authorize the manufacture of defense articles . . . for any foreign government whose defense he deemed vital," and to "sell, transfer title to, exchange, lease, lend . . . to any such government any defense article."

By the end of World War II the United States had given away $48.5 billion worth of arms and military supplies to 48 nations. The bulk of it went to Great Britain ($32 billion), the Soviet Union ($11 billion) and France ($3 billion).[27] The purpose of this aid was to help our allies carry some of the load in the war. It helped save the lives of American soldiers, although there is no way to measure how much. There was no thought at the time of being reimbursed for the material, and to this day very little has been paid back. The United States is still paying—in interest charges on the national debt—for its generosity.

The postwar growth in the arms trade stems from three pressures. The first was a direct response to the Soviet expansionist policies under Premier Stalin. Stalin wished to foment rebellion in the colonies and in the newly independent states, and the major tool he used was aggression, both overt and covert. The United States had no alternative but to contain this threat; to do it, Washington began a large-scale arms distribution program known as Military Aid. Anyone who wished to defend themselves against communist aggression could get arms from the United States. Thus there grew up a large trade in arms, flowing from U.S. arsenals into many countries threatened by communism.

The second pressure is a by-product of the central arms race between the Western and Eastern camps. As each side has improved its weapons, its inventories and armories have become cluttered with equipment that was obsolescent by their own standards but was otherwise quite serviceable. Rather than destroy this equipment, the arms-producing nations have passed it on to other nations.

The third stems from an enormous thirst for armaments in the third world. In the short span of 25 years, the number of sovereign nations has increased from 55 to 130. Only 13 of the 130 manufacture armaments in any variety or quantity: Belgium, Canada, Communist China, Czechoslovakia, France, Israel, Italy, the Soviet Union, Sweden, Switzerland, the United Kingdom, the United States and West Germany. Thus there are 117 nations—most of them poor, unstable and weaponless—that rely on outsiders to provide them with virtually all their military requirements. The demand for arms since 1945 among these countries seems insatiable. The pressure for weapons has been so strong, in fact, that the rate of obsolescence has not kept pace with demand. The world's leading military and industrial powers, therefore, find themselves more and more filling orders not with their castoff items but with brand new equipment.

For centuries the possession of modern armaments has been a symbol of power, and it is therefore not surprising that there is a strong and universal desire to demonstrate independence with an expensive array of such fancy hardware as jet fighters, missiles and tanks. Yet it is precisely these new nations—which can least afford this equipment—that actively engage in shooting wars. Fifty-four of the fifty-six "small" wars since 1945 have been fought in the underdeveloped areas of the world. Ironically, most of the weapons these poor, unstable nations buy are prestige items, not particularly suited to defending their territory.

This need for arms is so urgent that it overrides all other considerations. Dean Rusk, then the Secretary of State, put it best in a television interview on January 3, 1965. Said he: "I recall that at the United Nations General Assembly at a time when they were voting *unanimously* for disarmament, seventy members were at that moment asking us [the United States] for military assistance."[28]

Thus the doors to America's arsenals did not close with the end of World War II. Lend-Lease expired at the end of June 1946, but through a variety of legal authorizations and expedients arms worth $800 million were sent to China between 1946 and 1949 to bolster the forces of Chiang Kai-shek. In the Middle East, beginning in 1947 with the Truman Doctrine, the United States gave military assistance to Greece, Turkey and Iran, all of which were under intense Soviet pressure.

In 1949 the North Atlantic Treaty Organization came into being in order to protect Europe and the West from the expansionist designs of the Soviets. Later in the same year the Mutual Defense Assistance Act was passed by Congress; it was to become the basis for all subsequent U.S. military assistance legislation: that is, the Mutual Security Acts of 1951 and 1954, as amended, and today the Foreign Assistance Act of 1961, as amended.

The Korean War, which broke out in June 1950, accelerated America's military aid program. The war caught the U.S. government short of supplies, and industry was ordered to step up its output to meet the needs of the moment. By the end of the conflict the productive capabilities were so large, and the surpluses so vast, that the United States with little strain began supplying military equipment not only to our European allies but to other nations around the globe which appeared to be vulnerable to communist incursions.

With the Cold War at its height, the United States undertook to assume the role of protector of the entire free world. It was not a conscious policy at the time, but in retrospect it is clear that that is what it amounted to. No other country or combination of countries could have undertaken the job. The United States had already signed the Rio Pact in 1947, which declared that an attack on any American state would be considered an attack on all and that collective action would be taken to repel the aggression. In 1954 it became the leader in establishing the Southeast Asia Treaty Organization; it then encouraged the formation of, but did not join, the Central Treaty Organization (formerly the Baghdad Pact); it signed bilateral aid treaties with the Philippines, Korea and Nationalist China, among others; it established military bases in Spain and North Africa, and along with them went U.S. economic and military assistance; and it encouraged the rearming of both West Germany and Japan as early as 1954. All this activity led to a heavy outlay in military equipment.

U.S. military aid, both grant aid and sales, since 1945 has

averaged more than $2 billion per year. It rose to as much as $5 billion in fiscal year (FY) 1952 and fell to as low as $831 million in FY 1956.[29] The number of recipient countries rose from 14 in 1950 to a peak so far of 69 in 1963. In all, some 80 countries have received a total of approximately $50 billion in American military aid since the end of World War II. Except for 11 hard-core communist countries and certain nations tied closely to either Britain or France, very few nations have never received military aid of one kind or another from the United States.[30]

The fact that the United States has pumped some $52 billion worth of arms into the world market in the last 25 years is obscured by the sheer size of the figure. Put another way, it means that between the years 1950 and 1966, for instance, the U.S. government either gave away or sold 9,300 jet fighter aircraft, 8,340 other aircraft, 2,496 naval craft of all types, 19,827 tanks, 448,383 other combat vehicles, 1,445,194 carbines, 2,152,793 rifles, 82,496 submachine guns, 71,174 machine guns, 30,668 mortars, 25,106 field guns and howitzers, and 31,360 missiles of all types. One must add to these totals billions of rounds of ammunition and other explosives, thousands of supporting systems such as computers and radio sets, and millions of man-hours of training sessions both in the United States and in the recipient countries.[31]

This arms traffic is increasing in tempo. For instance, from 1945 to 1955, the world's arms markets were dominated by the United States and Great Britain alone. Both gave away or sold military equipment at an average yearly rate of $2 billion and an estimated $400 million, respectively. But then the Soviet Union entered the picture in a big way in 1955, and every year since has scattered an average of $500 million worth of additional arms around the world. Soon thereafter, a revitalized France broke into the market; she is currently selling another $400 million worth of arms each year. Ironically, it was America's economic aid under the Marshall Plan that hastened France's return to the arms sales field.

In the last seven years West Germany, Czechoslovakia, Belgium, Sweden, Switzerland, Israel, Italy, Canada and Communist

China have all plunged into the field, offering a variety of military wares to whoever shows interest. If military training programs and technical support from industry are included, the world's arms trade today runs to $5 billion a year, more than double what it was two decades ago. It is estimated that the market will double again by the early 1970's.

During the first ten years after 1945, the United States and Great Britain *gave away* most of their obsolete equipment. But by the mid-1950's it became apparent that more and more of the recipient countries were economically capable of paying their own way. Pressure was soon brought to bear, first in Washington and later in London, to *sell* military equipment (both obsolete and new) in order to recoup as much as possible of the high research, development, production and operating costs of the weapons. As other countries entered the arms trade it occurred to them as well that selling arms was a convenient and lucrative method of bringing in hard currencies. Not only did arms sales unclutter inventories, bolster allies, offset opponents and curry favor with neutrals, but it was—and still is—an easy way to balance the budget, to eliminate trade deficits, to ensure full employment. Thus today the arms trade is considered by most governments involved to be a moneymaking proposition, not an exercise in charity and military self-interest as it was twenty years earlier.

Eastern bloc countries, in order to retain and possibly augment their own influence around the world, have felt compelled to compete with the West. Russia's arms transactions have increased enormously in the last decade; Czechoslovakia has been given its head and today sells weapons wherever it can for the highest possible prices; Poland, East Germany, Bulgaria, Red China and several other communist countries are also involved in this trade.

In addition to this essentially government-to-government trade in arms, there still exist a number of private dealers, both legal and illegal, in the arms business. Their current annual volume of sales runs to $100 million or so. Although this figure is tiny in comparison to the trade carried on by governments, it cannot be discounted. In Napoleon's day relatively small wars could be fought with a large number of weapons. Today the reverse is true: because firepower per weapon has increased enormously, relatively large wars can be fought with few weapons. For instance, of the 750 million operable rifles and pistols in the world today, less than 2 million were used by both sides in a war the size of the Korean conflict. So with other weapons: the bomb load of one jet can wipe out a village, one squadron of jets can destroy a town, the firepower of a modern tank is so great as to have been unimaginable to a military strategist thirty years ago. It must be remembered that Fidel Castro had no more than 1,000 regulars under his command just before coming to power: until the last stages of the rebellion their arms came from private sources. Thus a small batch of weapons sold by a private arms dealer cannot be ignored.

It is these entrepreneurs to whom we shall turn our attention first.

PART TWO

FREE ENTERPRISE ARMED

II

Samuel Cummings of Interarms

"In the final analysis, the morality of armaments boils down to who makes the sale."
—SAMUEL CUMMINGS

1

The largest private dealer in surplus military weapons on the international market is Samuel Cummings, a forty-two-year-old American who is the founder, president and sole owner of the International Armament Corporation, otherwise known as Interarms.* For the past fifteen years Cummings' business, simply stated, has been to buy the surplus arms which are no longer of any use to a country and either sell them to another country or sell them as inexpensive sporting equipment on the domestic American and Canadian markets. Until the passage of the Gun Control Act of 1968, which among other things prohibits the importation into the United States of foreign military surplus weapons, there existed no other market like this one for small arms. Some twenty million people in North America are potential customers for inexpensive

* For many years the firm used the style "Interarmco" as the corporate title for many of its associate companies around the world. However, in 1967, after five years of litigation, the Armco Steel Corporation succeeded in enjoining the International Armament Corporation from using the word "Interarmco" as a trade mark, trade name or corporate name. While the company is now known legally as Interarms, it is still referred to informally by those in and around the industry as "Interarmco." For the sake of clarity I have standardized to the name Interarms throughout this volume.

but high quality foreign-made guns, and for most of the post-World War II years Cummings was the prime supplier to this market—a market the domestic manufacturers consistently failed or refused to fill.

Cummings is also an arms broker. That is to say, he will act as the middleman between two countries, one of which wants to sell obsolescent or surplus material, the other of which wants to buy. If any country wants new, up-to-date equipment, Cummings will be glad to supply that too.

By any standard of comparison, Cummings has been eminently successful at his job. He started Interarms as a one-man operation and in seventeen years has built it into an organization that today dominates the total free world market in private arms sales. He has had a hand in virtually every major private arms transaction, outside of the Soviet bloc, since 1953. Although Cummings is very tight-lipped about his finances, his annual volume of business today runs into eight figures—some say as high as $40 million, but this sum is probably exaggerated. No doubt a turnover of from $15 to $20 million would be a good year for him, and until a few years ago, he could count on anything from $3 to $5 million profit. Today profits are running slightly less. Some people estimate Cummings' personal fortune from this trade to be in excess of $10 million. Preliminary comparison between turnover and profit would indicate that it is probably far higher. No other arms dealer can come close to matching these figures today.

To give some indication of the size and breadth of the operation, Interarms maintains in Alexandria, Virginia, ten large warehouses with a total floor space of 100,000 square feet. At any one time there are from 500,000 to 600,000 surplus small-caliber weapons (usually up to 20 mm in size) in stock in these buildings. "That's enough for about forty infantry divisions," Cummings told me. Interarms also maintains another large warehouse in Acton, a suburb of London. An additional 150,000 to 200,000 similar types of weapons are in stock there. Cummings claims that he has more surplus weapons in stock than either the United States or the British military forces currently have in active service.

Walking through these warehouses is an experience in itself.

Stacked in crates that are sometimes piled twenty feet high are thousands of English Lee-Enfields, German Mauser rifles, Italian Mannlicher-Carcanos, Russian Tokarevs and Mosin-Nagants, American 1903 Springfields and M-1 carbines. There are also thousands of automatic pistols and revolvers: Lugers, Webley & Scotts, Glisentis, Nagants, Colts, Smith & Wessons, Mausers, Nambus and Walthers. His warehouses are always stocked with millions of rounds of ammunition, some of which is unobtainable elsewhere on the American and British markets.

On occasion he has stocked grenades, artillery shells and bazooka rounds; he has always carried a varied selection of mortars, submachine guns, bazookas, swords, sabers, bayonets and sometimes even lances. Every once in a while he will buy old military uniforms, and it is his practice to dress his employees in the stock of the moment; one week the Afrika Korps, the next the British Royal Navy or the Royal Tank Corps.

In one of his warehouses he maintains a $65,000 cartridge-loading machine, the only one of its kind in the United States. This machine can convert as many as nine different calibers of military ammunition into sporting ammunition at the rate of 8,000 rounds per hour. In his Acton warehouse, in England, Cummings maintains a large weapons reconditioning and converting shop. There, most of the weapons he buys are refurbished through the alteration of the stock, sights and finish.

No other private arms dealer in the world has anything like these facilities.

Interarms, at various times, controlled seven famous British sporting weapons firms: Churchill (Gunmakers), Ltd.; Hercules Arms Company of Birmingham; Grant & Lang of St. James's; Henry Atkin, Ltd.; F. Beesley, Ltd.; Harrison & Hussey, Ltd.; and Charles Harris & Sons. For five years Cummings owned a controlling interest in Cogswell & Harrison, another famous English gunmaking firm, but in 1963 he sold the name and retail store (but kept its inventory and warehouse facilities). Cummings' grip on the luxury gun market in England is so strong that the Worshipful Company of Gunmakers elected him to membership, the only foreigner ever to be so honored.[1]

Throughout the world, virtually in every free country, Cummings maintains either branch offices or independent agents. The men who work for Cummings are the best in the business: they know where the arms are, what it takes to buy them and what it takes to sell them. They are the men who guarantee that the volume stays high and that the profits continue to roll in.

Despite what his competitors seem to believe, Sam Cummings did not spring full blown onto the arms scene one day, his pockets bulging with banknotes and a worldwide organization at his disposal. Nor is Sam Cummings an aberration on the current arms scene: he is not only the product of selection in a very competitive, cutthroat business, but also the end result of historical processes that can be traced back to the nineteenth century. How Cummings has become the number-one private arms merchant in the world today, therefore, tells much of how and why this trade has flourished as it has in the last quarter-century.

Cummings was born in Philadelphia in 1927, the son of a fairly wealthy Main Line family. His father's sole occupation at the time was tending to his many stock-market investments. Young Cummings spent his first years in the care of governesses and at expensive private schools. At the age of five he became the proud owner of a German Maxim machine gun, a discarded World War I relic from the local American Legion post. Cummings spent many happy months dismantling and reassembling the weapon.

The stock-market crash wiped out the family investments, and his father went to work as the manager of an electric-supply house. When Cummings was eight years old his father died, leaving the family in poor straits. His mother went to work for a real-estate firm and was able to earn enough money to send her son to Episcopal Academy, an exclusive private school. The Academy's Latin motto—*Esse Quam Videri* ("To Be Rather Than to Seem to Be")—was adopted by Cummings later as the motto of Interarms.

Cummings reached draft age just as World War II was coming to an end. He served for a short period in the infantry at Fort (then Camp) Lee, Virginia, eventually rising to the rank of sergeant. His knowledge of every weapon in the nation's arsenal was so great at that time that the Army, duly impressed, made him a weapons instructor.

It was also at Fort Lee that Cummings first came to realize the extraordinary profits that could be made in the surplus military equipment market.

In the years immediately following the war, considerable military scrap was being shipped to the United States from Europe. Some of it ended up in a junkyard in Richmond, Virginia. Among the items there were thousands of German helmets which were going for 50 cents apiece. Cummings, on several occasions, loaded up his car to the roof with helmets and drove up to Aberdeen, Maryland, where he sold them for $4.00 apiece to Colonel George Burling Jarrett, the well-known military weapons collector. Jarrett in turn sold them for a slightly higher price to movie studios and costume shops. Cummings' car was usually so overloaded with helmets that he could count on blowing at least one tire per trip, the only extraordinary expense he faced in these transactions.

After his army career, Cummings enrolled at George Washington University under the GI Bill. As a sideline he bought antique guns and sold them for a profit to his fellow students. He tried a term at Oxford in 1948 but became bored and took a poor man's tour of Europe. When he got to France he was staggered by what he saw. There, lining many roads and sometimes stacked like cordwood, were thousands of abandoned military weapons. In the Falaise Gap, where the Allies had trapped ten German divisions, there were even more stockpiles of rifles and machine guns. Some of the weapons were still clutched by the hands of skeletons that the French had refused to bury for fear of booby traps.

Cummings reasoned that the French would be pleased to part with this technically obsolete material if someone had the means to transport it away. Unfortunately for Cummings, he did not even have enough money to put in a bid.

Cummings returned to America and graduated from George Washington in 1949 and immediately set about looking for a way in which to exploit what he had seen in France. He contacted Western Arms Corporation, a Los Angeles firm, hoping that he might be hired as a sales agent. But before he heard from them, the Korean War had broken out and he was hired by the Central Intelligence Agency to identify weapons that had been captured from the enemy. To no one's surprise the arms turned out to be mostly Russian in origin. Eighteen months later Cummings quit the agency and was soon thereafter hired by Western Arms as an agent at a salary of $5,600 a year plus one-eighth of one percent commission on all sales he could secure.[2]

Western Arms had a brief but interesting history. Not all of it is clear, and Cummings, one of the few men who knows all the facts, is reluctant to talk about the company. Nevertheless, some information is available.

In September 1945 the United States disbanded the Office of Strategic Services (OSS), its wartime intelligence agency. The Research and Analysis Branch of the OSS was assigned to the State Department where it still carries out intelligence duties; the rest of the OSS was first absorbed into the War Department under the name of Strategic Services Unit and later into the CIA.

The Central Intelligence Agency was not to be born until September 1947, and in this two-year period the bulk of America's intelligence needs were met by the R and A Branch in State. Its officials realized at that time that certain jobs had to be done that could not be done overtly. One was to keep an eye on the large amount of military surplus on distant battlefields that was still unspoken for and to make sure that it did not fall into the wrong hands. One way this could be done was to dispose of it in the United States.

Another problem facing the government during this period (and later on after the CIA had been established) was its need for large quantities of untraceable weapons to be given to hard-pressed governments friendly to America. Untraceable weapons, known as "clean" or "sterile" weapons in the trade, are usually foreign-made guns that cannot be traced by their serial numbers to United States or allied sources. They are vital to any clandestine operation where American support must be concealed.

In any event, into the breach stepped a Hollywood promoter named Leo Lippe. Lippe knew little about guns but he was very successful in convincing the State Department that it should set him up in business. In return, Lippe would make an inventory of all the world's armaments and bring as many of the surplus weapons as he could into the United States, supplying the government with all the clean weapons it needed and selling the remaining weapons to the public. This he did for a number of years under the name of Western Arms Corporation. He also operated through another government-backed company, Winfield Arms Company.

Lippe had hired two salesmen, Arthur Cecil Jackson, an Englishman,* and Seymour Ziebert. By the time Cummings came to work for Western Arms, Lippe seems to have faded from the scene. The effective control of the organization now lay in Jackson's hands. It also seems clear that the U.S. government was no longer subsidizing the company (which may be one reason why Lippy dropped out) and that it was being run along ordinary commercial lines. The CIA, by this time (1952), had apparently developed its own covert purchasing channels.

With Jackson in charge of Western Arms, a fierce rivalry soon sprang up between the two chief agents, Cummings and Ziebert. Both men were competing for the same orders and commissions, and the competition between them soon became acrimonious. Their dispute came to a head in Mexico City, and the upshot of it was that Ziebert either quit or was fired. Ziebert went off and formed Golden State Arms Corporation and Pasadena Firearms Corporation, import-export firms that were to compete in later years with Interarms. Both of Ziebert's firms were eventually to go bankrupt, mostly the result of more aggressive tactics by Interarms.

By the end of 1952 Cummings had come to realize fully how much money could be made in the arms business. He had seen the huge profits built up by Western Arms, part of which he was responsible for, and he saw no reason why all these profits should not be coming to him directly. His CIA work had also exposed him to all the important people in the arms trade, both in and out

* The fact that an Englishman was involved in the purchasing of weapons for the United States attests to how closely both countries cooperated in their arms buying policies during this period.

of government, and he believed that this advantage should be exploited.

Accordingly, he decided to strike out on his own. In February 1953, he says, after having registered with the Treasury Department and the State Department's Office of Munitions Control as an arms dealer, he sat down at his typewriter and wrote letters to ministers and chiefs of staff of many countries around the world, asking if they had any weapons for sale. Cummings, with a certain brashness, chose a fancy title for his letterhead—International Armament Corporation—and liberally sprinkled the corporate "we" throughout his letters, despite the fact that the "corporation" then consisted of Cummings alone.

In due course he received a reply from Colonel (now Brigadier General) Bolivar Vallarino, then the powerful head of Panama's national police force, who said that Panama did indeed have some weapons for sale. They turned out to be 7,000 small arms of many different makes and vintages—everything from Toledo rapiers, Molotov cocktails and nineteenth-century artillery pieces to the latest rifles and machine guns—that had been collected over the years from various visiting armies. Cummings bid $25,000, his entire savings, for the lot and got it. He promptly turned around and sold the material to his old employer, Cecil Jackson. Some sources say Cummings made a "modest profit" on the deal; others say he doubled his money.[3]

Cummings at this point in his career needed more capital to run the particular business he had in mind. Eventually he found Sidney Lerwin, a Chicago banker, who was reported to have backed him to the extent of $50,000, with the shares of the new arms company being divided equally between the two men. Lerwin was very much the silent partner; rarely if ever did he take part in the day-to-day affairs of Interarms. Lerwin was president and Cummings was vice president, and the company was operating primarily out of the Foreign Trade Zone in New York City.

In 1958 Cummings offered to buy out Lerwin. He divided the inventory in half and told Lerwin either to accept the offer or to take his half of the arms inventory. (Cummings had made sure that Lerwin's half contained the least salable goods.) Two new companies, Interarmco (now Interarms) Limited and Hunters Lodge, were set up in Alexandria, Virginia. Cummings planned to operate through them if Lerwin refused to sell out. Eventually a settlement was reached, Lerwin accepting a cash sum plus a quantity of leftover small arms.

Even before he acquired complete control there was no doubt back in 1953 that Sam Cummings was well established and fully primed to exploit the potential arms market that lay ahead. He was on his way and he was soon to make his first million dollars.

With Cummings poised to begin his swift domination of the arms market, several items should be noted at this point. One is Cummings' similarity to Bannerman. Prior to the Spanish-American War there had been no foreign military weapons, or even domestic military weapons, available in any quantity to the American public. Bannerman stepped in and filled this need. Cummings, in essence, did the same thing. It occurred to him that no foreign military weapons, particularly bolt action and semiautomatic rifles, had entered the American market in any numbers since the days of Bannerman. In effect there had been a forty-year drought on foreign weapons suitable for sporting purposes.

He also realized, as every gun buff knows, that a military rifle, properly reconditioned, makes an inexpensive but excellent if not superior quality sporting rifle. The demand for these guns in America, Cummings knew, was insatiable. Virtually all of the domestic gun manufacturers, particularly Winchester Arms and Remington Arms, were not satisfying this demand; their products were very expensive in comparison. Cummings realized as well that the foreign military weapons brought back by millions of servicemen in 1945 did not satisfy the demand; if anything they stimulated it.

Cummings, therefore, was, as is the case in many other fields of endeavor, the right man at the right time. He was extremely knowledgeable about weapons, particularly surplus military rifles and pistols. He also knew the market; he had good contacts, adequate backing and a keen business sense. He also started to build his own empire at the exact moment when the weapons used in World War II were beginning to flood the surplus market in volume. Furthermore, not only were the more industrial nations in the early 1950's beginning to shed their old weapons in favor of jet-age ordnance, but at the same time there began to emerge on the world stage a growing group of new nations, each one of which coveted all the weapons it could get. The demand here seemed just as insatiable as in the American market. Under such circumstances, Cummings' future in 1953 as a successful arms dealer seemed most auspicious indeed.

2

The Panamanian purchase which netted Cummings such a handsome profit was followed in close order by another large deal, this one in Guatemala. It is generally accepted now that the Central Intelligence Agency engineered the revolution in 1954 that overthrew the pro-communist government of President Jacobo Arbenz Guzmán. In the three years preceding the revolution, the U.S. government had sold a small quantity of weapons at very low prices to Arbenz in order to thwart his dependence on Eastern bloc countries for arms. Some of this business went to Cummings. He reportedly supplied several thousand small arms, which he had bought from the U.S. government for 50 cents each and had sold for $4.00 each, plus transportation.

The critical point leading up to the revolution came in May 1954, when it was learned through "arms-dealing circles" that Czechoslovakia was in the process of shipping 2,000 tons of small arms to Arbenz. The weapons were being delivered to the Polish port of Stettin from which a Swedish ship was to transport them to the Guatemalan harbor town of Puerto Barrios. This move gave the CIA a valid pretext to ship arms to a group of anti-communist Guatemalans, led by Carlos Castillo-Armas, which was exiled in Nicaragua. In short order, Castillo-Armas' rebels, armed with U.S. weapons, invaded their homeland.

The general supposition is that the "arms-dealing circles" which spotted the Czech arms shipment was Cummings or one of his agents. Thus, when Castillo-Armas took power after ousting

Arbenz, Cummings was, in his own words, "in on the ground floor."

"The new government," he said, "decided to scrap its entire Czech military inventory and re-equip on the American .30 caliber. The trouble was that America could not be too overt about supplying them. The Guatemalans were advised to get their weapons on the open market, and one way or another they came to me."[4]

Cummings, over the course of five years, bought all the surplus Guatemalan weapons—some 80,000 pieces, which included a number of ancient Hotchkiss cannon—and shipped them to his warehouse in Alexandria where they were later sold off to collectors through his mail-order and retail outlets. In England he found the arms he needed to re-equip the Guatemalans: old M-1 Garands that Britain had purchased from the United States in World War II. But Cummings learned to his dismay that, as an alien, he could not tender for British surplus weapons, not even American-made ones. This is standard practice in many European countries; it provides the selling government with someone local to blame if any laws are broken. Only a company owned by a national, he learned, was eligible to bid.

To get around this ruling Cummings persuaded an Englishman, R. Stuart Murray, the sales director of Cogswell & Harrison and a past Master of the Worshipful Company of Gunmakers, to tender for him, a perfectly legal move. Murray's bid was successful, and the Garands desired were duly sold to the Guatemalans for $500,000. Since the quantity was bigger than the Guatemalan requirements, the remaining Garands were sold via intermediaries to Haiti and Indonesia in 1961. Cummings was later to sell Guatemala a number of Lee-Enfield rifles, also purchased at auction in Great Britain.

As luck would have it, the Garand purchase paved the way to broadening Interarms' base. It was Murray who advised Cummings to invest in Cogswell & Harrison, a company that has supplied large quantities of weapons to Commonwealth countries. Cummings took a minority position in 1954 and acquired controlling interest, 55 percent, in 1958. During these years he also acquired control of the other quality gunmaking firms noted previously.

The profitable Panamanian deal of 1954 led Cummings two years later to another major sale. Part of the payment he received from Western Arms for the 7,000 weapons was in the form of .50 caliber machine guns. One person in Washington who expressed interest in the machine guns, and other weapons as well, was the Dominican military attaché. Cummings flew down to what was then Ciudad Trujillo and began negotiations. He met the late dictator of the Republic, General Rafael Leonidas Trujillo Molina, and it was the beginning of a long friendship. Trujillo, observed Cummings, was "a pleasant person to deal with" and was not as unsavory as the press made him out to be. Dictators, he added, "have a sense of order and they pay their bills promptly." Cummings was to become one of the major armaments suppliers to the Dominican Republic until 1960 when the United States placed heavy restrictions on all arms shipments to the Caribbean.

In the course of conversations over the supplying of .50 caliber machine guns and other arms, Trujillo mentioned to Cummings that he was interested in purchasing some jet fighters and asked if Cummings knew where he might get them. Cummings said he thought he might be able to fill the order. It so happened that the Interarms agent in Sweden had heard that the Swedish government might be willing to part with twenty-six of its *Vampire* Mark I jet fighter-bombers. Cummings put in a bid to the Swedes and it was accepted. The price quoted to the Dominicans was $3.5 million. What the difference was between the purchase and sales price is something Cummings is still not willing to discuss. But it is obvious that *Vampire* Mark I's were going cheap at the time (about $25,000 each), since they were an older generation of jet, too slow for a country such as Sweden, which feels that its air force must be constantly brought up to date.

Sweden, however, was reluctant to assume the responsibility of arming Trujillo, so it accepted Cummings' bid on the condition that the jets be shipped through U.S. ports. This allowed the State Department to veto the transaction if it felt that power relationships would be upset in the Caribbean. According to Cummings, the sale was allowed to go through in order to balance the air power between the Dominican Republic and Venezuela. Relations between these two countries were most strained at this time, and Venezuela had just purchased twenty-five *Vampires* from Great Britain. A balance was needed, since the two antagonists were only one hour apart by jet. Cummings got his license, and the Swedes sent the jets to New York where they were picked up by Dominican freighters.

Cummings was to see these jets in action a few years later, in June of 1959, when he was in the Dominican Republic again to sell the government some 25,000 AR-10's, the American-designed rifle that was being manufactured under license by the Dutch armaments firm of Artillerie Inrichtingen. It so happened that at the very moment Cummings was in the Republic a small band of Castro-backed rebels landed near Puerto Plata. The take-over bid was a fiasco: the Dominican *Vampires* strafed the invaders on the beach, and the local inhabitants finished off the survivors with their machetes.

The weapons the rebels left behind, however, happened to be brand-new AR-10's. General Kovaks, Trujillo's Hungarian-born military adviser, was examining one of the captured rifles on his desk when Cummings entered with Trujillo. One word led to another, and Cummings eventually was forced to admit that he had indeed sold the captured rifle to Castro. Trujillo was reportedly furious with Cummings, and undoubtedly the intrepid arms dealer had to do some fast talking. One report had Cummings dismissing the incident with the remark to Trujillo: "You know I wouldn't tell him [Castro] to use it against you."[5]

The first five years of Interarms' life, from 1953 to 1958, were difficult ones. Although Cummings had begun to broaden his base of operations, he still was short of cash on occasion and he still had formidable competition. They were frantic years, years in which a hectic pace was maintained buying and selling surplus weapons, making the right contacts and establishing well-connected sales agents.

Although Cummings is most reticent to talk about what he does, some of his transactions are known and can be recorded.

In 1955 Costa Rican exiles, aided by Nicaraguan dictator Anastasio Somoza, invaded their homeland in an attempt to overthrow the democratic government of President José "Pepe" Figueres. The rebels were armed with Italian Beretta pistols and Danish Madsen submachine guns supplied by Somoza but originally bought from Interarms. The Figueres loyalists repulsed the invasion with 2,000 M-1 Garands, 1,000 .30 caliber Browning machine guns and two million rounds of ammunition—also bought from Interarms.[6]

The following year Cummings bought 2,000 Israeli small arms which had been captured from the Egyptians in the Suez campaign. Cummings insists that he actually bought them through a third party, not directly from the Israelis. The weapons were predominantly Russian in origin, purchased by the Egyptians from the Czechs who, in turn, had acquired them from the Soviets. Cummings had the goods shipped to Alexandria, where they were then sold to the public through his usual outlets. "Most of them," he told me, "now hang over the fireplaces in American homes."

In the same period Cummings managed to sell Austria the entire ordnance needed to equip its border police. He was also one of the first to benefit from the rearming of West Germany: he bought from the Dutch government several thousand German MG-42 machine guns which had originally belonged to the Wehrmacht; he then sold the entire lot to the Bonn government. He sold submachine guns and a great deal of other equipment to Batista. Through Cogswell & Harrison he supplied the Kenya police with many Lee-Enfield No. 4 rifles to fight the Mau Mau.

He equipped the Finnish army with 75,000 Sten guns; he pleased President William V. S. Tubman of Liberia by providing his army with 2,000 .30-06 Springfield rifles with extra-long chrome-plated bayonets; he bought from Ireland several hundred Thompson submachine guns, all of which had been confiscated from members of the outlawed Irish Republican Army; he even sold 144 cavalry lances (complete with guidons) to the Sudan that were originally part of a batch of equipment purchased from Argentine arsenals. (The Sudan maintains one of the few remaining mounted camel cavalry units in the world.)

One of Interarms' most profitable deals took place in 1958 when British authorities put up for auction approximately 600,000 Lee-Enfield rifles. Cummings found that he did not have enough money to cover the cost of such a potentially large purchase so, with Stuart Murray, he went into temporary partnership with Birmingham-based Parker-Hale Limited, which, in turn, was acting as a purchasing agent for Golden State Arms. It is not clear what percentage either party underwrote the bid. John Le Breton, Parker-Hale's energetic sales director, claims his company had a 50 percent interest; Stuart Murray told me that Interarms had a 75 to 80 percent interest. Nor is it clear what the partners bid for the Lee-Enfields. Apparently many of the rifles went for as little as two shillings (then worth 28 cents) apiece, while others went for several pounds each. The average cost seems to have been close to one dollar. In any event the Interarms–Parker-Hale combine won the bid and subsequently made handsome profits. For example, a "sporterized" Lee-Enfield sells for $24.95 in the United States, and considering shipping, tariff and renovating costs, it seems reasonable to believe that profits of at least 300 percent were realized. Cummings also managed to sell 50,000 of these Lee-Enfields, on an "as is" basis, to Pakistan's border patrols.

Another big purchase was consummated in 1958, this time with surplus equipment from Finland. Cummings bought a total of 300,000 weapons which included Lahti antitank guns (later to achieve a certain notoriety), Tokarevs, Mosin-Nagants and a miscellaneous assortment of automatic weapons (which ended up, for the most part, in the Quantico and Aberdeen museums). Included in this purchase were 70 million rounds of ammunition, mostly in Russian 7.92 mm and 7.62 mm. The entire purchase was so large that it took three years to ship to the United States.

Cummings was the first person to bring into the United States in any quantity Italian Mannlicher-Carcano rifles and carbines.* He

* The rifle is known by three names: "Carcano," after one of the major designers; "Mannlicher-Carcano," after the magazine system designers; and "Parraviccini-Carcano," after the two who were credited with developing the original bolt action. The carbine version carries the same designations

brought in 70,000 in 1957, reportedly paying 75 cents apiece for them. They usually sold for $14.95 on the domestic market. Most of what he imported were 7.35 mm carbines, or "Ternis," which are lighter in weight and far more versatile than the rifle version. They are also more easily converted into inexpensive sporting weapons and, because of their relatively short barrel, have a greater appeal to hunters than the rifle. There was a huge demand in America for these Italian-made weapons during the late 1950's, and Cummings was able to sell this and subsequent batches without any difficulty.

Although Cummings has always had competitors, especially during these early years, one particular rival deserves mention at this point because it, too, wanted to share in what appeared to be the easy profits in Mannlicher-Carcanos. The name of the company was Adam Consolidated Industries, Inc., domiciled in New York and Rome, Italy. Its flirtation with buying and selling surplus Italian weapons presents a good example of what can happen to an amateur in the arms trade who thinks he can make a quick financial killing. Adam Consolidated is also the firm that imported Mannlicher-Carcano Model 91/38 in 6.5 caliber, serial number C2766, the rifle Lee Harvey Oswald used to assassinate President Kennedy.

Adam Consolidated's roots, incongruously enough, date back to the incorporation of Adam Hat Stores, Inc., under New York law on July 17, 1924. This company was perhaps best known for its radio sponsorship of championship boxing matches from Madison Square Garden. In 1954 Adam Hat found itself in fiscal difficulties and was bought out by Harold N. Leitman, who ran a family-owned junk and retail tire business. Two years later the new combine changed its name to Adam Consolidated Industries, Inc.

Adam Consolidated became a most diversified company. Its main business was selling tires through such firms as The R. H. Macy Company, Gimbels and Montgomery Ward. At one time the

---

but is more commonly known by those in the gun trade as a "Terni," after the town fifty miles from Rome where they were manufactured. Neither rifle nor carbine is ever referred to as a "Mannlicher" alone, since such would refer to an Austrian rifle designed by the same individual.

company had seventeen wholly or partly owned subsidiaries, none of which hinted that part of the firm's activities included buying and selling surplus foreign military weapons. It was also completely out of the hat business; but it was and still continues to be referred to derogatorily by the professionals in the arms business as "the hatties." By 1959 Adam Consolidated began a round of name changing which has clouded the picture somewhat, perhaps intentionally. First Adam Consolidated was dropped in favor of Vanderbilt Tire and Rubber; then the name was changed to VTR, Inc., which it is today, selling on the American Stock Exchange in the $30.00 range. From all indications, the company's branch in Rome kept the name Adam Consolidated.

To further muddy the waters, another firm was chartered under New York law in 1959 called Crescent Firearms, Inc. All guns imported by Adam Consolidated–VTR, Inc., were invoiced to this company for distribution in the states. There is no record that Crescent and VTR were or are financially linked in any way, but they maintained nevertheless an interesting relationship. In August 1965, an article in *Life* noted that VTR had its offices on the sixth floor at 404 Fifth Avenue, New York, and that Crescent maintained its offices at 2 West 37th Street, New York. It was, the article said, the same building, same floor, same receptionist and the same telephone number, WI 7-4700. The article also noted that the vice president, secretary and treasurer of VTR was Joseph Saik, an attorney, and that as late as 1964 VTR's controller was one Irving Weiss. Saik was also secretary-treasurer of Crescent Firearms, and Weiss was its controller.

Today, VTR is located at 370 Lexington Avenue, New York. A male voice, which refused to identify itself, told me over the phone that VTR no longer sells weapons and that Crescent Firearms "is no longer operating." The voice added that it would be futile for me to stop by the office for more information. Joseph Saik told me that he had severed his connection with both VTR and Crescent; he now runs Vanderbilt Automotive Centers, a tire company, from the same 2 West 37th Street office.

In any event, by 1958 Cummings had just begun to succeed in selling wholesale quantities of his weapons to large chain and department stores. Previously his sales in America were limited to retail gun dealers and his own mail-order sales. One of Cummings' wholesale customers was The R. H. Macy Company. Adam Consolidated, through its own sale of tires to Macy's, heard of the apparently large profits Cummings was making in bulk sales of Mannlicher-Carcanos and decided that if Interarms could do it, so could they.

So, in 1960, when the Italian Ministry of Defense offered 570,745 surplus Italian small arms for sale, Adam Consolidated (domiciled at Via Serte 62, Rome) thought it saw its opportunity and put in a bid. It won the contract, and the prices for the weapons ranged from $3.60 for the newer ones down to $1.12 for the older models. The entire contract called for Adam Consolidated to pay the Italian government $1,776,658.54. This meant that the cost of all the weapons averaged slightly more than $3.10; hence most of the weapons were of the relatively newer variety.

Not all these weapons, however, were in usable condition.* So Adam Consolidated contracted with a Luciano Riva, who ran a small gun renovating and manufacturing firm in Brescia in northern Italy, to recondition, process, pack and ship these rifles at a unit price of $1.72. Riva's contract with Adam Consolidated was made through a Louis Feldsott, who was as late as 1965 president of Crescent Firearms and treasurer of H & D Folsom Arms Company, Inc., of Yonkers, New York.

Soon after the contract was made, Riva and Adam Consolidated had a falling out. Riva complained he was due money for work he had completed; Adam Consolidated charged that Riva's work was unsatisfactory and that he was so slow in completing the contract that the market for Mannlicher-Carcanos in the United States was being filled by others. Adam Consolidated eventually found another renovator, and by October 1963 had imported into the

* This is not unusual in the surplus arms business. Most every surplus gun needs some reconditioning; others require a great deal of work, and usually a few—but sometimes as much as 10 percent of the whole batch—are unusable. Working parts from the worthless guns are invariably used as replacements on the salable guns.

United States approximately 125,000 units. Rifle No. C2766 was among them.

The rifle that Lee Harvey Oswald used to assassinate President Kennedy left Italy on September 30, 1960, aboard the Italian steamer *Elettra Fassio.* It arrived in Jersey City seventeen days later and was consigned to a bonded warehouse, Harborside Terminal, near the dockside. It remained there for twenty-eight months and then, along with a batch of other Mannlicher-Carcanos, was shipped by Crescent Firearms to Klein's Sporting Goods, Inc., of Chicago. Klein's is a large retail and mail-order firm specializing in sporting equipment, including firearms. It is a regular advertiser in *The American Rifleman,* the organ of the National Rifle Association.

In the February 1963 issue of the *Rifleman,* Klein's ran a full-page illustrated advertisement in which they offered a "6.5 ITALIAN CARBINE. Only 36″ overall, weighs only 5½ lbs. Shows only slight use. . . . Specially priced . . . $12.88. Carbine with brand new good quality 4X scope—¾″ diameter as illustrated. . . . $19.95."

On March 13, 1963, Klein's received a money order for $21.45 (to include postage) and a coupon clipped from the advertisement ordering this particular weapon with scope. Both the money order and the coupon were in the name of A. Hidell, P.O. Box 2915, Dallas, Texas. One week later rifle No. C2766 was shipped to the customer without demur, for indeed there was no law against it. The name A. Hidell, of course, was later determined to be an alias used by Lee Harvey Oswald.[7]

While the advertisement offered for sale a Mannlicher-Carcano *carbine,* the actual weapon illustrated in the ad was what is known as a "short rifle," which is not the same thing. Mannlicher-Carcanos underwent many modifications during Mussolini's dictatorship and to the uninitiated the results may seem confusing. But any standard weapons manual will show that the ordinary Mannlicher-Carcano *rifle,* in its various modifications, has an overall length of 47 inches or 50.7 inches; that the *carbine* has an overall length of approximately 36 inches; and that the *short rifle,* model 91/38 (in both 7.35 mm and 6.5 mm) has an overall length of 40.2 inches. Oswald received the third-named weapon in 6.5 mm. Klein's, which should have known better, did not notice the difference. Nor did Lee Harvey Oswald, who, in all probability, was primarily interested in the price and not the make or model. The "carbine" as advertised was the cheapest item Klein's was offering that month in rifles.*

When one looks back on Adam Consolidated's venture into the Mannlicher-Carcano market, several things are apparent. First of all, Adam Consolidated paid what was considered a large sum for the weapons. At an average of $3.10 per weapon this was over four times the price Cummings reportedly paid for his. A number of people close to the arms market feel that it was Cummings who forced up the price once he realized that Adam Consolidated was determined to buy, come what may. How Cummings did this is not clear, but one of the most common and most effective ways is to lay down a carpet of rumors just prior to the bidding to the effect that Interarms is determined to outbid everybody and is willing to go to such-and-such a price to do it. If this is the case, Adam Consolidated fell for the bait and Cummings let them take it.

Second, Adam Consolidated was not aware of the fact that it was buying primarily Mannlicher-Carcano rifles and short rifles, less salable items than the carbines. They not only cost more to purchase but are more expensive to refurbish into sporting

* The Klein's ads in *The American Rifleman,* as a rule, make interesting reading. For instance, Mannlicher-Carcanos were first advertised in the March 1962 issue of *Rifleman* and continued to appear in subsequent issues until October 1963. Klein's has never since run an ad for Mannlicher-Carcanos.

The specific manner in which Klein's advertised these rifles is also noteworthy. For instance, in the April 1963 issue of *Rifleman,* Klein's advertised its "carbine" as 40 inches overall and weighing 7 pounds, thus adding 4 inches to its length and 1½ pounds to its weight. The price, photograph and stock number remained unchanged. Three months later, in the July 1963 issue, the "carbine" price was reduced by ten cents. In the August issue, everything—stock number, weight, length and new price—remained the same except that the photographic illustration of the Mannlicher-Carcano now showed, for some reason, an Enfield .303 Jungle Carbine. Finally, in the September 1963 issue, the previous illustration—of a short rifle—was reinserted; the stock number, price and description (a "carbine") remained unchanged.

weapons. Furthermore, they were unaware that Cummings had bought his carbines from Spain at a much lower price and that he was selling them "as is" on the American market. By reconditioning its weapons outside the United States, Adam Consolidated ran up the cost of the guns to such a point that it had to pay a higher import duty, further reducing its profits.

Even a cursory glance at Adam Consolidated's expenses will show that the firm made very little if any money on the deal; some believe it lost heavily. If one were to add to the $3.10 average initial unit cost the $1.72 refurbishing cost, plus the cost of shipping from Italy to Jersey City, plus the high import duty of $2.00, plus 22.5 percent *ad valorem,* plus the storage fees at Harborside Terminal, and then deduct the standard 40 percent discount from Klein's $12.88 price, one is left with no profit at all. In addition, only some 125,000 units of the 570,745 Mannlicher-Carcanos were imported prior to the assassination. After that the market dried up. Adam Consolidated surely unloaded the remainder, perhaps even for a small profit, but certainly not for the financial coup it expected.

Cummings often says that he likes to "help his competitors out"—that is to say, out of business. His treatment of Adam Consolidated is a classic example. From 1958 until August 1961, Cummings, through Hunters Lodge, sold his Mannlicher-Carcanos for $14.95 apiece. But his purchase of cheaper ones from Spain in 1960 allowed him to reduce his prices. However, he maintained his $14.95 price until he heard that Adam Consolidated was ready to sell its Mannlicher-Carcanos. Then, in September 1961, as the bulk of Adam Consolidated's goods were on the high seas on their way from Italy to the United States, Cummings dropped his price to $9.95—a price at which he could turn a profit but one that his competitor could not match.

An indication of how effective was this whipsaw treatment is in the length of time both companies took to sell their Mannlicher-Carcanos. The last advertisement Hunters Lodge carried for its carbines was in November 1961, two months after it had dropped its price to $9.95. Adam Consolidated, however, through mail-order houses such as Klein's, was still attempting to sell them for

$12.78 two years later in October 1963, a month before the bottom fell out of the market.

3

During the years 1958–59, Interarms became undisputed leader in the private sphere of the international arms trade. It was perhaps not apparent then, but in retrospect it is clear that from those years on Interarms has pulled away from its competitors, slowly but surely tightening its grip on the market.

There are two major reasons why Cummings and his company became dominant. The first is the huge inventory Cummings built up during the preceding years. Most of his competitors maintained no inventory at all. They would buy weapons and then unload them as quickly as possible, much in the manner of Adam Consolidated. Some dealers would broker arms: that is, they would hear of a tender—in, say, England, Belgium, Italy or Finland—then hunt around for a buyer—in, say, Israel, Venezuela, Pakistan or Nigeria—before they even bid on the weapons. What they bid was determined in large part by what they had been provisionally offered by the potential buyer. This is a very risky way to sell arms and is usually considered the quickest way for an individual to go bankrupt.

Sam Cummings did none of this. He assiduously began from the start to store ever increasing quantities of weapons in his warehouses. Such a huge inventory as he eventually was able to build up inevitably had an inhibitive effect on his competition. For instance, if a tender for, say, 10,000 bolt-action Mauser rifles were about to be let by the Spanish government, Cummings, through his agents, could pass the rumor that his eleven warehouses were stuffed with Mauser rifles. They might not be; they might be full of Lee-Enfields, Tokarevs, Mannlicher-Carcanos and Krag-Jorgensens, but it made no difference because no one except Cummings knew for sure. The competitors were thus faced with a dilemma. If his warehouses were *in fact* filled with Mauser rifles, then it meant that Cummings could flood the American market with Mausers—usually at a price below what his competition *paid* for them, much less *sold* them for—until his adversaries went bankrupt. At this point Cummings would then withdraw Mauser rifles from the market until prices went up.

On the other hand, if his warehouses were *not* filled with Mauser rifles, then the competition had to be prepared to pay very high prices for the items in competition with Cummings. No matter what the price was or who secured the bid, Cummings usually won out. The reasons are quite apparent. If Cummings *won* the bid—say, paying nine dollars for a Mauser that ordinarily would go for three dollars—he simply stored these weapons in his warehouses and withheld all his subsequent purchases of Mausers from the market until the demand for them was, say, fifteen dollars. Then he would unload them. (He might just as well try this with Mausers he bought for three dollars.)

If, however, he *lost* the bid at ten dollars, there would be little or no profit in the deal for the winner. Cummings knows that Mausers command only so much and no more on the retail American market. At ten dollars he knows that no retail outlet will buy the weapon from his competitor at the price that has to be offered for anyone involved to make a profit. He also knows that if he bought the weapon at that price that the cost of storing it over a long period of time would appreciate faster than the value of the weapon itself.

The second major reason why Cummings came to dominate the private arms market around the world was the development between 1958 and 1963 of what is called his "purchasing fund." This fund was part of a complicated financial device used to great effect not only by Cummings but by many businessmen in international enterprises, particularly the oil industry. In its most simple form, Cummings' financial structure, with his purchasing fund at its core, was set up and run in the following manner:

At the time he was beginning to broaden the base of his empire with the purchase of the controlling interest in Cogswell & Harrison, Cummings was also establishing additional Interarms companies around the world. They are known as Interarms S.A. (in Panama), or Interarms (Greece), Ltd., or Oy Interarms AB (in Finland), or some similar name. Several of them are little more than paper companies, run on a part-time basis, whose existence allows Cummings to bid on surplus arms tenders when they arise. Others are fully staffed offices with sales and purchasing agents who spend all their time on Interarms business. The extent of activity in any one of these companies depends essentially on the amount of surplus arms being bought and sold in that country.

But one of the branches is different: it is called Interarms (Canada), Ltd., and is domiciled not in Canada but in Monaco. This company was set up by Cummings in 1958 to take advantage of the principality's low corporate tax rate, at that time set at 1 percent of gross profits (the current United States rate is 48 percent). Interarms (Canada)'s bank is the Banque Commerciale, S. A., located in Geneva, Switzerland. Although the rumor persists that Cummings owns this bank, it is not true; but Cummings would never deny it because the tale enhances his image, flatters his ego and infuriates his competitors. No doubt Cummings is a very good customer with a very large and very private account there. This bank is the true home of his purchasing fund.

In addition, another development must be noted, since it bears on Cummings' financial structure. During the early years of Interarms, no one—not even Cummings—had adequate capital to bid alone on large tenders. Therefore, all the competing arms dealers used to join together to bid collectively. Each dealer would subscribe to a percentage of the total bid and, if the bid were successful, would receive back in arms the same percentage. Cummings' and Le Breton's cooperation in the 600,000 Lee-Enfield deal of 1958 is a case in point. On occasion Cummings also cooperated, singly or in groups, with Cecil Jackson of Western Arms, Jan Winters of Firearms International and George Rose of Seaport Traders. Although many of the competitors cordially despised one another (a few are genuinely good friends), from time to time they were forced by mutual poverty to work together. On rare occasions they got together on small bids even when each had adequate capital to bid separately. Their attitude, as one arms dealer told me, was, "Why carve each other's hearts out on a deal? Why bid up four or five thousand rifles when you can go in together and buy them for twenty cents apiece?"

The profits from some of the deals were often immense, sometimes running to 2,000 percent over investment. Several of Cummings' competitors could not manage such success, and they began to spend their money lavishly, as fast as it came in. They used their newfound, if temporary, wealth in a most unbusinesslike manner, spending it mostly on personal whims rather than on the expansion of their firms. They began to assume *nouveau riche* airs; they became loud, ostentatious, overbearing and, finally, overconfident, which contributed in large measure to their eventual business decline.

Others were more prudent and saved some of their profits for future purchases. But the most prudent of them all was Cummings, who saved every spare dollar he made. One arms dealer recalls that Cummings often went to unusual lengths to save money during this period. For instance, he once received a shipment of large antitank rifles from abroad which he wished to transfer from the Foreign Trade Zone in New York City to Washington, D.C. Instead of using the services of a trucking company, he strapped the lot to a ski rack on the top of his car and drove them down himself. While others paid themselves salaries of $25,000, $50,000, even $150,000 a year, Cummings seldom paid himself more than $9,500 a year; everything else eventually went into the purchasing fund. Thus by late 1958 Cummings was in a position to buy large batches of surplus weapons without having to ally himself temporarily with his competitors.

More important, however, is the fact that Cummings, with such a huge pool of funds in reserve, could say to a country that was selling arms: "Here is a check for the full amount of the weapons I just bought from you." This ability to make a quick payment in full should not be underestimated in its importance, particularly in a business where credit is almost nonexistent, where mutual trust is an illusion and where double shuffles are an occupational hazard. "They know that if we say we will pay, we will pay," Cummings told me; "and we won't ping-pong them around waiting for money or giving them a lot of excuses."

Many countries that were in the process of selling their old weapons needed the money from the sale as quickly as possible to use as a down payment on new, more modern equipment. During the days when Cummings was forced into a consortium arrangement with his competitors, there was often a last-minute scramble for money as the result of either members backing out at the last moment or the bids going higher than expected. This appearance of fiscal instability did not enhance the status of private dealers and tended to inhibit various nations from giving them any business. When Cummings came along and paid on the spot for his purchases, however, he became a most welcome figure to foreign military purchasing and sales agents. Their favorable attitude toward him subsequently helped him to win many bids that he might otherwise have lost.

From 1958 to 1963, then, Cummings channeled substantial sums of virtually untaxed money from his American operations into Interarms (Canada) quite legally and ultimately into his purchasing fund in Geneva. The process worked in the following manner: Interarms (U.K.) might bid on a large British offer of, say, surplus Lee-Enfield No. 4 Mark I's, the standard British World War II rifle, now obsolete. Assuming Interarms (U.K.) was successful in its bid, the cost per unit for these weapons might have been, say, $1.50 (an average price in the late 1950's). Interarms (U.K.) then, even before it paid for or took possession of the weapons, immediately "sold" the arms to Interarms (Canada) for $1.65 per unit (a 10 percent profit added). The Monaco-based company then drew a check against its purchasing fund and paid $1.65 per unit to its sister company, Interarms (U.K.), which in turn paid the British government in full. At this point the Lee-Enfields in question were technically owned by Interarms (Canada).

To maximize profits, it was important that these Lee-Enfields be invoiced into the United States at a value below $5.00 to take advantage of a relatively low import duty. According to the U.S. Customs schedule in effect during these years, item No. 730.23 of Schedule 7 noted that "Rifles: valued not over $5.00 each" taking a Class 1 rate (that is to say, a preferred GATT-member rate) were charged an import duty of 75 cents each plus 22.5 percent *ad valorem*. Rifles invoiced at a value over $5.00 brought higher, more prohibitive tariff rates which were financially unattractive to international surplus arms dealers.

The next step in this involved process was yet another transaction. Interarms (Canada) in turn sold the Lee-Enfields it had just bought from Interarms (U.K.) to International Armament Corporation, the parent company based in Alexandria, Virginia. The sales price per unit to International Armament Corporation would be, say, $4.95; this permitted the British-made weapons to enter the United States at the advantageous customs rate. The Alexandria office then paid Interarms (Canada) $4.95 per Lee-Enfield. Thus, for every one of these particular weapons imported, $4.95 in American money flowed out of the country into an account in Geneva. The Monaco-based company, Interarms (Canada), therefore, made $3.30 profit per weapon on this transaction; that is to say, $4.95 it received minus the $1.65 it paid. No American taxes were paid on the outgoing $4.95 because it was not being picked up by other American firms as part of their gross income, which was and still is ultimately taxable. It was being picked up by a foreign company owned by Cummings as gross income which, for all intents and purposes, was not being taxed at all.

Since all of Cummings' American-domiciled companies have large gross sales, it also paid him to have as large a figure as possible on his American balance sheet opposite the item "cost of goods purchased" (i.e., the money he sent abroad to pay for the weapons) because it is a deductible item. Thus his American profits and, ultimately, his American taxes were substantially reduced.

This transaction, from the initial bid for the Lee-Enfields to the final deposit in the Geneva bank, was, of course, quite legal. The amazing thing is that almost the entire transaction could take place before the actual rifles in question had left the government arsenals in Britain.

In 1963 a treaty was signed between Monaco and France which increased the principality's corporate tax from 1 percent to 25 percent (and subsequently to 35 percent). As a result the advantages to Cummings of having Interarms (Canada) domiciled in Monaco have been considerably diminished. Furthermore, the

United States passed several laws in the early 1960's which restricted the tax freedom of American citizens living and conducting their businesses abroad. Nevertheless, until these developments, Cummings was able to acquire legally so much capital that collectively his competitors have since been unable to match his bids at the major arms auctions. Coupled with his large stocks of arms held in warehouses, this purchasing fund has had a devastating effect on all of his competitors.

Cummings, because he has maintained offices in a number of foreign countries, used this financial device to best advantage. Most of his competitors were less successful at it. Some American importers, however, used another device that deserves brief mention here. It was called "averaging" and could be an illegal practice designed to import weapons into the United States at the cheapest possible price. The Gun Control Act of 1968, by banning surplus military arms imports, brought this practice to an end. Illegal averaging, however, is still practiced on a much reduced scale in other countries where small arms are still allowed to be imported. It must be emphasized here that Cummings and his organization have never stooped to using this device.

Averaging is legal with many items, particularly bulk commodities. A buyer pays so much per ton, per square foot or per some other unit. He then imports the material and pays duty on his declared average price. But with armaments it was more complicated. When surplus military arms came up for bid in a foreign country, often the weapons were broken down into various lots upon which a buyer bid separately—so much per weapon for these 1,000 pistols, so much for each of those 50 antique cannon, so much per weapon for another lot of 3,500 semiautomatic rifles, and so on.

Occasionally an arms buyer would strike a deal with the seller by offering an average price for everything up for sale. The seller would often agree to such a deal because it meant that while he might lose a few dollars on the expensive items he figures he would make it up on the unsalable ones.

More often, however, an arms buyer would bid separately on

each lot of weapons, for which he would pay differing prices if his bids were successful—anything from 28 cents per weapon for near junk up to $15 per weapon for mint condition surplus guns. Yet, on importing these goods into the United States, the buyer would declare to Customs that he paid such-and-such an average price for the entire shipment.

Customs frowned on averaging because it was apparent that many of the weapons, paying a duty derived from a legitimate average price, qualified for a higher duty rate; in the latter case it was a clear evasion of the law.

It was the U.S. Customs' unhappy task to separate the proper averaging transactions from the improper ones. The problem of combating the illegal aspects of averaging was complicated by several factors. First of all, there was and still is no standard world price range for surplus arms (as there would be for, say, scrap iron, wool or plate glass) by which Customs can judge the accuracy of the declared price. Second, Customs found that foreign countries were and continue to be most unwilling to divulge their arms sales figures; the need for military security and the belief that it was none of U.S. Customs' business were the two excuses most often given. A foreigner's reluctance to exchange or divulge information with U.S. authorities, moreover, was compounded by his own frantic efforts to cover his tracks—to hide payoffs, markups and even thefts from his own government. The arms importer, if he was questioned on the validity of his declared prices, often said, "Well, if you don't believe me, why don't you ask the people in the country where I bought the guns?" Thus the Customs inspector was caught between two mute parties with no one to turn to for aid.

One ironic aspect is that Customs inspectors often found that the easiest improper averaging transactions to uncover were those in which arms were being imported under the auspices of the CIA or some other branch of the U.S. government. Here it would appear that many arms dealers did not care to hide their tracks, since they knew that they were protected by higher authority. They knew that the inspectors would be told by their superiors to cease investigating this particular transaction. This was a dangerous game for a dealer to play; nevertheless, several American companies seemed eternally willing to take the risks.

To give some idea why it frequently paid to average the cost of weapons imported, assume a dealer imported 30,000 Mauser rifles, having paid 50 cents apiece for 10,000 older models, $5.50 apiece for 10,000 newer models and $7.00 apiece for 10,000 near mint models. If the dealer had followed U.S. Customs law, he would have paid $76,750 in import duties. That is, he would have paid 75 cents plus 22.5 percent *ad valorem* on the 10,000 rifles for which he paid 50 cents and $2.00 plus 22.5 percent *ad valorem* on two lots of 10,000 rifles for which he paid more than $5.00.

However, if he had chosen to average his costs, he might have stated on his Customs declaration that he had bought all 30,000 rifles for $4.33 apiece (the average price of $0.50, $5.50 and $7.00). Therefore he would have paid 75 cents plus 22.5 percent *ad valorem* on all 30,000 rifles because they would have been listed as costing less than $5.00. Thus his bill to Customs would have been only $51,727.50, a saving of over $25,000 or nearly 33 percent.

A refinement of averaging was used when all the imported weapons had been purchased abroad for more than $5.00 apiece. In a few arms dealers' minds, to import them legally at higher tariff rates would have required an extra expenditure of private funds, a practice they have always opposed. To reduce their Customs payments, an arrangement was made whereby the seller "sold" the weapons for, say, an average price of $3.50 apiece when, in reality, the actual privately-agreed-upon price was, say, $9.50 apiece. The arms were then duly imported, tariff being paid on the $3.50 declared price. Six months or so later, the dealer would pay the original seller a "sales commission" of $6.00 per weapon (perhaps slightly more to cover interest), which balanced the account. The payment was made by check and sent through the mails and was never seen by the Customs officials. Customs argued rightly that the $6.00 was subject to import duties since it was in effect part of the original sales price. However, it was extremely difficult to convict a dealer of falsifying import statements in such a manner, again because no one at either end was willing to talk. Indeed, so clever were those who practiced it that it is still difficult to prove that this variation of averaging ever existed at all in the arms trade.

There are other reasons why Interarms is the world's foremost private surplus arms supply company. One reason was the large sales to chain stores in the United States. At one point, particularly around 1956–57, Cummings found himself with enormous quantities of weapons in his warehouses that were being sold to retailers only piecemeal. That is to say, an average order ran to 50 rifles or pistols, a large order to 200. Cummings knew that, at that rate of sales, it would be years before he would witness one complete turnover of his wares.

By 1958, however, Cummings had succeeded in breaking into the chain-store market. Such companies as Montgomery Ward, Sears Roebuck, The R. H. Macy Company, Gamble-Skogmo, Gimbels and many other similar types of firms began to buy 5,000, sometimes 10,000 surplus weapons per order.

The fight for this market was not an easy one because there was considerable prejudice among retailers against foreign-made weapons. In addition, every sporting gun retailer was subjected to heavy pressure from the domestic manufacturers to stock only American-made guns. But, again, Cummings was fortunate because the market for inexpensive foreign surplus-turned-sporting rifles and the market for domestically made sporting guns were not in competition with each other. The retail price of foreign-made surplus ranged from less than $10 to $80 or $90; the retail price for most domestic arms ranged from $80 up to $300 or more. Cummings was thus tapping a market with a demand that the domestic manufacturers failed or refused to meet.

In fact, Cummings claimed and still claims that his surplus sales complemented domestic sales. He calls it his "Kodak Brownie to Leica" theory. In other words, an American, interested in guns but without too much initial capital, will continually upgrade the quality of his rifle. He might start off by buying an inexpensive rifle, say a Russian Mosin-Nagant model 91/30 at $9.95; then, as his finances improve, he might move up to a model M98 Paraguayan Mauser in 8 mm at only $29.95; then perhaps he will purchase a Belgian FN SAFN model 1949 caliber .30-06 semiautomatic rifle at $79.00; and finally he might buy the "Leica," say the American-made Remington model 742 semiautomatic big game rifle at $169.95. Before Cummings came along, the American gun buff had to start his buying cycle with an expensive rifle.

The bulk of Interarms' U.S. profits came from direct sales to these chain stores. Previously, most profits came from sales through Hunters Lodge, an Interarms subsidiary that at one time was the largest gun mail-order house in the country. In 1957 profits from mail-order sales were a high percentage of the whole, perhaps as much as 60 percent. But they began to shrink after 1958 when the chain store market opened up. They were to shrink to 10 percent soon after President Kennedy's assassination and they were to dry up entirely by early 1968 in anticipation of the passage in Congress of the Gun Control Act that now prohibits the inter-state mail-order sale of weapons.

Because Interarms is so large, Cummings can "create" his own rare weapons by cornering the market in a particular gun. Pistols seem to be the easiest to corner, particularly Luger pistols. A Mauser Nazi "K" Series Luger will sell for $125, some $55 more than an ordinary secondhand 9 mm 1908 model Luger. A Mauser Banner model Luger goes for $150, a Krieghoff model for $225, and a Bulgarian Luger, complete with the Royal Coat of Arms of the former kingdom stamped on the breechblock, will sell for as much as $700.

If there are only 2,500 Lugers of a particularly model extant in the Western world, and Interarms owns them all, then Cummings sees no reason why he should let the chain stores make a profit on them. He sells these stores the more ordinary surplus in order to maintain his volume, but he sells the rare models through Hunters Lodge (previously via mail-order, now over-the-counter). He is in a particularly advantageous position here because there is no competition, because he can set the price as high as the market will bear, and because there is no retail discount consideration to cut into his profits.

Cummings has been fortunate in his choice of assistants. Stuart Murray remains his closest confidant, and the decisions of these two men usually determine what is bought and what the bids shall be. The man in charge of the Alexandria complex is Richard Winter, a former bombardier who came to work for Interarms in 1960. Previously he had worked for Ed Flaig, the owner of a large retail and mail-order gun store in Millvale, Pennsylvania. For a number of years the general manager in Alexandria was Peter Christian Beer, an Austrian by birth. He fled to the United States after the Nazi *Anschluss* and later served with distinction as a combat intelligence officer with a U.S. paratroop division in Europe during World War II. Interarms' complicated financial structure was essentially the creation of Beer; he also has a reputation as a superb organizer. Recently, however, he has tried his hand at buying surplus weapons and was badly burned by the competition, particularly Bill Sucher and Manny Wiggensberg of International Firearms, who outbid him on at least five occasions in South America. Beer now is in London working with Murray.

Interarms' accountant is Frank Slye, a resident of Washington, D.C. He is emerging as a most astute financial manager. The technical expert is Tom Nelson, one of the world's foremost authorities on submachine guns. Until recently there was another cog in the Interarms wheel, Richard Breed, Jr., who was in charge of relations with the U.S. government and international shipping matters. But Breed, a direct descendant of General George Gordon Meade, had a falling out with Beer and resigned from the company.

Backing up this group is the world's largest and most efficient private intelligence system in the arms business. Cummings has agents in virtually every free nation of the world. He has no agents in eastern bloc countries, but he has contacts in Omnipol, the Czech overseas trading agency, and in other eastern European trading firms as well. The job of Cummings' agents is to spot when surplus arms are about to come onto the market and to grab them up as cheaply as possible before the competitors do. Perhaps their most important job is to cultivate the proper contacts and to influence those who control the sale and purchase of arms so that when a deal is ripe it will fall Interarms' way. They also attempt to sell new, more modern equipment to the country for which they are responsible. No one has set up a better, more dynamic organization in this respect than Cummings. Some of his agents operate under the Interarms label; others operate independently. Either way, there is no doubt that they are first in their field, and they are paid handsome commissions for their efforts.

One of the most notable qualities of his agents is the influence and the contacts they have. For instance, Cummings' Finnish agent is Major Kurt Touri, a hero of the Finno-Russian Winter War. He knows all the right people in Helsinki and, despite his reputation as a fiery-tempered individual, can smooth the way for a sale or purchase far better than anyone else in the country. Cummings' man in Thailand was David Cumberland, an American formerly employed by the U.S. Military Assistance Advisory Group there. Again, he knew all the right people, all the way up to the Prime Minister and King. Cumberland carried a pistol because, as he explained, "business competition out here can be kind of rugged." When Sukarno was in power, Interarms' Indonesian agent was the Prime Minister's cousin. Currently its agent is a lifelong school friend of Suharto's. The Interarms agent in Iran is Ali Dadshaw, who has the ear of the Shah. No major decision, particularly on the purchase or sale of arms, is ever made in Iran without the Shah's personal approval. On occasion Cummings backs up his agents with other influential people. For instance, in order to buy some old Mauser rifles from Iran it was necessary to bring in Ove Westergaard, a Dane who manufactures 81 mm mortar ammunition, because he had the "key" to the sale. What the key was is not clear, but apparently Westergaard knew the right Iranians to clinch the deal.

From time to time Cummings finds that some of his contacts give his company a bad name. Eventually they are weeded out. One of the better known agents was Hans Joachim Seidenschnur, who once claimed to be Cummings' man in Germany. The association came to an end in 1961.

Seidenschnur was reportedly a part-time agent for Western interests who wanted to buy weapons from behind the Iron Curtain. Many of these weapons were to find their way to the Algerian FLN. Seidenschnur was close friends with Georg Puchert and Paul

Stauffer, arms dealers, respectively, from Hamburg and Zurich. Both men were shipping arms to the Algerian rebels. In Stauffer's files police found letters offering guns to Interarms but, as many newspapers failed to report, the offers were declined. By 1961 Seidenschnur had become so involved in the Algerian gun trade that he began calling for police protection following threats made by terrorists against his life.

In the same year Seidenschnur went to prison and served three years and seven months for illegal arms trafficking and financial swindling. He no sooner had emerged from jail in 1965 than he announced plans to sign a contract for the sale of surplus American military transport and training aircraft to the Red Chinese. The West German government denied that it had any connection with Seidenschnur and said that export licenses for the planes would be refused.[8] The consensus among arms dealers that I met seems to be that Seidenschnur is almost as interested in the publicity he receives from his bizarre business dealings as he is in the profits that might come from them.

Interarms was the official representative for Artillerie Inrichtingen, a Dutch government arms factory, for all sales of AR-10's in Latin America, northern Europe and Africa south of the Sahara. The AR-10 was the first important new military rifle to be developed for production by an American firm independent of government financial support since before World War II. It was developed by the Armalite division of the Fairchild Engine and Airplane Corporation. Its chief designer was Eugene Stoner, who gave his name to the bolt-locking and gas-tube operating system incorporated into the weapon. The AR-10 was designed to take a 7.62 mm NATO cartridge. The rifle was never adopted by the U.S. armed forces because the Pentagon, for political reasons, turned it down first in favor of the M-14 rifle and then in favor of the AR-15 (now called the M-16) rifle. The AR-15 was also designed by Stoner, incorporating the use of a .223 caliber projectile. It is currently in use by American and Allied forces in Vietnam. Stoner gets 50 cents royalty for every M-16 sold and his wife gets another 50 cents.

In 1957 the Dutch government bought the license to produce

AR-10's, but the weapon was never accepted as a standard infantry arm by any major power, and production ceased in 1961. Cummings believes that the AR-10 is one of the finest infantry assault rifles in existence in the world today. He has considerable contempt for light weapons such as the M-16 and the old M-1 carbine. The carbine, he told a Senate hearing in the spring of 1967, "was a useless weapon. Everyone loved it because it was light, but it was a dog."

"Why is it a dog?" asked Senator Symington.

Ballistically, Cummings replied, "you can have a hatful of cartridges in your stomach and still live long enough to blast the man who fired at you. It is as simple as that."

At this point in the hearings, the anonymous recorder, bent in concentration over his stenotype machine, leaped to his feet and cried. "He's right, he's right! I was in the Battle of the Bulge and I shot a German six times with a carbine and he was still able to shoot me!"

These remarks went unrecorded as did Cummings' personal opinion that "if I was a Marine in Vietnam and was given one of those new Armalites, I'd throw it away and say I'd lost it and try to get one of the Russian rifles off a dead VC. They're the best."[9]

Interarms is also a representative for Walther and Mauser products. On an *ad hoc* basis it is the representative for the Danish and Finnish munitions industries. This close cooperation with both commercial and government-owned firms has helped, quite naturally, to broaden Interarms' intelligence system. Cummings is being constantly fed information supplied by his agents and industrial contacts with the result that very little of what goes on in the arms business escapes his attention. The discovery of the Czech arms shipment to the Arbenz regime is an example of how efficient it can be, and it must be remembered that back in 1954 Cummings' intelligence network was just in the process of being organized. Today it is a ubiquitous factor in the arms trade.

Being a worldwide company has its advantages. One of the most obvious is that it has the flexibility to outflank embargoes placed on one country by another. For example, the United States embargoed arms to Pakistan and India in September 1965 when these two countries clashed over Kashmir. Although the embargo against "nonlethal" arms was lifted in March 1966, the embargo against guns and ammunition remained in effect until March 1968. Great Britain, on the other hand, although it too initially placed an embargo on the two countries, lifted all its restrictions soon after the actual fighting stopped. Thus the British branch of Interarms could conduct business quite legally with Pakistan and India for over two years while the American branch could not. Of course, Cummings could not be too blatant about what Interarms (U.K.) sold because the U.S. government would have cracked down on him at home.

South Africa is a more difficult problem for Cummings. Both the United States and Great Britain support a U.N. arms embargo on South Africa that has been in effect since the end of 1963. Cummings claims that he has sold nothing to the country since the embargo. In light of this claim, however, it is interesting to note that it was only in 1966 that Cummings closed down his branch office in Pretoria. If Cummings sells nothing there now, he would have very little trouble doing so if he wished. France, Belgium, Israel and Italy, among others, have ignored the embargo and have sold military equipment to South Africa. All it would take for Cummings to participate would be the incorporation of a subsidiary in any country, such as those above, that was unwilling to go along with the embargo. But again Cummings knows that the American government would make life unpleasant for him if too many of his wares found their way into Afrikaaner hands.

Another advantage of being a worldwide company is that it puts Interarms in a good position to trade with eastern European bloc nations. It is not against the law for an American firm to buy arms from communist countries, but had it happened prior to 1968 the State Department would not have issued an import license. If the arms are destined for some other country, State Department pressure would be brought to bear, not only because Western public opinion would be aroused but because such a transaction would send U.S. foreign exchange into the Soviet sphere. Very few industrialized Western countries have such restrictions on arms trading with the East as has the United States, and there is some indication that through indirect routes arms that originated from behind the Iron Curtain have ended up in Interarms warehouses. Specifically named have been Bulgarian Lugers, certain lots of 98K Mauser rifles and carbines, Soviet 7.92 mm and 7.62 mm ammunition, and various odd-lots of fully automatic weapons.

The case of the Bulgarian Lugers is a typical example of eastern European bloc weapons being sold in the West. Five thousand of these pistols were shipped in the late 1950's or early 1960's from Bulgaria into Austria where they soon found their way into Cummings' hands. Cummings realized that Bulgarian Lugers were highly desirable items for the American market. He bought them from his western European source reportedly for $9.00 apiece and sold some of them for around $700 each in the United States. The pistols were imported into the United States under an ordinary State Department license. They were shipped via Finnish freighter direct from the port of Hamburg to the Interarms docks in Alexandria. Virtually all of these Lugers had been made in Germany, so U.S. customs men had no reason to question the shipment. The Bulgarian source had previously been disclosed by Interarms to the State Department.

There are more than the usual strands of evidence to substantiate this story. First, once in the United States, these Lugers were mostly sold off privately by word of mouth to collectors. Second, no one I spoke to in the arms trade could remember there ever having been a public offer of this item for sale in the West. Bulgarian Lugers are sufficiently coveted by arms dealers that surely someone would have heard of at least one public sale. Third, when it was finally learned that the Lugers had actually come from Bulgaria, a quantity of these items suddenly appeared on the U.S. retail market with the royal crest filed off. The crest, stamped on the breechblock, is what gives the pistol its value; without it, the Luger would be reduced in value to $35, the price of an ordinary model 1908 Luger. No one would so alter a weapon that is otherwise worth $700 unless there was some pressing reason. But whoever did the altering failed to file off the Cyrillic lettering from the pistol's extractor, so to knowledgeable gun buffs many of these Bulgarian Lugers have not quite disappeared into the anonymity desired.

Cummings is very much in favor of trading with eastern Europe. "We feel," he told me, "that it's good business for the United States firms that are engaged in this industry and if we were allowed to obtain that material it wouldn't turn up in competition with us in many areas of the world." As an afterthought, he added, "Would you rather have us sell it or Russia sell it? That is what it boils down to."

On one occasion, in 1960, Cummings openly bought a batch of Czech Mausers from Omnipol and then applied to the U.S. State Department for an import license. He wanted to test the government's policy but, in the end, the license was denied and the sale was off.

The Czechs, however, had already packed the materials, each crate stamped prominently with the word "Interarms." The next time the world heard of these weapons was when they appeared in Angola. The crafty Czechs had shipped the lot to the rebels and "forgot" to take off the Interarms markings. Articles in the press accused Cummings of feeding arms to hot spots for his own personal gain. The responsibility for the sale was thus deftly shifted from the Czechs to Interarms. Cummings never did succeed in convincing many people that he had nothing to do with it. This is but one example of clever Cold War one-upmanship, and Cummings, in this instance, was the sacrificial goat.

4

Samuel Cummings himself, of course, is the key to Interarms' success. He is an exceedingly clever businessman and no doubt would have done well in any other endeavor he might have chosen. Foremost among his talents is his sales ability. He dresses conservatively, avoiding the pomaded and loud look effected by some of his competitors. He talks straight and gives the impression of being an intelligent and well-bred country boy. Being a man of some education and taste should not be underestimated in its importance. Many of the people who control the sale and purchase of arms in foreign countries started their careers from mean and lowly stations in life. Batista and Trujillo are two examples. Nevertheless, the moment these people reached power they thenceforth considered themselves "gentlemen" and were pleased to associate with anyone who had an "upper-class" background. Cummings exudes respectability, something these people all crave, and he is therefore a most welcome visitor and friend.

By all accounts, Cummings is an extraordinary bargainer. He does not waste his time fighting his way through a country's bureaucracy but goes right to the top—in Winston Churchill's words, he "cuts off the heads of the tall poppies." The first thing Cummings says whenever he goes shopping for arms is, "I'd like to talk to the man who can make the decision." In many countries the people in charge are colonels and admirals, in other countries civilian bureaucrats. Whoever they are Cummings knows them. Once with them he will close the rulebook, promise to cut red tape, give them a beneficial offer, assure them that the weapons will not end up in the hands of their enemies, and agree to immediate payment in full. Usually this is sufficient to close a deal.

Sometimes, in his capacity as a sales agent for Artillerie Inrichtingen, he set up a firing demonstration of the AR-10. This always provoked interest because, he says, "everybody likes fireworks." As a grand finale he would fire tracer bullets at rows of tin cans filled with gasoline. "Did you ever see a tracer bullet hit a bean can full of petrol?" he asks. "It's better than a John Wayne movie. This little demonstration never fails to elicit delightful 'Oh's' and 'Ah's.' I saddle up and ride into the sunset, leaving the firing range a smoldering ruin."[10] This ploy not only helped to sell AR-10's but often opened the door to large purchases of surplus military equipment.

Although Cummings tries to avoid taking political sides in a country, he does strengthen his hand with the decision-makers by befriending the important people in the country, even when they are not directly concerned with negotiating arms sales. He personally knew Nehru, Anastasio Somoza and Trujillo; he knows Franco, the Shah of Iran, Batista, the powerful Balester-Molina family who have influence and interests throughout South America, Brigadier General Bolivar Vallarino of Panama, and many other powerful people. To some of them he has presented gold-plated Walther pistols as a token of his esteem. Cummings is also acquainted with quite a few members of the "jet set," particularly those from Latin America. These people have all the necessary contacts and, for a slight consideration, will arrange the proper introductions. "To them," one ex-arms dealer told me, "it's just a parlor game."

Cummings' greatest asset has been his knowledge of the American arms market. Prior to 1968 the genius of the business was to ask: how many of rifle X are there in the United States now? Are they still in demand? If so, how many can I import (or release from bond) and what can I sell them for? Ten dollars? Twenty dollars? Thirty-five dollars, or what? Cummings knew what he would pay for a rifle; then he backtracked in his thinking: how much profit, he asked himself, can I make if I sell the rifles through Hunters Lodge? Through Sears Roebuck? After sporterizing, shipping, taxes, etc.? In other words, what can I offer to bid for the weapons in the first place? If it is too high I'll let someone outbid me.

His ability to judge what a customer will pay for a rifle is still just as keen when he brokers weapons on the international market. In one instance he sold some American 60 mm mortars to the British government for $1,125 apiece. It was not until some time later that the British learned that identical equipment could be purchased elsewhere in America from private sources for $50 apiece. "And at *that* price," an arms dealer told me, "I'd be making a handsome profit."

Cummings, despite his wealth and connections, is personally somewhat Spartan. He does not smoke and seldom drinks, he has only a slight taste for fine food, he virtually never frequents nightclubs or gambling casinos, and his strongest expletive is "Rubbish!" He has no outside hobby or interest that is not connected with armaments, and he spends most of his time on his business affairs. He travels seven or eight months a year, and the only tool of his trade that he carries with him (besides blank contracts) is a magnet to ascertain the composition of the component parts of cartridges.

Considerable secrecy surrounds his activities. He will seldom discuss a purchase or a sale in detail with an outsider. He does not use a Telex between his many subsidiaries and agents; interoffice telephone calls are discouraged lest they be intercepted. He has devised an intricate code for countries and types of armaments which he uses in his correspondence.[11]

Some people claim they have detected similarities between Cummings and Bannerman in their personal dedication to the arms trade; but on second inspection too extended a comparison is not valid. While it is true that his zeal and personal qualities have an almost religious quality about them, Cummings has never tried to ally Christianity with selling arms as did Bannerman.

Cummings is a voluminous letter-writer, constantly corresponding with agents, contacts and anyone else he thinks might be of some help to him. His letters are one, but a very important, way he keeps in touch with his intelligence network. They are also the vehicle he uses to plant stories, a favorite tactic used to gain psychological advantage over his competition. Depending on his mood, he will promote a story that is designed to deflate, anger or amuse his competitors or critics. Then he waits to see how the story comes back to him. Occasionally, the feedback will provide him with the needed leverage to win an order.

His letters reflect a certain sense of humor. Much of his correspondence is conducted via postcard, the message being typed in capital letters. In the spring of 1967 Cummings was called to testify before a subcommittee of the Senate Foreign Relations Committee. "AH'S BACK! AH'S BACK!" he wrote to Val Forgett, an old friend who owns Service Armament Corporation of Ridgefield, New Jersey. "KUM AGIN TUH SAVE EVERYONE FROM LEGISLATIVE OBLIVION: MOSTLY WE-UNS! . . . PLEASE CALL (NOT COLLECT) SO I KIN HEAR ALL THE NEWS BEFUH AH GOES BACK TO RETIREMENT. [signed] THE VIRGINIA KNAVE." Sometimes he signs himself "RASPUTIN," "STRANGELOVE" or "BLABBER." "VAL!" he wrote on another occasion, "WHAT ARE YOU DOING

ABOUT DEFEATING S 2043 [a proposed law that would have banned military surplus imports] SO I CAN CONTINUE MY LUXURIOUS LIFE ON THE RIVIERA WITHOUT WORRY? . . ."

During the early years, when few people had heard of Interarms, Cummings had printed under the Hunters Lodge label a sales brochure, much like the Bannerman catalogue, in which were advertised a wide variety of wares. Many of the advertisements in it also reflected his brand of humor. For a Finnish Lahti 20 mm antitank cannon, a mean-looking weapon about seven feet long, one ad asked, "Why be undergunned?" A Soviet mortar was once described as "the ultimate attraction for you smooth bore fanatics." Yet another piece of heavy equipment, a bazooka, was offered as the perfect weapon to "get those charging woodchucks."

Cummings lives today in Monaco but retains his American citizenship. Previously he had run Interarms from Salzburg, Copenhagen and Geneva. "I'm an economic exile," he once said. "I don't prefer life abroad, but in America nobody starting from scratch can accumulate capital any more. It's an immoral situation." Cummings runs his empire from a fourteen-room complex in a stylish building on Boulevard d'Italie, ironically not too far away from where Sir Basil Zaharoff spent his declining years. The offices have a commanding view of the principality, including Prince Rainier's palace and swimming pool and the casino.

Cummings lives with his second wife, an attractive Swiss girl, in an apartment next to his offices. (His first wife, a German he met while shopping for arms in Central America, could not adjust to his extensive traveling, and they were divorced.) The entire complex is filled with the bric-a-brac of a weapons expert and arms collector. Cummings not only is an insatiable collector of rare weapons but retains one specimen of every type of gun Interarms has ever bought. His bookshelves are filled with military histories, reference and technical books. The walls are covered with military prints, old sabers and pistols, and a large map of the world—courtesy of the U.S. Army Map Service. There is a sixteenth-century suit of German armor facing his desk and nearby sits an eighteenth-century regimental two-pound mortar. His office in Alexandria, Virginia, is of the same order except that the hardware next to his desk is one of the Hotchkiss mountain cannon that he bought from Guatemala.

Cummings bridles at the thought that he is considered a "merchant of death" or that what he is doing is immoral. "I would call your attention to the fact," he said to commentator David Brinkley in 1962, "that two-thirds [*sic*] of the taxes you and every other American pay go into exactly the same hardware as we deal in. So in a sense we are all in the same business." He argues that he is no more responsible for what his customers do with his weapons than distillers are for drunks or automobile manufacturers are for highway deaths. He says that if Lee Harvey Oswald had been unable to buy a cheap rifle he probably would have tried to kill President Kennedy "with a Cossack saber."[12] Nor does he believe that selling to two countries which later go to war with each other is immoral; all large American firms—from Coca Cola to Standard Oil—he says, sell to both sides. In wartime, he notes, the U.S. government prohibits him from selling to either antagonist.

He believes that disarmament will never be achieved and that there is no end in sight to war. Arms, he has said, "are the symbol of man's folly throughout the ages. That's what civilization was, is, and always will be: 'Open up! Let 'em have it!' That's why this is the only business that should last forever."[13]

Cummings also believes that the press plays up the more sensational aspects of the business and omits the ordinary aspects. The arms business, he told me, "is really much more mundane than the press can believe; and in fact it's so mundane that if it were presented in its completely objective form it would not sell papers sufficiently; so they have to stoke it up a bit." One way the American press plays its stories on Interarms is as follows, and comes from a 1966 article in the Washington, D.C., *Star:*

> If you want a Tiger tank slightly used perhaps at Normandy or the Battle of Berlin, Interarms will be happy to accommodate you. For $19 million, you can pick up a modern, ocean-going submarine, replete with turtle neck sweaters for the crew and a monocle for you.

The pressure on Interarms from this type of public exposure sometimes becomes so intense that the only release is a form of grim humor. For instance, some employees of the firm refer to themselves as "your friendly, neighborhood merchants of death."

The stigma of the arms merchant of old—semigangsters living a corrupt and selfish existence—still haunts Cummings and it sticks in his craw. "We operate a legitimate business within the laws of the countries in which we do business," Stuart Murray told me almost desperately, and Cummings would certainly echo this thought. "We've worked in about I would say seventy countries," Cummings said, "and there's no man in the world that I can't look in the eye." He points out that at his level of the arms business there are no "goon squads" or bodyguards. The threat of violence upon himself, he believes, is so minimal that he has never carried a gun. "Too heavy," he told me.

Nor is Cummings a violent person. While he buys, sells and collects weapons, he seldom if ever fires any of them (although he is an excellent shot). Occasionally he will go target shooting but he virtually never goes hunting. "I dislike killing things," he says.

5

In the eleven years since he won the large Lee-Enfield bid, Cummings has succeeded in buying up 90 percent of all British surplus small arms that has come onto the market. He has been able to do this even in the face of a change of Crown policy which, subsequent to the 1958 tender, has kept the lots of weapons offered as small as possible in order to favor the less wealthy bidder. Some of the material he has bought includes approximately 20,000 pistols that had been turned in by the public to the British police in 1961 in return for immunity from prosecution. He also bought 17 million rounds of military .303 ammunition from Britain; one million rounds each went to New Zealand, Australia and South Africa, and the remainder was imported into the United States, converted into sporting ammunition and sold primarily to those Americans who had bought his M-60 Royal Enfields (sporterized Lee-Enfields).

He sold $2.8 million worth of AR-10's to the Sudan in 1960–61. His attempt to sell a large batch of the same weapon to Yugoslavia fell through at the last moment because the State Department did not approve of it. He bought 30,000 Mosin-Nagants from Finland and 60,000 rifles, mostly Mausers, from Colombia; he sold "several thousand" pistols to the Portuguese police in 1962 and, because he had been burned by the Czechs on a previous occasion, announced almost desperately that he first obtained the permission of the United States (where the guns were made), the Swedes (from whom he bought them), the British (who reconditioned them) and then NATO (who was interested in the deal). Cummings also says he obtained a written promise that the Portuguese would not use the weapons in her territories, a dubious guarantee at best.

In 1965 Cummings paid one million dollars for Spain's entire small arms inventory—in all a total of 600,000 weapons. Most of them were relics of the Spanish Civil War and included Mosin-Nagants, German and Czech Mausers, Italian VV70 sniper rifles, Remington rolling blocks and thousands of pistols—Astras, Stars, Mausers, and Steyrs.

In the same year, Cummings' agent in Germany at the time, Merex A. G. of Bonn, was involved in a sale of F-86 *Sabrejets* to Venezuela. It is clear that Interarms had been a heavy supplier of weapons to Venezuela in the past, and therefore when the country wanted to replace its forty aging De Havilland FB-4 *Venoms,* it turned to Cummings. Cummings knew that Germany had some sixty practically unused F-86's stored in an old Dornier company warehouse and that there were twenty more available from the Luftwaffe, which was planning to replace them with Lockheed F-104G *Starfighters*. The *Sabrejets* cost West Germany $232,000 each, and the usual disposal price of one-owner jets is approximately 20 percent of cost, or $46,400 apiece. It is unlikely that Interarms-Merex paid more than that. The sales price to Venezuela was $140,000 each, including modifying the plane for photoreconnaissance and interceptor capabilities. This still left a handsome profit even after the modifications were carried out. In all, seventy-four F-86's (with the designation "K") were sold to

Venezuela, deliveries being completed in 1966. Cummings insists that all the profits went to Merex and not to Interarms. The companies have split up since this deal and are now competitors.

Cummings emphasizes whenever he can that the sale of heavy ordnance—particularly jets, tanks, warships and missiles—is the exception rather than the rule in his firm. He will and does on occasion broker these weapons—his sale of *Vampires* to the Dominicans, for example—but only because it complements the purchase of surplus small arms. It is for this reason that Cummings advertised in his sales brochure such hardware as M-47 and M-48 tanks, jet fighters, napalm, artillery shells, tear gas, reconnaissance vehicles and the odd warship. He seldom stocked the equipment but he knew where it could be bought and was willing to sell it if it would pry loose surplus rifles and pistols in the process. For instance, if he heard that a Latin American country wanted some tear gas grenades, he would go to Federal Laboratories in Saltsburg, Pennsylvania, a producer of these items but a company that makes no special effort to sell abroad. Cummings would buy the quantity wanted (at discount prices), add on as much profit as he thinks the market will bear and sell the material to the country concerned.

One piece of heavy ordnance he hopes to broker in the future is the M-47 tank, 5,000 of which will come onto the surplus market in western Europe around 1970 as they are replaced by the U.S.-German Main Battle Tank. He also hopes to broker the thousands of Nike *Ajax* missiles that are to be replaced by the Nike *Hercules*.

Brokering weapons constitutes from one-quarter to one-half of Interarms' current business, much less than commonly thought. One ex-importer of guns told me, "If Sam Cummings had to live on his brokering deals, he'd have starved to death a long time ago." Each deal takes an extremely long time to set up, sometimes as long as three years. But when one is consummated the profits can be enormous, far larger than selling surplus in the American market. That is why brokering, despite its risky nature, is so attractive to so many arms dealers.

Even ordinary purchases of surplus weapons are time-consuming affairs. Cummings, for instance, is fortunate if he can transact five major deals in one year. One of his biggest, in which he purchased $20 million worth of weapons, involved three countries and took a year and a half to negotiate.

The period from 1959 to 1961 seems to have been Interarms' era of high explosives, or "HE" as they are known in the trade. Cummings was buying up so much of the material that his warehouse complex—a scant thirty feet from Alexandria's old residential section—at one point took on more the appearance of an ammunition dump than an arms depot. Besides his usual complement of small arms ammunition, Cummings began storing huge quantities of heavier material. There were thousands of Swedish bazooka rounds (which cost up to $50 apiece), thousands of British 2 inch mortar ammunition, thousands of 37 mm antiaircraft ammunition, and thousands of heavy artillery and recoilless rifle rounds.

In one instance, Cummings imported from Denmark 50,000 hand grenades.* Cummings explained to me that he had the idea of going into the commercial explosives business by repacking the foreign-made gunpowder in quarter-pound blocks for sale on the American market. Unfortunately, he continued, local, state and federal authorities took a dim view of his idea and forced him to empty his warehouses of the items. The grenades were put aboard two railway cars and then shuffled from one obscure siding to another while Cummings figured out what to do with them. For a while they were held in storage at the Federal Laboratories plant in Saltsburg. Eventually, at Cummings' expense, the lot was dumped into the sea off the coast of Georgia by the Coast Guard. "Don't ever mention HE to us again!" Cummings exclaimed to me.

The manner of shipping these grenades caused considerable apprehension among the authorities. The items were packed loose in boxes and some of them had spilled out into the hold of the freighter transporting them to the United States. Dozens of loose

* Approximately 5,000 of them were practice grenades. One person who saw this particular batch told me, "They scare the hell out of people; they just smoke a little."

German potato masher grenades were found by longshoremen as they were unloading the boat. One arms dealer, who was in Alexandria at the time, explained his reaction to me: "I went in there [the warehouses] and I got frightened. I went out of there and I walked three blocks and finally I said, 'To hell with this!' and I took a plane out of there; I was even afraid to stay in Alexandria. The way they were packed—*poured loose in boxes!* It was frightening! Somebody could have dropped a box and *whooosh!*"

Hand grenades are not the only items on which Cummings has failed to turn the profit he expected. In fact, he has had his fair share of business defeats. For instance, the 1958 Lee-Enfield purchase, while profitable, was not as profitable as Cummings had anticipated because Interarms angered Proof House, an organization run by the Worshipful Company of Gunmakers. British law forbids any weapon being exported unless it has been "proofed"—that is, inspected to ensure its suitability for firing. Because the Lee-Enfields in question came from government arsenals, Cummings thought that the proofing process would be a perfunctory one at worst and told Proof House officials so. Proof House thought Cummings rather high-handed in his behavior and soon made life difficult for him. The time it took to proof his guns stretched on and on, all the while costing him money. Some of the Lee-Enfields were forever ruined because proof marks were stamped on with such heavy blows of the hammer that the barrels were bent out of shape. Several influential members of the Worshipful Company of Gunmakers were convinced that Cummings was also too greedy for his own good. They persuaded the authorities to harass him at his Acton warehouse; soon Cummings found himself having to install better security devices and fire-prevention systems, and having to pay a higher insurance premium. All of this cost him money.

In 1960 Cummings imported 999 Finnish Lahti 20 mm semi-automatic antitank cannons, which he sold for $99 each. A single round for this weapon costs one dollar. Many gun collectors are devotees of this particular gun, including a prominent bank president in Washington's Virginia suburb, a millionaire owner of an auto accessories business in Maryland, a bank president from Concord, New Hampshire, a dentist from Arizona who hunts rabbits with his ("I don't hit many," he said, "but when I do—oh, man!"). The president of a New England manufacturing firm mounts his Lahti on his twenty-eight-foot power launch moored on Cape Cod. He takes his boat twelve to fifteen miles out to sea and booms away at oil drum targets.

Unfortunately for Cummings, some of the devotees included a group of Canadian bank robbers who used a Lahti in 1965 to blast open the twenty-inch-thick concrete walls and steel sides of a Brinks safe in Syracuse, New York. They made off with $415,998. In the same year another Lahti was found at the scene of an unsuccessful bank robbery in Quebec City. The FBI also discovered two Lahtis, along with a hoard of other weapons and ammunition, in an old barn in New York that belonged to notorious bank robbers Bobby Wilcoxon and Roger Nussbaum. This publicity put a decided crimp in Cummings' sales, since he was the sole importer and distributor of the weapon.

Cummings once lost a large deal in Ethiopia. His bid for surplus arms was so low that it angered the military officer charged with conducting the sale. In fact, the officer was so angry that he chased Cummings through the streets of Addis Ababa shouting curses at him in Amharic.

Perhaps Cummings' biggest loss took place in 1963. He had just sold his 55 percent controlling interest in Cogswell & Harrison; not too long after the sale had been consummated, Moise Tshombe, then seeking to continue the Katanga secession, charged into the retail store on Piccadilly and, not aware that the firm had changed hands, ordered one million dollars worth of weapons. E. H. Holden, the new owner and general manager, happily obliged. Cummings and Murray were reportedly furious at losing this large order.

"Every once in a while," a British gun dealer told me, "Sam drops a clanger and we all roar with laughter."

Notwithstanding these and other setbacks, Interarms had such success importing surplus weapons into the American market that it kindled the ire of a well-heeled trade group called SAAMI or, more precisely, the Sporting Arms and Ammunition Manufacturers' Institute. SAAMI was founded in 1926 and ever since then has been one of the foremost advocates of protectionism for the American gun industry. There are currently ten members of the Institute, all corporations: Colt, Du Pont, Federal Cartridge, Hercules, Inc., High Standard, Ithaca Gun, O. F. Mossberg, Remington Arms, Savage Arms, and the Winchester-Western Division of Olin Mathieson.

Since 1957 SAAMI has taken special pains to shut off the flow of surplus arms into the United States—in effect, to run Sam Cummings out of business. The Institute sees four threats to the industry. According to E. C. Hadley, president of SAAMI, in testimony before the House Foreign Affairs Committee in March 1958, they are:

> First, the importation of American made rifles declared surplus by our allies abroad; second, the importation of surplus used and new foreign made military surplus; third, the importation of foreign made commercial arms; fourth, the sale of surplus military firearms by the U.S. government within the United States.

SAAMI began its campaign against Interarms in 1958 by petitioning the Department of Defense and the Department of State to ban the importation of surplus arms on the grounds that it threatened America's national defense; both Departments dismissed the petition. SAAMI then turned to the Department of Commerce and the Office of Civil and Defense Mobilization; but the former saw no threat to the domestic firearms manufacturers, and the latter also ruled that imports of this nature did not impair national security. The Institute then turned the heat on the U.S. Tariff Commission and again was rebuffed. It then supported the "Dodd Amendment" to a State Department appropriation bill in 1960 which stated that it was "the sense of the Senate" that the State Department "should take action as may be necessary to prevent the importation of all military firearms."* Finally the Institute op-

* Cummings helped to set up an opposition group to the Dodd Amendment and subsequent bills called the American Council for Technical Products, Inc. It advertised itself as a "trade association of importers, exporters, distributors [and] dealers."

posed unsuccessfully the Trade Expansion Act of 1962 as it pertained to the reduction of tariffs on firearms imports.

Despite these reverses, SAAMI was instrumental in stopping the importation or sale of those surplus weapons in all four of E. C. Hadley's "threats" above. In 1958 Section 414 of the Mutual Security Act of 1954 was amended wherein the reimportation of U.S.-made arms originally exported as Lend-Lease or military assistance was banned. In the same year the Defense Department, by administrative procedure, banned the sale of surplus military firearms by the U.S. government in the United States. And in 1968 the Gun Control Act banned the importation of all foreign military surplus arms.

Interarms naturally feels itself threatened by these laws and rulings. Cummings complained to me that a large percentage of the billions of dollars of weapons the United States has given away or sold since the end of World War II is forever lost to the American market. Peter Beer specifically decries the government's refusal to auction off its surplus in the United States. He told me that, because of the ruling, some 20,000 nearly unused Colt pistols were once destroyed rather than sold. He also said that the market for the model 1903 Springfield rifle, caliber .30-06, perhaps the most popular military-turned-sporting rifle in the United States, has dried up and that they are no longer available in any quantity. The price for those few still on the market has doubled since 1958.

Those at Interarms have a few pungent thoughts on SAAMI. They say, first of all, that its vendetta against Interarms has been motivated by envy. They say that SAAMI is jealous that Cummings cornered the market he did. One thing that particularly irritates the Institute, they say, is that Cummings has significantly cut into domestic ammunition sales, which is where the money is in the business. (The cost of labor is so high that a rifle or shotgun, largely handmade, can only be competitive if sold near cost; ammunition, on the other hand is a mass-produced item and is most profitable.)

According to Interarms, Cummings had pleaded with the domestic manufacturers for years to produce ammunition for the guns Interarms was importing, most notably caliber .303 ammunition for the Lee-Enfields and 6.5 mm ammunition for the Mannlicher-Carcanos. The manufacturers, particularly Remington and Winchester, because they made both guns and ammunition, turned Cummings down because they made no rifles in those calibers. Interarms, therefore, was forced to import what it needed. Eventually the domestic producers came around and began to turn out a wider variety of ammunition, but only when they saw that Interarms was importing in such volume that, even with a 30 percent duty and a 10 percent excise tax, it was able to undercut the local product at the retail level. In many cases Interarms still sells its ammunition below the price of the domestically produced material.

Cummings has particularly strong opinions on two other points. First, he says, Senator Thomas J. Dodd, who held many hearings on the Gun Control bill, is not antigun as is so often thought. He could not afford to be, he said, coming from Connecticut where the small arms industry is centered.* Rather, he adds, Dodd is pro gun industry but anti mail-order and anti the importation of surplus weapons. In effect, Cummings claims, he is therefore pro SAAMI and anti Interarms. Second, Cummings points out that if a comparison were made between the number of weapons imported and the excise tax paid on the first domestic sale of new weapons by the American manufacturers between the years 1958 and 1968, it would show that the rise in the former was soon followed by a rise in the latter. This means, Cummings says, that far from hindering the sale of domestic weapons, as SAAMI claims, his imports have actually stimulated sales, thus validating his "Kodak Brownie to Leica" theory. This further reinforces Cummings' conviction that sour grapes are behind SAAMI's campaign to destroy Interarms.

Harry L. Hampton, Jr., SAAMI's secretary-treasurer and an articulate spokesman for the Institute, told me, somewhat surpris-

* Such well-known firms as High Standard, Marlin Firearms, Sturm Ruger, Emhart Corporation, Remington Arms, Colt Industries, O. F. Mossberg, and Winchester are located in Connecticut. Another supporter of the gun industry is former Senator Saltonstall of Massachusetts, in whose state are such well-known companies as Smith & Wesson, Harrington & Richardson, Savage Arms, Ivor Johnson and Noble Manufacturing.

ingly, that "in calmer moments many in the industry would have to agree that Sam's imports have helped sales in the long run." But, he added, "the importation of cheap surpluses has brought undesirables to the rifle matches. . . . This problem would have happened despite Cummings, but he accelerated it."

Hampton also complains that Cummings refuses to give the devil his due and to acknowledge that it is quite natural for the domestic manufacturers to be upset when they see their markets shrinking. Furthermore, he said, "he's full of baloney if he thinks the members of SAAMI have spent their time conspiring against Interarms. We have too many other things to do."

Almost wistfully, he concluded, "I wish we had had the foresight to have had our own bidders at the tenders; and then opened the seacocks of the ships as they came over. It wouldn't have cost us as much as one might think."

6

Unlike its predecessors earlier in the century, Interarms' activities are quite tightly controlled by the U.S. government. Every item that was imported into or exported from the United States had to be cleared through a variety of government departments. Technically, Interarms required government permission (that is to say, an import or export license) only for arms moving in or out of the country; it claims it still obtains clearance on all transactions regardless of whether or not the arms ever come near the United States. For instance, a shipment by Interarms of AR-10's from Holland to the Sudan would be cleared by the State Department beforehand. Interarms also cooperates closely with the British Foreign Office, particularly for sales that take place within the British sphere of influence. Any other approach to selling arms would appear to be foolhardy on Interarms' part, since enough profits can be made by following rather than evading the rules. Interarms is so close to the State Department and the Foreign Office, in fact, that another breed of arms firms—legitimate to be sure—has sprung up to fill certain voids which Interarms cannot fill. They have been given the name "munitions manipulators" and are discussed in the following chapter.

The government body actually charged with controlling the export of arms, ammunition and the implements of war is the Office of Munitions Control. Its authority stems from Section 414 of the Mutual Security Act of 1954, as amended; it gives the President of the United States the power to control the trade in the country. The President, under Executive Order 10973 of 1961, delegated this authority to the Secretary of State, who in turn gave the functional and administrative responsibility to the Office of Munitions Control, which is a section of the State Department itself. Until the passage of the Gun Control Act of 1968, the OMC was also responsible for controlling all arms imports. Now the authority is vested in the Alcohol, Tobacco and Firearms Division of the Internal Revenue Service.

All persons in the United States engaged in the business of manufacturing, exporting and importing articles listed on the Munitions List must register with the Department of State. Those who are registered must keep a record of all export and import business transactions in order to provide a basis for stiffer controls should they become necessary. The Munitions List, which changes from time to time, is essentially made up of "hard core" munitions and military hardware, everything from cartridges to military space vehicles. Nearly 1,400 U.S. firms are registered with the State Department, the overwhelming majority of which are, unlike Interarms, manufacturers.

John Sipes, the current director of the OMC, told me that the operative word in his job is "control." His task is to make sure that arms go where they are intended to go and that they do not go where they are not supposed to go. He is responsible for the resale of material; that is to say, if Cummings sells equipment to the West Germans, who in turn sell the same goods to Iran, approval for this secondary transaction must be acquired from his office. Interestingly enough, the OMC has no control over the sale or grant of weapons carried out by the U.S. government itself.

Prior to the passage of the Gun Control Act of 1968, there was no specific law prohibiting the importation of surplus Soviet weapons into the United States. Nevertheless, the State Department and the Office of Munitions Control as a matter of policy did not allow such items to be brought in. The purpose of the policy, according to Robert N. Margrave, a former director of the OMC, was to preclude the possibility that the United States might indirectly support the Soviet armaments industry by buying its obsolescent weapons. The OMC made a distinction between Soviet weapons that were captured (by the Finns, for example) or were otherwise in the possession of Western nations (those left over from the Spanish Civil War, for example) and Soviet weapons in the possession of Western nations that were specifically sold by the Soviets. If the latter category of weapons, no matter what their vintage might be, could be traced back to a sale by the Soviets, then they were not, by the rulebook, allowed to be imported into the United States. The other arms were allowed to be imported, and had been in considerable quantity prior to 1968 because they were technically Western arms.

But in reality the distinction was always fuzzy. Soviet arms and ammunition seem to have trickled into the West in small lots to be mixed in with other arms. This has been difficult to prove, even, it seems, by the OMC itself, because records in Europe have always been purposely made difficult to trace. The testimony of Margrave, under cross-examination by Senator Dodd in 1965, strongly hinted that this trade existed for some time. A researcher on Dodd's staff told me that one official in the OMC admitted under pressure that occasionally his office allowed weapons sold by the Soviets into the United States in order to keep the arms off the world market. Publicly the OMC denies this and denied it to me privately. Yet there seems to be no other way to explain why Cummings was allowed to import, for example, the Soviet and Czech equipment that the Israelis had captured from the Egyptians in 1956.

Senator Dodd and others once viewed with alarm the many crates in Interarms warehouses stamped with "Made in Russia" on them. This, I was told, was evidence enough that Soviet weapons were pouring into the United States straight from the Soviet Union. However, this can be misleading. United States Customs law requires that a crate be marked according to where the goods were manufactured, not from where they were purchased. Thus a crate marked "Made in Russia" would mean that the goods inside were manufactured in the Soviet Union, but it would not necessarily mean that they had been bought from the Soviets. The equipment might—and in Cummings' case often did—originate in Finland, Spain or Germany and was eligible for importation until 1968.

One of the most persistent rumors concerning Cummings is that he and his company are either controlled by, dominated by, or otherwise in the pay of the Central Intelligence Agency. There is almost no indication that there is any direct tie between the two organizations. "We have nothing whatsoever to do with any part of the U.S. government except Internal Revenue," Cummings told me. "All that [talk] is just baloney." Peter Beer concurs. "It started out with a Drew Pearson article several years back," he said, "where he mentioned in his column in the Washington *Post* [dated May 23, 1961] that Interarms was owned and financed by the CIA. I must say, if it were, then our auditors never found it!"

The article said that Chester A. Emerick, chief of investigations for the Customs Bureau at the time, knew that the CIA had invested $100,000 in Cummings' venture in 1956, or at least had that much in the operation at that time. One person close to Interarms' operations stated categorically to me that Emerick's statement was true.

"I was seriously thinking of suing Drew Pearson," Beer continued, "but how can you really sue a man for associating you with the U.S. government which presumably is the best association you can get? But you see, we could have lost a tremendous amount of business. If the military attachés in Washington had clipped this article and sent it to their respective governments, it could have meant a complete denial of visits to us to arsenals. Why should an arsenal in South America, or anywhere else, permit what is reputedly a CIA agent to visit their facilities? Based on that we could have suffered a tremendous loss of business."

But they will not let the matter rest there. Cummings complicates the picture, seemingly on purpose, which tends to raise doubts whether the two organizations are in fact distinct. For instance, several of his subsidiary companies flaunt the CIA initials. Two specific examples are Cummings Investment Associates (which owns real estate in Alexandria) and Cummings International Associates (a holding company). In truth, Cummings does this for two reasons: he likes to "muddy the waters," as he says, and he believes that it gives him a psychological advantage over his competition. His use of the CIA initials is perhaps more a reflection of his sense of humor than it is of any direct tie to the intelligence agency.

If there is no clear tie-in, there does exist a close working relationship, for there is no doubt that Cummings and Interarms are very convenient instruments to the CIA and other government departments. First of all, no government bureaucracy could maintain an arms intelligence system in such a high state of alertness nor as cheaply; second, Interarms allows the U.S. government the opportunity to buy weapons from an unofficial source; and third, Interarms is a convenient buffer between the government and critics of the arms trade. Cummings knows all this and exploits the situation. Furthermore, he is protected by the aura of his alleged connection with the CIA, so it profits him to keep the public wondering just what his status is. Nothing would be worse for him than to have everyone concerned state flatly that Interarms and the CIA are two entirely separate entities which never have had anything to do with each other—because it would reduce Cummings to the level of just another arms dealer in the eyes of his competitors, and because it would not be entirely true.

Although the Central Intelligence Agency, the State Department or the Defense Department will not talk about it, the general consensus among arms dealers with whom I spoke indicates that the CIA and other government departments keep stockpiles of foreign weapons in various restricted locations around the country. Common sense would dictate that this be so. The United States government, in the interests of protecting its own citizens, feels that it must keep in touch with the latest weapons technology coming out of foreign countries, as indeed it keeps in touch with the latest foreign developments in agriculture, medicine, industry and atomic research. All countries with any power, in fact, maintain stocks of foreign weapons. The foreign ordnance stockpiled by the U.S. government is tested by our experts, and any technological advances deemed essential to our defense presumably are eventually incorporated into our weapons systems.

There are two other reasons why these weapons are stockpiled by the U.S. government, and they complement the initial motive. First, they are used in familiarization training by Special Forces troops, whose job it is to operate behind enemy lines. Second, they are used to arm clandestine groups friendly to the United States. To avoid sticky diplomatic scenes, none of these particular weapons should be traceable to U.S. sources. One of the best ways to build up a supply of untraceable, or clean, weapons is to buy them in small lots from different sources and to keep only those of any particular make whose serial numbers are widely spaced. Better yet are those weapons with no serial numbers at all.

Between nations that are particularly friendly, the weapons desired by one can be bought (or be given) outright by the other. But with many countries this is not so, particularly with Western nations that want arms developed and produced by countries behind the Iron and Bamboo Curtains. Furthermore, even friendly countries sometimes do not want their allies to know what they are doing, so they acquire weapons by devious means. The British government's purchase of 60 mm mortars from Cummings, rather than directly from the U.S. Army, attests to the complexity of relationships between even the most friendly of nations.

The U.S. government often uses an oblique approach when it purchases foreign weapons. In many cases Interarms has been a party to the transaction. If the government for some reason wanted, say, 10,000 German 98K Mauser rifles that Czechoslovakia or Bulgaria was offering for sale, it would find a company domiciled in a neutral country to buy them. The company concerned might be a U.S. government front or it might be a legitimate enterprise. The arms, legally purchased, would then be shipped around Europe until the origin of the weapons was obscured by the paperwork involved. Eventually they would end up in the possession of one of Interarms' foreign subsidiaries. An import license for the record, showing that the goods originated in a western European country, would then be issued to Interarms, and the rifles would be shipped to Alexandria. This circuitous approach protected the government in case of any incident or unfavorable publicity. It also cheated Customs of the proper duty rate since a prohibitively higher duty was placed on arms originating in eastern Europe than on those originating in western Europe.

Soon after their arrival a "customer" would approach Interarms and offer a price for the rifles. Cummings, who usually had a good idea who his "customer" was, could do one of two things. First, he could sell the rifles outright. But he would only do this if 98K's were in demand on the commercial market, because he knew (or was reasonably sure) that his "customer" only wanted to pick out 2,500 or so of the best or least traceable 98K's from the lot of 10,000 and then return the remaining ones as "unsuitable"; these Cummings was free to sell on the open market. Second, if Cummings believed that there was no commercial market for 98K's (which, in this particular case, would not have been true), he could have, in lieu of money, swapped 98K's for surplus American arms. This tactic, according to several sources, was most lucrative. For instance, if the wholesale unit price of a 98K Mauser was $9.00, Cummings could swap on a one-for-one basis for Springfield .30-06 rifles, whose wholesale unit price at one time was approximately $27.00. Cummings, therefore, tripled his money.

This seems to be the only logical explanation for the fact that Cummings, alone among all the arms dealers in America, has what appears to be almost unlimited stocks of American surplus arms and ammunition—Springfields, M-1 carbines, .30-06 military ammunition, etc. He will tell you that he bought them from a foreign country and, in some cases, he did. But not all of them.

If the U.S. government wanted the very latest in Soviet or Czech arms—such as the Russian AK-47 assault rifle, the Russian SKS carbine or the Czech model 25 submachine gun—it usually must resort to more covert methods of procurement, since no Soviet bloc country is willing to sell its latest equipment in any quantity to unfriendly nations. Ordinarily Cummings would not be involved in this trade; his agents could pry a few samples loose from Omnipol without much trouble, but supplies in any volume would have to be acquired through the efforts of our intelligence agency. The Vietnam War has provided one source of supply, as did the six-day Sinai War of 1967. E. H. Holden of Cogswell & Harrison told me that soon after the latter conflict the U.S. government brought a boatload of captured Soviet and Czech equipment back to the United States. These weapons went straight into government arsenals and would not be seen by Cummings.

On many occasions the U.S. government will abandon the oblique approach to arms buying in favor of a direct purchase from Interarms. This is a convenient procedure for many government departments because it eliminates the need for approval up the long bureaucratic ladder, it cuts down on paperwork, and it saves time. The Agency for International Development (AID) once bought from Interarms in the early 1960's a substantial quantity of 9 mm Danish Madsen machine guns (which, interestingly enough, had no serial numbers) for use by the Venezuelan police force. In fact, AID is a large odd-lot buyer of weapons from Interarms, particularly 9 mm ammunition and riot control equipment.

During the early days of the Vietnam War, the U.S. government found itself short of Soviet 14.5 mm (approximately .50 caliber) antitank rounds which it needed for testing. It came to Interarms and bought a batch of the ammunition that had been purchased by Cummings from Finland. At the same time the government bought from Cummings a substantial number of secondhand AN/M-2's, which are American-made air-cooled .50 caliber wing guns. The demand for these weapons became most acute when the U.S. military began arming its helicopters in Vietnam. According to several sources, the CIA in 1960 and early 1961 bought a large quantity of American-made semiautomatic rifles from Interarms in order to arm the anti-Castro forces for the Bay of Pigs invasion. Interarms has imported large quantities of 9 mm pistols directly from Fabrique Nationale which do not appear to have been absorbed in the commercial American market. Several arms dealers believe that the CIA purchased all of them. (Cummings insists they were re-exported to a Latin American country in exchange for old Mauser rifles.)

From 1956 to 1961, it appears that both pro- and anti-Castro groups attempted to buy small caliber weapons from Interarms. Both groups invariably purchased their arms under the cover of dummy or front companies. No one walked into the Alexandria office and said, "I'm from the *Frente,* let me see what you have for sale."

In fact, it had to be subtle because, as one arms dealer told me, "In this business you know everybody; it's a closed shop business. Your eyebrows are raised if you've got a dealer who is a $5,000-a-year buyer and suddenly he comes in with a $20,000 order. You're suspicious of it because you know pretty much his market."

Often buyers were not sufficiently subtle in their approach. For instance, before Castro came to power, a number of "new customers" beat a path to Alexandria. All of them possessed domestic dealer's licenses (which then cost one dollar each) but legitimacy appeared to stop there. Many of the buyers were suspiciously Cuban in manner and accent and, according to Cummings, were duly turned away. One such group, however, did succeed in the late 1950's in buying a batch of small arms from Interarms, but then it raised suspicions when the account was settled with Morgenthau fifty-dollar bills. It is generally believed that this money came from backers of Castro.

The Drew Pearson article, noted above, also stated that Chester Emerick believed that there was little doubt that Interarms was selling arms to Castro through his confederates in the United States and later to the anti-Castro rebels in the Dominican Republic, although the latter was difficult to prove.[14]

It is obvious that the U.S. government, while deficient in many respects, was quite capable of stopping the flow of weapons to Castro before he came to power and to the anti-Castro forces before the Bay of Pigs. It is clear now that in both cases it did not want to. The overall government policy now seems to have been quite lenient in those periods, and there is little doubt that Interarms, among others, was used by the government as an instrument of its policy.

If further examples are needed to illustrate the close relationship between Interarms and the U.S. government, consider the following:

First, it is of interest to note that Interarms' "high explosives" era, which ran from 1959 to 1961, coincided with the Central Intelligence Agency's buildup of the Bay of Pigs force. Cummings has never succeeded in convincing many people that the true reason he imported this material was to enter the commercial explosives field. He is too shrewd a businessman to believe that he could compete effectively with the Hodgdon Powder Company of Mission, Kansas, which is the biggest independent distributor of smokeless powder in the United States, or with such highly automated, billion-dollar powder manufacturers as Du Pont and Olin Mathieson.

Furthermore, it is widely accepted by arms dealers that handling charges—including uncrating and defusing the shells, and remixing and repacking the powder—are exorbitant. The only instance when money can be made is when the market price of the metal casings is sufficiently high to warrant scrapping the shells. In this instance the powder is invariably burned as a waste product. Cummings has never been in the scrap copper and brass business.

It should also be recalled that those 999 Lahti cannons, clearly unsuitable as sporting weapons but ideal for amphibious assaults, were imported in this same three-year period.

Second, note should be taken of the close association Cummings' former partner, Sidney Lerwin, apparently maintained with the U.S. government. Some people believe that he was employed by the CIA. To justify their claim, they tell the story of how Lerwin disposed of the weapons he acquired in 1958 when Cummings bought him out. Cummings realized that Lerwin knew very little about weapons, that he had very few sales contacts, and that his share of the weapons was odd-lot pieces with little commercial value. He was curious, therefore, to see to whom Lerwin sold them. He learned that the final destination of the arms was a government depot in Franconia, Virginia, and that the driver of the truck had been changed enroute.*

* Before this incident had taken place, Cummings apparently had bought back from Lerwin all of his .30 and .50 caliber machine guns. These weapons were then sold to Val Forgett of Service Armament for the bargain price of $15 apiece. Forgett sold them as DEWATS—or deactivated

Third, Cummings has been selling ammunition that could only come from government sources. For instance, he has sold .30-06 caliber ammunition with a headstamp designation of C/N/40/9. All cartridges have a code stamped on the base end of their cases indicating the producer and year of manufacture. Thus FA 49 would indicate that a cartridge was produced by the Frankford Arsenal (in Philadelphia) in 1949; RA 64 would indicate a cartridge produced by Remington Arms in 1964; NWM 61 would be one manufactured by the Dutch firm of Nederlandsche Wapenen Munitiefabriek in 1961; and so on. All cartridges carry headstamps, even communist-manufactured ones.

I wrote to the FBI Laboratory, the National Rifle Association, H. P. White Laboratories in Bel Air, Maryland, the Centre of Forensic Sciences in Ontario, and the Firearms Information Service in Winchester, New Hampshire, and asked these experts what arsenal or producer carried the designation C/N. The FBI Lab refused to comment, but the rest gave me a variety of answers. Some said the cartridges were made "overseas," or in Canada or in the United States. All except H. P. White Labs hinted that they were used by the U.S. government at the Bay of Pigs. Several weapons experts told me privately that C/N was a phony headstamp mark. In addition this ammunition was packed in standard government boxes and crates that carried no markings whatsoever on the sides, a highly unusual procedure in a business where everyone normally wants to know exactly what he is getting.

The only conclusion that can be drawn is that this ammunition was specifically made for the U.S. government (the consensus seems to be at Frankford Arsenal) for a specific reason. It may have been clean ammunition. At some point in time, though, this material was found to be no longer useful for the purposes for

---

war trophies—which required that lead be poured down the barrels to render the guns inoperable. Shortly thereafter, however, someone had fitted the machine guns with new barrels, along with Thompson submachine gun butt stocks and Browning Automatic Rifle bipods, and sold these strange hybrids to Fidel Castro while he was still a guerrilla in the mountains.

which it was intended and was eventually sold or traded to Cummings. "And why not?" asked one arms dealer, shrugging his shoulders. "What's the CIA going to do with ammunition they can't use? Why not swap it to Sam for something they can use?"

Cummings also has been selling Chinese and Russian mortars that were shipped out of the Interarms warehouses in American-made military-type crates. Several arms dealers noticed that the sides to all the crates had been sanded in order to erase the original markings.

Finally, note should be taken of Interarms' relationship with a firm called American Firearms and Ammunition Corporation of Long Island City, New York. From what little information is available this company seems to be a front for government interests. There are a number of reasons for believing this: It has been a very large buyer of equipment from Interarms, particularly from 1960 to 1963; yet nowhere has there been an advertisement by AFAC offering its wares to the public, nor are there any AFAC retail stores or foreign subsidiaries to dispose of the material bought. What has the company done with all this material? The inevitable conclusion is that the arms disappear into government depots. In fact, the American Firearms and Ammunition Corporation was at one point such a large purchaser of weapons that special prices were quoted to it, known around Interarms as "AFAC units."

AFAC, it appears, conducts its business in a most unusual manner for a firm claiming to be an ordinary commercial enterprise. In 1968 three attempts by a credit rating firm to contact officers at the company's headquarters across the river from Manhattan were unsuccessful, and requests for interviews went unanswered. Two nearby banks could supply no information on the company. It can also be said that running AFAC is a fairly casual affair, at least according to the firm's answering service. A friend of mine telephoned the company at noon one day and was told that all the officers were out for lunch; at 2:00 P.M. the operator said that none had returned, and at 4:00 P.M. she said that all had gone home. At 10:00 A.M. the next day she announced that none had arrived for work.

My own personal reconnaissance efforts were almost as fruitless. On one visit to the company—a dingy one-room top-floor office with desk, telephone and empty filing cabinet—I found the door unlocked, no one present and an accumulation of several days' mail on the floor. By letter count over half of this correspondence came from the State Department and the Morgan Guaranty Trust Company.

In 1962 Interarms and AFAC were together included in a mysterious episode involving the return to Finland of 32 million rounds of Soviet 7.62 mm and 7.92 mm ammunition. The entire incident was hushed up: the story found its way into only two local country newspapers.

It appears that in December 1961, Interarms had imported this material through the port of Baltimore and had it shipped to the "American Firearms Corp." of San Antonio for (as one newspaper reported it) "possible sale to sportsmen." Several points should be clarified here. First, the San Antonio telephone directory listed no American Firearms Corporation nor an American Firearms and Ammunition Corporation for 1961–67. No company that wants to sell 32 million rounds of ammunition to sportsmen hides its light under a bushel. Second, newspaper reports stated that the ammunition was also to be used for the U. S. Army M-1 and M-14 rifles; but anyone in the gun business will quickly point out that Russian 7.62 mm and 7.92 mm ammunition does not fit American weapons. Third, most of the crates had "Made in Russia" stamped on them along with the notation "5-4-46," which would indicate that the material was of postwar origin and thus technically ineligible for importation for commercial purposes. Fourth, U.S. Customs agents were reported to have tested the ammunition and found it in good condition; yet the reason given for returning the material was that it was "defective." It so happens that military standards for ammunition are higher than commercial standards; Customs' judgment, therefore, was based on the assumption that it was for commercial use: it would not ordinarily pass judgment on ammunition imported for military use. Along the way, however, the material became "defective," which would indicate that it did not meet U.S. military standards. This material was almost certainly destined to be used in Soviet weapons owned by the U.S. government.

In any event, all 32 million rounds—22 boxcar loads—were shipped to Brownsville, Texas, in December 1962 and unloaded at Pier 3 at the port. To Interarms' and AFAC's embarrassment, the material sat there for several weeks because the ship destined to return the ammunition to Finland—a Swedish freighter called the *Bernard Ingelsson*—was late in arriving. An enterprising reporter took pictures of the cargo, and the story was played up in the local papers. Senator John Tower, after having conferred with State Department officials, attempted to explain away the shipment by saying, "It was a speculation on the part of the International Armament Corporation of Alexandria, Virginia. They found out, however, that the bullets could not be sold to U.S. customers."[15]

Cummings would have known that before he imported the material.

7

Despite its past successes, Interarms faces a number of difficulties in the foreseeable future. Foremost among its problems is the Gun Control Act of 1968. This law, one of whose provisions bans the importation into the United States of foreign military surplus rifles and pistols, will deny to Cummings in the years ahead his most lucrative market.

At first glance it would appear that the many years of effort by gun control advocates like Senator Dodd and protectionists like the Sporting Arms and Ammunition Manufacturers Institute had at long last borne fruit. But the victory is by no means complete. In the first place, Cummings anticipated by several years the passage of such a law, and he and his men worked overtime to import as many small arms as they could before the gates were closed. Some estimate that his stock of small arms in Alexandria has risen to over a million. (Cummings denies this, claiming only one-quarter this number, or several years' worth of stock.) Under present law these weapons can be sold on the American market. The Gun Control Act of 1968 also prohibits Cummings from selling his wares by mail order, but the lucrative chain-store market, which now comprises virtually 90 percent of his business in the United States, is still open to him.

Cummings, however, is concerned that additional laws will be passed that will prohibit the *sale* of these weapons in the United States. If that happens then he will be stuck with a huge inventory that is essentially unsalable anywhere else in the world.

In many respects the Gun Control Act of 1968 was passed too late. Over the years, Interarms succeeded in buying up virtually all of the surplus small arms in the world that are suitable for sporting weapons in the United States. The only completely untapped markets that Cummings had not touched were in the Near and Far East—markets that some day in the future will offer for sale an interesting array of small arms but in no great volume. Thus virtually all the eligible small arms not yet in the hands of American gun buffs are already in the United States, ready to be sold in the years ahead.

Since the early 1950's, the world's leading arms manufacturers have switched from making semi-automatic weapons to making fully automatic weapons. These latter arms are not suitable as sporting weapons, and even under the old U.S. gun laws would not have been a lucrative sales item in the United States. Therefore, Cummings would have seen the semi-automatic surplus military small arms market dry up even if there had never been a Gun Control Act of 1968. Thus the ban on the importation into the United States of foreign military surplus is virtually meaningless since, realistically, there are relatively few desirable semi-automatic small arms available in other parts of the world that can be imported.

Over the next ten or fifteen years, therefore, Cummings will be faced with several choices. He can move into the antique reproduction field, currently a low-volume market that is becoming increasingly more lucrative; he can turn to importing high-quality sporting weapons; he can become a domestic trader, buying and selling the many tens of millions of guns already in the United States (now that the gates are closed, the price of foreign military surplus arms in the United States will tend to rise sharply); or he can move wholeheartedly into the brokering business, trading U.S. and allied arms on the world markets, with all the attendant risks that such a business entails. If he chooses the last course, and the pressures for him to do so will no doubt increase, he will certainly lose his dominant position in the private arms sales field. His loss of tax advantages from living in Monaco and his large warehouse facilities in various parts of the world will give him less leverage than in the past and will force him to compete on more equal terms with his competitors.

One way in which Interarms may return to importing foreign military surplus arms is if the U.S. government finds itself unable to set up an acceptable alternative channel for the importation of clean weapons—a channel that will attract as little attention as Interarms did in the past. The U.S. government will certainly need quantities of foreign arms in the future, and it will certainly want to protect itself from criticism and embarrassing incidents by using nongovernment organizations as shields. Washington may find that a total ban on foreign military surplus imports, as the Gun Control Act of 1968 prescribes, will only emphasize the government's involvement in this trade. It may be to Washington's advantage to change the law, so that some foreign military surplus would be allowed into the country. In doing this, foreign military surplus arms destined for U.S. arsenals would not be so conspicuous as they certainly will be in the immediate future. Cummings may benefit from any changes that are made to this law.

Somewhat surprisingly, Cummings is not against the enactment of more stringent gun laws in the United States. He told a Senate hearing in 1965 that he was in favor of restricting the mail-order sale of revolvers and automatic pistols (since enacted); that he was in favor of prohibitive taxes on the commercial sale of heavy weapons such as machine guns, mortars and bazookas; and that he approved of a proofing test such as the one Great Britain has. He said he would like to see in the United States a situation similar to that in Switzerland, where everyone eligible for military service keeps at home his military rifle and a certain quantity of ammunition.

Cummings does not like embargoes, for obvious reasons, and

feels that the U.S. government maintains them too long and for the wrong reasons. He believes that the market in Cuba is forever lost because the investment in any one weapons system is so great that it prohibits the country from returning to a system that can be supplied by Cummings or a Western power. Stuart Murray notes that Britain's traditional market is lost in South Africa for the same reason. Cummings also opposes the tendency of the U.S. and British governments to approve his licenses on a case-by-case basis. This makes business impossible to carry on, says Murray. "One can't maintain an attack on a market unless there is some reasonable chance of success," he added. Once, in a moment of unconscious candor, Murray said to me wistfully, "We'd just like to be able to sell more weapons. . . ." Cummings and everyone else in the trade would surely agree with that.

III

Private Entrepreneurs, All!

"Between craft and credulity, the voice of reason is stifled."
—EDMUND BURKE

1

That part of the world's private arms market not dominated by Interarms and its many subsidiaries is served by a wide variety of firms, some of which compete with Cummings, some of which do not. They range in temper from old, respectable firms, to not-so-respectable firms, to professional and amateur gunrunners, to mercenaries and thieves. Generally speaking, they are run by colorful people who receive far more publicity and criticism than their relatively small volume of business would ordinarily indicate they deserve.

Cummings has six competitors worth noting. One is the English firm of Cogswell & Harrison, founded in the nineteenth century, in which Cummings had a 55 percent interest from 1958 to 1963. It is now owned and run by E. H. "Ted" Holden, a quiet, self-effacing man whose rather bland exterior hides a tough, competitive spirit. Like most arms dealers, Holden is vague about his volume of business; yet there are some indications of its size. He admits, for instance, that he sometimes keeps as much as one million dollars worth of small arms (up to .50 caliber and including fully automatic weapons) in his warehouses at any one time. His firm has lucrative sales agreements with Fabrique Nationale of

Belgium in certain parts of the Middle East, with the Czech trading firm of Omnipol in various Commonwealth areas, and with Vickers in the same general areas. Historically, Cogswell & Harrison has maintained a very close relationship with the Crown Agents, a semiautonomous government body that controls, among other things, the sale of surplus military equipment. This connection has given the firm a crucial advantage when surplus arms are to be auctioned. The best indication of Cogswell & Harrison versatility is the ease with which it supplied one million dollars worth of weapons to Moise Tshombe in 1963.

Cogswell & Harrison maintains a "retail" outlet on Piccadilly primarily to afford potential customers a point of contact. The hub of the business, however, is on the second floor. It is here that all the international deals are made. One of the offices has a display on the wall of the latest equipment available for sale. Most of the weapons are Czech, and most prominently displayed are the Model 59 machine gun and the Model 61 submachine gun. Also hanging on the wall at the time of my visit was a Welrod, a tubelike single-shot assassination pistol made by the Naval Gun Factory in Washington, D.C. It is in effect a silencer pistol that makes no greater noise on firing than a popping champagne cork and was used to great effect by members of the French Resistance. Holden told me that this particular item was definitely not for sale.

Of particular interest is Cogswell & Harrison's relationship with the firm of Omnipol; Cogswell & Harrison is one of its principal outlets in the noncommunist world. Many eastern European arms ending up in former British colonies in the Middle East and Africa pass through the hands of the London-based firm. Holden refuses to accept an exclusive dealership from Omnipol because it would give him less leverage in striking profitable bargains.

Omnipol officials, he told me, "are about the nicest people in Europe almost without exception and infinitely more trustworthy than most. I mean this quite sincerely, and they certainly know their business from A to Z." He told me that when one ordered a weapon from Omnipol it came complete with spare parts—spare magazines, bayonet, sling, cleaning kit and instruction booklet—while Western firms often sold their wares without spares. The

Czechs, he said rather proudly, "are extremely competent salesmen, not so aggressive . . . in, shall we say, in the context of Sam Cummings or an American salesman. They have a much more quiet, reasonable approach.

"But there are certain methods and ways of dealing with them," he went on. "For example, you are extremely careful about discussing price, destination—things like that—in the office or on the telephone because they're all recorded. If they come to your hotel room, or on the street, then you can talk openly and make your deals with them. Then they simply set it down on paper afterwards, you see, without the intervening negotiations and discussions having been recorded anywhere for Big Brother." Omnipol, he went on, is only an arms sales agency, but it can operate quite independently of the Czech political authorities because it is one of the country's major sources of foreign currency. It will take payment in many currencies, preferably hard ones, although it is not for some reason fond of Italian lire. The one currency it will not accept in payment under any circumstances is its own country's.

Another firm dealing with Omnipol, and also a Cummings competitor, is Parker-Hale Limited of Birmingham. This company differs from Interarms and Cogswell & Harrison in that it is essentially in the quality rifle business. It does, however, buy surplus small arms at auction and renovates them into sporting weapons. Each year some 10,000 surplus rifles are converted, of which 99 percent are exported. John Le Breton, the company's sales director, claims that his firm, like the others, maintains ample stocks in reserve—in his case 100,000 small arms up to 20 mm in size. Parker-Hale sells throughout the world, with particular emphasis on Commonwealth countries. It also has a variety of outlets in Europe, the Middle East and Africa which handle its sales of British, western European and Czech weapons.

Le Breton told me that when his firm buys weapons from Omnipol, the goods are always imported first into Great Britain, regardless of their ultimate destination. Parker-Hale, he said, does not want the Czechs to know where the arms are going; nor for that matter do the Czechs want to know. Furthermore, it is easier for Parker-Hale to import Czech weapons because the Foreign

Office knows that, when they are re-exported, it can exercise some control over their final destination. Le Breton accepts rigid Foreign Office control because, in the last analysis, there are many avenues available for sending weapons to an undesirable country that ultimately lie beyond British government control. For instance, he said, there are some countries such as West Germany, Italy and Denmark that have a reputation of keeping close watch on their own arms exports; thus an arms shipment from Britain to one of those countries is seldom questioned by the Foreign Office. Once there, however, the arms can be shifted around Europe until they enter a country that is not too particular about the ultimate destination of the arms. Austria, Spain, Holland and Belgium, says Le Breton, are the most lax of all western European countries. From there the arms can be exported to their true destinations. Parker-Hale has used this technique most successfully in providing arms to Arab sheiks.

Another Cummings competitor is Merex AG of Bonn, West Germany. It was founded in 1963 by Gerhard G. Mertins, an ex-paratroop major who served under Otto Skorzeny, the famous SS leader, and a holder of the Iron Cross. The company is essentially an arms broker. Most of its sales have been to Arab countries. Until 1966 Merex enjoyed a very close relationship with, if not the support and favor of, the West German Defense Ministry. The Bonn government used Merex as a screen to cover the sale and shipment of surplus Bundeswehr arms to customers in Africa and the Middle East.[1] One indication of how close Merex was to the Bonn government is the fact that the company, with fifty-nine employees and five salesmen, had a reported working capital of only $27,000 but annual sales of $7.5 million.[2] Other arms dealers generally believe that no company, particularly in such a competitive field, could generate such huge sales in so short a time on such small capital without considerable government help. In this respect Merex cannot truly be described as a private arms firm.

In 1966 Mertins purchased a large and handsome house in Bethesda, Maryland, and installed one Gerhard Bauch as his U.S. agent. Bauch's job is to buy surplus from the U.S. government for sale abroad. Exactly what he has bought so far is unclear, although he is in contact with the military arms sales office in the Pentagon. Before working for Mertins, Bauch was an agent in Cairo for Herbert Quandt, a well-known Hamburg banker.* In 1965 Bauch, along with a "horse breeder" named Sigmund Lotz and several others, was arrested by Egyptian police on espionage charges. Lotz was charged with spying for Israel and for carrying on a terrorist campaign against West German rocket and aircraft experts at Helwan. Lotz is supposed to have been responsible for sending a booby-trapped letter to rocket expert Wolfgang Pilz which blinded his secretary. In any event, Bauch was secretly released and returned to Germany without being tried; Lotz was given life imprisonment, others were given lesser sentences, and a few others were acquitted.[3] Shortly after his return to Germany, Bauch turned up in the United States in the employ of Mertins.

Mertins, like Cummings and other arms dealers, has provided arms to two mutually antagonistic countries. For instance, in August 1965, just before the Pakistan-India war (but following the Rann of Kutch imbroglio), India placed an order with Merex for twenty-eight *Seahawk* Mk 100's and 101's, obsolete subsonic jet fighter-bombers of British manufacture that had been used by the Luftwaffe. However, the arms embargo at the outbreak of fighting in September effectively stopped the sale. In June 1966, nine months after the cease-fire, Bonn gave Merex permission to sell the jets to an Italian firm, Tirrena, S.p.A., run by a Dr. Amadasi, on the understanding that the jets would not be resold to a third party. Merex reportedly bought the jets for $625,000 and had agreed to sell them for $875,000.

The twenty-eight *Seahawks* were loaded at the obscure north German port of Nordenham onto a Merex-leased freighter called the *Billetal* (previously chartered, some say, to preserve secrecy in some of Mertins' deals). The boat went to the Mediterranean and passed through Italian waters but did not stop at any port. Instead, it headed for the Suez Canal and from there continued on to India. On its way, the *Billetal* passed its sister ship, the *Werretal,* also

* See pages 304–5.

leased by Merex. The *Werretal* was headed, first, to Pakistan to deliver a cargo of *Cobra* antitank rockets and other armaments and, second, to Saudi Arabia to deliver a batch of surplus Bundeswehr weapons. Cummings claims Mertins may have had to use Iranian documentation in order to sell to the Saudis, since King Faisal broke diplomatic relations with West Germany in 1965. The crates containing this material had the words "Merex AG" painted on them. Mertins claims he cleared "only" $500,000 on these two deals.[4]

The close relationship between Merex and the West German Defense Ministry cooled in 1966, probably over the *Seahawk* deal. In the same year Mertins was also reported to be unwelcome in Switzerland, and shortly thereafter his firm ceased to operate in that country. The breakup of his association with Cummings in 1965 is another factor in the erosion of his influence in arms dealing circles.

In Merex's place, the West Germany Defense Ministry has turned to a new firm called Werkszeugaussenhandel GmbH of Dusseldorf. Known as WAH for short, it was founded in 1966 about the time of the *Seahawk* sale and is run by Gerhard Engel, an ex-lieutenant general and former adjutant of Hitler's.[5] WAH is capitalized at only $5,000,[6] which would indicate that, like Merex in the past, it is receiving considerable support from official West German sources. As late as 1968 WAH was Interarms' representative in Europe, and Interarms, in return, was WAH's representative in the United States.[7]

Two Interarms competitors are Canadian firms. One is called Levy Industries, Inc., of Toronto. Levy Industries is a holding company engaged primarily in the purchase, manufacture and sale of automotive, aircraft and heavy industrial machine components. It maintains a close working relationship with the American firm of Baldwin-Lima-Hamilton Corporation. Only a part of Levy's business is concerned with arms sales.[8] Its activities in this field, mostly brokering arrangements, are wrapped in secrecy. However, some of its deals are known. A typical one, and resembling in many ways the manner in which Merex operates, involved the sale of surplus U.S. M-47 tanks of the West German army to Pakistan through an Iranian intermediary, General Hassan Toufanian.[9] This sale took place at a time when there was an embargo on the sale of U.S.-manufactured "lethal" weapons to Pakistan.*

The other Canadian firm is International Firearms of Montreal. It was started in the mid-1950's and has considerable money behind it. Bill Sucher, more a businessman than a gun buff, owns it, and it is run by his son-in-law, Manny Wiggensberg. It maintains two subsidiaries in the United States, one just across the border in Vermont called Century Arms and another in Florida called Federal Arms. Like Interarms, International Firearms is a large purchaser of surplus rifles and pistols that until 1968 were sold "as is" to American sportsmen and collectors. Recently this firm has been outbidding Interarms on surplus weapons from Latin American countries—specifically in Colombia, Venezuela and El Salvador. Its success was the primary reason why there was a shake-up in Interarms' management. Wiggensberg also took a cue from Cummings' success story by imitating Hunters Lodge advertisements in *The American Rifleman.* Both were so similar that one had to read the small print to tell them apart. International Firearms sales in the United States rose steeply as a result.

Another competitor is called Sidem International, located in Brussels. It is run by a French-born American citizen named Jacques S. Michault, who limits his transactions to government-to-government brokering arrangements. This firm is very discreet in its operations, and very little is known about it, although there is some indication that it maintains close relationships with the Belgian, French, Spanish and Italian governments. Many arms dealers claim that Michault was the first to realize after World War II that West Germany would eventually rearm. They note that, when it became a fact in 1954, it was Michault who sold to the Bonn government the bulk of the equipment it required. Much of this material was German in origin dating from World War II; some of it was Spanish. Sidem, along with Parker-Hale and Golden State Arms, was instrumental in setting up the production

* This is by no means an isolated incident of Pakistan buying weapons covertly in contravention of the U.S. embargo. See pages 203–5.

of Mauser actions in Spain; it also made handsome profits selling surplus 1903 Springfield rifles to arms dealers in the United States.

2

As in any business where there are prospects of quick and large profits, there exists a shady side to the private arms trade. There are scores of arms companies around the world whose adherence to the spirit of the law has been less strict than others. Most of them are located in the United States because until 1968 that was where the market and profits were. The activities of two arms dealers, Haywood Henry "Hy" Hunter and George W. Rose, illustrate how this side of the trade operates.

The careers of these two men show surprising parallels. Rose was arrested in 1951 for violating a local Los Angeles ordinance against selling indecent writings. He was sentenced to pay a $50 fine and serve ten days in jail.[10] Hunter, a few years earlier, had pleaded guilty to contributing to the delinquency of a minor in connection with selling what he euphemistically called "photographs of women in semidraped condition."[11] Both men also operated under a variety of corporate styles. For instance, Rose operated under the names of Madison Import Co., Seaport Traders, Inc.,* George Rose & Co., and Merchanteers, Inc.[12] Hunter conducted his business under such names as H. H. Hunter & Co., Hy Hunter, Inc., General Arms Corp., American Weapons Corp.,† Crown International Firearms, Inc., and Krone Internationale Waffenshandelsgesellschaft mbH. All the above companies were located in California except Krone, which was located in Hamburg, Germany.[13] It became clear in testimony by both men before the

* This is the company from which Lee Harvey Oswald purchased (by mail-order) the .38 Special caliber Smith & Wesson revolver with which he murdered Patrolman J. D. Tippit. The weapon had been imported by Rose from Canada. See *The President's Commission on the Assassination of President Kennedy* (Warren Report), pp. 172 ff, 558 ff.

† Hunter testified before a Senate hearing in 1964 that this company was started by the CIA and that Leo Lippe was its first president.

Senate Subcommittee to Investigate Juvenile Delinquency in 1963 and 1964 that there was no clear delineation between each man's corporate entities, and that the differences were created on purpose to confuse anyone investigating their operations.

Rose built up a large business in cheap foreign pistols. Before importing them he would have the barrel unscrewed and a blank (or solid) barrel substituted. These hybrid guns qualified as "starter pistols" and were imported into the United States at a duty lower than that on ordinary pistols. The original barrels were imported separately and later reassembled to the pistols. Customs eventually changed the law, prohibiting this method of importing. Rose then had his pistols entirely disassembled abroad, each part being imported separately in order to take advantage of other low shipping rates and import duties.[14]

The Senate hearings, noted above, brought out the fact that many of Rose's pistols found their way into the hands of criminals and children. One police report showed that 23 percent of a quantity of pistols Rose sold in Chicago had been shipped to persons that were found to have criminal records.[15] Another report revealed that he had sold a .22 caliber gun to an eleven-year-old boy which blew apart in his hands. "And it was just a miracle it didn't severely injure him," said Senator Dodd.

"Well," said Rose in response, "you know children can do all kinds of things. They will crawl into refrigerators and kill themselves. It doesn't necessarily mean . . ."

"You don't sell refrigerators, do you?" interrupted the Senator.

"No, I don't," replied Rose.[16]

Hunter did not sell refrigerators either, but he operated in much the same manner as Rose. He imported large quantities of weapons as "scrap" which he subsequently sold as operable items.[17] He also, like Rose, built up a lucrative business importing "starter pistols" and converting them into regular handguns.[18] Under the terms of the subpoena requiring him to testify before the same Senate Subcommittee in 1964, Hunter was instructed to produce his business records. He presented the lawmakers with several boxes filled with fishing tackle and old sporting magazines among other things.[19] Hunter explained that the rest of his "U.S. records" had been transferred to Germany because, he said, his imports came from Germany.

> *Senator Dodd.* So the law provides that every dealer who is licensed under the Treasury Department must keep very accurate records and preserve them as long as he is in business, and if he goes out of business turn them over to the Commissioner.
>
> *Mr. Hunter.* This is correct, I understand.
>
> *Senator Dodd.* Now, does it make any sense to license Mr. Hunter as a dealer in Los Angeles and permit him to ship his records to Hamburg, Germany, where obviously the laws of the United States are not enforcible? Does that make any sense to you?
>
> *Mr. Hunter.* Well, sir, living as many years as I have in Germany, and being—
>
> *Senator Dodd.* I didn't ask you about Germany. I am asking you as a man with commonsense. Do you actually believe that a law can be interpreted that way?
>
> *Mr. Hunter.* I always considered that West Germany was just like a part of the United States, as far as the control of the the United States. I know that the American GI's are there.
>
> *Senator Dodd.* I can only say that is a remarkable viewpoint.[20]

A good example of the manner in which Hunter operated took place in 1963. In January of that year he bid successfully on a mixed lot of surplus arms offered for sale by the Singapore police department. Several months later, Hunter, on Krone Internationale stationery, asked the police commissioner to ship the material to the United States as "field scrap." The commissioner replied that it was not advisable to transport the arms as scrap since, he wrote, "most of them are still in fairly good condition." The material was eventually imported on the understanding by the Office of Munitions Control that the items were in most cases incomplete guns, replacements or parts. Twenty-four of the weapons were described on a Krone Internationale shipping invoice as Beretta carbines.

When the shipment was inspected by U.S. Customs it was found that all the weapons were completely assembled and fully operable. The Berettas in question turned out to be fully automatic machine guns. The value of the weapons was listed as $481, whereas Customs claimed that the domestic value of the shipment (for duty purposes) was $6,501 and that an additional $1,069.54 was due in duty. It was also revealed in the Senate Subcommittee hearings that Krone Internationale had gone out of business prior to the date on Hunter's shipping invoice.[21]

It is perhaps best to pause here for a moment to explain two aspects of the private arms trade that can be discussed only in a general manner. One aspect might be called "the dirty tricks of the trade." The other is bribery.

The prevalence of underhanded methods of operation in the arms trade stems from the type of people who gravitate into the business and from the fierce competition for supremacy. In many ways today's private arms dealers are throwbacks to an earlier entrepreneurial era. It is not so much that they are free from laws and regulations; rather, they seem to assume the characteristics and mannerisms one often associates with both the American and European robber barons of old. Generally speaking, they are right-wing in their political views, they are brutally competitive, they have an air of Texas braggadocio about them, they are extremely secretive, and what they lack in social sophistication they make up in their cunning and shrewdness.

One of the most noted characteristics of arms dealers is the enthusiasm they bring to the business. Nothing pleases them more than a successful "coup" in which all competitors are left nodding their heads in awe. In this respect they differ little from other entrepreneurs, but arms dealers seem to relish it more. Of particular pleasure is to cause a competitor to lose money. This calls for special celebrations and screams of laughter at the plight of their foe. But putting an opponent in financial difficulties is not their purpose: most arms dealers are happy only when their competitors have been driven out of business. When Cummings says he likes to "help his competitors out" (of business), *he means it,* and so do most other arms dealers I have met. There is a near absence of belief among arms dealers that competition is healthy, good or inevitable. Most dealers I have met hate the thought of competition and are forever scheming to destroy it.

The underhanded tactics often used in the arms trade to gain the upper hand are varied. Some have been mentioned previously such as Cummings' willingness to undercut the market by offering weapons at a price that his rival cannot match (but which is still profitable to Cummings) until his competitor has experienced a financial loss. Cummings is by no means the only dealer to use this or other similar tactics: most arms dealers do, and they can be just as brutal in their behavior as Cummings.

A fairly common tactic is to submit a number of misleading bids under a variety of names at an arms auction. If enough of these "bids" are submitted, it would take the selling authorities several months to sort them all out, by which time the buyer with no stamina has been driven to exasperation and quits in disgust. This device is usually worked by a last-minute bidder because the ensuing delay allows him time to "convince" the seller to award him the bid. If the purpose is simply to drive out the impatient bidders, the arms dealer with the more staying power will usually step back into the picture at a later date and say to the seller something to the effect of, "Look, I realize the bids are in a dreadful muddle; why don't you accept my bid of such-and-such for the whole lot which will clear the decks." More often than not the seller is only too happy to oblige, since a chaotic bidding session does not reflect well on his competence as a government official. Also, the dates of many arms auctions are set with the need of payoffs in mind; a two- or three-month delay usually is time enough for the seller's personal financial schedule to be thrown into disarray; thus a seller is often only too pleased to settle on the spot so that he can get his rake-off.

Another tactic is to report to the authorities concerned all the business indiscretions of a competitor. This is done as a matter of course; no arms dealer would ever think of passing up an opportunity to report a violation of law committed by a competitor. One American arms dealer, for example, attempted to import some arms from South America by illegally averaging the cost of the goods. Cummings, who learned through his intelligence sources that the weapons had in fact been bought at varying prices, immediately (and, according to one source, with considerable glee) notified the U.S. Customs authorities. Cummings realized that his competition would not have hesitated to do the same thing to him had he ever averaged arms prices improperly.

A third tactic is rumormongering. Since the world of the private arms dealers is a small one, a rumor properly dropped will reach all interested ears in a relatively short period of time. It makes little difference whether the rumors are true or false; usually one known uncomplimentary fact will be used to embroider other statements that perhaps are not true. Thus an arms dealer who has a reputation as a slow payer will find that his competition is spreading tales on how he plans to renege on a possible deal. Sometimes a rumor properly "interpreted" can mean the difference between winning and losing a bid.

One arms dealer used to wave the police record of one of his competitors before foreign military sales agents, which had the effect of excluding that individual from the bid. Another carries his passport in an expensive leather folder on which is embossed his country's seal; on casual inspection it appears as if the man is a diplomat. Sometimes spies are sent to work in rival companies. On other occasions elaborate practical jokes are hatched in order to make a competitor the laughingstock of the industry.

One arms dealer tells the story of two competitors he knew—one an old hand, the other a relative newcomer to the trade—who found themselves on the same plane on the way to a small arms auction. As they were passing through customs, the veteran dealer turned to an official he had known from times past and asked in a hushed voice: did he know that the person six or seven places back (pointing to his competitor) had a false passport and was a representative of the Algerian FLN? The veteran soon cleared customs and continued on to the arsenal where the sale of arms was taking place. He subsequently won many of the bids, deposited his down payment and returned to the airport for his flight home. While awaiting his plane he found his unfortunate competitor still being interrogated by the local customs and intelligence officials. Whether this story is true or not is difficult to say, but the fact remains that this type of behavior is common among arms dealers.

The sheer competitiveness of some arms dealers leads to an

almost total lack of business morality. Again, Cummings is the most competitive of them all. One of his most noted characteristics is his dislike of success in others, regardless of whether or not they compete with him; the only successful person in the entire arms trade, to his way of thinking, must be himself. Cummings, for instance, encouraged Leo Lippe and Cecil Jackson to set up a rival company to Val Forgett's Service Armament Corporation, even though Cummings and Forgett do not compete. Forgett makes quality replicas of old frontier rifles in Italy. Thanks to Cummings, Forgett now has a large competitor in Intercontinental Arms, which is owned by Lippe and Jackson and which also makes frontier replicas in Italy. It appears that Cummings could not bear the thought of his friend Forgett's being a success.

Soon after encouraging the formation of Intercontinental Arms, Cummings tried to destroy it. He sold Lippe 800 rare Mannlicher pistols from Argentina for $26 each. He also sold 200 of the same pistols to Forgett for a very cheap price. Forgett, unaware of the other sale, sold his pistols for as little as $19.95 each and made a good profit. Lippe took a great loss.

Perhaps the keynote to this whole approach was put best by Cummings himself when he once said in a moment of candor: "In the final analysis the morality of armaments boils down to who makes the sale."

Bribery is another matter; it is a fact of life in the arms business. It is a natural part of any conversation on the trade; arms dealers talk about it with no trace of discomfort. It is by no means unique to the trade, but it appears to be more in evidence here than in other fields of endeavor.

As a worldwide phenomenon, bribery is most entrenched in southeast Asia. It is also conspicuously present in the Middle East, Africa and Latin America. The areas most free of corruption of this nature are North America and western Europe. Although America has its Bernard Goldfines, Italy its Mafia extortionists and France its corrupt tax collectors, there is one essential difference between Western and Eastern-African-Latin bribery: In the West it is not an integral part of life's fabric. To corrupt through bribery in the West takes ingenuity, and the legal and social penalties for being caught can be severe. But from Manila to Bangkok, from Rangoon to Cairo, from Casablanca to São Paulo, bribery is a way of life; it is habitual, ubiquitous and, in places, traditional. It is accepted not only as a necessity but invariably as just. One hears the phrases "speed money," "tax farming," "creaming" and "skimming" with no trace of embarrassment in these parts of the world. In Japan they talk of *oshoku* (dirty job), in Pakistan it is *ooper ki admani* (income from above), and to Arabs it is the familiar *baksheesh.* Everywhere it means the same thing: a payoff.

In the Bribery Belt, an arms merchant does not stand out among other Western businessmen. Everyone—bankers, salesmen, contractors, arms dealers, even tourists—while deploring the existence of bribery, realizes that he cannot buck the system if he wants to get things done. Virtually every reputable Western firm—and I include the reputable arms merchants here—will leave the actual bribing to their local representative, who is usually a national of the country. The phrase I heard most frequently when talking with arms dealers and weapons manufacturers in America and Europe was, "We pay our reps a nice commission for all the sales they can make. What they do with the money . . . well, that's their business." It is a convenient arrangement: the Western company cannot be accused of corruption, and the reps are left free to bribe or not to bribe, whatever the local custom demands.

Arms dealers tend to grade countries by the degree of subtlety of bribery. In Indonesia during Sukarno's era a flat surcharge of 15 percent was added openly to the sales price of arms. This extra money was divided among the military officers, bureaucrats and politicians who negotiated the sale. In other southeast Asian countries the old Zaharoff ploy of leaving a wallet full of cash on a bureaucrat's desk is still a common practice.

In Latin America, and to some extent Africa, the bribe becomes more subtle. Usually it is hidden in bureaucratic paperwork, and is often so cleverly done that it becomes impossible to unscramble. The most common technique used is the multiple price list. It works in the following manner: To *sell* weapons to a country, an arms merchant makes out two sales receipts, one listing the retail price of the weapons—say $80 for a 15-year-old virtually unused M-1 Garand—the other listing the true (usually a wholesale) price, say $50 per rifle. The first receipt goes to the country's treasury, which pays the arms salesmen via the negotiators. The negotiators actually pay the dealer the agreed-upon price, $50 per weapon, which leaves them $30 per rifle to divide among themselves. When an arms dealer wishes to *buy* weapons, the situation is reversed. A bid of, say, $50 per weapon is agreed upon and forwarded to the country's treasury. The negotiators, however, privately agree with the arms dealer that the price should be $80 apiece. Thus $50 goes to the local treasury and $30 is split among the negotiators.

Bribes sometimes take the form of unsolicited contributions to the local ruling political party. This is the most common type of bribery found in Europe. Sometimes they surface as elaborate gifts or lavish junkets; occasionally they sink to the level of procuring unusual favors for prospective clients. These particular methods are not, as is readily evident, unique to the arms trade.

One of the reasons that the private arms merchant can survive in the face of what on the surface appears to be overwhelming competition from governments is that the private dealers offer the only source for payoffs. When Henry Kuss, the United States' chief arms salesman, sells some jet fighter-bombers to a nation, no one at either end of the deal is in a position to enrich himself. It is a straight government-to-government transaction that involves no money under the table. Kuss and the men who work for him are not corrupt; besides, they have too many other powerful instruments at their disposal to have to win a sale through bribery.

This explains why Venezuela, for instance, went through Merex in 1965 to purchase surplus F-86 *Sabrejets.* Everyone close to the situation said that Venezuela could have purchased the jets far cheaper had they gone directly to the German government. But the lure of self-enrichment at times overcomes national fiscal considerations, and this is true in virtually every country outside North America and western Europe. One irony is that even when the United States sells or gives away weapons to these countries, the lure of the payoff remains so strong that a nation still will buy additional items on the private market, thus wasting money and overloading itself with weapons it does not need. By maintaining a stock of privately purchased arms, a country is always in a position to sell them with near impunity, thereby offering yet one more opportunity for a payoff. (A country has no such freedom of action with arms it acquired at no cost through the U.S. Military Aid Program.) In other words, there exists a private trade in arms that has nothing to do with a country's military needs.

An illustration of how strong this desire for payoffs can be took place recently in the Far East. Thailand wanted a quantity of M-16 rifles from Colt Industries. The Thai negotiators, it was revealed, were particularly interested in receiving a rake-off (which would have been paid by an intermediary and not by Colt). But the U.S. government stepped into the picture during the negotiations and offered the same M-16's at a lower price. The Thais, realizing that there would be no payoff if the U.S. government negotiated the sale, rejected the lower offer. Colt, by this time, had withdrawn from the deal, so the Thais, still insisting on a rake-off, eventually bought AR-18's (an American weapon manufactured abroad under license) from a private Japanese source at a higher price than Colt had offered for its M-16's.

Bribery is not unknown among Western dealers. Shortly after one of the many large surplus rifle sales in Great Britain in the late 1950's, an unsuccessful bidder was approached by a successful bidder and offered some of the weapons just bought. This practice is common enough, particularly among those arms dealers who, for one reason or another, find that they do not have adequate cash to cover their carrying charges—proofing, storing, shipping, duty, etc. But in this instance the potential buyer was outraged to hear that the offering price from the successful bidder was lower than what he himself had bid originally. It was clear to him that someone along the line had been bribed.

One ex-arms dealer with whom I spoke, an Englishman, told me, "What these people do is say, 'Right, old chap,' or 'Right, lots of old chaps, anyone here interested in a Swiss numbered bank account?' Well, of course a lot of people are interested in that, aren't they? It's very much simpler to hand a man a piece of paper . . . [with] this number than to say, 'Look here, old chap, here's my suitcase, let's start counting.' " After a moment of thought he added, "I mean, who wants English pounds . . . ?"

This particular individual had been very successful in the arms trade and had given it up a number of years ago to turn his attention to other interests. Reflecting on his career he said to me in a matter-of-fact manner, "Every man has his price and in some cases it's surprisingly low."

This attitude is by no means confined to the world of the private arms dealer. To cite but one recent example, several powerful representatives of a large Italian firm approached Henry Kuss in the Department of Defense and said that their country was interested in buying a large quantity of M-60 tanks. But in order that Kuss get the contract, they added, it would be necessary to kick back $6 million, payable into the coffers of the ruling political party. Kuss, shocked by their behavior, turned them down flat and the meeting ended immediately.

E. H. Holden told me that he once offered two secondhand DC-6's to an African country. The president of that country wrote to Cogswell & Harrison after a preliminary agreement had been reached saying that the United States had offered the same thing for free. Obviously, said Holden, if this deal went through the president would not get his cut. Thus the U.S. offer was cancelled. The planes were eventually supplied by another arms dealer on the Continent. This presented the opportunity for the president of the African country to enrich himself.

One of the most noticeable trends in the Bribery Belt is the increasing willingness of countries to *trade* their old weapons for newer ones rather than to *sell* them. For instance, a country with 7,000 obsolete Remington Rolling Block rifles might trade them for 500 new Beretta pistols. This has the advantage of eliminating the possibility of questions being raised concerning rake-offs or bribes—or so many countries believe. In actual practice this trend is just another way to hide the corruption, to make it more subtle and to make it far more difficult to discover.

3

There is a distinct group of arms dealers who are sometimes referred to as "munitions manipulators," or "MM's." They differ from the Cummings-type of dealer in that they are the trade's true opportunists, and they differ from gunrunners in that their operations are technically legal. No clear lines can be drawn separating MM's from the other two groups, for there is some overlap. However, there are sufficient differences to warrant special comment.

MM's have flourished for two reasons. First, all successful MM's have recognized the fact that no government, particularly a democratic one, speaks with one voice. The United States, for instance, must be the benign anticolonialist in the United Nations, an ardent peace-seeker and tariff-cutter in Geneva, the protector of its domestic arms industry in Congress, the powerful military force to its allies and enemies, and so on. There is no way these many roles can be reconciled. Often they are the result of differing policies of various government departments. MM's have recognized that policy differences are often so great and so irreconcilable that a large power such as the United States has, in fact, many *coexistent* governments. Officially, the United States may have one foreign policy, a policy that is voiced by the Department of State; actually, all government departments have, in effect, their own foreign policy.

Large arms firms such as Interarms have grown used to dealing with governments. MM's know that it is sometimes far easier to deal with *departments.* For instance, if Cummings were denied a State Department license to ship arms to, say, Nigeria, that might be the end of the matter. There might be some behind-the-scenes wirepulling, but if the answer were still "No," Cummings would try to sell his wares elsewhere. But MM's realize that a "No" from the State Department does not mean that the entire government is saying "No." The CIA or AID or any other department might say "Yes," provided that the MM was sufficiently discreet in the manner in which the arms were delivered. Cummings, too, knows that the government speaks with many voices, but his firm is so large that a particularly delicate transaction would inevitably attract attention were he to handle it. MM's, because they are quick on their feet, small, versatile, and imaginative, have thus been able to fill this particular void in the arms trade.

The second reason why MM's have flourished has been the existence and proliferation of embargoes. An arms embargo is placed on a country by a large Western power, particularly the United States, usually for one of two reasons: one is military—to dampen the threat of war or to de-escalate an existing war; the other is for public opinion purposes—to show the world how peace-loving a power it is. However, there is another side to the coin. All nations realize that embargoes, while they may inhibit violence and bring applause to the peace-loving power, have the negative effect of creating a vacuum through the withdrawal of the great power's influence.

Into the breach have stepped MM's, and in many cases with the full but covert support of the great power itself. When the United States, for instance, placed an arms embargo on Cuba in 1958, American, Canadian and British MM's, among others, flocked to Havana, secretly offering arms to Batista. The U.S. government, for one, was hedging its bets through the American MM's in the event Batista prevailed. Embargoes laid on the Dominican Republic, the Caribbean in general, Pakistan and India, Nigeria-Biafra, the Middle East, South Africa and other areas have all resulted in opportunists flocking to the scene to fill the void—many of them with the tacit support of their own government.

Embargoed nations, seeing themselves threatened, are inevitably determined to acquire arms despite the ban and, unless the embargo is maintained by force (and virtually none since the end of World War II have been), usually have no difficulty obtaining them. Recognizing this, large powers, particularly the embargoing nation, figure that it is better that the business be handled secretly by its own MM's rather than secretly by someone else's. If its policy is successful, the embargoing nation has the best of both worlds: it maintains its influence and yet it can still tell the world how principled it is.

The weapons MM's deliver are limited for the most part to small arms, since speed of delivery and maintenance of secrecy are of the essence. Occasionally tanks will be delivered, but they are the exception. It appears that most of these weapons pass in and out of the hands of MM's many times before they are retired to museums or scrap heaps. The prospect of an MM selling a weapon that will never again during its operational life appear on the market is rare. The trail of such firearms can be fantastically far-flung, and the following bizarre trail of a weapon testifies not only to the long shelf-life of all small arms but to the consistently high level of activity in this sector of the arms trade.

The weapon in question is a 20 mm Lahti cannon, which was made in Finland during World War II. In the late 1940's this particular cannon was bought by a European-based MM in exchange for some Sten guns; it was then shipped to Italy, sold to another MM, who in turn sold the weapon to the Israeli Haganah. In 1950 it returned to the first-mentioned MM and was sold to Costa Rica. Five years later it was back on the market and was sold to the Algerian FLN. In 1960 this same cannon appeared briefly in Panama, then it was shipped to the United States as a DEWAT (deactivated war trophy). Somewhere along the line it acquired a new barrel and was sold to anti-Castro rebels for delivery by air drop into the Sierra Escambray Mountains, but something went wrong and it next surfaced in Santo Domingo during the crisis of 1965. The following year it returned to the United States and was purchased first by an anti-Castro rebel in Miami and then by Haitian exiles before it was confiscated by U.S. authorities, who presumably possess the weapon at this writing.[22] Someday soon, however, this veteran Lahti 20 mm cannon will be back on the market, and chances are it will be an MM who will buy it.

A typical munitions manipulator is a special breed of man. More often than not he is a combat veteran who talks in the vernacular of the British officers' mess. Usually he is highly intelligent, clever and the possessor of a variety of special skills. Many of them cut dapper and dashing figures, affect charming and eccentric manners and entertain old-fashioned and conservative viewpoints. Often they arrived in the arms supply business through years of devotion to firearms as collectors or inventors.

One such MM, for example, is Mitchell Livingston WerBell, III, of Powder Springs, Georgia. For years he made a living planting and shipping tropical fruits but became a full-time licensed arms dealer as the result of his interest in guns. He is, for instance, the developer of what many people believe to be the finest silencer in the world. Through his fruit business he was able to cultivate lasting friendships with many influential Latin Americans, most of whom at one time or another have called on him to supply them with arms. WerBell himself sports a Guards mustache, a monocle, a shoulder holster and Tyrolean jacket and, when in working clothes, his old paratrooper insignia.[23]

Another MM is Dominick de Fekete von Altbach und Nagyratoth, a handsome, shrewd man-about-the-world who once was an officer in the Royal Hungarian Horse Artillery. In the early 1950's he moved to South America and began buying and selling arms. One of his specialties is supposed to be the development of foolproof methods of delivering contraband by sea. De Fekete's clients are just as often rebels as they are legitimate governments—sometimes in the same country. He once told a friend that it is easier to make a sale to rebels because "they want whatever you can get for them"; with governments, making a sale is far more difficult but, he added, once made "you have an easier delivery."[24]

Another MM is Andrew McNaughton, an ex-RAF Squadron Leader and the scion of Canada's most distinguished military family. He was one of those MM's attempting to sell arms to Batista just prior to his fall from power. McNaughton believes that selling weapons with the covert blessings of a particular government department is quite risky; if caught, no one will come to your aid. As a result, he said, "you have to charge more." But then, he added, "you often make a bit more, too."[25]

Yet another MM is John Dawson-Ellis, an English Jew (born Ellis Jacob Jacobs) who sold surplus military equipment to Arab countries. In 1956 the British government reportedly published a White Paper admitting that one hundred surplus *Valentine* tanks without guns found their way from Great Britain to Egypt with guns. Dawson-Ellis was named as one of the men behind the $434,000 deal. Apparently the tanks were exported first to Belgium and then re-exported to Egypt.[26]

Two other MM's are Major William Robert Leslie Turp, MBE, and Thomas Clement Borrie, until 1967 partners in an enterprise called Intor, Limited, located south of London in Bexleyheath. In

1963 Turp and Borrie received an order from Sheik Ibrahim Zahid of Saudi Arabia for 10,000 Lee-Enfield rifles "complete with bayonets and scabbards, pull-throughs and oil bottles." The Board of Trade, however, refused to issue Intor an export license for these items. Undaunted, Turp and Borrie got the sheik to order 10,000 Lee-Enfields from a firm in Belgium called Transma, with which Intor was closely associated.[27] Later the sheik was to order an additional 10,000 rifles. All 20,000 rifles were shipped by Intor, with Board of Trade permission, from Great Britain to the Belgian associate and then re-exported, with the permission of the Belgian government, to the sheik. In a short space of time these Lee-Enfields were in the hands of Yemeni Royalists. Turp and Borrie both denied that they knew of the ultimate destination of the rifles but did claim that it was John Dawson-Ellis who had arranged the entire deal.[28]

The most colorful and perhaps the least successful of all MM's is "Colonel" Hubert Fauntleroy Julian, otherwise known as the "Black Eagle of Harlem." He was born in Trinidad in 1898 and learned to fly in the Royal Canadian Air Force in World War I. In 1924, three years before Lindbergh's flight, Julian attempted to fly the Atlantic in a seaplane, but he said that he forgot whether it was necessary to pull the stick back or push it forward on takeoff, and the plane crashed several hundred yards upwind from his starting point in the East River Basin.

In 1930 Julian went to Ethiopia and put on a parachute-jumping exhibition for Ras Tafari Makonnen, soon to be crowned Emperor Haile Selassie I. He landed 500 feet from Selassie and the monarch gave Julian, on the spot, the Menelik Medal (coveted by all Abyssinian braves), $5,000 and made him a colonel in the Royal Ethiopian Air Force at a salary of $2,000 per month. Selassie's entire air force at the time consisted of a Gipsy Moth racing plane and two Junkers monoplanes. During the coronation rehearsal Julian managed to destroy one third of the entire Royal Ethiopian Air Force by crashing the Gipsy Moth at Selassie's feet. He was relieved of his duties and banished in disgrace from the kingdom.[29]

In 1940 Julian challenged Hermann Göring to an aerial duel

over the English Channel but received no reply from the Reich Marshal. Two years later he was an American citizen and a sergeant in the Army. After the war he became a licensed weapons dealer. For a while he was an arms purchasing agent for the Guatemalan government, supplying everything from Swiss antiaircraft guns to bulletproof vests.[30] In 1953 he tried to sell 25,000 rounds of Italian antiaircraft ammunition to the procommunist Arbenz regime, but the shipment was seized by U.S. officials when the freighter transporting the material stopped in New York harbor. In recent years Julian's activities have become increasingly more secretive. He has been linked to secret arms transactions with the Dominican government of Trujillo and the Haitian government of Duvalier but denies any involvement. In 1961 Moise Tshombe appointed Julian his "roving ambassador-at-large," which many people interpreted as a cover title for arms purchasing activities. Julian stoutly denies that he bought guns for Tshombe. In April 1962 United Nations forces in the Congo arrested Julian as a mercenary. Several weapons, said to be samples, were found in his luggage. He was released in August and sent back to the United States.[31]

Like other MM's, Julian is somewhat flamboyant in manner and dress. He makes an earnest effort at an Oxford accent, and on occasion affects a monocle, bowler, morning coat, silk shirt and wing collar. When he was an Ethiopian colonel he designed his own uniform: pith helmet, pink silk polo shirt, white breeches with green stripes and deerskin boots with large, jingling spurs.[32]

There are hundreds of WerBells, De Feketes, McNaughtons, Turps, Borries, Dawson-Ellises and Julians in the world. All of them are opportunists, all of them are in the business for the money and, not surprisingly considering the unsettled state of the world, all of them are in great demand.

4

The men who run guns are also in demand. Like Cummings, his competitors and MM's, gunrunners fill a void in the international arms market: namely, the illegal introduction of armaments into a country or region. Gunrunning is a worldwide phenomenon that flourishes or withers solely on the criteria of supply and demand. The motives for smuggling are twofold: to make money and to exert influence. Usually the former is more important to a gunrunner than the latter.

Gunrunning today is, as it traditionally has been, a most diverse and complex sphere of activity. It involves all manner of people, organizations and situations. It would be a mistake to think, for instance, that it is exclusively the domain of independent operators; on the contrary, one of the most noticeable trends of the twentieth century has been the increasing involvement of governments as gunrunners. Some of the biggest gunrunners in the world today are the Central Intelligence Agency, MI-6, SDECE (the French secret intelligence organization) and various communist intelligence agencies. In addition such groups as the Pan African Movement and the Moslem Brotherhood engage in gunrunning; so too do special government agencies in such countries as Algeria, Egypt, Ghana and Cuba.

Gunrunning profit margins run two to three times higher than those on legitimate transactions, since the risks involved are so much greater. A $16 secondhand single-shot rifle in the United States will bring $100 in Mexico where, in all likelihood, it will be smuggled into South America via Panama and resold for $200. A single round of ammunition for an automatic pistol costs approximately 3 cents in Munich and will fetch 35 cents in the Middle East. Saarland smugglers can sell an $18 pistol for over $100 in Turkey.[33] A No. 1 Mark III Lee-Enfield rifle, sold by the British government (using Cogswell & Harrison or Parker-Hale as the agents) to an Aden sheik for 9 pounds ($21.60), will fetch ten times that amount when smuggled into the interior and sold to dissident tribesmen.

Since the invention of gunpowder, western Europe has remained the major hub of all gunrunning activities. Switzerland is a hotbed of activity, particularly in Berne and Zurich. Brussels and Milan are also major centers. The greatest volume of illegal guns flows through the port of Hamburg, followed closely by Antwerp, Marseille, Barcelona, Rotterdam and Genoa. From there the contraband may go to Tangier, or to Latakia in Syria, or Beirut; or it may be shipped through the Suez Canal to Aqaba in Jordan, or to Jiddah in Saudi Arabia, or to Dar-es-Salaam in Tanzania; or it may go to Dakar, Conakry, Macao or Hong Kong. More likely, the arms will be shipped to small, obscure ports that few people have ever heard of. The goods, particularly if they are being smuggled by commercial carrier, are packed in crates bearing such false labels as "water pumps," "engine parts" and "porcelain." A shipment of West German flamethrowers being smuggled to the Algerian FLN was once labeled "crop sprayers."[34]

There are a number of well-known European gunrunners. One is a scar-faced mailbox manufacturer from Vaduz, Liechtenstein. He once offered 40,000 rifles to Portuguese settlers in Angola in 1961 and guaranteed to deliver them within 48 hours by air. Another gunrunner is a legless Swiss merchant, one of whose competitors is a former chief of Swiss counterintelligence who operates out of Zurich. Another was Marcel Leopold, now dead, who ran his gunrunning operation from Geneva.

Of particular interest are three West German arms merchants: Dr. Wilhelm Beisner, Ernst-Wilhelm Springer and Georg Puchert. All three were deeply involved in supplying arms to the Algerian FLN during its war with France.

Beisner, during World War II, was chief of the *Sicherheitsdienst,* or SD, in Yugoslavia. The SD was the SS Security Service and was the most sadistic and inhuman of all the Nazi politico-military units. At war's end Beisner escaped to Italy and soon went to Egypt, where he became a friend of Prince Abbas Halin, Farouk's pro-Nazi cousin. He joined the Egyptian Secret Service, supplying arms for the government. After Farouk's downfall Beisner turned up in Damascus working with Springer and an individual named Hartmann Lauterbacher, an ex-Nazi Gauleiter. Lauterbacher was once quoted as saying, "I deal in anything, as far as I'm concerned even if it's dried out horse manure. The only thing that counts is that it must make money."[35] By the late 1950's Beisner had become one of the main contact points for arms flowing to the FLN.

Springer was an even larger arms supplier to the FLN. He once bought 2,000 crates, or 80 tons, of hand weapons and munitions from the Czechs; this material was shipped from Prague to Yugoslavia destined for Latakia in Syria. From there the arms were to be smuggled to the FLN. However, Tito had the shipment confiscated on its way through Yugoslavia; he had the barrels bent and the bolts extracted; then the shipment was allowed to proceed on to Latakia. The FLN agents were furious with Springer when they saw the material and refused to pay him.

In 1959 Springer tried to buy 120 tons of dynamite for the FLN from Dynamit Nobel of Troisdorf, near Cologne. Nobel refused to make the delivery to Springer because the Bonn government failed to issue an export license. Undaunted, Springer went to Chemo Impex, a firm in Budapest, and arranged that the same amount of material be sent to Tripoli via a Finnish intermediary named Samo Salo. However, the deal collapsed when Chemo Impex demanded payment in advance in Budapest. Because Springer was brokering this sale, he could not produce the payment until after the dynamite had been delivered to the FLN.[36]

Puchert also worked very closely with the FLN. As of May 1958 he was its official armaments representative in western Europe. He organized all aspects of the gunrunning operation: types of weapons to be bought, prices, delivery dates, smuggling routes, payment arrangements. Puchert's cover name was "Captain Morris," apparently because he smoked Phillip Morris cigarettes.[37]

There are considerable risks in this type of business, and few of these arms dealers have come away unscathed. Someone tried to assassinate Ernst-Wilhelm Springer by putting a bomb under the seat of his car. Dr. Wilhelm Beisner was badly injured when a shrapnel-laden bomb blew him through the roof of his car. Georg Puchert was killed when a bomb in his car exploded. And Marcel Leopold was to suffer the most bizarre death of all: he was killed in a hotel lobby in Geneva by a poisoned arrow.[38]

Many of these deaths were due to a right-wing terrorist organization known as the Red Hand. It was founded in 1950 in Tunisia by French Army Officers, shopkeepers and officials who sought protection from the terrorists in Habib Bourguiba's Neo Destour movement. It took its name from the red of the Sicilian Mafia and the Hand of Fatma, a Moslem sign for luck. The organization soon spread throughout the French-speaking areas of North Africa, gaining adherents among those who were frightened by the rising tide of nationalism.

The Red Hand built up a network of agents both in Europe and in North Africa whose job it was to provide intelligence and, when necessary, supplies of contraband guns in the event its members had to defend themselves. It also maintained a network of killers, some of whom had the type of training only a professional secret agent of the French government would receive. Its agents not only were experts at boobytrapping automobiles but were expert assassins of the old school. They once murdered a reputed FLN arms buyer, one Ait Ahcene, by machine-gunning him in broad daylight before the Tunisian embassy in Bonn. They also tried to assassinate General Raoul Salan in 1957 (at that time he was pro-De Gaulle) by firing an antitank rocket at his office.

It has never been conclusively established that the Red Hand was actually in the pay of any French bureau; but it is almost certain that it had the government's semiofficial blessing. For instance, there was one member of the Red Hand called "The Killer" who began to appear on the scene of every one of the gunrunning assassinations and bombings. This individual had once been a member of the French secret service; he had also worked in West Germany with General Rheinhart Gehlen's intelligence organization: and he traveled with two official French passports, which would indicate a close tie with the French government. This individual was also involved in a scandal which concerned a Swiss secret service officer who had committed suicide after turning over information to him about the smuggling of weapons from Egypt to the Algerian FLN.[39]

Eventually the Red Hand merged with the OAS, or Secret Army Organization, an outlaw French right-wing terrorist group which was born after the French Army revolt in Algiers in April 1961. In all probability the Red Hand has now ceased to function as an independent group.

There is no possible way to judge accurately the number of gunrunning rings operating out of Europe at any one moment.

Undoubtedly there is a relationship between the number of active rings and the amount of physical unrest in the world. By their very nature gunrunning rings are secretive; in the event they are discovered, not too much additional information is forthcoming, because of the political implications involved and because of the frequent involvement of governments themselves. Nevertheless, in spite of these obstacles, some information has come to light and deserves brief comment if only to illustrate the wide variety of gunrunning operations coming out of Europe.

The seven-year Algerian War, from 1954 to 1961, is a good example of how internationalized gunrunning operations can become. Supplying weapons to the FLN was by no means the exclusive preserve of such men as Beisner, Springer and Puchert. Governments themselves were unofficial participants and a partial list of them would include Morocco, Egypt, Czechoslovakia, Yugoslavia, West Germany, Belgium, Lebanon, Red China, Cuba and Ghana. Even a group of Argentines were involved: they planned to buy $625,000 worth of bazookas, cannons, rifles and ammunition in Italy and load the goods onto an Argentine-bound boat which was to be diverted at the last moment to Algeria. The plot was discovered when Argentine authorities questioned the plotters' forged documents.[40]

The arms traffic by 1957 was so heavy along the North African coast that the French government was forced to impose a tight blockade. Between 1957 and 1961 the French Navy stopped nearly a score of German freighters believed to be carrying arms to the FLN. At least seventeen Yugoslav gunrunning ships were seized in the same period. A Czech ship, the *Lidice,* was discovered to be carrying enough arms to equip a full division. Another communist ship, the *Bulgaria,* succeeded in running the blockade and unloading 1,800 tons of arms at Tangiers for the Algerian rebels. In response to all this, French agents blew up at least three ships carrying weapons from West German and Belgian ports. Some Lebanese gunrunners took to flying in their cargo by DC-4.

It was impossible for the French to stop this traffic for several reasons. The Algerian border, first of all, is so long that it is for all practical purposes impossible to guard. The fact that all of Algeria's neighbors were sympathetic to the FLN cause made the task that much more difficult. Second, the French Army, after its defeat in Indochina, was too busy and demoralized fighting the National Liberation Army to make the effort to cut off the flow of weapons. Third, and perhaps most important of all, the FLN was so well financed and was offering such good prices for arms that no gunrunner, neither professional nor amateur, could resist becoming involved.

A far more typical gunrunning operation was one discovered in Munich in 1965. This particular ring had been smuggling arms from Czechoslovakia, Spain and Belgium into Turkey and the Middle East. It had organized a smoothly run shuttle service of buses, cars and trucks, driven by Turks, Syrians, Iraqis, Lebanese and Germans, between points in western Europe and Istanbul. The drivers were hired from among the foreign workers milling around Munich's main railroad station and given $140 down and another $140 when their cargo was delivered intact. The vehicles were bought secondhand in Munich, given temporary ten-day export registration plates, and fitted out with false bottoms and secret caches. With thousands of tourists swarming through Austria, northern Italy, Yugoslavia and Greece, only cursory checks were made, since it appeared as if the vehicles were meant to be resold in the Middle East. Many of the weapons ended up in the hands of Turkish Cypriots, Yemeni Royalists and Iraqi Kurds.

One of the drivers of this ring had his load of arms confiscated by customs. (The easiest way to spot-check against this type of smuggling is to weigh the vehicle when it is "empty" and to check the result against standard vehicle weights.) He was reported to have been "executed" when he arrived in Istanbul because the ringleader did not believe his story, thinking he had sold the weapons and pocketed the proceeds.[41]

One of the more unusual postwar gunrunning plots took place in 1964–65 when a group of American, British, French and Canadian adventurers attempted to move 1,000 tons of Czech arms from Prague to what appears to have been either anti-Ben Bella or pro-OAS groups in the Cascade de Kefrida mountain area of Algeria.

In October 1964 two rather shadowy Frenchmen, Paul Bonte and Georges Starkmann, contacted in Amsterdam an ex-CIA operative named Urban L. Drew. It appears that Bonte was an OAS fixer and interpreter and that Starkmann, a former member of the French intelligence service, was the cashier. Drew, with twenty-seven decorations for gallantry, had been president of Seven Seas Airlines, which once flew under contract for the United Nations in the Congo. This airline was doing $3 million worth of business a year for the peace-keeping organization until Drew was caught smuggling crated Fouga jet fighters to Tshombe. Seven Seas was denounced by Adlai Stevenson in the U.N. and soon went broke. Drew next showed up in Vietnam, officially working for a civil airline but also engaged in aviation activities for the CIA. His work for the American agency, however, proved unsatisfactory and, he said, "I was furloughed—that means fired."

After many long and exploratory conversations, Bonte and Starkmann told Drew the nature of their plans and asked if he would be interested in taking part. He said he would and soon thereafter set about recruiting a crew and searching for a suitable aircraft. After many false starts, he happened upon an American, Captain H. Lucien Pickett, of USAIR, a chartered company operating out of London. Did USAIR have any DC-4's for hire? No, replied a spokesman, but they did have a Lockheed *Super Constellation* in London. Did the doors open inward (a standard gunrunner's question because outward-opening doors prevent para-drops)? Yes, they did, replied the spokesman. An understanding was eventually reached whereby USAIR agreed to run the 1,000 tons of arms into Algeria for a fee of $10,000 per flight.

Bonte then went off to Prague to prepare the shipment. The standard payment arrangement in an operation such as this is to set up a small "export-import" firm somewhere in western Europe and have it place sufficient deposits (for "machinery" and the like) in the account of a Czech cover firm usually located in either Switzerland or Luxembourg, the two most commonly used countries for such a purpose. Lest the Czech's love of the Algerian regime overcome their lust for hard currencies, Bonte told them that the arms were destined for Rwanda-Burundi.

On February 1, 1965, the *Constellation* was flown to Amsterdam where the crew had assembled. The next day, when Pickett arrived, he found the crew in near rebellion because the operation was not, as they had been led to believe, a "normal" gunrunning one from Prague to Leopoldville, but a parachute drop at night at 500 feet in the Berber Mountains. Drew had to give Pickett, who was to be the plane's navigator, an additional $1,000 to parcel out among the crew to mollify them.

The plane was then flown from Amsterdam to the tiny airport at Beek, a town in south Holland. Parachutes were loaded on board and the U.S. registration, N9642Z, was painted over and a false Ghanaian one, 9G28, was substituted. (A London-based Trinidad student had been paid $1,000 to get the Ghanaian registration.)

Because of bad weather Pickett radioed Prague, using the code LKPRYA, which meant direct contact with the Czech Air Ministry. He asked for a twenty-four-hour delay on "request for penetration Red 11/CHEB" and signed his message with the name of a nonexistent firm, Trans-African Airways. Under normal procedures, an aircraft would ask its take-off field to obtain landing clearance at Prague airport. Obviously Pickett was operating under a special procedure.

The *Constellation* was four hours late crossing CHEB checkpoint into corridor Red 11. Nevertheless no difficulties were encountered upon landing in Prague. Exactly forty minutes later the plane was once more airborne with seventeen tons of arms aboard (an overload of 18 percent). While at Prague, the pilot had filed a flight plan for Benina, Libya.

The plan, as worked out by the gunrunners, was to build up a picture to flight control centers along the way that the aircraft was in difficulties. Instead of going to Benina they were to request permission to divert to Palma, Majorca. Then they were to descend to 500 feet to avoid radar, divert again into the Berber hills, drop their load and skirt back to Palma before anyone realized what had happened.

When the plane reached Sardinia, Pickett radioed Rome control for permission to divert, having previously reported falsely that his No. 3 engine was feathered. Rome granted permission and the plane headed west. But soon the plane developed genuine engine trouble and it fell so far behind schedule that the arms drop would have had to have been made in daylight. A cloud cover at the time also made a low-level run through the mountains dangerous. Under the circumstances Pickett decided to call the drop off. He advised Rome control that he was continuing on to Benina but en route decided to land at Malta. He and the entire crew were arrested and the arms—rifles, submachine guns and ammunition—were impounded.[42]

Dutch authorities were aware of the flight's purpose from the start. So, too, were American agencies which Dutch security officials claim had been forewarned. So, too, were the Czechs and in all probability the British. Drew and Bonte had led Pickett to believe that he was on an official mission and that his flight was to be monitored by the U.S. Sixth Fleet in the Mediterranean. The U.S. State Department maintained on two occasions that neither it nor the CIA played any role in the incident and then dropped the matter. The plane's pilot and Lucien Pickett were fined only $280 (for violating Maltese air space). Dutch authorities arrested Drew and an associate, but both were soon released without being charged. The Dutch also impounded for false registration a Canadian DC-4 owned by Pickett which he had left at Amsterdam's Schiphol Airport. (This plane was to play a part in another gunrunning episode, this time to Nigeria.) And the last that was heard of Bonte and Starkmann, they were back in London with a briefcase full of dollars attempting to organize yet another flight.[43]

For centuries the greatest and most sustained market for illegal guns has been the Arab world, stretching from Pakistan to Morocco and from Syria to the Sudan. A seven-year war for independence such as experienced by Algeria would only temporarily increase the consistently high demand for weapons in the entire area. This demand remains high for a number of reasons, chief among them being the unsettled state of the area and the brutal competition between various factions jockeying for power. Also, an Arab tribesman, by and large, feels undressed without a rifle or pistol; arms are essential to him physically, socially and psychologically. Even if a gun is inaccurate or dangerous, its possession in his view is vital to his own well-being and life.

The British long realized the importance Arabs attached to rifles and worked out a system whereby colonial civil servants rewarded the local emirs and sheiks by allowing them to buy arms—usually no more than 300 per year—from the Crown Agents at controlled prices. The emirs and sheiks would then sell the rifles to loyal tribesmen in the hills. Whatever profit they received—and it was usually no less than 500 percent—was their practical reward for their loyalty to the British Crown.[44] The British used this tactic to good effect throughout their Near and Middle East colonies and were particularly successful among the emirs and sheiks in the East Aden Protectorate, the South Arabian Federation and Muscat and Oman. Even though the British have all but withdrawn from east of Suez, they still seek the loyalty of these groups through the bargain-price sale of guns.

Sometimes the emirs and sheiks would trade rifles for equipment they did not want the armed tribes to have, such as terrorist-type grenades and bazookas. In 1967, for instance, the recognized reward for the surrender of a landmine in the East Aden Protectorate was two Lee-Enfield rifles. The bottom fell out of this market, however, when it was discovered that the tribesmen were crossing into the war-torn Yemen where the price of a landmine was only one rifle, buying another mine and showing a 100 percent profit.

Virtually every Arab, given the opportunity, will smuggle weapons, so lucrative can it be. A big gunrunner at one time was Sharif Nasser ben Shamil, an uncle of Jordan's King Hussein. After Hussein himself he is the most powerful man in Jordan's army. In 1966 Sharif Nasser was caught smuggling weapons into Jordan, not, as many people thought, to overthrow the regime but simply to make money. It was and still is against Jordanian law to import weapons privately. Approximately 50,000 weapons were found by Jordanian customs officials at Aqaba while Sharif Nasser was in England. King Hussein was notified and he ordered that the entire shipment be confiscated. Hussein, while he was further troubled by his uncle's complicity in a large dope-smuggling ring, reportedly did not mention the incident to Sharif Nasser upon his return.

A month later King Hussein went to England on a state visit.

Sharif Nasser immediately took possession of all the confiscated weapons and sold them to his original customers. The arms import ban created such a large demand for arms that when Sharif Nasser sold his 50,000 units he was able to make a 1,000 percent profit. Hussein, upon his return, was told of what had happened, and he had his uncle and several confederates arrested. He reconfiscated what weapons he could find; those that he could not find in all probability were resold for even higher prices to Iraqi Kurds and Yemeni Royalists.[45]

Of recent interest have been the gunrunning activities in the Yemen. Like the Algerian War the trade has taken on an international flavor, and it has also made large fortunes for some of the individuals involved. The civil war which broke out in 1962 saw the polarization of forces between the conservative Arabs backing the Royalists and the radical Arabs supporting the Republicans.

On the Republican side, Egypt has given support openly, supplying at one point, among other things, as many as 55,000 troops. Red China has supplied arms secretly; so, too, have Czechoslovakia, the Soviet Union and Bulgaria. The Soviets have provided, either directly or through Egypt, all the heavy equipment, particularly fighters, bombers and field guns. At one point the Soviets were even supplying the pilots for the airplanes.

The most controversial weapon used by the Republicans was a gas bomb, the nature and source of which are still obscure. From first reports it appeared that the bombs had come from Bulgaria and were filled with tabun, sarin or soman, three deadly nerve gasses developed by the Germans in World War II. Others believe that the gas was a special one developed by German scientists in Egypt. Still others claim it was a mustard and blinding gas; witnesses spoke of a "greenish colored, sweet smelling gas . . . killing everything wherever the wind blew." Cairo, upon whom most of the responsibility was laid, denied ever using such a weapon, but the evidence is quite strong that some type of toxic gas was used. None of these claims have been proved or disproved at this writing.[46]

The Royalists, led by a group of feuding princes occasionally loyal to the Imam El Badr, have been supplied covertly from a number of sources although the secret has been very poorly kept. The greatest assistance has come from Saudi Arabia, which, along with arms and ammunition, has sent in a monthly allowance of gold guineas. At first the Saudis gave only small arms, but later the Royalists were given heavy machine guns, bazookas, mines and three-inch mortars. The Royalist commanders supplemented this equipment by offering to pay tribes for weapons captured from the Republicans; thus to many Yemenis a successful ambush often became a paying proposition. Other assistance has come from Jordan and Iran.[47]

One Bushrod Howard announced in 1966 that the Royalists, with Saudi gold, had contracted to buy $25 million worth of ammunition from Bulgaria for their captured Russian weapons. This material, he said, was shipped to Greece or Austria in cases marked "in transit," then picked up by charter planes and dropped by parachute to the Royalists. Howard, it must be pointed out, was then the registered agent in the United States for the Yemeni Royalists. He probably encouraged the dissemination of this story in order to advance his client's cause.[48]

One source of aid has been a secret organization based in London and Paris that has supplied arms and highly trained European mercenary soldiers. Reportedly it was run at one time by Major John M. Cooper, MBE, DCM, a colorful British military figure who was one of the charter members of the Special Air Services, an organization founded by Colonel David Sterling to fight deep behind enemy lines in the Western Desert. Cooper supposedly operated under the cover of the Yemeni Relief Committee, founded by the Dowager Lady Birdwood at the outbreak of the civil war ostensibly to provide medical supplies to the Royalists. This group seems to maintain some link with official British government authorities.[49]

The mercenaries employed by the Royalists—of which there were approximately 500 in 1967, mostly supplied by this secret organization—were predominantly British, French and Belgian in nationality. Most were veterans of the Congo; some were ex-

Legionnaires; others were ex-OAS ultras. They were and continue to be used to train troops and to operate some of the more complicated equipment. Some of them are being paid as much as $28,000 a year.[50]

In April 1962, King Faisal, Saudi Arabia's Prime Minister, and President Nasser of Egypt signed a "disengagement agreement" whereby the Saudis would cease aiding the Royalists if the Egyptians would withdraw their troops. The Saudis claim that they kept their part of the bargain for over a year and that the Egyptians from the start did not. Faced with a possible loss of supplies and a continuation of the war, the Royalists sought aid from the sheiks of the South Arabian Federation. One ruler, Sharif Hussein Bin Ahmed el-Habili of Beihan, was reported to have subsequently made a vast fortune in arms trafficking to the Royalists. He was also deeply involved in supplying arms to the anti-British rebels in Aden. Another group that grew rich from this trade was the Beni Jahm tribe, a greedy bunch of Arabs who ambushed Saudi caravans and then ransomed the arms to the Royalists.[51]

The Lebanese are a ubiquitous factor in the gunrunning trade. Beirut is a major center for the financing of gunrunning operations, and many of the world's leading smugglers at one time preferred to keep their business accounts at the now-defunct Intra Bank. Occasionally these Lebanese moneymen will become runners, but more often they will limit themselves to the financial aspects. So great is their desire for profits that they know no other loyalty. It is well known, for instance, that Lebanese traders financed private (and sometimes government-sponsored) gunrunning operations from both Western and Eastern sources in the Yemen and Aden. They have financed illegal shipments of arms to Congolese rebels, to both sides in the Six Day War, to Kurdish tribesmen, to both Greek and Turkish Cyriots, to Sudanese rebels, to both sides in the Nigerian Civil War, to Iranian dissidents, to white Rhodesians and to South Africans.

The Middle East has produced unique manufacturers-cum-gunrunners who deserve brief notice here. They are the Pathans, a collection of Moslem tribesmen inhabiting an area running from

Kashmir down through the princely states between the Himalayas and the Hindu Kush and all along the mountain borders between Pakistan and Afghanistan to the south. For centuries those Pathans living in the area of Malakand and Swat, by the Khyber and Kohat Passes, have been manufacturing their own weapons and then smuggling them into Afghanistan, Kashmir, Pakistan and even distant Iran. One group, the Afridi clan, makes weapons from old railroad tracks, suitably reworked on primitive hand-turned lathes. Usually their products are copies of more famous European models, complete with name and patent numbers.[52]

C. L. Sulzberger of *The New York Times* showed me a .32 caliber "Webley & Scott" revolver which had been reproduced faithfully in every detail except that the words "Birmingham & London" had been misspelled. He paid the equivalent of $18 for it. Besides revolvers the Afridis manufacture shotguns, rifles, submachine guns, machine guns and three-inch cannons—again, all faithful reproductions of well-known Western models. Throughout the gun trade these weapons are known as "Khyber Pass Specials," a term that has come to mean any weapon of inferior make.*

These weapons have been widely distributed throughout the Pathan tribal areas. Many of them are smuggled to their destinations; others are freely available in local markets. While a few arms dealers believe these weapons to be of superior quality (because of the high temper of the railroad tracks), it is generally acknowledged that the guns are good only for so long—perhaps the time it takes to kill a score of the enemy—before the receiver melts and the barrel begins to twist. But, then, few of the tribal wars in the area last longer than that. A Pakistani colonel told Sulzberger that a quantity of these arms had been bought by his government from the Afridis in the 1950's during a threatened crisis over Kashmir.

* Pre-Communist China engaged in the reproduction of well-known models of small arms, particularly Browning and Mauser pistols. These guns are known as "Chinese Wonders" in the arms trade, and some of them were used by the Chinese Communists in the Korean War.

5

Compared with the sustained and high volume of arms being shuffled around the Near and Middle East, gunrunning in the Western Hemisphere is quite small and has been a one-way street—from the United States outward. Most of the recent activity has centered around Cuba from 1956 to 1962, and Haiti and the Dominican Republic at sporadic intervals. The remaining attempts to run guns have been, on the whole, minor affairs such as the covert supplying of arms to both Arbenz leftists and Castillo-Armas rebels in 1953–54; the 1959 comic opera effort of Dame Margot Fonteyn and her husband, Roberto M. Arias, to smuggle weapons via fishing boat into Panama as part of a plot to overthrow the legitimate government; and a plot in 1966 involving a group of Texans who planned to smuggle arms into Latin America. Even Fidel Castro's efforts to smuggle guns to procommunist revolutionaries in Venezuela and Bolivia, among other countries, were relatively minor affairs.*

Fidel Castro's forces, before the fall of Batista, acquired their weapons almost exclusively from U.S. sources. Castro's arms purchasers first tried to buy in bulk lots from such firms as Interarms, but when eyebrows were raised they decentralized their operations, buying odd-lot weapons wherever they could. These weapons were then brought to staging points in Georgia and Florida and then smuggled, usually by boat and with U.S. authorities looking the other way, into Cuba. The guns were of a wide variety of makes and calibers, presenting Castro with a logistics supply problem of the first order. By 1958 sufficient quantities of U.S. military aid to the Batista government had been captured (mostly M-1 Garands) that the problem was somewhat eased.

* According to the Report of the Investigating Committee of the Organization of American States, dated February 18, 1964, the quantity of weapons discovered in Venezuela on November 1, 1963, consisted of 81 FN rifles, 31 Uzi submachine guns, five mortars, 20 3.5-inch rocket launchers, 9 recoilless rifles and a small quantity of ammunition. Most arms dealers believe that Castro acquired these weapons from third parties rather than from the original manufacturers.

After Castro came to power, legitimate European arms dealers and MM's flocked to the island offering arms for sale. The United States had clamped an embargo on Cuba in March 1958 which, because it was not backed up by force, had the effect of excluding only legitimate U.S. arms dealers from trading with the new regime. The aggressive Belgian firm of Fabrique Nationale was first off the mark: it supplied a large quantity of small arms and explosives to the new government. The Czechs entered the supply picture soon after Fabrique Nationale and were, in turn, followed by the Soviets themselves.

The anti-Castro rebels were forced to adopt the same haphazard methods of buying and gunrunning that Castro had adopted previously, except that, from 1959 to the spring of 1961, U.S. arms dealers were far more wary, the U.S. government began cracking down on offenders, and the Cuban people, by and large, failed to give the new rebels any appreciable support. Before the Bay of Pigs, independent gunrunning efforts were generally sporadic and ineffectual.

From what sparse evidence is available, the equipment supplied by the CIA for the Bay of Pigs invasion force was almost totally American in origin. Some of the small caliber rifles, as previously noted, came from Interarms. Much of the small arms ammunition appears to have been manufactured in U.S. government arsenals, given false headstamp designations and packed in unmarked boxes. Some of the heavier ordnance appears to have been foreign-made but purchased from U.S. sources. The military vehicles—B-26 bombers, C-46 and C-54 transports, trucks, jeeps and landing craft—appear to have been surplus stock taken directly from U.S. military inventory.

All this equipment was smuggled either first to Retalhuleu and Puerto Barrios in Guatemala, or to Puerto Cabezas in Nicaragua, and then to the Bay of Pigs with the invasion forces, or directly from the United States to the beaches. The mode of transportation to the beaches, unlike that suffered by independent operators, was strictly first-class: via U.S. Air Force planes, U.S. Navy ships, or similar equipment operated by subcontractors to the CIA.[53]

During the preinvasion buildup considerable confusion reigned among the various U.S. government agencies concerned with controlling the arms trade; none of their efforts seem to have been coordinated. While the CIA was busy gathering arms and the FBI was busy infiltrating pro- and anti-Castro groups, the Alcohol, Tobacco and Firearms Division of the Internal Revenue Service, the agency charged with enforcing the domestic firearms laws, was busy rounding up gunrunners; so too were the Immigration and Customs Services. According to Karl Meyer and Tad Szulc in their book *The Cuban Invasion,* the situation was so confusing at one point that "it became impossible to enforce the law without running the risk of one government agency handcuffing henchmen of another government agency."[54]

One is struck in the entire Cuban affair how at every turn the smuggling of weapons was ultimately detrimental to U.S. interests. That it helped rid Cuba of a brutal dictatorship is doubtlessly true; that it helped to bring to power a better regime has yet to be proved. Once Castro was in power, the U.S. authorities still allowed these activities to continue. Sporadic air drops to the anti-Castro underground, hit-and-run raids by rebels armed with U.S. weapons, and the blowing up of the French munitions ship *Le Coubre* in Havana harbor in March 1960, all contributed during the preinvasion period to Castro's break with the United States and his eventual dependence on communist countries for support. The Bay of Pigs disaster was just a cap to the whole affair.

Gunrunning activities that have the support of the United States government are not always spectacular affairs like the Bay of Pigs. In many cases they are minor; nevertheless, they are just as important in their own way. For instance, in mid-1964 Haiti requested permission to export from the United States fifteen T-28's, old World War II training planes that are easily converted into fighter-bombers. The Office of Munitions Control turned down the request on the grounds that such a sale would strengthen the regime of Dr. François "Papa Doc" Duvalier, the Caribbean's most oppressive dictator. Three months later, in September, it was learned that two T-28's had been smuggled out of the United States. The planes, for which Duvalier had paid the high price of $10,000 each, apparently were flown out of Florida at low level, to avoid coastal radar, and landed at the Haitian capital of Port-au-Prince.* Involved in the smuggling were three American pilots, a Florida aircraft broker, a former federal employee and a group of high-level Haitian officials.

The U.S. government at first expressed shock that such a thing could happen. Federal law enforcement officers and the State Department believed that they had an airtight case and were eager to prosecute. The conspirators, including the Haitians, were indicted by a federal grand jury on charges of violating munitions control regulations. But then suddenly the case was dropped and nothing more was heard of it. It appears that the State Department was forced to curb its enthusiasm for prosecution at the behest of the CIA. One of its former agents had been involved and apparently was willing to testify. Revelations by such an individual were held to be not in the national interest, since they could conceivably expose some of the agency's methods of operation.[55]

Those gunrunners not fortunate enough to have U.S. government backing must make do with their own wits. One plot to invade Haiti in 1966–67 had all the makings of a television spectacular; in fact it was indirectly financed in part by the Columbia Broadcasting System.

The plot was hatched by a group of Haitian and Cuban exiles in 1966. The Haitians wanted to overthrow Duvalier, and the Cubans went along in order to use Haiti as a jumping-off point for an invasion of Cuba. One of the leaders was the Reverend Jean Baptiste Georges, a former Education Minister under Duvalier and at the time a Spanish teacher in a New York City parochial school. Père Georges—sometimes addressed as "Señor Presidente" by his Cuban admirers—hoped to replace Duvalier with a more democratic regime. The other leader was Rolando "The Butcher" Masferrer Rojas, a brilliant, ruthless, if often charming adventurer who was one of the most hated men in Cuba during Batista's rule. In his early life Masferrer was a communist and served in the

* So distrustful is Duvalier of his own air force that reportedly the propellers to these and all his other prop-driven planes are locked in a basement room of the Presidential Palace.

Spanish Civil War as a political commissar. He was wounded several times and his right heel was shot off. He still limps from that action. Under Batista, Masferrer swung to the right; he became a senator, a publisher and a very wealthy man. In his home province of Oriente he formed a group of vigilantes called Los Tigres (The Tigers), whose several thousand members were specialists in extortion, murder and stealing from priests. He escaped to Florida on the day Batista fell from power.

The invasion plan, as envisioned by Georges and Masferrer, first called for the capture of a small airfield at Cap-Haïtien. Then U.S.-based B-25's, B-26's and P-51's, supposedly owned by the rebels, would be transferred to the airstrip. How these planes were to be smuggled out of the United States was never made clear. These planes were then to be used to support a 100-man seaborne commando raid on Port-au-Prince itself. The size of this force was considered sufficient to overthrow Duvalier's government. To finance such a venture, Masferrer was reported to have raised a fund variously estimated between $100,000 and $700,000 from Haitian and Cuban exiles and American and Canadian well-wishers. Recruiting of volunteers took place openly in New York City and along Miami's Cubanized Eighth Street.

While all this was going on, two free-lance writer-photographers under contract to CBS, looking for gunrunning footage, happened upon the plot and convinced Masferrer that the invasion should be recorded for history. A sum of money—"slightly over $1,000"—was paid by CBS to cover the cost of lodgings and meals for a three-man television crew to accompany the invasion force. For the next six months CBS filmed the developments: a secret meeting in a New York basement, target practice in New Jersey and Florida, the smuggling of arms from New York to Miami, a full dress rehearsal on Coco Plum Beach 110 miles south of Miami.

But as is often the case in an amateur attempt such as this, dissension broke out in the ranks. Most of the Cubans quit, some complaining bitterly of the quality of leadership, others charging that the equipment was broken down and worthless. At this point CBS decided that the show would never come off and pulled out, at an overall loss of $100,000.

A new invasion date was set for late January 1967, but at another beachside rehearsal shortly before D-Day, U.S. Customs officials moved in and arrested the entire group on a charge of trying to export weapons without a license. "The United States is protecting Fidel Castro!" cried Masferrer as he was taken off to jail. Some observers, in the wake of this fiasco, believe that the entire operation was more a plan to make money than a serious military undertaking.[56]

What concerns many people with cases like this is that U.S. authorities seldom close down such an operation until it is well under way and has had the benefit of considerable publicity. There were numerous occasions before the final arrests where laws had been broken. Had the authorities made their move earlier, there would not have been so much wasted time and money, so much unfavorable publicity. Like the Bay of Pigs with Fidel Castro, the Georges-Masferrer "invasion" served only to strengthen the two regimes its perpetrators wished to destroy.

The Mafia in America, contrary to what many people believe, is not deeply involved in gunrunning. The primary reason is that there is more money to be made in the less bulky items of narcotics and diamonds.* Charles H. Rogovin, formerly an Assistant District Attorney for the Commonwealth of Massachusetts and a member of the President's Task Force on Organized Crime, told me that a Mafiosi would seldom back a gunrunning operation with a general contribution of cash in the vague hope of winning any exclusive concessions from the new regime. The risks, he said, are too great. Rather, a Mafiosi would prefer to lend money to a conspirator with a personal guarantee of repayment. Thus, no matter how the plot turns out, there is someone specific to whom he can go to collect his money. The Mafia, said Rogovin, is less interested in the politics of an arms plot than in making large profits from the high interest rate (the "vigorish") charged on the loan. However, if a plot—say, against Haiti—were successful, the

* They are, however, involved in the smuggling of guns domestically, usually untraceable items known as "hit" guns.

Mafia would be only too pleased to move in, citing their loan as the deciding factor, and demand the hotel, gambling, narcotics or prostitution concessions.

If the Mafia is not deeply involved, it does have, however, several free-lance operators in the business. One is Joe "Bayonne Joe" Zicarelli, a Bonanno *capo* who reportedly bosses bookie and lottery action in New Jersey's Hudson County. Zicarelli has extensive holdings in Venezuela and the Dominican Republic and is the man to see if guns are needed, price no object. Through the years he sold over one million dollars worth of arms to Trujillo, a close personal friend of his. Zicarelli has also sold arms to the men who overthrew Trujillo. Another friend was Venezuela dictator Pérez Jiménez. During his presidency Zicarelli landed a contract worth $380,000 to supply aircraft parts to Venezuela; the profits in this deal were reportedly $280,000.[57]

Another free-lance gunrunner is Gabriel Mannarino, a gangster from western Pennsylvania who was one of the sixty hoodlums at the 1957 Mafia meeting in Apalachin, New York. According to Harold A. Serr, Director of the IRS's Alcohol, Tobacco and Firearms Division, Mannarino "was trafficking in firearms, shipping them to Latin American countries." It was during the time that Castro came to power that Mannarino was most active because, said Serr, he sensed that there were large profits to be made. Exactly what Mannarino sold the Castro regime is unknown. The U.S. government, added Serr, was fully aware of Mannarino's activities; on occasion the gangster was tailed by airplane. However, no indictments charging arms control violations have been brought against him as of this writing.

Concluded Serr: "It is very rare that these people, at the higher echelon in the Cosa Nostra family, or the Mafia, or whatever you want to call it, will get active in this area."[58]

Gunrunning activities in the Far East, exclusive of the Vietcong, which is treated separately in Chapter VIII, are also, somewhat surprisingly, primarily an American affair. What little arms traffic exists is small in comparison with the volume in other areas of the world. This stems from the absence of both large sources of supply and surplus stocks. Governments and their military establishments possess the only large sources of arms, and they believe, by and large, that they never have enough. Thus few surplus weapons are put up for auction. What surplus arms *do* become available are usually sold to Western dealers because they can offer higher prices. The illegal arms market in the Far East is fed from four sources: arms are either stolen from government arsenals, forcibly requisitioned from the populace, put on the illegal markets by governments themselves, or bought legally by traders and sold to smugglers.

Indeed there is a constant hum of small-scale gunrunning activity in the Orient. There is a brisk trade in illegal arms among the opium growers and buyers in the hills of Burma, Thailand and Laos. Small quantities of arms are regularly smuggled to the procommunist Hukbalahap guerrillas in the Philippines. Indonesian nationalists in Malaysia and West Irian were smuggled arms by the Sukarno government. There was considerable arms trafficking during all the civil wars and wars for independence—in Burma, Thailand, Cambodia, Mainland China, Indonesia, Malaysia, etc. And there still continues to be a small trade in illegal arms through Macao and Hong Kong of which very little is known publicly.

But the largest traffic has been conducted by the U.S. government, specifically by the Central Intelligence Agency. For instance, between the years 1949 and 1961 the CIA actively supplied arms to a group of Chinese Nationalists in Burma. When Chiang Kai-shek fled to Formosa in 1949, not everyone who wanted to could go with him. Some 12,000 Nationalist troops fled across the Yunnan border and set up camp in the lush poppy-growing area of northern Burma. Occasionally they conducted hit-and-run raids into Red China, but soon they grew tired of it and decided to settle down and become rich by growing opium. Nevertheless, the CIA saw these troops as a thorn in Mao's side and continued to supply them with arms and money. Many of the supplies were air-dropped by a CIA-backed company called Air America, a firm that still exists today supplementing the U.S. military effort in Vietnam.

The Burmese government, however, beset by its own economic and political difficulties during this period, found the Nationalists a continuing source of embarrassment and on occasion was forced to send its own army into the hills to do battle with them. Indeed the situation had so reversed itself by 1961 that some elements of the Nationalist irregulars reportedly had accepted arms from Mao to fight the Burmese. It took a four-power conference to settle the matter: 6,000 of the Nationalists were airlifted to Formosa, and the remainder were forcibly scattered throughout Thailand and Laos.

In the early 1950's the CIA secretly supplied arms to Chinese Nationalist guerrillas who conducted hit-and-run raids—some of battalion size—from Quemoy and Matsu onto the mainland. The agency operated under a dummy company called Western Enterprises, Incorporated, which purported to be a trading firm. Between 1951 and 1954 the CIA was deeply involved in running guns to agents within Red China. A number of Americans engaged in this trade were captured by the Chinese; two of them are John Thomas Downey and Richard George Fecteau—still officially listed by Washington as "civilian personnel employed by the Department of the Army." Both received long sentences and at this writing are still in Chinese jails. In 1958 the CIA was involved in smuggling arms to the anti-Sukarno rebels in Indonesia. Its men ferried half a dozen B-26's in and out of a rebel airstrip in the North Celebes from Clark Field, a U.S. Air Force base near Manila. Some of its men flew missions for the rebels, and at least one agent was captured.[59]

6

Since 1960 it has been boom times for gunrunners selling their wares in Africa south of the Sahara. The greatest volume of smuggled guns has come out of communist countries, specifically the Soviet Union, Czechoslovakia, Red China and, to a lesser extent, Cuba. The reason why these countries are such large gunrunners is quite apparent: invariably they have backed the rebels, or "outs"; if arms are to be supplied to these groups, it must be done clandestinely. Communist gunrunning activities in sub-Sahara Africa are explored more fully in Chapter VIII.

Noncommunist gunrunners have been just as active in the area but collectively not as large. Egypt, for instance, has sent old British military equipment left behind at Suez to the Angolan rebels led by Holden Roberto. It has trained and armed Eritrean exiles for guerrilla warfare against the Ethiopian government. In 1964 it sent a shipment of arms (originally Cuban) to Zanzibari rebels that was in part responsible for a successful procommunist *coup d'etat*. Egypt has also been a transit point for Soviet and Czech weapons smuggled to the rebel Congolese Simbas in 1964–65.

Algeria, which can barely feed itself, has also funneled Soviet and Czech arms to the Congo rebels, and it too has supplied weapons to Roberto's rebels in Angola. (Both these and other transactions were carried out by Ben Bella for ideological reasons, despite the domestic problems they created; they were among the determining factors that led to his overthrow by Colonel Houari Boumedienne in June 1965.) Tunisia and the Congo have also smuggled arms to Roberto, while Ethiopia, Nigeria (before its civil war) and the Organization of African Unity have given him money to buy weapons.[60]

Ethiopian gunrunners have supplied Turkana tribesmen with weapons which have been used in bitterly fought cattle-rustling raids in Uganda and Kenya's Northern Frontier Province. The Sudan has run Czech-made guns to the Beni Amer tribe in Ethiopia whose members are anti-Haile Selassie; it has also supported an armed revolt by Moslems in Chad (a country run by Christians); and it has helped to channel arms into the Congo for the Simba rebels. After their own revolt failed, the Simbas ironically sold many of their weapons to antigovernment rebels in the Sudan called the Anya Nya.*

Uganda, Zambia and Tanzania all smuggled arms to the Con-

* The name comes from a native word for a snake poison that kills a person by forcing him to scratch himself to death—an unusually appropriate name for a guerrilla organization.

golese and Mozambique rebels; Morocco, Guinea and Senegal have run guns to rebels in Portuguese Guinea. Pro-Tshombe troops, following the collapse of the Katanga secession in 1963, secretly sold arms to both blacks and whites in what is now Zambia. Zambia, in turn, has run guns to two competing Rhodesian freedom movements. And at least ten member countries of the OAU have given military aid to the banned African National Congress in South Africa.[61]

Ghana under Nkrumah was a center of subversion in Africa. Through an organization called the Bureau of African Affairs, guns were run to rebels in, among other countries, Niger, Angola, Sierra Leone, Cameroon, the Congo and its own neighboring states of Togo and the Ivory Coast. In addition, the Bureau was responsible to see that as many nationalist movements as possible throughout Africa were penetrated by pro-Nkrumah men. It also set up in Ghana secret espionage and guerrilla training camps—run by Red Chinese and East German instructors—for political exiles who, after finishing the courses, were to return to their homelands as "freedom fighters." It was hoped that these individuals would sacrifice themselves for socialism and Nkrumahism—defined as "African in context, but Marxist in form."[62] All this came to an end when Nkrumah was deposed in February 1966.

As is evident from the above, small-scale gunrunning operations in sub-Sahara Africa are so numerous and so complex that they are virtually impossible to examine with any sense of perspective.

Three particular instances of gunrunning are worthy of special comment. One was the attempt in 1965–66 to smuggle ten B-26's to the Portuguese which were to be used against Angolan rebels; another was the gunrunning activities in the Nigerian civil war; and the third was the arms traffic to secessionist Katanga from 1960 to 1963.

The smuggling of B-26's to Portugal qualifies as gunrunning because the United States, which allowed the planes to be delivered, has publicly only given arms to this particular NATO ally under the proviso that none of them be used in its colonies. Why the United States permitted such a sale to be made is still a mystery, since this type of plane today is good only—as has been proven in Vietnam—for antiguerrilla activities. Certainly B-26's would be of no use in Portugal itself.

Briefly, the affair began in April 1965 when Gregory Board, the owner of Aero Associates, Inc., in Tucson, Arizona, asked an ex-RAF ace and acrobatic pilot, John Richard Hawke, whether he would be interested in ferrying ten B-26's to Europe. Hawke said that he would and a fee of $3,000 per flight, to cover all expenses, was agreed upon. Hawke later learned that a number of other people were involved in the deal: one was the broker, a fifty-eight-year-old French count by the name of Henri Mari François de Marin de Montmarin, and another was a Canadian named Woodrow Wilson Roderick, a middleman in the purchase of the planes.

Hawke's first flight in May 1965 was relatively uneventful. He flew his B-26 from Tucson to Rochester, New York, then to Torbay, Newfoundland, and then to Santa Maria in the Azores. His radio went dead in midocean, precipitating a general alert across the North Atlantic, but he received nothing worse than a tongue-lashing from the Portuguese authorities. He then flew on to the Portuguese Air Force base at Tancos, delivered the plane and returned by commercial flight to the United States. His second flight was more eventful. On the way up from Tucson he ran into bad weather and decided to land his B-26 at Washington National Airport. While in the flight pattern he developed engine trouble and drifted, at low altitude, over the White House—a forbidden zone. When he landed he was met by squads of men in dark suits. "I always worry about men in dark suits," he said with reason. These turned out to be from the Federal Aviation Agency. Hawke was questioned for several hours by both FAA and FBI officials. He claims that before his first ferrying flight he was given a code word, "Sparrow," that he was to use if he got into any trouble. After invoking this word several times to his interrogators he was allowed to proceed. The next five flights from Tucson to Tancos were uneventful.

But then in September 1965 Hawke was arrested in Miami. A four-count indictment, charging violation of the State Department's Export Control Act and the Neutrality Acts, was brought against him, De Montmarin, Board and Roderick. Board went to Jamaica to avoid arrest; the charges against Roderick were later dismissed for lack of evidence. Hawke and De Montmarin stood trial in 1966 and, surprisingly, were acquitted.

The trial—which, for some obscure reason, was held in Buffalo, New York—brought out the fact that the CIA had been aware of these flights at least four days before the first one had begun. The agency, it was revealed, had passed on the information to intelligence units in the State Department, Department of Defense, the Army, Navy, Air Force, the Joint Chiefs of Staff and ten other government agencies. While it is fairly certain that the CIA, for once, was not the villain in the case, it is clear that a number of high U.S. government officials chose to ignore the information. One indication of the government's attitude was the FAA's refusal for eight months after the fact to admit that the White House incident had ever occurred. It is clear that someone important in the government wanted Portugal to have those planes, particularly, as one person noted, "when an amateurish agent like Hawke can buzz the White House with a B-26 and still be in the illegal export business five planes later."[63]

While it was surreptitiously supporting Portugal in its war against guerrillas by allowing it to buy B-26 bombers, the United States was and still is supporting the guerrillas themselves, a fact that is not widely known. In Angola, for instance, it has been supporting Holden Roberto. In Mozambique, also a Portuguese colony, it has been supporting a rebel group led by a pro-West nationalist named Eduardo Mondlane. Both men were educated in the United States and have been looked upon with discreet favor by Washington officials. They both have received a small amount of financial aid from U.S. sources. Several African experts have told me that the money has come and still comes from both private and government funds. One authority claims that the CIA has been directly involved with these rebels but he could not prove it. The United States has realized—as, surprisingly, do many Portuguese leaders—that someday both territories must be given their freedom and, until then, it is in the U.S.'s interest to keep potential leaders from turning away from the West.[64]

The Nigerian civil war—the Federals versus the Biafrans—is a classic example of the forces at play in the gunrunning business.

The Federals under Major General Yakabu Gowon had a larger army and air force and the advantages of controlling the bulk of the country's revenues. Biafra, the breakaway eastern state, maintained a smaller army and air force, but its troops, under the command of Oxford-educated Chukwuemeka Odumegwu Ojukwu, were considered superior fighters. Biafra is also the center of Nigeria's budding oil industry.

The Federals viewed the secession as a rebellion to be crushed; the Biafrans, mostly Ibo tribesmen, considered the fight the only alternative they had to being dominated—perhaps indeed exterminated—by the country's larger ethnic groups, particularly the Hausas of the north and the Yorubas of the west.

Biafra began arming itself well before the October 1966 massacres in the north or the formal breakup of the Federation in May of 1967. The first inkling that Biafra was planning to arm itself was in early 1966 immediately after the political assassinations of the January coup. Paul Favier, a former senior employee in the French Sûreté Nationale, was one of the first to realize the Ibos' need for arms. He owned a large quantity of small arms dating back to World War II days that were stored in Holland. Several Nigerians living in Geneva (it was unclear at first with whom their loyalties lay) expressed interest in the weapons and a bargain—price unknown—was struck. The only trouble was that the Dutch authorities would not give Favier an export license to ship the arms directly to Nigeria. Refusing to be put off, Favier went to Major Robert Turp of Intor in England and convinced him that he should import the weapons. Turp was unaware that Favier had a client and agreed to go along.

In October, a DC-4 under the command of a forty-four-year-old German-American adventurer named Captain Henry A. Warton landed at Zestienhoven Airport in Rotterdam to pick up the guns. Dutch authorities were well acquainted with this particular DC-4: it was the one that had been impounded from Captain Lucien Pickett after the Algerian gunrunning episode; and for the ten months that it sat on the asphalt at Schiphol Airport, officials watched fascinated as rain washed away the Panamanian registration number to reveal a previous Canadian one. Warton told

Dutch authorities that Favier's guns were going to Birmingham, and since all his papers were in order, the authorities had no choice but to let him proceed.

The plane, 3,000 pounds overweight at takeoff, headed for Birmingham, but before it landed Warton radioed the tower that his "company" had diverted the plane to Majorca. He landed at Palma, refueled, and proceeded on to Hassi Messaoud in Algeria and from there "to Fort Lamy in Chad," which is near the Nigerian border. On the way Warton ran out of gas and crashed near Garoua, Cameroon. The plane broke into four sections, scattering arms all along a marshy riverbank. Warton suffered a mild concussion and the co-pilot a broken leg. Several months later a Cameroon court convicted both men of illegally transporting arms; they were each fined a small amount of money and sentenced to a month's imprisonment.[65]

This arms supply effort, while ill-fated, was a portent of things to come. In 1966 Biafra spent over a million pounds sterling for arms. This money came from a Swiss bank account. It is generally agreed, in retrospect, that Biafra paid very high prices for these arms. On top of this, many of the arms were never delivered: some of the ships were intercepted by the Federal government; other arms dealers, having been paid in advance by the desperate rebels, simply reneged on the theory that Biafra did not or would not have the means to catch them.

At the time of the formal break in May 1967 both Great Britain, Nigeria's traditional supplier, and the United States declined to take an active part in supplying arms to either side. Undoubtedly their motivations were rooted in a sincere desire to keep the civil war from growing into a major arms competition. But neither country made any effort to keep other arms suppliers out. Because both the Federals and Biafrans wanted arms and could not get them from either Great Britain or the United States, a vacuum was created which was promptly filled by all manner of arms supplier: legitimate private dealers, gunrunners, and interested governments.

The big buildup of arms on both sides began when fighting broke out in July 1967 and ran through the end of the year. The

Czechs delivered to the Federals two Delfin trainers, at a cost of $238,000 each, which were equipped to carry rockets and bombs. The Soviets delivered six MiG-17's and four or five additional Delfins; the latter were bought through Omnipol. Later, in August, the Soviets shipped in fifteen additional MiG-17's. By late 1968 the Soviet Union had become Lagos' major source of arms.

The French government sold Gowon some Panhard armored cars and the Poles delivered a ship full of munitions. Great Britain relented—primarily to offset the Soviet and Czech influence—and allowed a quantity of Swedish Bofors 40 mm light antiaircraft guns to be shipped to the Federals. The United States, later in the summer, also relented and began to deliver arms, but it has never been determined exactly what was sent. Throughout the entire arms race, the U.S.'s role was very quiet.[66]

Interarms (U.K.), which had been approached by both sides, was at first denied an arms export license by the Board of Trade, much to Stuart Murray's irritation. Later in the year the British authorities relaxed their restrictions on the firm's arms sales activities. Exactly what equipment was sold to the Lagos government Murray will not say.

On the Biafran side, things were much more complicated. French, West German, Swiss, British and Spanish arms dealers converged on the scene. So too did Lebanese and Greek merchants willing to run the Federal blockade; some of their agents bid openly on the Baltic Exchange for the best shipping rates. They sold to Ojukwu Spanish, French, Czech and American weapons and munitions. Other arms began to filter in from South Africa via Angola. Small deliveries of arms and ammunition were made to the Biafrans by Air Trans-Africa, a Lisbon-based charter company. One of the firm's executives is Major Alistair Wicks, formerly second in command of Major "Mad Mike" Hoare's 5 Commando in the Congo during the 1964–65 Simba revolt. While Henry Warton languished in a Cameroon jail, two other Americans, one of them Geneva-based, attempted to take up the slack by flying in Czech arms with the aid of a British charter airline operator who was then engaged in the lucrative and illegal Pakistani immigrant business.

Two B-26 bombers were delivered to the Biafrans and a reliable source claims that they were "obtained from a French arms dealer through intermediaries." In October 1967, the French government sold twelve T-6 trainer aircraft to the rebels, and they arrived with the French Air Force insignia still painted on them. A transport under French registry, traveling from Ireland, also brought in a load of Czech arms.[67]

Biafra's greatest support during this period came from Portugal. The Lisbon government allowed a Biafran arms-buying mission to be set up in the capital. This group coordinated purchases and deliveries with its many scattered suppliers. The Portuguese allowed gunrunners and legitimate firms to refuel at Lisbon, at São Thomé Island off Gabon and at Portuguese Guinea on the run into Enugu or Port Harcourt. The Portuguese also tolerated a secret shuttle of supply planes, many of them under false registry, between Lisbon and Biafra. One of the pilots of this sixteen-plane fleet was Captain Henry Warton, who reportedly charged $22,000 per flight. Some of these planes were bought from Air France, Iberia Airlines and TAP, the Portuguese airline. Portugal also tried to smuggle 11,000 shotguns and 800,000 shells to the Biafrans aboard a 500-ton freighter called the *Jozina,* but the ship was impounded by the Federals before it reached its destination.[68]

The bulk of the money to pay for these arms did not come, as many people believed, from the foreign oil companies in Biafra. One large sum was acquired just prior to the May 1967 breakup of the Federation when Biafra, without Lagos' permission, transferred abroad six million pounds sterling. Ojukwu also tapped foreign accounts under his control and sold the Nigerian pounds at a discount. Furthermore, he also succeeded in having a tanker full of palm oil—a very valuable cargo—smuggled out of the country and sold for hard currency in Rotterdam. Another large sum also came from Lagos itself. It appears that Gowon, at the time of secession, authorized the transfer of a large shipment of currency by air to the north to protect his government financially in the event the Ibos captured Lagos. The Biafrans heard of the shipment and had some of their allies in Lagos divert the plane from Ibadan to Enugu "until the weather cleared" in the north. The man in the

Lagos radio tower who actually caused the plane to divert was later shot.

Ojukwu, with all this money in his hands, knew that it would be worthless if Gowon decided (as he subsequently did) to issue a new currency. So he set about spending it for arms as fast as he could. He spent approximately $5 million in Brussels in two weeks, and another $1.8 million in Frankfurt in an even shorter period of time. Later, as this money began to run out, several sources reported that Ojukwu arranged a $16.8 million loan from the Rothschild Bank in Paris supposedly in exchange for exclusive mineral rights, including oil, for ten years in the Biafra area. The bank has denied it ever made this arrangement.[69]

The naiveté of the Biafran purchasing agents and the treachery of the arms merchants is often difficult to believe. Shortly after secession, for instance, the Biafrans expressed a desire to score both a psychological and strategic victory by sinking the Federal destroyer *Nigeria,* then blockading Port Harcourt. One of the schemes seriously considered by the Biafran High Command was put forward by an Englishman who suggested that the destroyer be rammed by a small remote-controlled craft filled with napalm. The arms dealer told the Biafrans that 50,000 pounds ($120,000) would cover initial costs and that an additional 450,000 pounds ($1,080,000) would be needed to enable him "to employ the best technicians in every phase of the operation." Had the scheme been carried out, it would have cost this arms merchant no more than $3–4,000 for all the equipment needed to sink the destroyer.

In the meantime, another group of arms merchants suggested that the job could be done with a single torpedo. To their chagrin, however, they found that there were no spare torpedoes available in Europe's arms markets. Undaunted, they arranged for a film company to construct a dummy—a film prop—for 2,000 pounds ($4,800). This item was offered to the Biafrans for 100,000 pounds ($240,000).

In any event, both schemes fell through because in the interim the Federals captured Port Harcourt and Biafra lost its access to the gulf.

Both sides also hired white mercenaries. A mercenary is considered here to be part of the gunrunning trade because he is, in a very real sense, a "hired gun." He is smuggled from one crisis to another according to the laws of supply and demand; he is expensive to purchase and expendable once the crisis has passed—just like any other weapon. He is not too far removed from the "hired gun" of American western lore: he is a quasi-outlaw and a professional killer. He is good at his job, he cares nothing for his victims, and he is widely despised and feared by the general populace. Generally speaking, nations hire mercenaries whenever there exists a gap between a soldier and his ability to operate complicated modern military equipment.

The Federals first hired British, Rhodesian and South African pilots in July 1967 at a reported $2,800 per month tax-free salary delivered into Swiss numbered bank accounts. When the Soviet and Czech jets arrived it was found that there were no Nigerians qualified to fly them, so Egyptian and Czech mercenaries were imported. The Soviet Union forbade any of its nationals to fly the planes. A minor Cold War developed between the English-speaking pilots and the Egyptians and Czechs. The English-speakers, for instance, taunted the Egyptians with loud renditions of "Jerusalem the Golden" (the Six Day War was in June of that year) and many fights ensued. The English-speakers were also dubbed the "whisky pilots" because of their heavy drinking habits. One pilot, named "Boozy Bonzo" Bond, a South African veteran of the RAF, was renowned for consuming a bottle of whisky before reaching target. He flew in a Moslem praying cap and regarded a mission as a failure if his plane returned without bullet holes. No Nigerian would fly with him.[70]

Biafra began by hiring eighty-three French mercenaries to train its troops. This group was under the command of Colonel Roger Faulkes, a former Foreign Legionnaire who left the army under a cloud after opposing De Gaulle's Algerian policies. Faulkes, considered a brilliant and heroic officer, is a battle-scarred veteran. Before coming to Biafra, Faulkes fought in World War II, Indochina, Algeria, Katanga and the Yemen, in the latter two instances as a mercenary for Tshombe and the Royalists. His right thumb is missing, a long scar decorates his right cheek, he walks with a limp because of a disjointed hip, and his legs are heavy with shrapnel.

Faulkes' mercenaries were soon augmented by another French contingent under the command of Robert Denard. Denard was an officer in 6 Commando in the Congo when Tshombe was Prime Minister; he and his men had retreated into Angola only a month before they showed up in Biafra. A third group of French mercenaries, under one Michel Declary, another old Congo hand, joined the fight later. Many of these men were to quit the service of Biafra when they realized that they were never going to get the equipment needed to train their charges properly. Others were to quit when they came to believe that the Biafran cause was hopeless. By the summer of 1968 the entire mercenary contingent had been reduced to five.[71]

Some African political experts claim that the reason French mercenaries have been so eager to fight in Africa stems from an old OAS ultra belief that, with only a few well-trained men, white beachheads could be established on the continent. This, so the argument goes, would encourage the whites of Rhodesia and South Africa to hang on, confident that a small group of professionals could master a larger force of untrained blacks.

By the spring of 1968 it was clear to most that, barring a political and military miracle, Biafra's cause was nearly a hopeless one. What little money the breakaway state had remaining was spent on arms and medicine for the troops and food for the populace. In those most desperate hours of the secession, an airlift of supplies into Biafra was organized by many interested parties. Some of them, such as Caritas (a Roman Catholic relief organization), the World Council of Churches (a Protestant body), and the International Committee of the Red Cross, were motivated by humanitarian considerations. Others, however, became involved for different reasons. One who was in it for the money was Captain Henry Warton, by this time operating under the name of North American Aircraft Trading Company. For a fee, usually $12,000 per flight or $60,000 for six flights, he was willing to run food, medical supplies and arms to the beleaguered Biafrans. He was eminently successful at his task and reportedly made large profits from it. "I never miss a chance to make some money and do some lucrative business," he once said. Warton subsequently received many tributes for his "humanitarian action" in Biafra from the Red Cross and various church groups.

Another blockade runner who took part for the money was Captain Lucien Pickett of USAIR. Pickett considered himself a major competitor of Warton's and the two battled bitterly to win supply contracts from the European relief organizations. USAIR's vice president in charge of Middle Eastern and African operations is Colonel Otto Skorzeny, a Nazi war hero, who was responsible for "liberating" Mussolini from an Allied-held mountaintop in 1943. Skorzeny, when not making money from the plight of Biafrans, is a successful Madrid real-estate broker.

France, even at this late hour, was still seeking some political advantage from the civil war. While it had sold arms to both sides earlier in the secession, France was by the end of 1968 concentrating its aid on the rebels. Paris gave Biafra a modest amount of foreign currency with which to buy arms and other supplies. It also underwrote the cost of ferrying arms to the rebels. The reason why France chose to aid Biafra in this manner is unclear. At one point it appeared as if Paris sought to create a military stalemate from which the French presumably could extract some political advantage. Some believe the French hoped eventually to replace British influence in the area; others saw the aid as a means to control the mineral reserves; still others saw it as a wedge to influence—by what means was not clear—the Lagos government after the country returned to some form of normalcy.[72]

Back in October 1967 the Federals shot down an F-27 airliner that was bombing Lagos. The plane was hit while flying at 300 feet over a suburb where diplomats live and seemed bent on a suicidal course toward the Federal supreme military headquarters. Four white mercenaries and four others were killed in the crash. The body of one of the men killed smashed through the roof of the Czechoslovakian Embassy and fell into the sitting room of the ambassador.[73] Another version of this story is that the four mercenaries were intoxicated and the four others were female companions, also intoxicated. According to this source, these eight in a drunken moment decided to "bomb Lagos." They commandeered an airliner, loaded on board a quantity of bombs (reportedly barrels filled with shrapnel and gunpowder), flew over Lagos and threw the bombs out the side door at whatever targets caught their fancy. Ojukwu, it is estimated, lost 20 percent of his mercenary pilots in this one crash. Wherever the truth may lie, either story in its own way is symbolic of the tragedy of Nigeria.

Secessionist Katanga, which existed from July 1960 to the spring of 1963, was also the focal point of sizable gunrunning activities. Early on in the secession, Katanga's Prime Minister Tshombe purchased a number of Fouga *Magister* and Dornier aircraft. It is believed that these planes came from private European dealers. Most of them were smuggled into Katanga in crates and later assembled. The activities of Seven Seas Airline—working for both sides at the same time—were the exception rather than the rule among arms suppliers. Twelve *Harvard* aircraft, equipped with guns and French rockets, and an unspecified number of World War II P-51's reportedly were bought in South Africa and shipped to Katanga via Angola. One report stated that the crates carried Red Cross markings and were declared to be medicines at the Angolan border. Portugal disclaimed ever seeing such a shipment.[74]

Tshombe also received considerable help from the Rhodesian government of Sir Roy Welensky. He also bought Israeli submachine guns either directly from the factory or from private dealers. He bought American-made tear gas grenades, 40 mm Bofors antiaircraft shells (smuggled through Angola) and odd lots of equipment from a variety of free-lance operators.

His secessionist effort was financed primarily by dividends, franchise charges and taxes from the large mining concern of Union Minière du Haut-Katanga, now nationalized and called GECOMIN.* This firm poured some $52 million a year into the

* One of the most intriguing aspects of Union Minière was its ownership at the time of secession. Officially the large holding company Société Générale de Belgique owned 4.64 percent of the stock. Tanganyika Con-

Katanga treasury.[75] Although the company denies it, it also constructed armored cars for the Katangese gendarmerie and hid the presence of the mercenaries by putting them on its payroll.

The Katanga secession also witnessed the hiring of white mercenaries. They were used in the early years of the secession to stiffen the local gendarmerie. Later, when Tshombe became Prime Minister, the mercenaries were reorganized into their own small battalions—designated 1, 2, 3, 4, 5, and 6 Commando—and were used to good military effect to put down the Simba revolt of 1964–65. According to reliable sources the number of white mercenaries in the Congo totaled no more than 400 during secession and no more than 1,500 during the Simba revolt.

These mercenaries came from a wide variety of backgrounds. There were British colonials from the old Indian Army, combat-hardened Frenchmen from Algeria, World War II RAF pilots from Rhodesia and South Africa and veteran Belgian paratroopers.

---

cessions, Limited (commonly known as "Tanks"), owned another 14.47 percent, Compagnie du Katanga owned 8.77 percent, and the Belgian government held 18.14 percent "in trust" for the Congolese government. The remaining 53.98 percent was distributed among 120,000 private stockholders, three quarters of whom were Belgian.

But beyond this the picture became somewhat cloudy. It appears that Société Générale held significant interests in both Tanganyika Concessions and Compagnie du Katanga; so while it appeared on the surface that Société Générale held the smallest investment share in Union Minière, it in fact held effective control over the entire operation. Tanganyika Concessions, furthermore, had a 20 percent voting power in Union Minière, slightly more than its percentage in stock. Reportedly closely connected with Tanganyika Concessions were the British South Africa Company and the Anglo-American Corporation of South Africa, both large and diversified mining firms operating in Rhodesia and South Africa. There appeared to be at the time of secession considerable overlap in the board memberships of all these companies.

Collectively, these men and those sympathetic to them were known as the "Katanga Lobby." Their vigorous activities in favor of secession were in large part responsible for the singular refusal of Britain, Belgium or France to back up the U.N.'s Congo policy with armed strength. That Union Minière actively encouraged secession with money, influence, facilities and arms there is no question. The chairman of Tanganyika Concessions admitted as much in the company's 1961 annual report when he referred to Union Minière's activities as having "played no small part in enabling the independent African government of the province to establish itself on a firmer basis than had been achieved in any part of the Congo."

Some were "officers and gentlemen" infused with a heightened sense of idealism (Colonel Mike Hoare, leader of 5 Commando and perhaps the most famous of these mercenaries, claims that he fought in the Congo primarily for idealistic reasons). Others were drunkards and dope addicts from the gutters of Marseilles and Salisbury. There were the romantics, the adventurous, the racists, the bored and the rootless. Some homosexuals joined seeking the company of men; others were jobless; still others were running away from their troubles; and there were a few who joined for the sheer desire to kill.

But more than anything they joined for the money. A Congo mercenary was well paid: a raw recruit received a minimum of $500 per month with special incentive pay for dangerous assignments. Their lives were insured for $20,000 each, and whatever a man could pick up as loot he could keep. (Safecracking was the mercenaries' favorite off-duty activity.) An officer with combat experience could count on a minimum of $2,800 a month or more, plus all *he* could steal. Combat-experienced pilots were the princes of the trade: some of them commanded salaries of $1,000 per mission.

From my conversations with them, many mercenaries—particularly the middle-aged ones—appear to yearn for a return to the excitement, passion, danger and horror that they experienced as youths in World War II. For example, one part-time mercenary with whom I spent a number of hours recounted his exciting days as an RCAF pilot and later as an Army Air Force pilot in the European Theatre. His voice was full of emotion as he rattled off story after story—some amusing, some serious, most of them exaggerated—of the days that meant the most to him. Today he runs a garage, feels boxed in by family life and is driven to distraction by the sameness of his day-to-day peacetime existence.

In the early 1960's, he said, he hired himself out as a pilot to a group of Haitian exiles; his job was to airdrop a load of small arms to a band of rebels in the hills. For reasons of economy the weapons were broken down into sections and packed separately in suitcases. Because there was not enough money to buy parachutes, each suitcase had been wrapped in pillows to cushion the impact.

He brought in his ancient B-26 (purchased in Puerto Rico for $5,000), he said, at 100 feet, spotted the rebels' marker, dropped the arms precisely on target, and escaped, leaving behind a cloud of chicken feathers. His eyes flashed with excitement at the thought of it. Later on he told me that he accepted the job only in order to relive the exciting days of his past. He told me that he could not even remember how much he got paid for this task, but he did say that, were another opportunity to arise, he would take it.

War seems to breed a type of man that cannot readjust to civilian life. Many of these individuals become part- or full-time mercenaries who skip from war to war. Roger Faulkes and Robert Denard, to pick only two, have both been in at least six wars in the last quarter-century: World War II, Indochina, Algeria, the Congo, the Yemen and Biafra. Hundreds of others—British, Dutch, Belgian, Poles, Czechs, Egyptians, Germans, South Africans, Rhodesians, Algerians, Greeks, Swiss, Cubans and Portuguese, to name but a few of the more common nationalities—have fought in Cuba against Batista, in Malaysia against Indonesia, in South America against guerrillas, in the Congo against the U.N. and the Simbas, in the Yemen against the Republicans, and in Nigeria against each other. Doubtless in wars to follow they will be there, too.

The Congo was the first time that the post-World War II world witnessed the overt employment of mercenaries fighting as a unit. Because they were whites fighting in a black country, they provided an explosive ingredient both to that troubled land and to a world that is currently preoccupied with racial problems. There seems to be no reason to suppose that their presence in the Congo as a unit was an isolated incident; nor is there any reason to believe that future mercenary units will not be composed of other races of men; nor is there much doubt that such units, no matter what their racial composition, will be just as explosive an ingredient in future crises as they have been in the past. The rise in de facto wars since the end of World War II not only ensures that all types of mercenaries will be constantly in demand, but guarantees that a new generation of mercenaries will be bred to carry on as before.

PART THREE

BUREAUCRACY ARMED

IV

The Pentagon Drummers

Monstrum horrendum, informe, ingens, cui lumen ademptum.

"A monster fearful and hideous, vast and eyeless."

—VIRGIL'S *Aeneid*

1

Room 4E-820 of the Pentagon may at first glance seem far removed from the steamy competitive jungles of the private arms dealer, the munitions manipulator, the gunrunner and mercenary. The quiet is broken only by the clacking of several typewriters, by the bustle of efficient secretaries and by the occasional murmur of executive voices floating out from the adjacent offices. There is nothing martial about this or the nearby rooms: artificial flowers and family pictures decorate the desks; no military uniforms are in evidence; no war trophies command the scene; no combat art catches the eye. To the casual visitor room 4E-820 would seem almost out of place in that vast and machinelike building.

But appearances are deceiving. This room is the home of the International Logistics Negotiations Section of the International Security Affairs Division of the Department of Defense—the U.S. government's arms sales office. The man who runs this section, America's chief arms salesman, is Henry John Kuss, Jr., a longtime civil servant.*

Kuss will tell you, as he has told me, that selling arms at the rate

* In March, 1969, as the hardbound edition of this book went to press, Kuss resigned from ILN to work for American Trade and Finance, a private consulting firm, a small part of whose business is to act as an arms broker between American companies and foreign governments. Kuss' place

of $2 billion per year promotes the collective security of the West, that it furthers the idea of logistical cooperation among allies, and that it helps to offset the cost of our troops stationed abroad. He will also tell you that he will never sell equipment to a country that cannot afford it or should not have it. He claims that he has never forced a foreign country to buy from him. Nor will he, he avers, sell something that a customer needs but can buy cheaper elsewhere.

He will also claim that the U.S. government's control over arms sales and resales is excellent, that decisions to sell are coordinated with and approved by a large number of his governmental peers, that information on his activities is freely available, that he and his office work smoothly with private industry, and that Congress is kept fully informed of all his activities. He will state just as emphatically that his sales efforts create no major political repercussions, that selling arms by his methods promotes no arms races, and that his team of salesmen shun the tactics of high-pressure salesmanship.

One would conclude from listening to Kuss that the overall U.S. arms sales program which he heads is a model of restraint, compassion and wisdom in a restless and violence-prone world. One can almost believe it sitting in his office, far from the tumult in the outside world. However, the actual facts differ quite markedly from the glowing picture he would have one believe.

The roots of the U.S. military sales program can be traced back to the immediate post-World War II years. It began with the concept of giving, under a variety of legal authorizations, free military aid to our allies. Additional military aid was authorized several years later by the Military Defense Assistance Act of 1949, which was, in turn, augmented by the provisions of the Mutual Security

---

at ILN has been taken by Lieutenant General Robert H. Warren, a career Air Force officer with no previous arms sales experience.

There have been several minor reorganizations in and around the Pentagon's arms sales office since Kuss' departure: some titles have been changed, some personnel reshuffled. I have let this chapter stand largely as originally written in December 1968 since the basic objectives and activities of the office have not changed significantly since that time.

Acts of 1951 and 1954, as amended, and the Foreign Assistance Act of 1961, as amended. In the early years the U.S. government felt that it was in its own interest to give away surplus military equipment in order that our allies be able to maintain a credible military posture both at home and in their respective spheres of influence around the world. The recipient countries—mostly European but also including South Korea, the Philippines, Taiwan and a number of Middle East and Latin American countries—welcomed the material because none was healthy enough economically either to manufacture or to purchase it. European countries especially welcomed the aid because they were fearful, particularly in the immediate post-Korean War years, that the Soviets were about to march.

One of the sidelights of the Military Aid Program during these years that has been little appreciated was that it gave the three U.S. military services an additional source of funds without their having to ask for more from Congress. In other words, the Military Aid Program, which was administered by the Defense Department, bought from its own Army, Navy and Air Force, war surplus that was then given free to foreign countries. The three services, therefore, not only had a lucrative means of clearing their inventories but also acquired in the process large sums of money to buy new equipment that was outside the purview of direct Congressional control.[1]

The demand for military equipment from the very beginning was so great that the U.S. government eventually ran out of surplus material. No precise date can be fixed when this happened because shortages of different surplus items came about at different times. Some time in the mid-1950's the U.S. government, through the Military Aid Program, began to buy from the three military services brand new equipment to be given away free to its allies.

By 1955 most European countries were back on their feet economically. Although all were producing their own military equipment of one sort or another, only two, Great Britain and France, were manufacturing very sophisticated weapons such as jet fighters and bombers. The idea soon arose in U.S. government circles that our allies should begin to pay for the material we were giving them. But although the European countries had revived, they had not accumulated adequate surpluses of dollars to pay for the arms; they only had a surplus in their own currency.[2] Thus, slowly, there evolved the concept of co-production. The idea behind co-production was to allow our allies to manufacture U.S.-designed military equipment at home. The benefits to all were obvious: It gave such countries as Italy, West Germany, Belgium, Holland and France, among others, an opportunity to use their own surplus currency to build military equipment; it cut down on their need to spend their foreign reserves; and it brought these countries up to date in the technology of arms making. The United States benefited because private manufacturers of armaments received income from licensing fees; it also stimulated a heavy transatlantic traffic in technicians and technical data that was eventually to bring more foreign-held dollars into the U.S. Treasury.

It took several years to convince Congress and the countries involved to accept and agree to the idea, although precedents had been set as far back as 1949 when Canada began making F-86E's under license from North American Aviation, the prime U.S. contractor. In 1953 Fiat began assembling F-86K's under license; and the next year Mitsubishi also began producing another version of the plane under license in Japan. By 1959 the concept of co-production was fully accepted by most industrialized Western countries as a lucrative way to re-enter the armaments market. Production licenses for the Raytheon *Hawk* surface-to-air missile were granted to companies in Belgium, France, West Germany, Italy and Holland in 1959. In 1960 licenses for the production of the Lockheed F-104G *Starfighter* aircraft were granted to companies in West Germany, Italy, Belgium and Holland. In the following two years licensing arrangements for the General Electric J-79 turbojet engine (for the F-104G), the *Bullpup* air-to-surface missile and *Sidewinder* air-to-air missile were granted to a number of European firms.[3] Today, co-production has expanded to the point where the United States and virtually every industrialized European country have had part of their own designed equipment produced by some other industrial country.

Co-production was the transition point between the U.S. government's policy of giving away its military equipment and its policy of selling it. The emphasis shifted sharply and decisively in favor of arms *sales* when Robert S. McNamara became Secretary of Defense in 1961. It has been said that the idea of selling arms was solely the product of McNamara's fertile mind. The facts are that he took what was previously a vaguely articulated sales policy (co-production) and changed it into a dynamic sales effort—an effort that in retrospect has been not too far removed from what the Secretary might have demanded at an earlier time of his Ford Motor Company salesmen.

One of McNamara's prime concerns, as he surveyed the United States' and the West's defense posture, was the unhappy state of the allied logistics system. Every nation in the Western alliance seemed to have different equipment which in time of war would create a chaotic supply situation. One NATO member country was using nine different rifles; and each nation had its own supply depots which often led to a shortage of an item in one allied army area and a surplus in another area. The Berlin crisis of 1961, for instance, found the U.S. forces short of 105 mm armor-piercing shells. The shortage had actually been discovered several months previously, and a high-priority order worth $11 million was quietly placed with Great Britain, but the crisis arrived before the shells did. Faced with similar problems, McNamara asked: why not integrate all of the allies' logistics systems? What gave the problem a special urgency was the knowledge that the United States needed to do something drastic to stem the outflow of gold, which had been going on virtually uninterrupted since the end of World War II and which became serious from around 1956 onward.

During the summer of 1961 a task force of specialists headed by McGeorge Bundy and Paul Nitze, and including Henry Kuss and several high-powered American businessmen, studied the problem, particularly as it applied to NATO. One of the recommendations this group made was the creation of an office in the Department of Defense that would promote the integration of allied equipment through the sale of American armaments. This was soon thereafter to become the office of International Logistics Negotiations, which was to report to the International Security Affairs Division in the

Pentagon, which, in turn, was to report directly to the Secretary of Defense. Deputy Under Secretary of Defense Henry Kuss was put in charge. He explained to me that "Negotiations" referred to the fact that the *sale* of weapons required much bargaining while give-aways (or grant aid) apparently required none.

Kuss himself was a Navy supply control officer in World War II and after hostilities ended remained in government service handling financial and production inventory problems for the Navy. In 1955 he first became exposed to international problems when he was sent to Paris to handle military financial matters there; he also served on a NATO cost committee. He then returned to Washington and became ISA's director of overseas resources. His job was to reduce American aid to allies who were financially capable of paying. In 1961 he was an observer in Bonn at the Anderson-Dillon conference on means of offsetting U.S. costs of maintaining military forces in West Germany. It was here that the United States and West German defense leaders worked out a plan for cooperative logistics which, according to Kuss, was the true beginning of the U.S. export sales program.[4]

Kuss' entire staff numbers forty-two people. He has four teams of assistants, each of which specializes in selling arms to a particular area. The "Red Team" is responsible for sales to Canada, the Far East, Scandinavia, France and the NATO "infrastructure"; the "White Team" is responsible for sales to West Germany alone; the "Blue Team" is responsible for sales to Latin America, Italy, Spain and the Benelux countries; and the "Gray Team" is responsible for the United Kingdom, Switzerland, Austria, the Middle East and Near East. Sales to African nations, it appears, are handled on an *ad hoc* basis. These four teams also divide up the jobs of long-range planning, industrial liaison, export support and financing.[5]

Kuss' staff is one of the most loyal that I encountered in my travels through the U.S. bureaucratic maze. His subordinates are passionately, almost fanatically, devoted to their work and put in many extra hours of effort in his behalf. Philosophically they seem to be hard-line hawks. I happened to interview Kuss in October 1967, the day before a large contingent of anti-Vietnam War protesters planned to lay siege to the Pentagon. The opinions expressed by some of his staff indicated that, had the Pentagon permitted them to do so, they would have gone out and personally pummeled every one of the demonstrators.

The Deputy Under Secretary himself is a large man with several extra chins. He is extremely bright, with a good analytical mind, somewhat idealistic but not impractical. One veteran of his staff said, "I don't think he has a hobby in the world except his work. He once sat with me at ringside in the Crazy Horse Saloon [a Paris striptease nightclub] and we wrote an ILN paper in forty-five minutes. He didn't look at the stage once."

Kuss is also a consummate salesman. He thinks in terms of "optimum optimized sales" as he calls it. "If we possibly can," he once said, "we want to sell, first, the whole airplane. If we can't, then we'll settle for selling major parts or for licensing. But to optimize sales, we've got to shoot first for the bigger package." A businessman once described Kuss' ability as an arms negotiator as "something of a cross between a Yankee horse trader and a Lebanese jewel merchant . . . a shrewd and tough bargainer . . . and a red-tape cutter extraordinary. . . ."

More than anything Kuss is ambitious, and it shows in an abrasive, pushing manner that often raises the hackles of his peers. In his early days at ILN, one businessman told me, "he was pure carborundum." Although he has calmed down in recent years—he talks less loudly and his pushing is less obvious—his dominating personality can cause considerable dissension in government circles. For instance, the caution of diplomacy is still almost completely absent in his manner, and according to one military equipment exporter, "he gives the State Department fits." In fact, several U.S. ambassadors in Europe have suggested that he keep out of their area because his hard pressure and somewhat rough methods have irritated both our embassies and the local defense establishments.

One critic on Capitol Hill calls Kuss a "bureaucrat's bureaucrat" who is not used to being cross-examined by outsiders. When he finds himself on uncomfortable grounds before a congressional committee, he often slows down the dialogue in order to drag it out, much as if he were stalling on an arms deal. "Kuss is the archetype of the new arms salesman," said this critic. "He can sell $2 billion worth of arms a year, sleep soundly and struggle on his $25,000 a year salary; he represents the abstractions in our society."

Kuss has undoubtedly been successful at his job. He has succeeded in reversing in a few short years the emphasis on military grant aid to one of military sales. He will point out with some pride that in FY 1953, for instance, the United States gave away $1.96 billion worth of arms and sold only $230 million worth. In FY 1968, in contrast, grant aid had shrunk to $466 million while sales had climbed to $1.5 billion. Since 1962 Kuss has averaged sales of $2 billion a year. Kuss' sales prowess was recognized in May 1965 when Secretary McNamara presented him with the Meritorious Civilian Service Medal, the highest peacetime award available to civil servants.

Kuss will also point out that 75 percent of all U.S. sales since 1962 has gone to Canada and the industrialized countries in Europe (in particular Great Britain and West Germany), all of which can afford the material. Only 12 percent went to Far Eastern countries (not including our investment in South Vietnam); only 10 percent went to Near and Middle Eastern countries; 2 percent went to Latin America, and only 1 percent went to Africa and the rest of the world.

Kuss claims that only 6 percent of all these sales has been made to the underdeveloped countries. This does not appear to be borne out by the facts; a more accurate figure would probably be between 25 and 30 percent. Such a charge is not difficult to prove even though the Pentagon issues no list of nations that qualify as underdeveloped. What the Defense Department does when pressed for such a list is to reverse matters by citing Executive Order 11285 of June 10, 1966, which names only those free-world countries that are *not* "economically less developed," namely Australia, Austria, Belgium, Canada, Denmark, France, Iran, Iraq, Ireland, Italy, Japan, Kuwait, Kuwait-Saudi Arabia Neutral Zone (*sic*), Libya, Liechtenstein, Luxembourg, Monaco, Netherlands, New

Zealand, Norway, Portugal, San Marino, Saudi Arabia, Spain, Sweden, Switzerland, Union of South Africa, United Kingdom, and West Germany. These twenty-nine nations (out of some 117 non-communist nations in the world) presumably qualify as "developed" in the Pentagon's eyes and are supposedly the recipients of 94 percent of all U.S. military arms sales.

A cursory glance at this list will show that it is obviously padded with five names: Kuwait-Saudi Arabia Neutral Zone (which is not even a country), Liechtenstein, Monaco, San Marino and the Union of South Africa. The U.S. government sells no military equipment worth mentioning to these nations. Furthermore, according to the Arms Control and Disarmament Agency's "World Wide Military Expenditures and Related Data, 1965," Iran, Iraq, Libya, Portugal and Saudi Arabia have average per capita Gross National Products of, respectively, $241, $233, $548, $407 and $354—all of which are well below the world average of $641. Thus by any definition these five nations quality as "economically less developed."

In addition, while the Pentagon will classify Iran and Saudi Arabia as "developed" according to the list above, it will also classify them as "underdeveloped" when it comes to qualifying them for high-risk (i.e. poor country) arms purchasing loans available until 1968 through a Pentagon device known as the Country-X Account (see pages 212–18). Finally, it should be noted that Israel, with a relatively high average national per capita GNP of $1,325 and currently a recipient of U.S. military hardware, is not included in the above list.

Thus there remain nineteen recipient countries that qualify as "developed." From all available sources it appears that they receive between 70 and 75 percent of all U.S. arms sales each year. The rest goes to the 98 or so remaining non-communist "economically less developed" countries. It is my estimation (there are no hard figures available) that the U.S. sales to Iran, Iraq, Libya, Portugal, Saudi Arabia and Israel alone account for between 10 and 15 percent of U.S. arms sales each year and that an additional 15 to 20 percent is acquired by the remaining "economically less developed" states.

Even if it were true, as Kuss claims, that only 6 percent of U.S. sales goes to the underdeveloped countries, the statement would lose some of its magic when compared to the fact that these same countries have only 18 percent of the world's Gross National Product but 71 percent of its population.[6]

Perhaps the prime reason why McNamara saw a need for a Kuss-type operation was the knowledge that only 5 percent of all military equipment produced in the United States goes to foreign nations. The other 95 percent is absorbed by the U.S. military establishment. He knew perfectly well that very few businessmen were willing to go to the expense of setting up a worldwide sales organization just to sell 5 percent of their products. The best solution, he reasoned, was to have the government do the selling for them, thereby centralizing the effort, eliminating the duplication of facilities and theoretically giving the government some control over the program's direction. The subsequent establishment of the ILN office has led to criticism that its staff is nothing more than a government-financed sales force for private industry.

In retrospect it was quite easy for the U.S. government to become deeply involved in the sales of weapons. Before the change of emphasis in 1961, industry, according to Charles Shuff, the Director of Supplies for the IBM World Trade Corporation and a member of the 1961 task force that recommended the establishment of the ILN office, was "like a blind dog in a meat market: it ran from carcass to carcass seeking 'quick sales' "; no long-term policy was considered. Because of its past experience in giving away armaments, he said, the U.S. government found that *it* rather than industry had all the proper contacts abroad. Thus, when McNamara decided to emphasize sales, he saw no reason to give any special incentive to private industry to do the job alone.

Of the approximately 1,500 industrial enterprises in America that make military equipment of one kind or another, only 20, according to Kuss, export their wares in any quantity. Most of this business has accrued from Kuss' personal sales effort abroad. Who these firms are, Kuss will not say, but some of the names are readily apparent from the membership list of the Committee on

Military Exports, which is part of the Defense-Industry Advisory Council, or DIAC, the leading liaison group between the ILN office and the domestic arms manufacturers. Among the firms represented on the committee, of which Kuss is chairman, are United Aircraft, North American Aviation, Bendix, Chrysler, Lockheed, Northrop, Boeing, General Electric, General Dynamics, McDonnell-Douglas, Raytheon, IT&T, FMC Corporation, Avco, IBM, American Machine and Foundry, and Philco. A number of banks are also represented on this committee—namely, First National City Bank, Chase Manhattan Bank, Riggs National Bank and, in the old tradition, the Morgan Guaranty Trust Company, whose executive committee chairman at this writing is Thomas S. Gates, Jr., the very able former Secretary of Defense.

It is also of interest to note who is *not* represented on this committee—specifically, Du Pont, U.S. Steel and large shipbuilding firms, all of which were zealous traders on the international arms market before World War II. American powder makers such as Du Pont have found that most countries with any industrial capacity have powder factories of their own; U.S. steelmakers have found that there is no longer any foreign demand for their armor plate; and American shipbuilders, because of high costs and archaic practices, have lost their competitive position to more aggressive foreign firms.[7]

One of the most striking aspects of the U.S. sales effort abroad is the extent to which the entire government is involved to ensure its success. It is the nature of a government department to set up a group of experts under its control whose job it is to cope with a government policy as it affects that department. In other words, a policy to promote, say, tourism in the United States would find experts on the subject in the Treasury, Commerce, State, Labor and Interior Departments, among others. It is the same with the arms sales policy, only more so.

The *Military Export Guide,* a private publication established to encourage U.S. industry to sell military equipment abroad, lists at least forty-one branches or subbranches of government with a direct stake in the arms business.[8] They should be examined briefly because their involvement explains in large part how our arms sales policy works (or does not work), why it has taken the course it has, and why it is criticized as much as it is by those few who are aware of the problem.

First of all there is the Executive branch of government. The President's decisions are usually reserved for only the most delicate of questions. Should Morocco get $100 million in arms it requested in 1967? (No, only $15 million.) Should West Germany be allowed to ease its $675 million yearly offset arrangement by buying $500 million medium-term U.S. Treasury securities instead of arms? (Yes.) Should Kuss be allowed to resume "nonlethal" sales to Pakistan and India? (Yes.) Should Israel receive U.S. military aid in 1968? (That depends on what the Soviets do in the Middle East.) Most of these decisions are based on extensive consultation with the Secretaries of State and Defense and the heads of other agencies concerned.

Also under the jurisdiction of the Executive branch is the National Security Council which passes judgment on many of our secret military commitments. The Office of the Special Representative for Trade Negotiations, the National Advisory Council on International Monetary and Financial Problems, and the Export Control Review Board are also involved one way or another in promoting arms sales.

Since the policy is an important part of the overall U.S. foreign policy, the Department of State is also deeply involved in arms sales. At the top is the office of the Secretary of State, which theoretically makes all the final departmental judgments on whether or not a sale is to be made. At a lower level there are the Country Desks, which give specialized opinions on their particular areas. At each desk is a group that is expert on arms sales. In addition there are two coordinating committees which, again in theory, bring the often divergent views of State and Defense together for settlement. The more important one is called the Senior Interdepartmental Group, or SIG, consisting of under secretaries in both departments. During the Johnson Administration, Under Secretary Nicholas deB. Katzenbach chaired it and Paul Nitze represented the Department of Defense. This is a policy-making group that passes on its recommendation to the Secretaries of State and Defense. At a lower level is the Defense-State Coordinating Committee, which meets every Monday afternoon. It brings together the deputy assistant secretaries, and it is where the actual sales decisions are hammered out. It used to be known as the "Kuss-Kitchen Kabinet" after Henry Kuss and Jeffrey Kitchen, now reassigned but formerly Deputy Assistant Secretary of State for Politico-Military Affairs. Kitchen's job was inherited by Phil Farley, a highly regarded career State Department officer.

An orphan of the State Department is the Arms Control and Disarmament Agency. Its 200 employees are housed in one corner of the State Department building in Foggy Bottom. Contrary to what many people believe, ACDA is neither a policing agency nor a group that shouts "No!" to Kuss' "Yes!" According to Charles Van Doren, ACDA's Deputy General Counsel, his agency accepts the government's arms sales policy but tries at the same time to work in the direction of restraint. Nathan Rich, Executive Officer of ACDA's Arms Transfer Coordinating Group, told me that for ACDA to take an absolutist position against arms sales would be unrealistic "because no one would pay any attention to us." Besides, he added, "it's not very professional." ACDA's principal role, he added, "is to participate in establishing policy, not to pass judgment on an individual sale of arms." As will be pointed out later, there is some question as to how much influence, if any, ACDA has over the policy-making process.

It is of interest to note that, in order to cope with ACDA's arms control policy, the Defense Department has created its own arms control office part of whose job has been to give the Defense Department's views on ACDA's views. This particular office until recently shared—probably for public relations reasons—the same reception room as the ILN office.

Another State Department orphan is the Office of Munitions Control. Its job, as noted, has been to control the importation and exportation of lethal items through the issuance of licenses. It handles 30,000 requests a year, all of which are nongovernmental transactions. John Sipes, the OMC's current director, told me that he has absolutely no authority to control the $2 billion yearly sales of the ILN office. His department, he adds, is responsible for controlling the resale of American military equipment around the world regardless of who originally sold it. When I pressed him on the point of how his twenty-eight-man office could possibly keep tabs on such a huge volume of transactions, he admitted that first-line enforcement invariably falls on Military Assistance Advisory Groups, military attachés and industrial competitors stationed abroad. Sipes, it must be pointed out, has no enforcement authority or control over any of these groups; if they do not choose to pass on information on violations or loopholes, there is no legal way he can demand it.

Also involved in weapons sales are American ambassadors. Where the weapon-buying process in a country is diffused through a series of committees and consultative processes—such as in Great Britain, Italy, France or Israel—the American ambassador's involvement is minimal. Usually the day-to-day bargaining is left to lower-echelon military representatives of the respective nations with only overall policies and recommendations left to the ambassador himself. But in authoritarian countries, where weapons buying is the decision of the head of state alone, then U.S. ambassadors often become deeply involved. An ambassador's reputation usually rests in large part on what is known as "access to the palace." If a king or shah or dictator wants arms from the United States, the ambassador, in order to maintain his "access," often becomes a fervent advocate of arms sales.

Weapons sales by the Department of Defense, despite what ILN literature will tell you, are not limited to the initiative of the executives operating out of room 4E-820 or their immediate superiors. In fact, the Defense Department sales effort is so powerful, so immense, and with so many layers of bureaucracy aiding it that no one in the U.S. government fully comprehends the extent of its influence and power. Be that as it may, the known major Defense agencies helping the ILN office with its sales effort should be noted.

First of all, there are the Departments of the Army, Navy and Air Force. They are responsible for, among other things, the development of all military assistance sales activities; they furnish training and technical assistance to foreign armed forces; they advise on force levels, types of equipment, supply levels and maintenance procedures; they procure from U.S. industry and arrange for the foreign armed forces to use U.S. logistics systems if desired; and they furnish the personnel for Military Assistance Advisory Groups in various countries.

The MAAG's are the principal contact between the Defense Department and foreign armed forces. In FY 1966, according to Kuss' own statistics, there were nearly 11,000 individuals assigned to these Advisory Groups abroad.[9] Despite Kuss' repeated and sometimes heated denials, these men have been and continue to be a sales force for the ILN office. According to the pro-arms sales publication, *Military Export Reporter,* MAAG's "will cooperate with U.S. contractors in furthering U.S. military exports." Because these individuals administer the U.S. military assistance programs, they are in a good position to know the needs of foreign armed forces and are usually friends of the key personnel in foreign defense establishments.

The following exchange took place in April 1967 between Townsend "Tim" Hoopes, then Deputy Assistant Secretary of Defense for International Security Affairs, and Senator Eugene McCarthy during a Senate hearing on arms sales to Near East and south Asian countries:[10]

> *Mr. Hoopes.* Military Assistance Advisory Groups were all of course initiated when we had large grant programs, and we never established a MAAG where we did not have a grant program. There are some countries in Europe where MAAG's continue to exist, even though the grant program is phased out.
>
> *Senator McCarthy.* They have become primarily a sales agency now?
>
> *Mr. Hoopes.* Where we have a sales program and there is a MAAG, usually the MAAG assists in the sales function.

Another group in the Defense Department that pushes sales is the Unified Commands of which there are eight around the world. They are often called upon to help recommend force levels and equipment to foreign military establishments within their areas of responsibility. There is, in addition, the Defense Supply Agency, which procures, if requested to do so, items for foreign governments to support their weapons systems. The Advanced Research Projects Agency is a hush-hush research empire within the Defense Department, part of whose job it is to provide technical guidance to underdeveloped countries on arms procurement. The Defense Industrial Security Clearance Office and the Defense Contract Audit Agency also help ILN in its sales effort. The military attachés in our embassies abroad (one step up the chain of command from the MAAG's), Military Missions (not to be confused with MAAG's or attachés), which operate in virtually every noncommunist country in the world, and the large military staffs assigned to NATO, SEATO and the Inter-American Defense Board, all help in their own way to sell U.S. military equipment to foreign countries.

The U.S. government's involvement in arms sales does not stop with the State Department, Defense Department and the Executive branch of government. For instance, the Treasury Department works with the ILN office, the Export-Import Bank and commercial banking institutions to further military exports through adequate financing and arranging of credits and loan guarantees.

The Department of Commerce will cooperate with armament manufacturers to sell their wares abroad. With the U.S. balance of payments deficit becoming more and more critical—particularly because of the Vietnam War—the Commerce Department has of late become one of the most fervent exponents of arms sales. The department also encourages the exhibition of U.S. military hardware at the fifteen to twenty international trade fairs at which the United States is an official exhibitor each year. Furthermore, the department exhibits arms at the permanent trade centers that it has established in major commercial centers such as Bangkok, Frankfurt, London, Milan, Tokyo and Stockholm. The United States Information Agency also takes part in the arms sales program by advertising through its outlets military equipment exhibited at the various foreign trade fairs. Although Kuss would deny it—indeed, he says he is not allowed to do it—his office has supplemented USIA efforts with an advertising campaign of its own. For instance, there was a Defense Department booklet called *Information and*

Guidance on Military Assistance which instructed its many arms salesmen on how to go about securing sales. It stated, in part:[11]

> The Department of Defense has embarked on an intensified military assistance sales program. . . . Success in this endeavor will be dependent in large measure upon effective sales promotion. The Department of Defense has taken several steps to assist in the successful conclusion of military sales. . . . Foreign customer preference is being generated by developing an appreciation of its technical superiority, price, availability, and the offer of follow-on support through U.S. logistics systems. . . . In many cases, credit arrangements may be made to facilitate military sales, on short- or long-term basis, as needed.

In FY 1965, reported Senator McCarthy, $500,000 of military assistance funds was programmed for sales promotion.[12] Presumably this practice has continued up to the present, although ILN denies there is such an allocation in its budget. Kuss told me with a slight smile on his face, "We follow the principle that you should 'let your light so shine before men that they may see your good works.' "

Another sales pitch is conducted through the extensive training programs which bring scores of foreign military officers to the United States each year. General Robert J. Wood, at one time the director of the Military Aid Program, told a House Appropriations Committee in 1964 that foreign officers are trained with the view that they might buy equipment that interests them. "Then," he said, "we have a program to train certain countries in some of our equipment in the expectation they will buy [it]. This is really sales promotion."[13] In addition, sales are promoted through the liberal distribution of technical manuals to interested foreigners.

Finally, there is the biennial Paris Air Show, the largest and the most prestigious in the world, into which the Defense Department puts considerable sales promotion effort. The department spent "more than $750,000" promoting U.S. arms at the ten-day 1967 show.[14] In this instance it was overshadowed by private U.S. firms, which collectively spent $2.25 million pushing their wares. The U.S. Embassy in Paris, not to be outdone, spent an unspecified amount on a "small" cocktail party for 6,000 leading members of the free world's aeronautical community.

Still again there are other government agencies tied closely to the arms sales policy. As has been noted previously, both AID and the CIA are large purchasers and distributors of weapons in their own right. AID officials are also consulted on occasion when sales problems overlap with the economic aid program. The CIA, and sometimes the Defense Intelligence Agency, are consulted when specific intelligence is required. Also involved in arms sales is the Atomic Energy Commission, particularly when technology falling within its domain is exported. Another participant is the Small Business Administration, which will gladly lend money to qualified companies in order to help them sell their military products abroad. The National Aeronautics and Space Administration, another participant, helps out with its advice if an application for export involves international space programs, products and technology. So does the Federal Aviation Agency assist the sales effort, particularly when military air traffic control equipment is concerned. So, too, are the Bureau of the Budget and the watchdog General Accounting Office involved in the sales program. Even the Department of Agriculture is involved through its Commodity Credit Corporation, which takes part in a sale when arms are bartered in exchange for a country's agricultural produce.

As is evident, the machinery in operation to ensure the success of the arms sales program is vast. Several knowledgeable experts estimate that the total number of people employed by the U.S. government whose jobs depend directly on the continuance of the policy exceeds 500,000. Not all of these departments or individuals push sales; most simply complement the policy in one way or another; some actually oppose it. But what they all have in common is a vested interest to see that the policy continues unchanged, for without it their jobs and/or departments have less, and in some cases no, reason for being. These facts in themselves do not make the arms sales policy right or wrong. What they do illustrate, however, is that there exists a built-in resistance in the U.S. government to any change in this policy.

By their very nature, bureaucrats—and they are not alone—

promote their own careers by seeking to expand the programs and policies for which they are responsible. To a bureaucrat it is the only measure of success. Thus they are empire builders: they hire more people, request more authority, and seek larger appropriations. For instance, between 1966 and 1968 Kuss' staff increased from 28 to 42 and his office costs increased from $564,000 to $700,000. Any cutback in a program or policy is a cutback in a bureaucrat's career; therefore, his survival and success are based on the augmentation and expansion of his responsibilities. Often this leads to a situation where, in order to preserve a career, a program is continued along other avenues even in the face of an order from higher up ordering that the program be cut back. The best and most recent example of this phenomenon with regard to arms sales is the "Jackson Amendment" incident which took place in 1967 and is described in detail on pages 216–18. Sometimes it leads to a situation where a particular group—the Defense Department's arms control office, for instance—has a vested interest in maintaining a policy that in general it opposes.

One would suppose, with so many people involved in the sale of arms, that every decision to sell would be thoroughly checked and rechecked by all interested parties. But in actual practice this does not happen. To be sure, all the most sensitive decisions are weighed carefully by the President, the Secretaries of State, Defense and perhaps Treasury; but there are thousands of "minor" decisions that the President and his Secretaries never see. Taken collectively, they can and often do add up to decisions of major importance. For instance, in February 1967 Senator Albert Gore asked AID, ACDA, Treasury and the Bureau of the Budget to describe their individual roles in four U.S. decisions to sell jet aircraft in 1966—namely, the sixteen F-4's to Iran, the twelve F-5's to Morocco, the thirty-six F-104's to Jordan and the twenty-five A-4's to Argentina. A summation of their answers showed that the Senior Interdepartmental Group—at which representatives of all these groups should have been present—*did not even meet* on the F-104 and F-4 sales; SIG had not been formed, the Senator pointed out, until after the F-5 and A-4 sales had been made. In addition, the Defense-State Coordinating Committee (the "Kuss-

Kitchen Kabinet") did not meet on the F-4 sale, the F-104 sale or the A-4 sale. It did meet on the F-5 sale, but neither ACDA, Treasury or the Bureau of the Budget took part.[15]

The fact is that, beyond the most sensitive decisions, the head of the ILN office and very few other people determine to whom the bulk of all arms shall be sold. Kuss admitted to Senator Fulbright during hearings of a subcommittee of the Senate Foreign Relations Committee in 1967 that the decision to sell arms was his responsibility and that it was he who determined a country's capacity to purchase arms without endangering its economy.[16]

The reason why Kuss wields such power and why other departments are bypassed in the decision-making process is not difficult to understand when one considers the dominating position of the Defense Department in governmental matters. With a yearly budget currently in the neighborhood of $72 billion (roughly 40 percent of the entire federal budget), it dwarfs all other governmental departments. The State Department, for instance, operates on a budget of approximately $382 million, almost one two-hundredths the size of the Defense Department's.

The Defense Department is so large that it is almost impervious to outside influences. There are so many layers of leadership and bureaucracy in a place as big as the Pentagon that even a Secretary of Defense as astute as McNamara could be tuned in to only so many of them. Significant "wars" are being fought at a lower level that he never heard about. What bothers many people is that Defense Department employees are, on the whole, decent and competent people; they have no evil intent. But with 27,000 employees in the Pentagon itself, another 3.5 million men and women in uniform, plus all the ancillary groups (industries and private research companies, for example) that feed off the department, the operation becomes virtually impossible to control and can often veer off onto a course that no one intended it to take. It is so vast that it has a motion and life of its own.

Senator Eugene McCarthy once described it as follows:[17]

> A department as large as the Department of Defense must develop a state of mind similar to the situation reported to exist in the great dirigible hangar in New Jersey. That hangar was so big

> that it had its own weather inside. There might be sunshine on the outside, but rain inside; there might have been calm inside, but a tornado outside; there might be storms inside and calm outside. They were never aware of the weather outside because the hangar was so big. They were never aware of the realities. This seems to be what is happening in the Department of Defense.
>
> . . . The Department of Defense has developed its own educational system. The Department operates one of the largest educational systems in the world. The Department has developed its own public relations program, its own propaganda program, its own diplomatic corps. It runs the largest retail distribution operation in the world in the PX.

This kind of power is felt far beyond our own shores. Ralph Dungan, a former U.S. ambassador to Chile, tells the story of his difficulties trying to convince Chileans that the U.S. military establishment was actually under the control of civilians. He said that it was particularly difficult to convince them when both a high-ranking military officer and a career diplomat happened to arrive simultaneously at the Santiago airport. The military brass, he said, would arrive in their own jets accompanied by a huge retinue of assistants; the Foreign Service officer, unless he were an ambassador, would arrive alone, by commercial jet, traveling tourist class. If he were an ambassador, he could travel first class, but he would not have a State Department jet or a large retinue of assistants at his disposal.

Furthermore, Dungan says, "there are platoons of military brass gingering up the military in these countries and only squads of civilians gingering up the civilian sector." He notes that it is impossible to figure a true ratio of State Department employees to military brass in an American embassy by counting heads. Often, he says, the military men are hidden away in other buildings. The MAAG in Chile, for instance, is physically housed in the Chilean Defense Ministry building, a constant source of embarrassment to the State Department and to America's friends in the country.

These men are often not content to advise the local military establishment or to sell them arms. They are so powerful that they often openly interfere in a country's internal politics. Victor Paz

Estenssoro, a former civilian President of Bolivia, stated that a former Air Force attaché at the U.S. Embassy in La Paz was a "key influence" in the 1963 military coup that ousted him. In Brazil, a U.S. Army brigadier general was largely responsible for the success of the 1964 military coup that brought General Humberto Castelo Branco to power. This particular brigadier was a former roommate of Castelo Branco's in Italy during World War II and was still a close enough friend to lunch privately with him on the day after his inauguration. He once expressed his belief in the folly of arms ceilings for Latin America, particularly for Brazil, and also voiced the conviction that all arms negotiations with that large South American country should be left to the Rio MAP mission, which numbered in 1966 more than 100 men. This type of meddling is common among U.S. military officers stationed abroad.

Such power inevitably takes its toll elsewhere. A staff study on arms sales and foreign policy issued by the Senate Foreign Relations Committee in January 1967 pointed out that testimony had shown that ACDA, "despite its charter, does not sit at the high table when decisions on the sale of arms are made."[18] Charles Van Doren admitted to me that the staff study had an impact on his agency but claimed that what it said is less true now than before it was published. Thus he was admitting that ACDA had not been heard in many past meetings. He also said that whenever he did sit in on a Defense-State Coordinating Committee meeting it was only for information purposes. Little or no attempt was, or still is, made by him or other ACDA officials at such meetings to affect the course of decisions.

Another toll is taken in the State Department itself. For instance, Area Desks in the Pentagon, with all the wealth of the Defense Department behind them, find they have the power to intimidate the Country Desks of the State Department. At times, says Ralph Dungan, the Country Desks are "in the hip pocket of the Pentagon—lock, stock and barrel, ideologically owned by the Pentagon!" The power of the Defense Department over a long period of time has been so overwhelming, he adds, that many State Department officials think in Defense Department terms. They are "prostitutes to the rich uncle," he concluded.

The decision-making process, particularly with such a critical policy as arms sales, is neither simplified nor clarified by the conflicts that exist even in the best of times between one department and another. For instance, the Atomic Energy Commission has been at war with ACDA ever since the latter was founded in 1961. The commission believes that it is threatened by ACDA's move into the arms control field, and periodically feels it necessary to restate the areas of prime responsibility which it is convinced are being eaten away. The Alcohol, Tobacco and Firearms Division of the IRS from time to time finds itself at odds with the CIA: the job of one is to stop the flow of arms and the job of the other is (when it feels necessary) to promote the flow. Likewise, the CIA and the Defense Intelligence Agency, distrust each other: one sees the other as a competitor bent on usurping its intelligence-gathering prerogatives. AID and MAP are constantly at war over exactly what constitutes economic and military aid. There is even a running battle between legislators and various appropriations committees, and between supporters and detractors of the arms sales program. Here again a toll is taken. Throughout all of these battles, the Department of Defense, with all its power and influence, can often orchestrate these conflicts to its advantage.

2

None of this has helped to strengthen the mechanisms that control the end-use of American equipment sold to foreign nations. Ever since it first began supplying its allies after World War II, the U.S. government has always insisted that it have ultimate control over how its allies were to use the material. It has insisted, for instance, that a weapon be used only for "defensive" purposes, not "offensive." In other words, strings have been attached to the grant or sale of U.S. arms. At the same time, Washington has sought to control the resale of American equipment by our allies. Nearly every postwar bilateral arms agreement involving the United States has contained an article which reserved to the United States the right to veto any third-party sale of its equipment.

The number of times these controls have broken down is legion, and only some of the better known instances need be mentioned here for the purposes of illustration. In the Pakistan-India War of 1965, for instance, U.S. *Sherman* tanks of the Indian Army battled U.S. *Patton* tanks of the Pakistani Army. These tanks had been provided to both countries (perhaps somewhat naïvely) on the understanding that they were to be used "defensively" against communist aggression. In the 1967 Sinai War, U.S. *Pattons* of the Israeli Army faced an equal number of *Pattons* of the Jordanian Army. Neither sale was made with the thought in mind (again, perhaps naïvely) that the two countries would use the tanks offensively. "Defensive" American weapons were used "offensively" in the 1967 Greek military coup. At least half a dozen other coups, particularly in Latin America, have seen "defensive" American arms used in an "offensive" capacity. The sight of *Sherman* or *Patton* tanks invading a presidential palace is not too uncommon an experience.

As of this writing there have not been many breakdowns in the mechanisms designed to control the resale of U.S. equipment to third parties. But this is due less to the efficiency of resale controls than to the fact that third-hand equipment is just now beginning to flood the market in any volume. The vast quantities of equipment given away or sold in the late 1940's, the 1950's and the early 1960's are now being discarded for newer equipment.* For example, many countries are phasing out their F-80's, F-84's and F-

* Technically, all grant aid material belonged to the U.S. military, no matter who the recipient was; it was to be returned when it was no longer capable of fulfilling the function for which it was given. In practice, however, much of the original grant aid—that given during the 1949–55 period—had no operable life after 1959 and was junked locally since to return it to the United States served no useful purpose and was a waste of money. The third-hand equipment which is now coming onto the market is post-1959 in origin with the exception of certain highly desired prop and jet aircraft and certain tanks of an earlier vintage.

West Germany was treated somewhat differently. Between 1956 and 1958, as part of its rearmament program, it received one billion dollars in military equipment from the United States. In 1962, rather than return the equipment, the U.S. government, through the provisions of the Nash List Agreement of that year, permitted Bonn to purchase the equipment for seven cents on the dollar. Strings, however, were still attached: Bonn was allowed to sell this equipment freely to other NATO members, but for sales to non-NATO members it had to get U.S. permission.

86's of Korean War vintage and replacing them with the faster and more sophisticated F-4 *Phantoms,* F-104 *Starfighters,* F-5 *Freedomfighters,* and the F-111 variable-wing jets. Nike *Ajax* missiles are being replaced by Nike *Hercules;* and M-47 and M-48 tanks will soon give way to the U.S.-German-designed MBT-70 tank. All of this older material is now in the process of being resold to third parties.

The best example to date of a breakdown in control procedures, and one that is worthy of considerable comment, is the case of the ninety F-86's that West Germany sold in 1966 to Iran, which was acting, as it turned out, as a secret intermediary for embargo-bound Pakistan. Kuss claims that this violation of resale control mechanisms was "an aberration." It may be, but with more of this type of equipment coming onto the market every day, it may also be a portent of things to come.

The incident began in 1957 when West Germany bought from Canada 225 F-86 *Sabrejets.* By 1965 the Luftwaffe had moved up to the F-104G *Starfighter* and was anxious to unload the phased-out planes. In the autumn of that year the Pakistanis and Indians went to war over Kashmir, and a general worldwide arms embargo was promptly clamped on both nations. Shortly after the cease-fire on September 22, an arms-buying delegation from Iran arrived in Bonn. It was headed by a former Chief of the Iranian General Staff, General Hassan Toufanian. Accompanying him was an armaments expert of the Pakistani Army, Colonel Hussein Zaidi. Apparently Zaidi's presence raised no suspicions in Bonn.

Toufanian expressed an interest in purchasing ninety F-86's, and the Germans agreed to sell if certain conditions were met. The U.S. resale control procedure in a case like this requires that West Germany (the current seller) obtain permission from Canada (the manufacturer and original seller), who, in turn, obtains permission from the United States (the licenser and controlling government). The State Department insists that it received assurances from both Canada and West Germany that the *Sabres* were indeed for use by the Iranian Air Force. Thus the deal was approved.

Merex AG acted as a broker and reportedly purchased the ninety jets for $6.75 million. It then sold them to the Iranians for

$10 million. Cummings claims that Gerhard Mertins, Merex's owner, had to give the Iranian middlemen $300,000 of his profits as their fee.

Beginning in March 1966 and continuing until November of the same year, the jets were transferred from West Germany to Iran by Luftwaffe pilots reportedly dressed in civilian clothes. The Shah is supposed to have given each pilot as a reward a souvenir cup. Soon these jets began to appear in Pakistan, ostensibly to be "repaired," and the Indian press complained loudly that this was a violation of the embargo. A diplomatic scramble began: Washington queried Ottawa, who queried Bonn, who queried Tehran. A crisis was averted "when the planes were returned to Iran," although as late as March 1967 Kuss could not state categorically that all of them had in fact been returned.[19]

Here then was a clear attempt to evade the embargo. One of the reasons it could happen, according to the then Deputy Assistant Secretary of Defense Townsend Hoopes, is that no "end-use" inspections by American military officials had been conducted for the previous two years in either Pakistan or India. In other words, no one was checking to see that the U.S. military aid was being used for the purposes for which it was provided.[20]

This breakdown in controls was emphasized by Cummings of Interarms when he told Senator Symington during hearings in March 1967:

> . . . it seemed to me that the United States was almost indifferent to what happened to the material because, for instance, there were thousands of rounds of tank gun and artillery ammunition which were shipped out of Germany and France to Iran for Pakistan. [Deleted.] All of that material was U.S. standard material or even U.S.-produced material, and there was no licensing problem experienced by Merex. [Deleted.]

Furthermore, he said, "it is my understanding that only certain categories of weapons [sold to West Germany] were subject to that ultimate U.S. control. In other words, the light weapons were not, but heavy weapons were." Therefore, at least with weapons the United States sold to West Germany, there are virtually no controls at all: none for small arms because there is no contractual obligation to notify the United States of a resale, and none for large weapons because, as is apparent, no one is bothering to make end-use inspections.

Cummings also claimed that it was "common knowledge" among weapons dealers, himself included, that the ninety F-86's were from the start destined for Pakistan. Kuss, on the other hand, told Senator Symington that he suspected nothing until the violation had occurred.[21]

It is quite clear now, as more facts have emerged, that despite Kuss' apparent ignorance of the violation, the U.S. government not only knew what was going on but was actually aiding the Pakistanis to violate the embargo. Several salient facts come to mind. First of all, according to the most reliable source, the Institute for Strategic Studies, the entire Iranian Air Force in 1965–66 numbered no more than 110 planes of all types.[22] To double virtually the number of planes in a nine-month period would indicate that Kuss was either irresponsible or incompetent, or both, neither of which he is. On the other hand, Pakistan lost an estimated seventy aircraft in the war, which would suggest to even a rank novice that there was a void that needed to be filled in the area. Under the circumstances it seems reasonable to believe that someone in authority in the U.S. government knew the ultimate destination of those jets.

Second, during 1965 and 1966 Iran was in the process of negotiating with the United States for F-4 *Phantoms* to replace some of its aging F-86's. Eventually the Shah was promised at least one squadron of sixteen planes. No country that is trying to upgrade its air force is going to overload itself with the same type of jet it is trying to get rid of.

Finally, the German weekly *Der Spiegel* reported Senator Symington as saying in a closed session of the same hearings, "Our own intelligence service knew exactly at the time that these F-86's were meant for Pakistan."[23]

It is clear that the United States' overall procedures for controlling both the use of its military equipment and its resale by foreign countries are, at best, haphazardly administered. Undoubtedly Washington currently leans heavily on the hope that the system will police itself—that it is in the interest of the recipients to keep obsolescent material out of the hands of undesirables. The Office of Munitions Control is also unequal to the task of controlling sales under its jurisdiction, and it does not even have responsibility for handling, cataloguing or controlling the transactions of the greatest arms exporter of all—the ILN office. Furthermore, there is ample evidence that the Defense Department itself does not keep adequate records. For instance, when Senator Symington asked a high-ranking official in the department for a list of sales and commitments that Merex had made in reselling *U.S.* equipment, he was told that the information was not available.[24]

This apparent lack of information is perhaps the largest single factor hindering anyone—public servant or private citizen—from understanding the true nature of the U.S. involvement in arms sales around the world. One truism is that when arms sales were promoted by private industry or by independent arms dealers, as they were prior to World War II, information was ultimately attainable; but with arms sales dominated by a government bureaucracy, as they are today, virtually no information is available. Most of this is due to the bureaucracy's obsessive concern for secrecy and self-preservation. Although considerable information is suppressed legitimately for reasons of national security, a great deal more is suppressed for other reasons.

Anyone perusing congressional hearings or debates on arms sales, for example, is confronted with an overwhelming number of deletions that often render a manuscript incomprehensible. Senator Albert Gore is particularly incensed by what he considers unselective censorship. Said he:[25]

> I do not see how putting this kind of information on the public record violates our national security. Surely, if any foreign foe wished to know how many fighter bombers Argentina has or how many *Sherman* tanks Brazil has, they could find out by sending an intelligence officer there. However, the American people, who are paying the bill, cannot find out what they helped to pay for.

Officials in the Defense Department will reply, however, that such deletions serve several purposes. First, they say, aside from national security, the deletions help protect one country from another that might have territorial ambitions against it. Many countries, they claim, hesitate to act if they do not know their opposition's strength. Second, to publish figures would demonstrate to our own enemies the efficiency of our intelligence service. Defense Department officials will also say privately that by not releasing figures it preserves the fiction that the U.S. government is neither involved nor interested in the internal military affairs of other countries.

Whenever there are complaints that no information is available, the Defense Department will immediately press stacks of statistical tables upon the plaintiff. Henry Kuss is always quick to hand out copies of ILN's latest sales figures. But on second inspection, these statistics are often confusing, conflicting and obscure. It appears that this is done on purpose, to satisfy on the one hand the incessant demand for information, yet on the other hand to ensure that not too many facts are divulged.

For example, the Defense Department issues a series of unclassified reports called either *Foreign Military Sales Facts, Military Assistance and Foreign Military Sales Facts,* or *Military Assistance Facts.* All three give what appear to be considerable data on both grant aid and sales—how much equipment is being sent abroad, when it was sent, who is getting it, and what its value is. But it is virtually impossible to collate the information in one report or to compare in depth one report with another. One issue of *Facts,* for instance, will break down into six categories the number of cargo aircraft sold; the next issue will group into only one category all cargo aircraft sold. In another issue of *Facts,* the number of *Freedomfighter* jets delivered is listed under the designation "Aircraft Fighter F-5"; in the next issue of *Facts,* F-5 totals are combined with T-38 trainer totals, so there is no way these two figures can be compared. In the opening statistical tables in both the May 1966 and 1967 issues of *Facts,* entirely different figures for "Funds and Programs, Military Aid Program, Cumulative FY 1950–66" are given with no explanation. Sometimes an issue of

Facts will list sales or grant aid by the actual number of weapons delivered; in other areas it will show the sale or grant aid in dollar volume. Thus, there is no way the figures can be compared.

Some information is not available at all. For instance, it would be of interest to show how ILN sales grew year by year, with particular emphasis on which countries bought what material. One can find out the total dollar value of all items sold or given to, say, Brazil since 1945; but no *yearly* dollar totals are available for Brazil or, for that fact, for any other country. Nor is there any way to find out how many, say, tanks the United States has given or sold to Brazil. All this is hidden, as Senator Gore notes, under a dollar figure (which is meaningless because it bears little relationship to the true economic value of the equipment) and behind such obscure descriptions as "general defense equipment to be mutually agreed upon."[26]

Still other arms sales information is hidden in the yearly Defense budget requests to Congress. These estimates of expenditures and proposals for new fiscal authority, with all their supporting data, are extremely long and complicated documents that no legislator, no matter how interested, has the time or the staff to plumb properly. Some of the itemizations in the estimates are so woolly ("contingencies," for instance) that monies maintained in one area by Congress can easily be transferred later by the Pentagon to another area where funds were slashed by the lawmakers. The sheer complexity of Defense estimates, appropriations and the implementation of funds precludes outsiders from knowing exactly how the Pentagon spends its money. What is more, Congress can do very little to control this switching of funds; usually it is reduced to hacking away indiscriminately at the most vulnerable aspects of the estimates in order to show that it has some control over the Pentagon; but Defense officials usually anticipate this and go to Congress asking for approximately 15 percent more than they hope to come away with.

There is also some indication that considerable information is suppressed even when demanded by Congress. One of the best and most recent examples occurred in 1967. Senator Dodd, Chairman of the Senate Subcommittee on Juvenile Delinquency, was holding hearings in that year on bills to amend the Federal Firearms Act of 1938. He had heard that Sam Cummings had sold weapons to both sides in the Costa Rican revolution of 1955. Cummings has never denied it; in fact, as pointed out earlier, he feels justified in selling to antagonists as long as there is no actual fighting going on between them. Dodd, therefore, was interested in knowing who in the U.S. government had given permission for the two sales, since he believed that neither was in the "furtherance of world peace."

On August 17, 1967, John Sipes, the Director of the Office of Munitions Control, wrote a letter to Senator Roman L. Hruska, a member of Dodd's subcommittee. In it, Sipes said that his files showed that no such transactions occurred. Hruska, believing that this letter would end the matter, passed it on to Senator Dodd for inclusion in the subcommittee's records. On October 3, Dodd, unsatisfied with the explanation, wrote back to Sipes asking that a further search of his files be made. Enclosed in the letter were copies of two articles—one from the *Saturday Evening Post* and the other from the *New York Times Magazine*—both of which supported Dodd's view that indeed Cummings had made the sales.

Three weeks later, Robert A. Clark, Jr., Acting Director of the OMC in Sipes' absence, replied that "a thorough search of the Office of Munitions Control files and retired records has failed to produce any documentation that would confirm the allegation that Interarms supplied firearms to both sides in the 1955 Costa Rican revolution." He then went on to say that records of all licenses issued through 1955 had been destroyed in accordance with various legal authorizations to do so.[27]

Critics point out that Clark was not as quick to say, as did Sipes, that no such transactions occurred. All Clark said was that a thorough search produced no documentation; he did not deny that Cummings made the sales. The destruction of old records of licenses issued, the critics add, is difficult to believe. Perhaps, they say, the licenses themselves were destroyed, but surely not the record of licenses issued, which presumably would show what was sold, when it was sold, who sold it and who bought it. One member of Dodd's subcommittee staff said to me, "If we [the United States] don't have some record of what arms Costa Rica bought and sold from 1955 on back—and I would include all the other countries in the world—then we're in deep trouble. The security of this country, indeed of the entire world, depends on us knowing." And then he added, "In fact, they [the OMC] know damn well what Costa Rica got in 1955, but they won't tell us [the subcommittee] because it would be admitting that they allowed Cummings to sell to both sides."

Congress, particularly since 1961, has become increasingly frustrated over its inability to influence the course of arms sales. Many of its members have come to believe that its "advise and consent" function has been ignored by zealous and independent-minded bureaucrats. The example most often cited by Congressmen is the sale of sixteen F-4 *Phantom* jets to Iran in 1966. Senator Symington complained that Congress ordinarily would not have been informed until six to nine months after the sale had been completed. It was only through testimony at a special hearing, which he chaired, that the facts were brought out in advance. "What are members . . . supposed to do if we are not even to know of these things?" he asked. "I realize the position of Congress is not respected by some of the administration," he continued. "Nevertheless it is a fact and you [speaking to Townsend Hoopes] know it just as well as I. Some agree, give us a pleasant grin, and do as they please."[28]

Congressional pique at being bypassed boiled over in the spring and summer of 1967. In January of that year, the Senate Committee on Foreign Relations' Staff Study called into question the entire U.S. arms sales program. It stated in effect that the policy was ill-conceived, that its implications with respect to overall U.S. foreign policy objectives were far more grave than previously had been supposed, and that the control mechanisms were unequal to the task. This study sparked other investigations. In March, April and June, hearings were held by the Senate Subcommittee on Near Eastern and South Asian Affairs at which Cummings, Kuss, Hoopes and Kitchen testified. It was these hearings that brought to light the sale of the ninety F-86's which ended up in Pakistan. During the summer, considerable time was spent by both the

House and Senate in debating the merits of various aspects of the U.S. arms sales program as it applied to the Foreign Assistance Act of 1961, then in the process of being amended.

At issue—far more so than control mechanisms and the availability of information—was the question of credit arrangements available to the Defense Department in selling weapons. The importance of credit arrangements to the ILN office cannot be ignored, because they not only have given the United States tremendous sales leverage over other nations selling weapons, but have increased the power and independence of the Pentagon by putting it in the banking business.

Until 1968 there were three major sources of financing available to foreign countries interested in buying U.S. arms. Depending on the situation, each one could be used to "sweeten" a sale by making package loans, mixing interest rates and offering long-term credit. This breadth and flexibility of credit tools at ILN's disposal has accounted in large measure for the success of the U.S. arms sales program.

The first source of financing was and still is cash sales negotiated either by direct contracts between foreign governments and private U.S. manufacturers and lending institutions, or through a military assistance sale negotiated directly between two governments. This has been the most common means of financing arms sales and accounts for approximately 70 percent of all arms sales since 1961. The largest cash customers have been West Germany, Australia, Canada and the United Kingdom.[29]

The second source was the Military Assistance Credit Account. The idea that the Defense Department should have its own funds available for use in providing credit for arms sales dates back to 1957 when, under the Mutual Security Act amendments of that year, $15 million was authorized for this purpose. It was felt at that time that a source of credit should be available in the transition period from grant aid to sales to help countries that could not afford to pay cash and whose credit was not up to the standards required by private and independent lending institutions. Over the years, through yearly appropriations ranging from $21 million to $83 million, the fund grew to approximately $383 million by

1967. Additional legislation in 1961 authorized the fund to be a "revolving account." In other words, future repayments were to be pumped back into the fund in order to finance more loans. Approximately 10 percent of all arms sales by 1965 were being financed through this account.[30]

The third source of credit was the Export-Import Bank of Washington, D.C. This institution, commonly known as the Eximbank, was created in 1934 for the purpose of helping to finance commercial exports. After 1964, when the ILN office was first given the authority to insure credit arrangements, the Eximbank moved more and more into the financing of arms sales, a purpose for which it was not established. By the end of FY 1967 this bank had lent a total of $1.6 billion for arms purchases to seventeen countries, fourteen of which were and still are underdeveloped. In FY's 1966 and 1967, between 25 and 36 percent of the bank's loans went for arms. This vast sum represented the remaining 20 percent of all arms sales financing.[31]

The Eximbank made two types of loans for arms purchases. The first was direct loans, usually at Defense Department request, to low-risk countries such as Austria, Great Britain, Italy and Australia. These loans were made on a five- to seven-year medium-term basis at an interest rate of approximately 5.5 percent per year. The first two loans by the bank were in 1963 when $163 million went to Austria and Italy, which at that time were arguing for control over parts of the Tyrol. From FY 1963 to FY 1967 slightly more than $1 billion of the $1.6 billion were direct loans such as this.[32]

The second type of Eximbank loan was an indirect one and was made through a device known as the "Country-X Account." Under this arrangement, Eximbank opened a line of credit to the Defense Department, usually at from 3.5 to 5.5 percent interest. The Defense Department, using the ILN office as its vehicle, then lent this money to unspecified countries with low credit ratings. The funds were guaranteed by the Military Assistance Credit "Revolving" Account. An amendment to the Foreign Assistance Act of 1964 gave the Defense Department the authority to guarantee 100 percent of all credit extended on arms sales while only obligating 25 percent of the total as a reserve. Thus the $383 million in the revolving account (in 1967) allowed the Defense Department to put the full guarantee of the U.S. government behind over $1.5 billion in credits. In other words, the total in the revolving account, instead of being the maximum amount of government funds available for arms loans, now represented only one quarter of all the funds available. For every dollar held in reserve in the revolving account, the U.S. government was willing both to lend and to guarantee the repayment of three more dollars. Under such lucrative conditions, the Eximbank was willing to plunge headlong into financing arms sales, for it could not lose. Between mid-1965 and June 1967 alone, the bank had extended $604 million in Country-X loans to the Defense Department, and was planning to extend an additional $1 billion in the following two years. From 1963 to 1967 military sales to underdeveloped countries increased thirteenfold through the use of this revolving fund.[33]

The full implications of the U.S. arms sales credit arrangements were understood by very few people at the beginning of 1967. This want of knowledge stemmed in large part from a general lack of official information on the subject. Slowly, however, information began to leak out during the summer.

In closed hearings before the House Banking and Currency Committee on July 17, 1967, Harold Linder, the Eximbank's president,* revealed for the first time the extent of his bank's involvement in the financing of U.S. arms sales. He is supposed to have told the committee that the bank had obeyed its legal requirements to give Congress full and complete details each year on its loans. Some members of the committee were said to have been incredulous—even derisive—at Linder's testimony. At one point in the hearings, Representative William B. Widnall, Republican from New Jersey, was reported to have asked, "I want anybody in this room who knew anything about these Country-X loans before

* Linder was appointed by President Kennedy. Congressional records show that Linder was also the largest single contributor to President Johnson's campaign for re-election in 1964, giving a total of $61,300 through various committees.

last weekend to hold up his hand." Apparently no hands were raised.[34]

What irritated Widnall and the other members of the committee, such as Henry S. Reuss, Democrat from Wisconsin, and Chairman of the Full Committee Wright Patman, Democrat from Texas, was their belief that the bank's new role was instituted through stealth, if not outright deception. The Foreign Assistance Act of 1964, they say, gave the President the authority to furnish military aid by "guaranteeing, insuring, coinsuring and reinsuring any individual, corporation, partnership or other association doing business with the United States against political and credit risks of nonpayment arising in connection with credit sales financed by such individual, corporation, partnership or other association for defense articles procured in the United States by such friendly country." This, say the critics, was not intended to authorize the supplying of credit by the Eximbank for arms sales.

Several observers have pointed out that Eximbank annual reports gave no hint that between 25 and 36 percent of its loans were going for arms purchases. A foreword in one report spoke of "the contribution which its long-term loans have made to the economies and thus the development of the recipient countries." There followed a series of photographs, one showing a cargo plane being exported to Zambia, another showing a generator being shipped to Japan and a third showing U.S. machinery making tin plate in Brazil. A spokesman for the bank reluctantly admitted, after the uproar in the House Banking and Currency Committee hearings, that arms loans were concealed under such headings as "various U.S. exports." "I thought it was in the national interest," Linder told the committee, "not to define these exports. . . . We did not particularly like to have the thing widely known. I had good reason to think it was unwise for the bank to indicate in its annual report that it was conducting military business."[35]

Soon after the Country-X Account exposure, other previously unknown aspects of America's arms sales credit structure entered the public domain. For instance, Neil Sheehan, a *New York Times* reporter, pointed out in a three-part series on the entire world's arms sales activities and trends that the developing countries paid out approximately $4 billion in foreign exchange for debt service alone in 1964. This amount was equal to about half of all the new economic aid extended to them that year. Much of this debt had been incurred through large arms purchases. In other words, the United States, through its liberal credit arrangements, not only was supplying weapons to poor nations that did not need them, but was also encouraging debts which were an intolerably heavy burden for most of these underdeveloped countries to carry.[36]

Harold Linder, in further testimony, asserted that until his appearance before the House Banking and Currency Committee he had not known—indeed, did not want to know—the names of the countries that had received Country-X loans. It was Eximbank policy, he said, simply to trust the Defense Department in its judgment (which in reality meant trust in the ILN office), since it had the responsibility to see that the loans were repaid.

A week after Linder's testimony, Sheehan, in another *Times* article, listed the fourteen underdeveloped countries and the amounts reportedly lent, heretofore a secret kept by the ILN office. Five of the countries were in Latin America: Brazil, Argentina, Peru, Chile and Venezuela; five were in the Near East: Iran, Saudi Arabia, Jordan, Israel and Morocco; and four were in the Middle and Far East: Pakistan, India, Malaysia and Taiwan. Approximately 75 percent of all Country-X loans went to the five countries in the Near East—one of the most explosive areas in the world today. The loans to Pakistan and India, totaling $21 million, seem to have contravened the U.S. embargo established after the 1965 war since part of these loans was used reportedly to buy "lethal" weapons.[37]

The following week it was revealed that the Defense Department was subsidizing interest rates on arms sales loans. In other words, when Eximbank opened a line of credit for a Country-X loan, it would charge the Defense Department normally from 3.5 to 5.5 percent interest. The Defense Department would then lend the money at a lower interest rate to its arms buying customer and absorb the difference itself. For instance, India was paying 3 percent interest on an $18 million loan; the Eximbank's interest rate to the ILN office, however, was 5.5 percent. Thus 2.5 percent, or $450,000 per year, was absorbed by the Defense Department.

On at least one occasion the Defense Department made a little money by charging more interest than it was paying. Chile, on a $1 million loan, was paying 5 percent interest on a Country-X loan for which the Eximbank had charged the Defense Department only 4.875 percent interest.[38]

As more and more information such as this came to light, many senators and representatives became convinced that the Defense Department in general and the ILN office in particular were intentionally attempting to deceive Congress. Senator Allen J. Ellender, Democrat from Louisiana, in testimony before the Senate Banking and Currency Committee, quoted a statement by Secretary McNamara in 1964 that the Defense Department did not intend to use the bank for arms loans. The fact that the Eximbank three years later was a prime instrument of the ILN office's credit sales scheme convinced many legislators that Pentagon officials were telling Congress one thing and doing another. Under Secretary of State for Political Affairs Eugene V. Rostow conceded that the Administration had not kept "some members" of the House and Senate Banking and Currency Committees adequately informed, although he insisted that both the House Foreign Affairs and Senate Foreign Relations Committee members were kept informed. Senators Fulbright and Symington, among others, stoutly denied it. Said Symington, "All I can say is that we have been taken."[39]

If, however, Congress had any illusions that these revelations had chastened the ILN office, or the Defense Department in general, it was rudely jolted the following month during debate in the Senate on the Foreign Assistance Act of 1968 (which proposed amendments to the Foreign Assistance Act of 1961). Part of the Senate Foreign Relations Committee bill contained an amendment, known as the Church Amendment, which sought to remove the Defense Department's authority to finance credit sales to underdeveloped nations through the revolving fund. It asked that Country-X loans be abolished by June 30, 1968, and that the money in the revolving fund be turned over to the Treasury.

Senator Henry M. Jackson, Democrat from Washington, moved to counter this amendment with one of his own. On the surface his amendment proposed that Senator Church's amendment be deleted from the bill as reported out by the Foreign Relations Committee. It was strongly backed by the Joint Chiefs of Staff, Henry Kuss and other Pentagon officials.

But in the early afternoon of August 15, as debate got under way, it was discovered that a new provision had been added to Jackson's printed amendment that gave the Defense Department even broader authority than it previously had. The new section allowed the Pentagon to purchase from U.S. arms suppliers or manufacturers promissory notes or other evidence of indebtedness given them by foreign governments; these notes the Defense Department could then discount at the Eximbank. In other words, while Jackson's amendment appeared only to retain existing powers, it in fact gave the ILN office one more string to its credit sales bow.

A careful headcount on both sides of the Senate chamber earlier in the day showed that the Jackson amendment—as most senators understood its intentions—stood a fair chance of passing. But at a meeting in Majority Leader Mansfield's office the full facts of the matter became known. Present were sixteen Democrats, six Republicans, Paul Nitze, the Deputy Secretary of Defense, Nicholas Katzenbach, the Under Secretary of State, and William S. Gaud, the Administrator for AID. The purpose of the meeting was to win support for the bipartisan effort to retain the Pantagon's existing arms credit authority and to restore funds cut from the bill by the Senate Foreign Relations Committee. It was a massive lobbying effort by the promoters of arms sales. Most of the legislators present favored the Administration's position on the Eximbank and the continuation of the bank's financing of arms to underdeveloped countries.

The new—and previously unrealized—section of Jackson's amendment, however, changed all that. One Republican and six Democrats switched sides and the proposal lost 50 to 43. Aside from cries of being "hoodwinked" and "duped," senators were furious to learn that the offending section had been written in Henry Kuss' office in the Pentagon.

Supporters of the arms sales credit program, fully aware of the revolt, nevertheless tried to recoup their losses. Senator Tower proposed an amendment that would have retained only the existing Defense Department credit authority without the controversial section. The new mood, however, militated against its passage. It was defeated by a vote of 46 to 45.[40]

Said Henry Kuss during the early days of the crisis, "It's been a tough year. What with Vietnam, the Near East, and the like—doves all over—people just won't listen to you."[41]

V

The Problems of Success

"To create what sounds like an arms race, it doesn't take a lot of weapons. You talk of 90 airplanes; well, for God's sake, 90 airplanes is nothing. Somebody talks of 150 tanks going to Israel; it's a drop in the bucket, 150 tanks."

—HENRY KUSS to the author

1

The machinery set up by the U.S. government both to sell and to control arms, it has been pointed out, is neither simple in structure nor clearly defined. In many instances it is not even fully understood by those in charge. Congressional impotence and wrath, bureaucratic obscurantism and the general unavailability of information have infinitely complicated the picture. Far more important than this, however, are the implications and repercussions of the government's arms sales policy, for the justification of such a policy in the last analysis rests, not on how well or poorly the mechanisms work, but whether the policy itself accomplishes the tasks for which it was created. The question that must be answered is: has the U.S. arms sales policy achieved what it set out to do?

The motives behind U.S. military aid in the immediate postwar years tended to emphasize almost exclusively political and strategic objectives—a direct response to Stalin's Cold War. Arms were given or sold to a country essentially for military reasons. Over the years, however, as the character of the Cold War changed, as the immediate threat of nuclear war receded, as nationalism gained in voice, the emphasis shifted from political and strategic to political and economic objectives. The shift was formalized with the establishment of the International Logistics Negotiations office in 1961 and is clearly reflected in the three objectives of the foreign military sales program. The first objective is "to promote the defensive strength of our allies, consistent with our political-economic objectives"; the second is "to promote the concept of cooperative logistics with our allies"; and the third is "to offset the unfavorable balance of payments resulting from essential U.S. military deployment abroad."[1] All three objectives deserve special attention here.

A policy "to promote the defensive strength of our allies," as the first objective seeks to do, must, if it is to be responsible, promote at the same time the political, social and economic stability and strength of our allies. A country whose military strength is based on fiscal insecurity, social unrest and political vulnerability is a weak link in any alliance. In this context, then, there is considerable evidence to support the view that the U.S. arms sales policy has often failed in this particular objective.

The sale of F-104G *Starfighters* to West Germany is a case in point. In the mid-1950's, Franz Josef Strauss, the Federal Republic's Defense Minister, was particularly anxious to have West Germany included as a part of NATO's atomic strike force. The F-85 and F-86 jets in the Luftwaffe, he knew, would be unsuitable for such a role. In 1957, therefore, he formed a team of experts to look at various aircraft capable of meeting the new requirements. Fifteen different possibilities were considered and eventually the list was pared to three: the Grumman *Super Tiger,* the Dassault *Mirage III* and the Lockheed F-104 *Starfighter.* For strategic and tactical reasons it was necessary for the Federal Republic to have a plane that would combine several capabilities—namely, assault, attack, support, reconnaissance and bombing. It also had to have good climbing, acceleration and long-range striking capabilities.

Because the F-104 seemed to combine all these capabilities to the best degree, and because it weighed half as much as the other two possibilities and seemed cheap at the price, the Lockheed product was chosen. The contract, signed in March 1959, called for West Germany to purchase 250 *Starfighters* modified to meet its specifications. In 1960 Strauss increased the order to 700; later an additional 264 F-104's were ordered. Altogether, this weapons system is the most expensive the Bundeswehr has bought to date; it is estimated to have cost the Bonn government in excess of $2 billion.

In 1957 the German team of experts was looking at an ordinary F-104, a simplified plane not loaded down with all the gear required by the Luftwaffe. The team was counting on Lockheed to turn the ordinary F-104 into the all-purpose craft that they had in mind. By the time Lockheed had made all the required modifications, the plane, according to *Interavia,* a Swiss aeronautical journal, was a completely different piece of equipment with entirely different handling characteristics.

Lockheed, during the 1950's, had fallen on hard times, and its case was pushed with unusual vigor by both company officials and representatives of the U.S. government. The full facts of this sales offensive have yet to be revealed, but it is known that a number of German politicians—among them Kurt Georg Kiesinger, then the head of the Parliamentary Foreign Affairs Committee and later Federal Chancellor, and Kai-Uwe von Hassel, then Bundesrat President and later Defense Minister—reported that they were forced upon occasion to bar their office doors physically to the aggressive salesmen. Large amounts of money were spent in Bonn to convince the government that it should buy the *Starfighter.* So overwhelming and insistent was the lobbying, so high-handed and crass were the tactics used, that there still exists a residual bitterness among many Germans today.

The problems of modification facing Lockheed and the German government were so complex that they were never properly worked out. As a result the *Starfighter,* once deliveries began in 1961–62, never was able to achieve the capabilities for which it was bought. This was particularly true of its ability to operate at night and in bad weather. There were also snags in the radar, bomb release and ejection seat systems that defied correction.

In addition the Luftwaffe was extremely short of trained mechanical and electronic service personnel. From 1945 to 1957 the Germans had virtually no experience in aeronautical technology. They therefore initiated a crash program of military schooling in this art. But here again it proved inadequate: the equipment in the F-104G (as the plane was designated) was so complicated that it took virtually the entire eighteen-month enlistment period to train a mechanic properly, by which time he was prepared to leave to seek more lucrative wages in private industry. In 1966 the Luftwaffe still had a service personnel shortage of 40 percent. The Federal Republic, as a way to save money, also bought no spare electronic equipment: this increased the "down time" of the aircraft and cut heavily into the number of hours flown by Luftwaffe pilots. Finally, and in spite of the problems of modification and maintenance, the F-104G was still so swift an aircraft that its pilots had very little room to practice maneuvers in the restricted and crowded West German airspace.*

Soon after delivery, F-104G's began falling out of the sky in alarming numbers. By last count (October 1969) 100 *Starfighters* had crashed. The planes were nicknamed the "Flying Coffin" and the "Widow Maker." So bad was the publicity that between 1957 and 1965 the number of Germans volunteering each year to fly the planes fell from a high of 471 to only 134.[2]

The sale of *Starfighters,* quite clearly, did not promote the defensive strength of one of America's staunchest allies. The planes were never up to the mark required of them, the pilots were and still are ill-trained, service personnel are still in short supply, and vast sums of money were spent for no lasting improvements in West German defense capabilities. The representatives of Lockheed and the U.S. government, with their aggressive, hard-sell tactics, did not promote the defensive strength of an ally; on the contrary, they succeeded in convincing many individuals in the West German government that their country's best interests lay outside direct U.S. influence. The U.S. also failed to provide adequate training schemes for Luftwaffe service personnel, yet it still disclaims any responsibility for the high accident rate of the planes.

* This is reminiscent of a problem Andorra had in the late nineteenth century. It bought a gun from Krupp which it could not fire without sending the projectile beyond its own frontiers.

The *Starfighter* Affair, as it is known in Germany, led to a number of crises. In August 1966 the three highest-ranking generals in the West German armed forces resigned over the plane's poor performance record. The purchase of these planes contributed to economic and budgetary crises in West Germany, both of which were extremely serious. Most damaging of all, the Affair was to play an important role in bringing about the downfall of the pro-American Erhard government in 1966.*

Another example of how the U.S. arms sales program "promotes the defensive strength of our allies" followed closely on the heels of the *Starfighter* Affair. In 1961 there was an exchange of correspondence between Chancellor Erhard and Roswell Gilpatric, then Deputy Secretary of Defense, in which West Germany said that she foresaw the possibility of her military financial needs equaling the foreign exchange costs of stationing U.S. troops on her soil. From this exchange emerged the idea of an "offset arrangement" by which Bonn agreed to purchase through the ILN office $1.3 billion worth of U.S. military equipment over a two-year period. This arrangement has subsequently been continued for two-year periods.

The results of this agreement were to have far-reaching consequences. Despite denials from Secretary McNamara that West Germany was a dumping ground for U.S. weapons, it is clear in retrospect that the United States was forcing on West Germany's military establishment weapons that it did not want or need. By 1965 the Bundewehr had so much excess equipment that Bonn found itself deeply involved in its own military aid program: that is to say, as Bonn was forced to buy quantities of U.S. equipment, it had to unload its older equipment out the back door in order to recover some of the costs and clear its inventories.

One specific example of back-door aid was Bonn's efforts to supply arms to Israel, with whom it had no diplomatic relations at the time. This particular effort dates back to 1960 when Chancellor Adenauer met Israel's Prime Minister, David Ben-Gurion, and

* Other aspects of the *Starfighter* sale, involving Lockheed, Litton and officials of the West German government, are examined in Chapter VII.

secretly agreed to supply arms worth $80 million to the embattled Middle Eastern state. Defense Minister Strauss put the agreement into effect in the summer of 1962. He was encouraged by Washington, which wanted to strengthen Israel without being blamed for it by the Arabs. In June 1964 the new Chancellor, Erhard, asked the United States to relieve him of this arrangement drawn up by his predecessors, but he was given no comfort by U.S. officials. The arms thus continued to flow from the reluctant supplier. Part of a 1964 consignment included 200 U.S. tanks formerly used by the Bundeswehr.[3]

The $80 million arms aid was given by Bonn under the guise of a strictly German-Israeli arrangement. The material, said Bonn, was in payment for a "moral debt" to Israel. In the hope that this explanation would mollify the Arabs, the U.S. denied that it was involved at all in the transaction. But in February 1965, as the story became more prominent in the press and as a crisis began to boil, the United States reluctantly admitted that it had secretly agreed to the transfer of the 200 tanks. Several weeks later, in mid-February, in an attempt to ease the subsequent diplomatic furor, the State Department acknowledged that it had supported the aid effort since its inception in 1960.[4]

President Gamal Abdel Nasser of Egypt, meanwhile, displeased with West Germany's aid to Israel, took countermeasures of his own. They were to result in one of the most agile diplomatic coups of the year. In the summer of 1964, Nasser invited East German leader Walter Ulbricht to visit Cairo with no set date in mind. There were two major motives that prompted this move: it was first a clear warning that unless West Germany dropped its arms aid to Israel, Egypt would recognize the Pankow government, and second it was an effort—undoubtedly with Soviet encouragement—to undermine the Hallstein Doctrine.* The Egyptians also ex-

* The Hallstein Doctrine, named for a Permanent Head of the West German Foreign Office, denied Bonn's diplomatic recognition to any state (with the exception of the Soviet Union) that recognized East Germany. It has proved to be a two-edged sword: Bonn could squeeze states wishing to recognize the Pankow government, but states could also squeeze Bonn by threatening the same recognition.

pressed their displeasure with the United States by burning down the Kennedy Memorial Library in Cairo.[5]

Bonn's reaction to Nasser's move was immediate. It announced on February 10, 1965, that its arms aid to Israel would cease forthwith. But the crisis did not end here. Once started it seemed to assume a motion and life all its own that no amount of back-tracking could halt. Nasser refused to cancel Ulbricht's proposed visit. Bonn, in retaliation, threatened to cut off economic aid to the UAR, which it eventually did when the Ulbricht visit came off as later planned in February.

Israeli leaders, in the meantime, were annoyed with Bonn's withdrawal of aid. Said Prime Minister Levi Eshkol in a speech before the Knesset, "No compensation or monetary substitute can exempt Germany from this duty" of supplying arms. To appease Israel, Bonn proposed an exchange of ambassadors which culminated in the establishment of full diplomatic relations in May. As a result of this action, ten Arab states promptly broke diplomatic relations with West Germany; at this writing none of them have been resumed. So far, the same ten have not recognized East Germany. It is believed that this action is being held as a threat against Bonn in the event it ever again sends arms to Israel.

France, in the meantime, sensing an opportunity, announced in early March that it would resume arms sales to Arab countries for the first time in ten years. French officials also stressed that this new tack would not change France's long-term arms aid program to Israel (but the 1967 war was to change their minds).[6]

The U.S. government, the cause of this disruption, was eventually forced to assume the task of supplying Israel, the one thing it did not want to do. For a full year, from February 1965 to February 1966, it was done secretly. At the same time the United States was openly supplying surplus *Patton* tanks to Jordan. Though this made little sense, Washington then announced in May 1966 that it agreed to sell Israel a small number of tactical jet bombers "as a deterrent against the numerically superior air power of the Arab nations." Then, with equal inscrutability, the U.S. government announced in December 1966 that it would soon send several million dollars' worth of arms to Jordan, as *The New York*

Times announced, "to bolster her against Israel." All this equipment (plus that of Great Britain, France, Czechoslovakia, the Soviet Union and Sweden) was to be used six months later in June 1967.[7]

The force-feeding of West Germany by the United States was to have an even greater impact on domestic German affairs than on her external affairs. As long as West Germany's economy maintained its vigorous pace, there was little difficulty in meeting the $1.3 billion biennial arms bill from Washington. But by 1966 Germany's economic boom began to show signs of strain. Industrial investments were in decline, the stock market slumped, unemployment rose, and living costs began to soar. By June of that year Bonn had fallen more than $600 million in arrears in its pledge to buy arms.

In the previous month, on May 13, Secretary McNamara, in an unprecedented and blunt note, told West German Defense Minister von Hassel that henceforth the United States would reserve the right to reduce its forces in Germany "proportionately" should Bonn's purchases of American arms fail to offset troop costs. This announcement followed shortly after McNamara had ordered 15,000 American troops in Germany to Vietnam without consulting with Bonn. The German government vainly protested, to Secretary Rusk, both the note and the troop transfers.[8]

The mood in German government circles at this time was one of retrenchment. The Germans were prepared to honor their agreement with Washington but sought to purchase space equipment or other goods in place of arms which were of no productive value and which they claimed they did not need. A cartoon in the German newspaper, *Die Welt,* expressed local sentiment best: it showed McNamara as a quartermaster sergeant loading down a German soldier with five rifles, five helmets and four packs. With a money box in one hand and putting yet another helmet on the soldier's head, McNamara is saying, "It fits! It fits! It fits! Pay me! Pay me! Pay me!"[9]

McNamara, faced with his own problems in Vietnam and with the dollar drain, was in no mood to compromise. He insisted that Bonn carry out the agreement as originally drawn up by buying arms and not other equipment. Bonn at first appeared to capitulate to the demand, but later in the summer, with more doubts being raised on the wisdom of such an arrangement, it became clear that Germany faced a prospective budget deficit for 1967 of a billion dollars. Few Germans saw the efficacy of buying arms it did not need with money it did not have. The German Constitution also forbids deficit budgets.

The crisis was serious enough to force Chancellor Erhard to come to Washington in September in an effort to seek some form of relief. He was given no comfort by President Johnson or Secretaries Rusk and McNamara. Erhard had no choice upon returning home but to propose a tax increase to cover the budget deficit. This was the note on which the Free Democratic Party ministers in Erhard's coalition cabinet decided to withdraw their support of the government. Thus Erhard's government fell, ostensibly on the issue of a tax increase, but in large measure over the force-feeding of arms to the country by the United States.

The creation of a new coalition government under the leadership of Kurt Georg Kiesinger marked the end of the American era in Germany. It may have been inevitable, but it was brought about with particular insensitivity on the part of America's leaders. The single-minded insistence of Washington in demanding that its arms sales policy be promoted ruthlessly in the face of other more important considerations was the spark that led to this change. Bonn, in spite of it all, still is willing to offset U.S. troop costs; it agreed in 1967 to purchase $500 million worth of medium-term Treasury securities in place of unwanted arms; the next year it agreed to purchase $625 million in bonds and $100 in military equipment. It is a mark of Washington's inflexibility in its arms sales policy that it first took the fall of a pro-U.S. government before U.S. officials considered changing their policy.

Several other instances of arms sales "to promote the defensive strength of our allies" are worth noting. There is the case of the proposed sale of *Skybolt* missiles to Great Britain. The story is an exceedingly complicated one that has been told many times; it need only be highlighted here.

In 1960 President Eisenhower and Prime Minister Macmillan agreed at a Camp David meeting that the United States would provide Great Britain with *Skybolt* missiles; the United States was to pay all research and development costs, and Britain was to pay only for the operational missiles she required. At that time the missile was still in the blueprint stage.

Skybolt was conceived as a bomber-launched air-to-surface ballistics missile capable of carrying nuclear warheads. Although extremely intricate and completely untested, the missile appealed to Macmillan because he saw it as a means of maintaining the "independence" of Britain's deterrent; he realized that it would prolong the life of Britain's V-bomber force and would, at the same time, obviate the necessity to transfer funds to a *Polaris*-type submarine building program. In the face of stiff opposition from the Labour party, Macmillan succeeded in selling the idea of this weapon to the British public.

When he took over the Defense Department in 1961, McNamara decided, despite cautions from some quarters, to allow the program to go ahead. But by 1962, after considerable money had been spent and with very little progress to show for it, McNamara came to the conclusion that further investment in *Skybolt* would be a mistake. On November 7, 1962, McNamara officially recommended cancellation of the program.[10]

Apparently very little thought was given in Washington to the possible British reaction. McNamara claims that he had previously intimated to Macmillan his intention to cancel *Skybolt,* but he appears not to have made himself clear at the time. A crisis of confidence in the Macmillan government arose immediately following McNamara's announcement. Because of its relative decline as a world power, Britain was particularly sensitive to the fact that its nuclear "independence" rested upon a foreign missile system over the supply of which it had very little control. When *Skybolt* was cancelled, the British were rudely reminded of their relative political and military impotence; their claim as a world power—as a nation that sat at the high table—lay shattered in an American bureaucratic decision based not on consideration for its allies but on negative cost-effectiveness studies. It also meant that until

Britain developed some other "independent" deterrent, which conceivably could be four or five years later, the country lay nearly helpless in the atomic arena.

At Nassau, Macmillan, faced with this *fait accompli,* was able to salvage some of his own and his country's prestige by getting the United States to agree to supply *Polaris* missiles (less warheads) for a soon-to-be-built British nuclear submarine fleet. So the cancellation of *Skybolt* forced Britain to do the one thing it did not want to do: scrap its V-bomber force and transfer the money to an expensive shipbuilding program.

Today, Great Britain has an "independent" deterrent, but it was acquired at heavy costs in other areas. For instance, the affair seriously damaged the "special relationship" between the United States and Great Britain. To the Europeanists in the U.S. government—those who talk of a Grand Design incorporating the political, economic and social activities of all western European countries, including Britain, into a single, powerful world force—the disintegration of such a relationship was and is long overdue. This may be true, but on the other hand the Europeanists can find no solace in it because it did not move Britain any closer to becoming integrated into Europe. Britain's dependence on *Skybolt* and then *Polaris* convinced France that Britain's loyalty lay primarily to America and not to Europe. Thus the *Skybolt* affair was a contributing factor in De Gaulle's veto of British membership in the Common Market.

There is no question, too, that the British embarrassment over their claims of an independent deterrent had much to do with encouraging Macmillan to resign from office in the fall of 1963.

In 1967, after several years of negotiations, Britain decided to buy fifty variable-geometry (or swing-wing) F-111 fighter-bombers from the United States. The sales price was approximately one billion dollars to be paid over a twelve-year period, with first delivery guaranteed by 1970. Secretary McNamara, along with Henry Kuss and his office, agreed with their British counterparts that Great Britain would be exporting 240 million pounds (then worth $672 million) worth of arms by 1977 to meet the dollar cost of the F-111 deal. Part of this offset arrangement included the understanding that the United States would buy at least $325 million in arms from the United Kingdom.

Britain agreed to the deal because it still had ambitions east of Suez, because the F-111 was cheaper than the untried TSR-2 (developed by the British Aircraft Corporation), and because the arrangement, involving the production of many component parts in Britain, would help to keep Britain's aeronautical engineering industry, among others, alive.

However, events were to alter radically the original assumption that this arms sale was really promoting the defensive strength of America's closest ally. Part of the offset agreement included an understanding that the United States would allow British companies to tender on equal terms with American companies (i.e., without having to overcome the 50-percent-or-less price difference required by the Buy American Act) for sixteen wooden-hulled minesweepers worth approximately $80 million. But in September 1967, John W. Byrnes, Republican congressman from a shipbuilding district in Wisconsin, introduced an amendment to a defense appropriations bill which proposed that all U.S. naval vessels be built in U.S. yards. The amendment was accepted by both the House and Senate and eventually passed into law.

The British were understandably annoyed with this development. It was pointed out in a number of newspapers that Britain's obligation to buy F-111's was subject to a binding contract, while the United States' obligation to buy minesweepers from the United Kingdom was the result of a series of ministerial understandings. "It is not clear," stated a London *Times* editorial with some bitterness, "why Britain should sign contracts while the United States only agrees to understandings."[11]

The British also complained that such a capricious act as the Byrnes Amendment makes it extremely difficult for Britain ever again to accept the word of a Defense Secretary or an arms salesman. McNamara's waiving of the Buy American Act for Britain, only to have the barrier re-erected by Congress, underscored the belief held by many Britons that the United States would ride roughshod over anyone—friend or enemy—who threatened the interests of American industry. "The spirit of the offset agreement," continued *The Times,* "has been broken in Washington to an extent that must jeopardize British confidence in the future of artificial arrangements of this kind."[12]

United States officials gave numerous assurances to the British that, despite the ban, the overall F-111 offset deal would still continue. Yet, somehow nothing too specific was offered to replace the minesweeper contract. Nevertheless, Britain retained the F-111 order for the moment because other offset arrangements tied into the sale were so complicated that they were impossible to unscramble. In other words, all the other offset agreements that Kuss and his men had made with their British counterparts were so intricate that it was considered better to let them run their course—good or bad as they might be—than to stop or redirect them, because of the financial penalties involved and the ruffled feelings such a move would provoke. Thus, this arms sale, like political crises, created its own motion that, once initiated, was impossible to stop.

In spite of U.S. efforts, Britain was forced for several reasons to cancel its F-111 order in January 1968. Primarily, costs had more than doubled since the earliest estimates, and Britain had less need for the planes in the wake of its decision to retreat back from east of Suez; second, the F-111 system, up until cancellation (and indeed beyond), had proved a most contrary piece of machinery, and many people voiced doubts as to the craft's ultimate worth; and third, Prime Minister Wilson wanted to ensure that his devaluation of the pound in late 1967 would work, and the only way he believed he could do it was to cut back drastically on his military expenditures. The fifty F-111's were at the top of his list to go.

What, then, are some of the visible results of this abortive transaction? It certainly did not cement any economic or military friendships; nor did it do much to promote the concept of cooperative logistics. By encouraging Great Britain to undertake such a financial burden, it led to the devaluation of the pound and a stepped-up retreat from its worldwide responsibilities. Although there are those who argue that both the devaluation and the retreat were long overdue and that they will ultimately benefit the country, it is not in the United States' interests either to weaken an ally financially or to promote the creation of power vacuums that may ultimately have to be filled by an American military presence. Thus it can be argued that, in reality, the F-111 "sale" not only promoted both the military and financial weakness of Great Britain but increased American military weakness as well by stretching American military commitments.

2

Promoting the defensive strength of our allies often leads to arms races and sometimes to war. The Pakistan-India clash of 1965 in Kashmir is an example.

Pakistan, for many years a staunch U.S. ally, first began receiving U.S. military aid in 1954; the amount of equipment supplied over the succeeding years has totaled approximately $730 million, although there is no way to verify this figure from U.S. government statistics, since Pakistan is one country for which Washington releases no military aid figures. Nevertheless, reliable independent sources show that by 1965 Pakistan had a military strength of 253,000 men who were armed in large part with U.S. equipment such as M-47 tanks, F-104 and F-86 jets, T-33 trainers used as reconnaissance aircraft and C-130B transports. Most of the small arms were American in origin. At the outbreak of the conflict in 1965 the dominant influence in the Pakistani military establishment was overwhelmingly American.[13]

India since World War II had been more eclectic in its military tastes. Before 1962 its military establishment was relatively small and ill-equipped, its material coming primarily from Great Britain and France. In October 1962, however, there were limited Red Chinese attacks on India's Himalayan frontier in which Indian troops were outmaneuvered and outgunned. Indian forces were immediately bolstered by arms supplied by Britain, France, Australia, Belgium, Canada, Japan, the Soviet Union and the United States.

With American guns being rushed in to aid the Indians, Pakistan became increasingly concerned over the eventual use of the arms. Its press, particularly after the Chinese attacks had ceased, grew hysterically anti-American and anti-Indian. Some quarters in Karachi argued that the Chinese border attacks were an Indian hoax designed to obtain U.S. arms for use against Pakistan. It made no difference to the Pakistanis that U.S. arms aid to India was relatively small—$83 million between October 1962 and September 1965, or one ninth of all U.S. arms aid to Pakistan—compared to the value of arms given or sold to India by all the other suppliers; Karachi was frightened of what New Delhi would do with the American equipment and took countermeasures of its own. It built up its forces in Kashmir and throughout 1963 and 1964 repeatedly provoked skirmishes with India along the cease-fire line. All this culminated in the war that broke out in early September 1965. Here, then, is a good example of U.S. arms aid, originally given to stop one war, being instrumental in beginning the next one.

When the Pakistan-India War broke out, the world was presented with the curious spectacle of Pakistanis in American *Patton* tanks fighting Indians in American *Sherman* tanks, and Pakistanis being transported to the front in C-130B *Hercules* to fight Indians who had been transported to the front in both C-119's and C-47's, all American built.*

An arms embargo was laid upon the two antagonists by the major suppliers and was instrumental in bringing the war to a speedy halt. Because the United States was its main supplier, Pakistan suffered most by the cutoff in arms. India, on the other hand, while adversely affected by the embargo during the actual fighting, was soon after the cease-fire receiving additional equipment from Britain and the Soviet Union—countries that lifted their embargoes the moment the firing stopped. The United States, however, maintained a total embargo on both countries until February 1966 when the suspension was lifted to allow the purchase of "nonlethal spare parts and end items."[14]

Pakistan, already angered by Washington's aid to India, once

* This is not to imply that other nations' equipment was not used. French, British and Soviet arms were also conspicuous by their presence.

again became frightened, this time by the continued Indian buildup between September 1965 and February 1966 when, at the same time, its own military establishment, mauled by its neighbor in the war, was not being equipped by its major supplier. Ayub Khan, Pakistan's Prime Minister, realized that, like India, his country could not afford to rely upon one supplier alone, no matter how close an ally the United States might be. So he turned to other sources, first the Chinese Communists and, two years later, in 1968, the Soviet Union. Pakistan was eventually to receive some obsolescent MiG-19's, Chinese-made T-59 tanks and some other unspecified Soviet equipment, all of which are still part of Pakistan's military arsenal today.

One previously unknown aspect of the arms sales to emerge from the war was the existence of a loophole in both the U.S. and British aid pacts which, in effect, did not tie India specifically to using the weapons solely against Chinese aggression, as the two suppliers had wished. India, therefore, felt free to use them against the Pakistanis and never made excuses for doing so.[15]

The resumption of "nonlethal" sales to the two countries in February 1966 by the United States re-emphasized the fact that selling such spares is a subterfuge designed to calm public opinion. Everyone in the arms business knows that nonlethal items—gasoline, tires, spare engines, radios, electronic gear, and so on—activate the lethal items—guns, bombs, tanks, missiles and jets. Apparently Washington, among others, does not believe that outsiders realize this.

The resumption of nonlethal sales in this case once again brought home the fact that an embargo denies the donor country any significant influence over the recipient country. Townsend Hoopes touched the quick of the problem when he told a Senate subcommittee in 1967, "A further reason for the policy shift [allowing nonlethal sales] was a growing awareness that, with the passage of time, a policy of total arms suspension was dissipating our influence and producing side effects of serious concern. All these developments are destabilizing and their cumulative effect could produce an uncontrolled arms race which no one wanted or intended. They clearly run counter to both United States and

Indian interests in the subcontinent. Yet a U.S. policy of total arms suspension made it increasingly difficult for U.S. diplomacy to cope with [those developments]."[16] This is perhaps the closest that any American bureaucrat has come to admitting that to control arms races one must sell arms.

In March 1968 the United States quietly approved the resumption of "lethal" arms sales to Pakistan. Typically, it was done in an oblique manner so as not to arouse the ire of ILN critics. The arrangement, still not completed at this writing, calls for a consortium of Italian firms to provide Pakistan with 100 refurbished *Sherman* tanks that had originally seen service in the West German army. The entire sale will cost Pakistan from $3 million to $4 million.[17]

Former U.S. Ambassador to India, John Kenneth Galbraith, entertains no doubts as to the cause of the 1965 war. "The arms we supplied under this policy," he said, "caused, and I underline the word, the war . . . between India and Pakistan. I do not pass on the merits of the Kashmir dispute or the rights of Pakistan in this regard. I have a great deal of sympathy with the position of Pakistan in this dispute. But if we had not supplied arms, Pakistan would not have sought the one thing we wanted above all to avoid; namely a military solution."[18]

The results of that war find Pakistan today more of a neutral, less of a staunch American ally. India, always neutral, is just as much so today, yet is far more willing to accept Soviet and Chinese aid than it was before the war. The conflict also led India to seriously consider manufacturing atomic weapons in order to maintain its superiority over its enemy. Both nations still maintain large and expensive military establishments, both receive their arms from a variety of sources, and both still hate each other with as much passion as they did in 1965 and before. Thus not too much has changed, not counting the destruction wrought, except that throughout it all the United States half lost an ally—and largely because of its arms sales policy.

The most frustrating of arms races, from the U.S. point of view, is the one in the Middle East. It is complicated by the fact that it is not just a race between two antagonists but a race among at least ten competing groups. There is, first of all, what might be called an "influence race" between the United States and the Soviet Union. Then there is an arms race between the radical Arab states—Egypt, Syria, Iraq and Algeria—and the conservatives—Saudi Arabia, Jordan, Morocco, Tunisia and Iran. There is, of course, the major arms race between Israel and all Arab states. There is also a race in the area between the Moscow and Peking factions of the communist world. And finally there is an arms sales race among various arms-manufacturing Western nations.

What makes the situation so explosive is not only the existence of old antagonisms among the many countries, the nationalistic ambitions, the grinding poverty, the corruption and the Arab capacity for almost unlimited self-delusion, but the fact that virtually all the weapons of war used by these nations (with the exception of a few minor items) are imported into the area. Middle Eastern countries have almost no capacity to produce their own weapons; thus their ability to fight a war is dependent on outside suppliers. All these factors, plus a seemingly insatiable appetite for weapons, have created a highly unstable situation.

Prior to 1955 the United States, Great Britain and France, acting in consort, were able to maintain something like a military balance among various hostile groups, particularly between Israel and her Arab neighbors. But in 1955 the Soviet Union entered the picture when it sold a large quantity of arms to Egypt. Ever since then the arms race in the area has become increasingly more difficult to control. The United States has been in the unenviable position of possessing the ultimate regional deterrent in its Sixth Fleet while at the same time watching almost helplessly as the Arabs and Israelis armed to the teeth.

United States policy for many years has been to stabilize the area, to balance the military power of one group against another. It has been, in retrospect, a reactive rather than creative policy. Thus when the Soviets began upgrading Egypt's arsenal, the United States sought a balance with aid to Israel, Jordan, Saudi Arabia, Iran and other countries. Likewise, when Egypt went to the aid of the Yemeni Republicans, the United States quietly encouraged Faisal of Saudi Arabia to provide aid to the Royalists.

When the Israeli Air Force upgraded its inventory with modern French jets, the United States sought a balance by providing F-104's (in this case via Taiwan), *Hawk* missiles and A-4 *Skyhawks* to Jordan and (with Great Britain) missiles and jets to Saudi Arabia. When the balance between Algeria and Morocco—at odds over their common border—shifted in favor of Algeria, owing to large arms shipments from Czechoslovakia and the Soviet Union, the United States moved to counter the disparity with additional arms to Morocco.

The Middle Eastern arms race has been complicated by other factors. The extraordinary demand for arms encouraged other nations to enter the market. Besides the United States, Great Britain, France, the Soviet Union and Czechoslovakia, such nations as Belgium, Sweden, Italy, Switzerland, Poland, Bulgaria, Japan and both Chinas have plunged in. West Germany, as noted, was once anxious to take part. On top of this are the independent arms dealers, many of whom have long believed that the Middle East is their own private market.

In addition, every major power that wishes to exert influence in the Middle East is subject to blackmail. Blackmail is a tool used by nearly every noncommunist country seeking arms from Western sources, but it is used most blatantly by Middle Eastern countries against the United States. There is also some indication that the Soviet Union, now with its own stake in the area, is likewise subjected to it. With nations seeking Western arms, the blackmail usually begins with a story in the press or diplomatic circles that such-and-such a country is thinking of acquiring Soviet arms. A short while later representatives of this particular country will go to Washington to negotiate directly for the desired items. By this time the Pentagon and the State Department have been sufficiently softened up by the possibility of their influence being replaced by the Soviets' that they are willing to listen to the plea. A large quantity of arms is demanded; the State Department and Pentagon whittle it down; a bargain is struck and both groups part happy—the U.S. government because it got off cheaply and did not throw the balance too far out of kilter, the purchaser because it acquired the weapons it actually sought from the beginning.

A case in point is Iran. In July 1966, articles appeared in the press indicating that Iran was considering buying Soviet missiles, ostensibly to defend the Persian Gulf against Egyptian aircraft. Two months later it was reported that the Shah had been dissuaded by U.S. officials from this course and that in place of the missiles the United States would supply a squadron of F-4 *Phantoms*. The seriousness with which the United States viewed the Iranian request for Soviet arms is attested by the fact that the subsequent F-4 agreement was made when these planes—the mainstay of U.S. air power—were in exceedingly short supply in Vietnam. The crowning irony was that Iran, in February 1967, announced in spite of the F-4 sale that it had signed a pact with the Soviet Union for the purchase of $110 million worth of other arms and equipment.[19]

Another case is Morocco. King Hassan II in late 1966 let it be known that he needed approximately $100 million worth of arms to offset large Algerian acquisitions of Soviet weapons. The hint was given that if the United States did not provide the arms, Morocco would go elsewhere. In February 1967 the King, accompanied by an entourage of 136 people, arrived in Washington for consultations with government officials. A week later he returned to Rabat with a pledge of $15 million worth of U.S. arms on the condition that they not be used in Morocco's border and territorial disputes with Algeria, Mauritania or Spain. Officials in the Pentagon and the State Department were visibly pleased with the deal because they had gotten off relatively cheaply. Morocco (so it seemed) was still firmly pro-West, Algeria had not been sufficiently alarmed to appeal for even more arms from Moscow, and French and Spanish suspicions of U.S. intentions in Morocco were not aroused. But Morocco acquired the arms it wanted, and as a result, the entire Middle Eastern arms level was raised one more notch. Like Iran, Morocco's purchases in the United States did not stop Hassan three months later from buying one million dollars worth of replacement parts from Moscow to reactivate a quantity of Soviet equipment it owned.[20]

Jordan is still another example. After the 1967 war with Israel, King Hussein, angered not only by his loss of territories but by the knowledge that his Western friends sympathized with the Israeli cause, felt obliged to seek military and economic aid from the

Soviet Union. Hussein, following four days of consultation in Moscow in October 1967, came away with vague offers of Soviet help. It is clear that Hussein's apparent rapprochement with the Soviets was intended primarily to persuade his traditional suppliers, Great Britain and the United States, to renew their arms shipments. The King's actions undoubtedly were a contributing factor in influencing the United States to lift its Middle Eastern embargo in February 1968, for very shortly thereafter the United States was sending F-104 *Starfighter* jets, M-48 *Patton* tanks, 105 mm and 155 mm guns, jeep-mounted antitank weapons and other arms to the kingdom. Much of this equipment has been used in the sporadic border clashes between Israel and Jordan that have continued ever since the end of the 1967 war.[21]

One of the major weaknesses of U.S. policy in the Middle East is what appears to be an unconscious desire to be everyone's friend, a clearly impossible task in such an explosive area. To satisfy both Arabs and Jews, for instance, the United States long ago deemed it wise to split its arms policy in two: first to give diplomatic recognition to Israel but at the same time not to sell it arms and, second, to sell arms to Arab states on a cautious case-by-case basis. This presumably would please everyone: Arabs because they could buy U.S. arms and feel assured that none were going to Israel, and Zionists because, unlike Arab states, the United States recognized and gave moral support to Israel.

But this policy has not pleased anyone. Although the United States would not supply arms to Israel, it encouraged its allies to fill the void. (France was to take best advantage of this policy, and it explains why the Israeli Air Force was at one time composed almost entirely of French aircraft.) However, this often produced results the exact opposite desired. The United States was forced, for instance, to step in and supply arms openly to Israel when West Germany's back-door aid program collapsed. The United States was also forced to supply arms to Israel when France, following the 1967 war, switched its allegiance for political reasons from Israel to Arab nations. At the same time the United States was forced to step up its supplies to certain Arab states. Such an ambivalent policy creates more enemies than it does friends.[22]

The desire to balance the forces of opposing factions has led over the years to a progressive upgrading of the balance. During the days of Partition in the late 1940's, the balance of arms between Arab and Jew consisted of the most basic military weapons: rifles, pistols, grenades, prop-driven planes. This was maintained until 1955 when the Soviets first sent arms to Egypt. Soon the balance was upgraded to include jet fighters, tanks, submarines and patrol boats. Then, in the late 1950's and running into the early 1960's, both Arabs and Israelis upgraded their arsenals to include even more modern arms—all the while any disparity in destructive power being "balanced" by U.S. arms—until by the time of the 1967 war each side had missiles, offensive bombers, the most sophisticated jet interceptors, and the most advanced weaponry. This is a far cry from the balance maintained in the late 1940's and is due largely to the United States' desire for balance with what appears to be little regard for the level of that balance.

The Egyptians, who reportedly lost approximately one billion dollars worth of Soviet-supplied equipment during the Six-Day War, were quickly resupplied by their benefactors with even more modern equipment. So, too, were other Arab nations resupplied, much of this material coming from Western sources. Israel has likewise increased its military materiel far beyond what it had at the outset of the 1967 war, its main military benefactor now being the United States. So today, after a bitter war—the third of its kind in twenty years—all the opposing groups are armed to the teeth, better than they ever had been before. All the ingredients for war are there: poverty, hatred, irresponsible leaders, lack of controls, big power inertia and, above all, swollen military establishments. If there is ever to be a resumption in large-scale worldwide warfare, chances are that it will start in the Middle East. But as several officials in the U.S. government pointed out to me, for the moment there is "peace" because there is a balance.

The policy of promoting "the defensive strength of our allies" has also led to a continuing arms race in Latin America. In October 1965 the United States agreed to sell fifty A-4B *Skyhawk* attack jets to Argentina. Because of the demands of the Vietnam

War, this order was soon reduced to twenty-five jets. The sale, even though reduced, prompted Chile, which has long considered Argentina a threat, to begin negotiations for more advanced aircraft. The United States offered the Santiago government sixteen A-4B's and sixteen F-86's, the latter of Korean War vintage, for $5.5 million, but the Chileans wanted the faster F-5 *Freedomfighter.* The United States was at that point not prepared publicly to sell F-5's to Latin American countries, so the offer was rejected. Chile then turned to European sources and in October 1966 announced that it planned to purchase twenty-one British Hawker *Hunter* jets for $20 million.

This sale in turn prompted Peru, which has a border dispute with Chile, to seek newer equipment for its own air force. Reluctantly the United States agreed to supply some F-86's, but the sale bogged down in early 1967 owing to Peru's severe economic troubles, which forced a devaluation of her currency. For this reason the United States also blocked in August 1967 a British sale of six *Canberra* jet bombers to Peru for $2.5 million. Undeterred, Peru went to France and agreed to purchase twelve *Mirage V* fighter-bombers—one of the most advanced jets in the world at the time—for approximately $20 million.

The arms race soon spread to other countries. Venezuela bought seventy-four F-86's from the Interarms-Merex combine, and Brazil expressed an interest in purchasing a hundred French jets belonging to the Luftwaffe. In the meantime, the United States had agreed to sell fifty M-41 tanks to Argentina but stopped the sale when the military junta seized power in mid-1966. Argentina then bought fifty new French AMX-30 tanks for $200,000 apiece. All this activity by European competitors, particularly France, prompted the United States to change its policy against supplying Latin American countries with the most sophisticated supersonic jet aircraft. Henceforth, it announced in October 1967, F-5 *Freedomfighters* would be available for purchase.[23]

Until 1962 the primary purpose for extending military aid to Latin American countries was to strengthen the collective security of the Western Hemisphere. The concept of collective security dates back to ideas first articulated by Simon Bolivar in 1815 and was adopted in principle by all the American nations in 1936 as a direct result of Nazi-Fascist penetration into the area. The concept was subsequently reaffirmed on numerous occasions and was first formalized by the Rio Treaty in 1947.

Military aid from the United States, particularly after World War II, was also designed to contribute to the political stability of Latin nations, to counter British, French and German arms sales efforts, to coordinate hemispheric military efforts, and to augment U.S. influence over the training and supply of the various military forces. This entire policy rested on the assumption that Latin America was threatened by communist aggression both from without and from within.[24]

Critics have been quick to point out that the United States has failed in these objectives. They say, with considerable truth, that U.S. arms entrench the military in power, stifle reform and divert money from badly needed economic and social programs into wasteful military ones. An area that has the world's highest birth rate, some of the world's worst poverty and some of the most archaic political and social institutions, they say, cannot afford to spend collectively, as it does, nearly two billion dollars a year on its military establishments, particularly since only one war of note has been fought in the area in the last fifty years. Although Latin American countries spend for military purposes a relatively small 12 percent on average of their entire budgets (versus roughly 40 percent for the United States and 25.6 percent for NATO countries), critics claim that that is no consolation, since their military expenditures, combined with approximately one billion dollars they receive each year in economic aid, exceeds what they spend yearly on public health and education together.[25]

This failure has deeply worried Washington. The creation of the Alliance for Progress was one manifestation of concern and was and still remains an attempt to divert interest from military matters to the economic sector.

The policy of encouraging Latin American nations to take a collective part in the hemisphere's security was changed in 1962 to an emphasis on internal security. The shift was prompted by three developments: Cuba's conversion into a communist state and the realization that the exportation of Castro's brand of revolution might cause serious internal problems in many Latin American countries; the realization in Washington that when it came to overall hemispheric defense the Latin military amounted to little; and the realization that the Soviet Union was not a direct threat to the area.

Such a shift implied that the tools needed to promote regional security would be changed to those needed to promote internal security. In place of jets, tanks and warships, the United States would, it was hoped, supply such antiguerrilla equipment as helicopters, spotter planes, jeeps, radios and light weapons. In large measure the United States was able to make this shift, but it has never been able to break away completely from supplying those expensive and complicated prestige weapons that none of these countries need.[26]

Moreover, the United States no longer even pretends that the prestige items are being sold for military reasons. Secretary McNamara acknowledged during congressional testimony in early 1966, for instance, that the sale of the twenty-five A-4B's to Argentina had been made for economic rather than military reasons to help offset the U.S. gold drain. Asked what relationship the sale had to the maintenance of internal security in Argentina, the Secretary replied, "The answer is nothing, absolutely nothing."[27]

Blackmail, as in other areas of the world, is another reason why these items are sold. Consider the statement that came from Peru's President Fernando Belaúnde Terry in 1966. Said he, "If the United States is not willing to sell us the planes we need, we will buy them from any other country willing to sell to us."[28] There are some bureaucrats in Washington who tremble at the thought that the United States might lose such a sale.

Because of its desire to maintain its influence with these nations, because it wants to keep European competitors out, and because of constant pressure from its own military equipment manufacturers, the U.S. government is often forced to succumb to this blackmail by selling its most advanced operational equipment. Sometimes, in order to get the business, prices are cut drastically and liberal credit terms are arranged. Often these sales are justified—as many of them were to me by government officials—on the grounds that *less foreign exchange is wasted* by the purchaser accepting the beneficial U.S. terms than would have been wasted had the country bought the arms from some European supplier whose products, because of the poorer terms offered, would have been more expensive.

Ex-ambassador Ralph Dungan is especially concerned by two aspects of the Latin American arms policy of the United States. First, he says, despite the fact that the emphasis has shifted to internal security, the U.S. military still continues to whet the appetites of Latin military leaders for useless equipment they cannot afford. The hunger for this equipment is sparked by joint U.S.–Latin American maneuvers—such as the yearly naval exercise called "Operation Unitas"; by exchange and educational programs between the U.S. military and its various counterparts below the border; and finally by the zeal with which the MAAG's distribute the operational manuals of the latest U.S. equipment available for sale. "All those fancy black boxes, antisubmarine warfare gear, and rocketry are displayed," said Dungan, "and the locals naturally want some of these toys. They see year by year they're slipping further behind. . . . The problem here is of whetting appetites and then saying, 'Sorry, we don't think you should have the material'; we also tell our allies they have a vital role to play and then we only give them part of the equipment to play it with."

Second, he said, questions are seldom raised in Washington over the effect a sale to one country will have on another. The sale of the twenty-five A-4B's to Argentina, he noted, is an excellent example of what can follow. "Each country," he said, referring to Chile, Argentina, Peru, Bolivia and Brazil in particular, "watches the others like a hawk," and what one country gets affects what all the others want.

The basic strength of the U.S. arms policy in Latin America is that, except for the ILN office and a group of other interested individuals, few officials see any long-term benefit in selling arms to the nations to the south. Congress, for instance, has put an $85 million yearly limit on arms sales and grants in the area. In 1967 Congress also amended the Foreign Aid Appropriations Bill to require a cut in economic assistance equal to the amount a developing nation spends on advanced weapons. (This is known as the Conte-Long Amendment.) Exactly who qualifies as a developing nation or what exactly qualifies as advanced weaponry has never been made clear. In any event, this provision was used in 1968 to halt all development aid loans to Peru in response to that impoverished country's insistence on carrying through with its plan to spend $20 million on French jets. The Peruvians were irate but, editorialized *The New York Times,* clearly reflecting official U.S. views, "it is unreasonable to expect United States taxpayers to underwrite, directly or indirectly, Peru's military whims." This cutoff of aid was done without any prior warning to Peruvian officials, and was intended to give other nations pause before they went off and bought arms with money they could not afford to waste.[29]

The weaknesses of the U.S. arms policy in Latin America lie, as elsewhere, in its implementation. Washington seems reluctant to draw up clear-cut policies and then stick to them. It seeks to channel the military into an internal security role; this it has done with some success. But at the same time it still entices nations with new military gear, it still sells them expensive and useless weaponry, and it still flatters their hemispheric ambitions. Furthermore, Washington is still not sufficiently prepared to say "No." The few times that it is firm, such as the above, appear to come after all the damage has been done.

3

The second of ILN's three major objectives—"to promote the concept of cooperative logistics with our allies"—was conceived, like the first, essentially with political and strategic goals in mind rather than political and economic ones. However, almost from the start, the economics of this objective have outweighed the strategic.

The desire to integrate allied defense purchases—known as

cooperative logistics—dates back to the days of offshore procurement and co-production in the 1950's, both of which emphasized the cooperative production of military goods. The idea of integrating purchases with production was first spelled out clearly by Secretary McNamara on May 30, 1965: he called for a common arms production market within NATO—a "Defense Common Market"—in which military hardware made by one member country would be available to all members at an agreed uniform price. The idea envisioned the maximum practicable degree of standardization of equipment, the elimination of duplication of scientific and productive effort, and the creation of closer military ties. What McNamara was actually asking, said IBM's Charles Shuff, was: since the United States had the largest free-world military production establishment, why not throw our allies' requirements in with ours so that they could get the benefit of a cheaper price? The U.S. government, he added, expressed its willingness to buy some of its requirements in foreign countries if our allies in return bought from or through us. Since so many NATO members were complaining of high defense costs, particularly of locally produced equipment, said Shuff, here was a way to buy more cheaply.

But persuading another nation to forego the manufacture of its own weapons in favor of foreign weapons, no matter how much cheaper, is no easy task. It meant that the buying governments had to sacrifice a certain amount of national prestige (such a desire is not, as is readily evident, confined to the ranks of the underdeveloped countries); it also meant that they had to face the outcries of their own manufacturers, labor unions and opposition politicians; and that they had to be prepared to be dependent upon a foreign nation for part of their defense needs.

It was hoped that Great Britain, which had been experiencing the greatest difficulties in the development, production and cost evaluation of its military equipment, would benefit most from the scheme. But from the start the plan has proved to be most disadvantageous to her. For instance, by encouraging Great Britain to scrap the development of its TSR-2 fighter-bomber for the American F-111, the United States effectively crippled British military airframe technology. By encouraging Britain to scrap its development of the Hawker Siddeley HS-861 STOL (Short Take-off and Landing) and P-1154 VTOL (Vertical Takeoff and Landing) airplanes for the American F-4 *Phantom,* the United States undercut British technological competence in these fields. The leadership as a result has shifted to the United States and West Germany. By cancelling its own *Blue Streak* missile in favor of *Skybolt,* Britain in effect gave up any lead it might have had in this area of the missile field.

British critics will point out that, in these three instances, it is probably better in the long run that Britain get out of the airframe, vertical and short takeoff, and missile development fields and stick to the technology where it has no peers, such as jet engine and ejection seat design and production. But, they add, by giving up certain technological experience—all in the name of "cooperative logistics"—it has received none in return. It did not even get, as British aerospace officials will heatedly and sometimes sarcastically point out, an operative system of weapons in exchange from the United States.

With West Germany, the United States' largest arms customer, the case was different because the Germans had no existing arms industry whose products needed to be "integrated" into a common manufacturing and purchasing plan. Any cooperative arms scheme implies a certain give and take between the partners: the United States, as it has insisted from the outset, doing most of the selling but on occasion buying items in return. Since West Germany had no arms industry of its own, the United States had to create one in order to make the Defense Common Market plan work. This it did through a series of bilateral arrangements (actually dating back as far as 1954) that encouraged West Germany to make its own arms. This encouragement was particularly intense following the birth of the Defense Common Market in 1965. Thus, today, West Germany is back in the arms manufacturing business, specifically in jet fighter aircraft, 20 mm cannons, light weapons, tanks and naval craft. There seems to be every indication that in the next decade West Germany will be manufacturing a full range of military equipment.

Some of the items bought by the United States in return for

heavy purchases from its own stock include Rolls Royce *Spey* engines for the U.S. Air Force A-7 attack jet, Martin Baker ejection seats and $75 million worth of 20 mm cannons (for the M-114 armored personnel carrier) made by the German firm of Rheinmetall.

Where direct purchases are not feasible, the United States will sometimes encourage joint ventures. A specific example is the U.S.–West German development of the MBT-70, or Main Battle Tank of the 1970's. This venture, incidentally, angered the British, who believe that their *Chieftain* tank, already developed and considered superior to anything in Western arsenals today, should have been the common NATO tank of the future.

Sometimes, in order to make cooperative logistics work with small NATO countries that have no products of interest to the United States, a licensing arrangement has been worked out for the production of U.S. equipment. For example, Canada, Spain and the Netherlands produce the F-5 *Freedomfighter* under license. There are a number of these types of arrangements in effect today, and they are examined more fully in Chapter VII.

Criticism of the Defense Common Market scheme—even though it is still suffering birth pangs—is extraordinarily heavy and comes mostly from European quarters. The most persistent and most valid is the belief that the United States, after all the oratory has been stripped away, is not prepared to be dependent on a foreign supplier for even a small percentage of its requirements. Conversations I had with State Department and Pentagon officials confirm this: they say that no world power can afford to be so dependent. These same officials will also add that the scheme was not conceived as an "even-Stephen switch," as one person put it, but as a way to cut costs, eliminate duplication and to give our allies, as Kuss likes to say, "the biggest bang for the buck."

Europeans, nevertheless, believe that the only reason the Defense Common Market has survived as long as it has has been due to emergency U.S. purchases for the Vietnam War. They cite, for example, 2.75 inch rocket ammunition purchased from Belgium, 105 mm artillery rounds from Italy and Japan, radio equipment from Denmark, Italy and Japan, 7.62 mm ammunition from

Australia, a variety of Korean-War-vintage bombs from West Germany, Greece, Holland, Norway, Belgium and Italy, 750 lb. fragmentation bombs from West Germany* and 20 mm Vulcan-type ammunition from Holland.† They say that once the war is over the U.S. interest in buying from abroad will evaporate.

Other criticisms abound. Europeans say that the U.S. effort to eliminate duplication of scientific research is actually a ploy to corner the world's scientific talent; they say that the desire to eliminate duplication of production effort is actually a means of destroying European competition; they say that the United States is asking its allies to produce individually only what they are technically competent to make, while the United States produces all of the same items in competition, thus ensuring that, because the U.S. production base is so large and because the production base of individual European countries is relatively so small, whatever competition remains is small and of no threat. They also say that standardization, while desirable, is an unrealistic goal. Finally they say that in practice the Defense Common Market program is a huge U.S. arms sales smokescreen designed to obscure the true U.S. motive: to milk the maximum amount of foreign exchange from its allies—and when there are complaints, to buy just enough in return to appease them.

Criticism in the United States centers on Pentagon indecision,

* Some 7,500 of these bombs were sold as surplus in 1964 to a West German firm for $1.70 each. Because of its needs in the Vietnam War, the U.S. government decided to buy back 5,500 of them in 1966 for $21 apiece. A Pentagon spokesman said that the goods were cheap at the price because new 750 lb. bombs would have cost the government $440 apiece.

† The United States placed a $22 million contract with the Dutch firm of Nederlandsche Wapenen Munitiefabriek for 20 mm ammunition in 1966. In such short supply was the U.S. Air Force in the Far East that the material was taken straight out of the NWM factory in Kruithoorn in U.S. Army trucks, loaded into military cargo jets and flown over the Pole to Vietnam. It was in use within 36 hours after it left the factory.

One European arms dealer of impeccable reputation told me that this $22 million contract infuriated U.S. Military Aid Program brass stationed in The Hague because, as indirect salesmen for ILN, their target goal for the year of $25 million sales to the Dutch (net above what the U.S. bought from Holland) had been upset, and not only would be difficult to explain to their superiors but would reflect poorly on their records.

contradictory conversations with allies, the splintering of authority, what appears to be a subconscious desire that the program fail, and congressional hostility (the Byrnes Amendment was one manifestation of this). More relevant, however, despite European fears to the contrary, is the criticism that the program is reviving needless arms industries in Europe. Thus, say the critics, the United States has created its own competition and has ensured that arms sales in the foreseeable future will become increasingly more difficult to control.

4

The third of ILN's three major arms sales objectives is "to offset the unfavorable balance of payments resulting from essential U.S. military deployment abroad." To everyone in the U.S. arms sales establishment, it is perfectly legitimate for the United States to sell arms strictly for monetary reasons, given the parlous state of the country's finances. By Kuss' reasoning, international trade is the " 'staff of life' of a peaceful world," and selling arms will help to achieve the peace. Kuss himself is proud of the fact that in the first six years of ILN's existence (1961 through 1966), he and his men reduced the gold drain by $6.1 billion; that is to say, while Defense Department expenditures abroad (not counting Vietnam) totaled $17 billion in those years, Kuss' arms sales receipts reduced it to slightly less than $11 billion.[30]

This third objective has resulted in considerable criticism of the ILN operation. One ILN claim, often voiced by Kuss, is that selling arms through its office has resulted in returning to Fort Knox the maximum amount in gold. Private arms manufacturers, among others, disagree. They say that if acquiring foreign exchange is the object of the exercise, then private industry could do a better job because it would sell its wares only at the true market price, not at reduced prices as they claim ILN has often done to secure sales. Kuss heatedly denied that ILN has sold below the market and added that, in fact, it was and still is against the law for it to do so. But what Kuss means by this is misleading because his market price is different from an ordinary market price. The

Defense Department is such a huge buyer of arms that the price it pays for an item is usually 10 to 20 percent lower than what someone else would pay on ordering independently a smaller quantity of the same item directly from the manufacturer. In other words, ILN can buy a million M-16 rifles cheaper from Colt Industries than Australia, for example, can buy 10,000. Thus if ILN sells M-16's to Australia they are bound to be cheaper. While ILN does add a Pentagon overhead factor to its sales price to foreign customers, it does not add a profit factor (as Colt would), which also allows it to sell that much more below the true market price.

Even if ILN has a slight price advantage with newly manufactured items, it has a decided price advantage when it sells second-hand items taken from U.S. military inventory. Here there is no market price: an F-80 jet that has seen fifteen years service with an Air National Guard unit can be sold for $1,000 or $15,000. ILN has considerable leeway in the price it sets, and usually it is a political price based on a country's ability to pay. Those members of American industry with whom I spoke were almost unanimous in their belief that ILN is not bringing back the maximum in gold; in fact, they say, it is selling the maximum amount of weapons for the minimum amount of gold.

An idealized view of the policy to balance the payments deficit through arms sales would have the United States, through the ILN office, sell weapons at the highest price to allies who would in turn pay immediately in dollars. The sale would be concluded at this point, with our allies possessing arms and the Treasury experiencing the maximum inflow of gold. But the policy does not operate in a vacuum. There are other countries that also have balance of payments problems, and which seek to correct them through arms sales. Other countries have no reserve pool of dollars to pay for the U.S. arms; others want to build up their own arms industries; others want to pay for arms with commodities. Whenever there is pressure from a customer, as there invariably is, to accommodate local problems, the United States is forced to seek some form of compromise in order to keep the business. Each compromise—whether it is called offshore procurement, co-production, a Defense Common Market, offset agreements or Country-X loans—inevitably cuts down on the amount of gold that ultimately flows back into the U.S. Treasury, since the purpose of the compromise is to ease the financial burdens of the recipients. In time these arrangements have become so complicated and so tied to the problems of a particular country that every year less and less gold is being returned to the United States in relation to the number of weapons being sold.

For example, Colt was denied permission to sell its .223 caliber M-16 rifles to Nationalist China. Had the sale gone through, there would have been a maximum inflow of gold into the Treasury, since Colt would have sold the rifles at the highest price. (Colt would also have paid more taxes into the Treasury as a result of higher earnings from the sale, which is a phenomenon not known to government enterprises.) However, ILN decided that, instead, Taiwan should be given the rights to produce the 7.62 mm M-14 rifle. The terms of the arrangement were most advantageous to the Nationalists. The result: Chiang's forces get the maximum number of weapons and the U.S., through license fees, gets only a minimum return in gold.

Another good example of how complicated it can become, and how little gold flows back to the Treasury, is the case of the M-113 Armored Personnel Carrier. The M-113 was developed by the Ordnance Division of the FMC Corporation and first went into production in 1960. In 1963, with Kuss' encouragement, FMC granted a co-production license to the Fiat, Lancia and OTO Melara companies to manufacture M-113's in Italy. It is a popular military vehicle and the Italian consortium subsequently has sold thousands of them—to Australia, Canada, Denmark, West Germany, Norway, Switzerland, and to its own military in Italy. The only gold coming back to the United States is in the form of license fees paid by the Italian companies to the FMC Corporation and several other component manufacturers. These fees are minuscule compared to the foreign exchange that would have been acquired had FMC made and sold the vehicles itself.

Despite its ineffectiveness, so strong is ILN's zeal to bring back gold that it often leads to a situation in which a country is sold not *too many* weapons or *too few* weapons but the *wrong* weapons. For instance, it is generally conceded now that it was a mistake to sell West Germany F-104G *Starfighters* (even though negotiations began before the creation of ILN), that the Luftwaffe needed a less sophisticated airplane at a time when its technical competence in aeronautics was so inadequate. Many also believe that the Northrop F-5 *Freedomfighter,* while being sold to U.S. allies as a first-line fighter, is actually by current standards a second-rate jet that could not possibly compete on equal terms with the best Soviet fighters. Although no one at Northrop will admit it, others say the F-5 was originally designed for the U.S. Air Force, but the stiff requirements were never met and the plane was soon being billed as a "combat aircraft designed specifically to meet the needs of foreign air arms rather than a specialized U.S. military requirement."[31] There are many knowledgeable authorities in the armaments business who say that the reason the F-5 is being sold abroad with such fervor is to keep the Northrop company in the airframe business in the event its technical knowledge is needed by the U.S. government at a later date.

The *Lightning-Hawk* sale to Saudi Arabia in 1965–66 is perhaps the best and most recent example of the wrong weapons being sold. In May 1965 McNamara offered a $100 million "package" of U.S. arms, including the F-5, *Hawk* missile, and radar and communications equipment. The British and French offered similar quantities of weapons. Throughout the summer of 1965 the three-way competition became fierce. Various combinations of weapons were proposed, parties haggled over prices and deliveries, and a considerable amount of money was used by all sides to influence the outcome. In November 1965 King Faisal settled on a Great Britain–U.S. package consisting of thirty-six English Electric *Lightning* interceptors and a quantity of Raytheon *Hawk* missiles and U.S. radar and communications equipment, all worth approximately $300 million. It was later revealed that the Saudis had been prepared to buy all of its military needs from the United States but that Kuss himself had interceded, suggesting that the sale be split with Great Britain. Kuss realized that London at that moment was annoyed with the United States for having cornered so much of the world's arms markets and that it needed a "victory" to appease the electorate at home. Kuss also knew that by giving the British this order he stood a better chance to land the F-111 order. His strategy worked, although events were eventually to nullify that deal.

But *Lightning* jets and *Hawk* missiles are inadequate to the tasks desired of them in Saudi Arabia. *Lightnings* are short-range jets designed to protect the relatively restricted United Kingdom airspace; the Saudis were convinced that these planes could protect an airspace over nine times as large, which they are obviously incapable of doing. *Lightnings* are also extremely complex machines that require expert maintenance crews, which the Saudis did not and still do not have. Nor do they have the pilots to fly them; in fact, the planes are still being flown by British mercenaries. *Hawks,* to compound the error, are surface-to-air defense missiles designed for close-in defense of static areas. Although carriage-mounted, they are not meant to be dragged long distances to the scene of the fighting such as would be the case in Saudi Arabia. It would have been far better had Saudi Arabia bought the longer-range and more easily maintained U.S. jets—the F-5 or even the F-104. Instead of *Hawks,* Faisal should have bought perhaps British or French air-to-air missiles. This type of equipment would have given the Saudis the range, versatility and flexibility that their air defenses require.

Selling arms for balance of payments reasons is clearly the least defensible of all the U.S.'s arms sales objectives. It is an attempt to apply a business objective—the maximization of profits—to a field of endeavor where the dividends paid upon the success of such a policy are not necessarily in cash. It might be justifiable to the stockholders of the Ford Motor Company, but the rationalization cannot be applied *ipso facto* to the stockholders in mankind.

Taken at its face value, the policy implies that the United States is more interested in dollars than it is in the control of arms or the maintenance of peace. It implies that what weapons are sold and how they might be used are of secondary importance.

It is, judging from results, a rationalization for selling weapons for truly unsavory reasons. If, for instance, the United States believes that it must, as the lesser of two evils, prop up a corrupt dictator with arms, it can justify the move for balance of payments reasons. It can trumpet the "good" aspects of bringing home gold and minimize the "bad" aspects of helping to maintain a dictator in power. It can, in the last analysis, justify virtually any arms sales—particularly to those areas or countries that least need them.

The United States is faced with several unresolved problems of major importance in the international arms trade. The first is the lack of any agreement with the Soviets. "As long as the Soviets stand free to do what they have done after the [1967] Israeli battle," such as re-equipping the defeated Egyptian forces, Kuss told me, "then we've got problems. So if I were living in a dream world I'd love to have an agreement with the Soviets on arms." This lack of agreement, he added, "puts you in a position that even if you deem yourself to be out [of the supply picture], you still haven't controlled world arms." Kuss believes that a U.S.–Soviet understanding would effectively control future sales and grants by Red China and the arms-producing nations in the West. "There won't be an agreement on *no* arms," he continued, "but there will be a control that means you can turn on the spigot and turn off the spigot when you think it's in the benefit of the political realities of the world."

Kuss is fully aware that it does not take much to start an arms race. "To create what sounds like an arms race," he told me, "it doesn't take a lot of weapons. You talk of 90 airplanes [going to Pakistan]; well, for God's sake, 90 airplanes is nothing. Somebody talks of 150 tanks going to Israel; it's a drop in the bucket, 150 tanks. [Red] China could do that any time it wanted, it could do it right now if it wanted to. And if it took the kind of policies a communist nation can take, where it can deprive itself of wheat to send it abroad for political purposes, it can deprive itself of weapons it's got and send them abroad. I think that's the most critical problem."

Another major problem is nationalism. "We still have people who desire to defend themselves," Kuss said. "We still have countries in the Middle East, for example, who say, 'Well, all great and swell for you to tell us that we don't have to be prepared to fight communism—in fact . . . we don't think we can fight 'em anyway if they come across the border—but we want an ability to [say] control the Persian Gulf situation. A couple of short, lightning-like attacks by a neighboı and we're out of the oil business. We want that minimum ability.' "

That minimum ability, continued Kuss, "leads a country like Saudi Arabia to buy 36 air defense fighter airplanes and some *Hawk* missiles. Nationalism leads them to do that. And it leads the Shah of Iran to do that. It leads Argentina to do that. It leads Brazil to do it."

Nationalism is such a strong force, he went on, that it turns many political leaders into avid buyers of weapons. It is a mistake, therefore, he said, for his American and western European critics to call him a "supersalesman." His job, he said, is to fend off the demands of foreign nations. "I haven't had, in fact, to take the lead on a single solitary [sale]," he told me. "Now once they make the move with us—once Belgium says, 'We'd like to negotiate F-5 aircraft,' and West Germany says, 'We'd like to negotiate helicopters,'—then it's my job to see what I can do to make the thing work. We help people buy; it sounds silly but that's literally what happens because it's strictly a follow-on from the kind of mutual security planning that was going on before. So it gets written up in the newspapers as a rather glamorous kind of operation; but in terms of a commercial [operation], it just isn't that at all." Essentially, he added, his job amounts to facilitating. "Now I'm a damn good facilitator," he told me. Few would deny that Kuss is a competent and honest civil servant, but there are many who would argue with his own assessment of his job. The problem, continued Kuss, is actually one of superpurchasers. "We sell to ministers, prime ministers and defense ministers and, believe me, they are superpurchasers. Now they don't want to tell everyone else about it, mind you," he added. As long as there remains this extraordinary demand for arms, he concluded, there will be no easy solution to controlling the world's arms trade.

All these problems put the ILN office in a dilemma. Its officials are charged with supplying an essential element to the military security of both the United States and its allies. Yet at the same time they must provide that security within the financial and legal limitations imposed upon them by Congress. In many cases it is not always possible. Sometimes the only way it can be done is through extraordinary twists in logic, by double-think and by unusually liberal interpretations of the rules. This central difficulty explains, perhaps more clearly than anything else, all that has gone before.

It also may be a hint of things to come.

VI

Competitive Governments

> *"He will ensure, within limits of Government policy, that as much military equipment is sold overseas as possible and also develop research to stimulate interest of potential buyers."*
>
> —Government Directive to Britain's first supersalesman of arms

1

The relative importance of the other major Western arms suppliers compared to the United States is that of a corner shop to a supermarket. Although reliable statistics are difficult if not impossible to obtain in many countries, it is estimated that Great Britain, the free world's second largest weapons supplier, currently maintains an annual arms sales volume in excess of $400 million. France, the third largest, maintains a slightly lesser volume but in recent years has been narrowing the gap.[1] The remaining free world suppliers—West Germany, Belgium, Sweden, Switzerland, Canada, Italy and Israel, among others—together maintain yearly arms sales of no more than $100 million. The annual U.S. effort is currently over twice as large as all of these combined.

Great Britain, in the years immediately following World War II, enjoyed some success in exporting its arms. Compared to its European allies, its weapons industry emerged from the war fairly well intact. Sales, particularly of jet aircraft, went mostly to captive markets: colonial regimes and Commonwealth countries.

The primary effort to export arms lay in the hands of private industry rather than with the bureaucrats in Whitehall.

In the early 1950's, however, sales began to fall off for a number of reasons. British foreign policy, first of all, was changing radically to adjust itself to a smaller role in the world. As its military aid began to shrink, its traditional customers turned to other suppliers. The country's lack of adequate financial resources and its inability to offer liberal credit terms also made it increasingly difficult to compete with the large U.S. aid effort. Britain found, furthermore, that it could not afford to give away material to the extent the United States was doing; and it watched helplessly as the massive U.S. grant aid effort stole away its traditional customers wholesale. In the mid-1950's other suppliers, specifically the Soviet Union and France, entered the market, thus further eroding Britain's position.

An example of the decline of Britain as an arms supplier is reflected in its aircraft sales to the Middle East and North Africa: before 1955 Great Britain supplied 95 percent of all the jets delivered to the area; since 1955 its percentage of the market has fallen to less than 10 percent. The same decline is reflected in its sales to Latin American countries. Between 1945 and 1955 it sold 255 jets in the area; in the following decade it sold only 108. United States sales, on the other hand, soared from 32 in the 1945–55 era to 323 in the 1955–65 decade.[2]

In addition, British defense policy from 1950 to 1957 was directed at the defense of the United Kingdom, leaving the defense of Europe to NATO. The weapons Britain manufactured, therefore, were designed to a narrow national requirement. As a result much of the equipment Britain wished to sell abroad did not have a wide appeal. Production runs of military equipment, furthermore, were relatively short (due to the cutback in its worldwide commitments) compared to runs in the United States; this had the effect of driving up a weapon's unit price and thus decreasing its competitiveness.

Britain did not begin to take corrective steps until 1958. A memorandum submitted by the Minister of Supply to the Select Committee on Estimates listed six reasons why the British government should sell and should assist private industry to sell military equipment abroad. It is the closest the country has come to defining its arms sales policy. The memorandum said that arms sales help to promote standardization among allies, that they help to recover the research and development costs incurred by the government, that they help to preserve the Royal Ordnance Factories, that they provide an outlet for surplus equipment, that they strengthen political and military ties, and that they bring into the country considerable earnings of foreign exchange.[3]

Having defined its policy objectives, however, nothing concrete was to follow until late 1965 when the Committee of Inquiry into the Aircraft Industry issued a report, known as the Plowden Report, which predicted that the world demand for military aircraft and missiles would be approximately $35 billion in the following decade.[4] It also went on to suggest that if Britain wished to sell arms abroad in a competitive fashion, it should reorganize its machinery for doing so in Whitehall and should appoint someone to look into the measures needed to be taken.

In anticipation of the report's publication, the Secretary of State for Defense, Denis Healey, in July 1965, appointed Sir Donald Stokes, managing director of Leyland-Triumph, as the British government's adviser on arms sales. Stokes was impressed by the U.S. arms sales machinery, namely the ILN office, and suggested that a British "supersalesman" be appointed and that he be given sufficient rank to reach the ears of Cabinet members. Thus, in January 1966, Healey announced the appointment of Raymond Brown, a dynamic, self-made businessman in the electronics field, as "Head of Defense Sales." Brown's first term was for two years at a relatively high—by British standards—government salary of $22,400 per annum.

The pressures to create such a position stemmed largely from the successes of the ILN office. There was considerable bitterness at U.S. arms sales methods, and Britons felt the need to defend themselves. The U.S. Embassy in London was fully aware of this bitterness, but apparently it escaped the attention of the men in ILN. When the Embassy in June 1965 sent a memo to the Defense Department outlining Britain's plans, it was received in the ILN office with mild astonishment. The memo was couched in terms that made it clear that such an appointment "would receive enthusiastic approval in Britain" and was designed to counter American "high-pressure salesmanship." One member of ILN sent a note to Henry Kuss: "Is the Embassy giving you the shaft?" he asked. "Personally," he continued, "I think it is a great compliment. You have shaken them [the British] up like nothing since Napoleon."

Raymond Brown undertook his job laboring under several misconceptions. He thought that his work entailed sitting at a bargaining table hammering out sales with the assistance of various clever financial tools. But, as he was quick to learn, the problem was not one of selling but of administration. The machinery in Whitehall was not geared to arms sales. As a short-term measure, Brown suggested that a "loss leader" program in small arms and ammunition be initiated in order to win back some of the foreign markets. He also suggested that a dual production scale—one for the British military, the other for foreign markets—be created.[5] These two suggestions were greeted with stony silence by Whitehall, and nothing further was heard of them. Whitehall, from the outset, was so hostile to an outsider coming in to redirect its efforts toward arms sales that Brown had very little time to sell arms. He had to spend all his time on administrative matters. In fact, not one significant arms sale during his first two-year term was due to his personal efforts.

Brown was faced with many prickly problems. One was a longtime cleavage in thinking between the Treasury, which wanted to promote arms sales for financial reasons, and the political administration, which generally opposed the sale of arms as inconsistent with the country's overall foreign policy objectives. There was also considerable confusion within the British bureaucracy over exactly which department determined what could be sold: was it the Minister of Technology, whose job it was to determine whether or not a weapons system was classified? Was it the Minister of Defense, who had to take into account the military repercussions? Was it the Treasury "Mandarins," who sought the maximum inflow of gold? Was it the Board of Trade, which issued export licenses? Was it the Foreign Office or even the Minister for Disarmament? Or did the decision devolve on the Prime Minister and him alone? No one, either in government or in industry, even knew to whom an arms export inquiry should be directed.

R. L. Nobbs, head of the Market Intelligence Unit of the British Aircraft Corporation's Guided Weapons Division, reflected at the time all of British industry's frustration with such a situation. He said, for example, that when BAC wished to sell supersonic aircraft to, say, Peru, every department even remotely concerned with the possible sale would deal with the problem separately. The Minister of Technology would perhaps clear the sale but pass it on to the Minister of Defense, who would give a conditional approval. The Foreign Office, next in line, would say, "No, such a sale would offend the Americans," and Treasury would follow with, "Yes, sell all you can." All of this, said Nobbs, would take a year before BAC received a reply. Usually the answer was so full of hedges that the sale would be lost. One standard government answer, for instance, was, "We do not know until the time arises," which was sufficiently obscure virtually to assure that both Peru and BAC lost interest. Another typical answer was, "Give us the contract then we, Whitehall, will approve or disapprove." This attitude made any concerted sales drive impossible to undertake with any hopes of success.

Brown was also plagued by an inordinate amount of government secrecy, a situation by no means unique to him. Whitehall made it a practice to divulge no information on the export of military weapons.[6] Thus Brown had no way to estimate future targets; nor did Parliament itself have the information necessary to pass laws either to augment or to restrict arms sales. Nevertheless, the flow of information has increased somewhat, most of it due to the personal efforts of Brown.

If industry's efforts to sell abroad were stifled by muddled thinking and obscure chains of authority in Whitehall, they were further hindered by a special segment of the government bureaucracy—namely, the Ordnance Factories and the Research & Development Establishments.

These organizations, all government-owned and -financed, have mushroomed in both number and size since the end of World War II, until today there are several hundred of them. Some of the more famous ones are the Royal Small Arms Ordnance Factories, the Royal Radar Establishment, the Armaments Research & Development Establishment, and the Royal Aircraft Establishments. There are also those Establishments that concern themselves with, among other things, underwater weapons, surface weapons, fighting vehicles, missiles, gunnery, computers, biological warfare, and communications equipment. Instead of there being one such Establishment for all three military branches, there are usually separate and independent ones for each service. Some of them just design weapons; others design, test and actually manufacture weapons. Virtually none of them sell their wares in the accepted sense because they have a captive customer in the Ministry of Defense. Like all bureaucracies, each has its own specialized experience and each jealously guards its own interests. Each must constantly justify its existence by having as many of its own weapons adopted as possible, so that, in turn, more people can be hired, more money appropriated and larger programs undertaken.

Obviously these Establishments compete with private industry for military orders, a situation that is practically unknown in the United States. While the competition for domestic sales is clear, it is often not apparent why the Establishments and Factories have hindered the sale of weapons abroad. The reasons date back to the 1950's. At that time it was recognized that, because there were so few "off-the-shelf" weapons that appealed to foreign customers, it was necessary whenever a new weapon was designed to take into account not only domestic requirements but also foreign requirements, combining them both wherever possible. The plan was subsequently put into effect, and many major weapons since have been designed, not always successfully, for the two markets.

When Brown became Head of Defense Sales he found that no clear distinctions had been made between what new items were strictly for the British military, for the export market, or both. For example, the ill-fated TSR-2, a low-level supersonic attack bomber, was originally designed solely for a British requirement, but as costs mounted and worldwide commitments shrank, it suddenly became a product for export. The government hunted around desperately for customers. Particular pressure was put on the Australians, but to no avail; the plane did not meet its requirements. All the while there was considerable argument between the private and public sectors in Britain over who was to make the sales, who was responsible for design modifications, and how much each was to be reimbursed in the event of a sale.

Because even a privately financed weapons development program is usually today partly underwritten by a government grant, the Establishment with the greatest expertise in that particular field, while it may not be a party to the program, will still insist on having its say. Often this advice was welcomed by industry, but in most cases it proved to be a hindrance to the speedy development of a new weapon. The Establishments, bent on preserving their prerogatives, ofttimes delayed projects for many months out of sheer pettiness and jealousy. Sometimes, in their capacity as adviser to private industry, they would sit for a year or more on some newly developed weapon from the private sector until their own version of the weapon had passed its field tests; then they would blandly suggest to Whitehall that *their* version be sold abroad instead.

Colonel H. Lacy, a special director and military adviser to the British Aircraft Corporation, told me that when he was employed by Vickers he often attended meetings at which there were two company men and as many as forty civil servants from the various Establishments. Each one of the forty would say to the two Vickers men, "That won't work," or "We don't like the design," or some similar criticism of a new product. When Lacy would ask, "Well, will you write it down?" the forty would reply in chorus, "Oh, no, these are just our views."

This type of foot-dragging is indicative of the bitterness that exists between the private companies and the government-owned organizations. The depths of this bitterness is seldom appreciated. Lacy told me, for instance, that BAC had had extraordinary difficulty selling its *Vigilant* antitank missile to the Ministry of Defense and, at a later date, to foreign military departments. Since several Establishments themselves were developing antitank missiles, pressure was brought to bear on Whitehall to turn down the *Vigilant* in favor of the Establishment-designed missiles. Lacy was forced to sell the idea of the *Vigilant,* not to the potential primary user (the British Army), but to the competing Establishments, which exercised enough power to determine what the government's decision would be. At a field trial of prototypes in 1958, he said, "We had eleven shots; we hit seven tanks out of eleven, and when we missed the Establishment representatives cheered." These bureaucrats disliked the *Vigilant,* he said, for the sole reason that they themselves did not design it. In this particular case, Lacy's views prevailed, and the *Vigilant* was adopted despite Establishment criticism and subsequently has been sold to several countries.

This bitter infighting and bureaucratic exclusivism have resulted in delaying for as much as two to five years new weapons designed for the export market. By the time they are ready to be sold abroad, technical obsolescence has usually rendered them just as unsalable as the weapons previously designed for a narrow national requirement. These delays also meant that the more efficient and more ruthless Americans and French would move in and secure the sale with up-to-date equipment.

Brown spent his entire first two-year term trying to make some logic out of this confusion. He changed departments around in the Exports and International Relations Division in the Ministry of Technology. The EIR Division, while it denies it, is the Whitehall export arms sales office and reports directly to the Head of Defense Sales.

Brown convinced the Contracts Department to alter their ways of writing contracts; he persuaded the Treasury to alter some of the government's methods of financing export sales; and, more than anything, he strengthened the overseas sales forces in the embassies. In Saudi Arabia, for instance, there were (in 1966) approximately 222 Americans, including technicians to service the *Hawk* missiles, concerned with arms sales and only one Briton; in Bonn there were roughly 118 Americans and only two Britons. Brown sought to narrow this ratio not only by placing additional men in the field but by changing the role of the existing military attachés from that of reporter to active salesman.[7]

The results of Brown's considerable efforts have been mixed. He succeeded in getting most of the Whitehall departments to think in terms of export sales; he also succeeded in reducing the time lag between export application and ministerial reply from nearly a year to several days; and he has changed the thinking from selling *repair* parts to one of emphasizing *replacement* parts, a particularly American philosophy. In other words, instead of trying to sell, say, spare radio tubes, his men are told to go out and sell more modern versions of the entire radio set. The British government's policy today appears to be to conclude any sale that can be made, even at the risk of offending the United States, except in the most sensitive cases (such as South Africa). Now the usual answer from Whitehall, said Nobbs, is, "Yes, you can sell, unless . . ."*

One of the most noticeable trends resulting from Brown's work has been the move away from large sophisticated missiles to smaller and cheaper ones that are easier to maintain. Since around 1965 there has been keen competition in missile sales among the Americans, British, Italians, Dutch, French, West Germans and Swiss. The British, in spite of their difficulties with the Research & Development Establishments, were successful in producing quickly several inexpensive types of missiles with broad applications. It is one of the few types of arms that they have had any success in selling in recent years. *Vigilants,* for instance, have been bought by Finland, Kuwait and Saudi Arabia; *Bloodhound* antiaircraft missiles have been bought by Sweden and Switzerland; and the popular *Seacat,* a ship-to-air missile, has been bought by Holland, West Germany, Sweden, Australia, New Zealand, Brazil, Chile and Malaysia.[8]

Another noticeable result of Brown's efforts has been to create an even larger bureaucracy which might, in time, clog the machinery still further. By mid-1968 there were signs that Whitehall wanted to take over all arms sales activities. To British industrialists this would be a disastrous turn because it would surely guarantee that the Research & Development Establishments would

* Brown was sufficiently successful at his job to earn a knighthood in 1969 for "services to the Ministry of Defence." Like the United States, Britain, too, has learned that it pays to decorate its arms salesmen.

gain control. Since the Establishments are not motivated by economic considerations, they say, the cost of new weapons would increase unchecked, and time lags would widen immeasurably. Therefore, say these industrialists, if the Establishments or Whitehall, or both, take over the sale of arms abroad, everything accomplished by Brown would revert to its former state, the only "bonus" being a larger bureaucracy. In 1967 it was estimated by several knowledgeable sources that, like the United States, there is a vast army of British bureaucrats—as many as 200,000—whose jobs now depend one way or another on the continuance of Britain's current export arms sales policy.

Many businessmen believe that the success of the policy depends on the private sector of the economy taking an active part. No company with its own resources at stake, they say, can afford to drag its feet; nor can it plod along with an unsalable item; nor can it afford to make decisions strictly for political reasons. They see themselves as spurs to bureaucracy, goading it to make decisions more quickly, and to be more aggressive and pragmatic.

One indication of Whitehall's eagerness to take over the sales function is its reluctance to give any particular incentives to arms industries to sell their wares abroad. A levy is added to all arms sales prices that must be paid into the Exchequer to recover some of the government's development costs. It varies from 7 to 10 percent of the net price. "If you sold the Jordanians a completely new air force," Nobbs told me, "you'd get an OBE, but you'd still have to pay the government up to 10 percent out of profits."

Sometimes Whitehall gives incentives to its own. Alastair Buchan, Director of the Institute for Strategic Studies, recalls one acquaintance who was due for retirement after serving as a British naval attaché in a Latin American country; the officer was offered retention and promotion if he could sell a cruiser to that government.[9]

The latest trend has been collaboration with European and Commonwealth countries in the research, development and production of new equipment. Britain has collaborated with Belgium in the production of rocket engines; with France in the development of the *Jaguar* strike-trainer aircraft; with Holland on the *Sea*

Dart ship-to-air guided missile; and with Australia on the development of the *Ikara* antisubmarine weapon.

These arrangements are viewed favorably by the British government because they spread the heavy financial costs among several parties and encourage a wider exchange of technological information. At the same time, however, they reduce the amount of foreign exchange flowing into the Exchequer, since profits are shared by all parties. Private industries favor such arrangements because, with others involved, it becomes far more difficult for the government to cancel a project in midstream. They also force the Treasury to free money earlier along in a project, which gives industry a better chance to estimate its costs accurately. Collaboration has also forced the British government to guarantee a certain number of export sales, something it was not prepared to do when it financed a project unilaterally.

Yet another trend is an increasing willingness by the British government to forego embargoes in the interests of increasing its arms sales. Historically, Britain maintained embargoes only for the minimum amount of time and would usually drop them entirely immediately after actual hostilities had ended. For instance, Britain resumed its military aid in full to both Pakistan and India a scant six months after the two countries had gone to war in 1965. (The United States, it will be recalled, resumed "nonlethal" sales at the same time, but it was another two years before "lethal" sales were resumed.) In the Six-Day War Britain placed an embargo on both antagonists for only forty-eight hours.[10]

At this writing Britain maintains a full arms embargo on South Africa. It dates back to 1963 when both the United States and Great Britain declared that they both would not send arms to South Africa that could be used to enforce apartheid. Soon after the Labour party took office in October 1964, Prime Minister Wilson changed the policy, banning all arms exports to the country. It was estimated that this action would lose equipment orders worth $420 million to British industry in the years 1965–68.[11] At the same time Labour party dogma dictated against selling arms to the United States that could be used in Vietnam. This policy put Raymond Brown on the spot: he was charged with maximizing arms sales but found that one large market was completely closed to him and that another was partially closed.

However, there are indications that, in time, both these bans will be relaxed, so pressing is the need for foreign exchange. The Conservative party, along with many industrialists, has been making an all-out effort since late 1967 to persuade the South Africans to postpone placing any long-term arms contracts with other European countries, hinting that when the Conservatives return to power the arms ban will be partially lifted. The Tories do not favor a complete lifting of the ban; they would still bar weapons used for "internal repression" but would resume sales of aircraft and naval vessels.[12] When peace is restored in Vietnam, it is believed—and hoped—that sales to the United States will increase as well.

Holding up spare parts to a country as a means of controlling a conflict is viewed with considerable skepticism by many Britons. No country likes to be controlled by its suppliers, and there is increasing pressure in Britain to guarantee the delivery of spares under all circumstances, and to both sides if necessary, in order to win back arms markets previously lost. "Every conflict brings out this dependence of the operator on the supplier," one aircraft manufacturer told me. "I think that unless we can get into a position of not taking sides in these things, it immediately jeopardizes our chances of selling in the future. The Indo-Pakistan and Israeli-Arab conflicts have brought this out bloody clearly. And certainly the Pakistanis and Indians won't buy from us in the future unless we guarantee that we won't hold up spares."

Britain's frantic efforts to revitalize its lagging arms export trade have been partly due to the successes of the United States in this field of endeavor. The British government has been stung by a long series of American sales coups. As far back as 1956 it was complaining that the United States was giving away F-86's to the renascent Luftwaffe "like free samples of detergent." It complained in 1959 that it had been rudely shouldered aside in its efforts to sell English Electric *Lightning* jets to West Germany, and in 1962 it grumbled that its own *Blue Water* surface-to-surface nuclear missile should have been chosen by the Bundeswehr over the United States' supposedly inferior *Sergeant* missile. Considerable resentment was expressed in 1965 over the Italian decision to purchase U.S. M-60 tanks instead of the British fifty-ton *Chieftain* tank.* These complaints rapidly developed into cacophonous cries of resentment and bitterness over "high-pressure salesmanship" and the "free-spending attitudes" of the Americans. "Ruthless" is the most common adjective ascribed to American arms salesmen by the British. A typical British attitude is that held by R. L. Nobbs of the British Aircraft Corporation. "One tends to think of Kuss and his organization as fantastically dynamic and sharpshooting," he said. "Our lawyers tend to treat them as simpletons . . . as being commercially not as acute as one would expect them to be. I tend to think of them as an *enormous* bloody great machine bulldozing its way around, not really concerned with the details. I think it is U.S. policy to be ruthless, to sell maximum at any means at your power. I think Kuss is pretty ruthless when it comes to selling."

American companies, he continued, "are large enough to operate independently on a very large scale which British companies are not capable of doing. They can send over a fifty-man team to Germany, spend their way around and buy the market. We can't do that."

Nobbs believes that Kuss "knifed" BAC in the Saudi *Lightning-Hawk* deal of 1965. "He would have done more," he said, "but for the fact that he couldn't deliver F-104's in time. As it is, he promised them *Hawks* in a time scale that was completely unrealistic." Kuss, he added, "will promise anything and then argue it out later." Nobbs rejects the idea that the United States "allowed" Britain to make the *Lightning* sale so that it would be less resistant to buying F-111's.

Many British businessmen would second these views. Several

* So bitter was their reaction to this particular loss that, ever since, British critics have rarely missed an opportunity to point up the superiority of British tanks over U.S. tanks. This was particularly true in the Pakistan-India War and the Six-Day War, despite the fact that neither *Chieftains* nor M-60's faced each other in either conflict. Both wars saw British *Centurions* facing U.S. M-48 *Pattons,* and, it is true, in most cases the British tanks proved superior.

with whom I spoke also believe that the ILN office operates far more at a political level than is apparent on the surface. For instance, one knowledgeable businessman told me that Kuss had a "standoff agreement" with Britain on supplying arms to Libya; that is to say, the United States would sell to Libya while Britain would not. But if British forces stayed in Aden for two more years, then the United States would "allow" Britain to sell certain planes to Libya. British arms salesmen, said my source, do not have this kind of power.

Whatever agreement Kuss may have had with the British was broken in May 1968 when Whitehall announced that it had won a 150-million-pound order to provide and install a complete missile air defense system in Libya. (Until 1969, it was the largest missile system order ever won by a British firm.) It is of interest to note that no one in Britain has ever asked why Libya needs these weapons, who its enemies are, or from what quarter the country is being threatened. Nor was Britain really interested in selling Libya weapons until it became rich through oil revenues; then all of a sudden the country needed extremely sophisticated weapons.

A few British businessmen with whom I spoke believe that during the 1950's Military Aid Program grant aid policy was to capture all the arms markets it could. The United States, said one Briton, "obviously figured out the amount of money involved in MAP giveaways and then how much it could get back in second-generation sales of the same equipment to those captive countries."

All of Britain's problems, however, do not stem from American aggressiveness; some of them are self-inflicted. The British arms industry, like other segments of the economy, is sluggish, having fed for years on the uncompetitive domestic market. One export order for $28 million worth of 1,000 lb. bombs was lost because of the inability of a Royal Ordnance Factory to begin manufacture within eighteen months. Another large order was lost because one Establishment refused to introduce improved manufacturing techniques in order to cut production costs. Britons also have an inferiority complex about their own military weapons. They constantly are telling themselves how superior their arms are, as if that were sufficient to ensure high export sales. "Britain *Has* Better

Arms for Sale," read one recent newspaper headline. It is typical of the mood.[13]

The Defense Common Market is viewed with deep suspicion in Britain; it is seen as a way to dominate sales to NATO. Offset arrangements are just as suspect. "We've been trying it with the Americans for years," Colonel Lacy told me, "but interdependence with the Americans only means one bloody thing: that we take yours but you never take ours."

He and others also complain that the United States has let Britain down on a number of occasions. Most often cited was the informal arrangement whereby neither country would sell missiles to certain Middle Eastern countries. The United Kingdom, they say, held off selling *Bloodhounds* to Israel in order not to escalate the arms race in the area, but before they knew it Kuss had secretly sold *Hawks* to the Israelis. Later he was to sell them A-4 *Skyhawks,* and then he was to sell some F-104's to the Jordanians. They complain that a similar understanding over Iran was also broken. In addition, they complain that a strict agreement between the United States, Great Britain and several other nations not to supply supersonic aircraft to any South American country had been broken behind their backs: they learned that the United States had secretly offered Venezuela some F-5's for delivery in 1969 if it did not buy anything in the meantime. This agreement has been confirmed by several reliable sources. Anger over this apparent double-cross is what drove the British to push the sale of Hawker *Hunters* to Chile and *Canberra* bombers to Peru in 1966 and 1967.

Britons are also angry over the reluctance of the United States to buy its military needs abroad, even when a country such as Britain has a superior weapon for which there is no counterpart in the American arsenal. They cite the case of the ET-316 *Rapier* low-level antiaircraft missile. The British government cancelled the *Rapier* (then called the PT-428) in 1959 because of high costs. It told English Electric, the prime contractor, that instead it would buy the American *Mauler* missile, which at that time was still on the drawing boards. English Electric replied, in effect, that Whitehall had made a poor decision—that *Mauler* was too sophisticated, that the techniques were wrong, that it was too heavy for two soldiers to carry in the field (as they could with *Rapier*), that it was too complicated to be maintained in the field by ordinary soldiers, and that it could not shoot down a low-flying supersonic jet on three seconds' notice. *Mauler,* they said, was a relatively slow heat-seeking proximity missile that could only chase a plane, while the *Rapier* was an optical-tracking, direct-hit missile capable of reaching Mach 3 speeds.

English Electric, despite the loss of government funds, carried on its development of *Rapier* as a private venture. In 1965 the United States cancelled *Mauler* (at a loss of $200 million) for many of the reasons cited by English Electric six years earlier.[14] Red-faced, Whitehall went back to English Electric and expressed renewed interest. The *Rapier* eventually went into production in 1967.

The British government then went to the United States and suggested that it buy the *Rapier,* since the Pentagon had no comparable item. The United States expressed some interest but claimed that it still did not believe in the optical-tracking system, despite many successful tests. Eventually *Rapier* was turned down by the Pentagon.

In the meantime, U.S. Army Ordnance had developed the *Chaparral,* which was nothing more than a *Sidewinder* air-to-air heat-seeking missile mounted on a tracked vehicle. The British complained, as subsequently have others, that the *Chaparral* is a proximity-fused missile that, because of its relatively small warhead, still cannot destroy a supersonic jet. Only a direct-hit missile such as *Rapier* with a delayed fuse (so that the small warhead would explode *inside* the aircraft), they claimed, can do the job effectively. The Pentagon at first appeared impressed by the British argument and said that it would continue to look into the possibilities of somehow combining *Chaparral* with *Rapier,* but nothing was to come of it.

To many Britons, this was a typical instance of the refusal of the United States to be dependent for *any* of its military needs on a foreign supplier. Keeping discussions open is viewed both as a political move to appease London and as a means to glean as much technical information as possible from the *Rapier* for its own use—which is what eventually happened when the U.S. Army later produced the TOW (for Tube-launched, Optical-tracking and Wire-guided) missile.

While Britain is the second largest free-world arms trader, its sales of weapons, particularly since 1955, have not had as great an impact on events as have U.S. sales. It must, however, share in the responsibility of arming both Pakistan and India prior to the fighting in 1965. At the outbreak of war, India's air force had been supplied with 220 British jet fighters and 68 British jet bombers, which together represented 71 percent of India's air attack force. Britain had supplied 50 *Canberra* bombers to Pakistan, which represented 25 percent of its entire air force. India also fought the war with one armored division equipped with *Centurions*. With the exception of one submarine, which had been supplied to Pakistan by the United States, both countries' naval ships were of British origin.[15]

Britain must also share in the responsibility for the Middle Eastern arms race. Israel, for instance, had been sold 250 *Centurions;* and except for one destroyer (which had been captured from the Egyptians in 1956), its entire navy had been bought from Britain. On the other side, Egypt's navy, while mostly Soviet in origin, consisted of at least two British ships, specifically "Z"-type destroyers; Jordan's army boasted a quantity of *Centurions* and its air force 12 *Hunter* and 16 *Vampire* fighter-bombers; Saudi Arabia, while it did no fighting in the 1967 war, kept its 6 *Hunter* and 6 *Lightning* (the first of the 36 to be delivered, and all piloted by British mercenaries) jet fighters on alert along with some British *Thunderbird* surface-to-air missiles; Iraq's arsenal included *Centurion* tanks, *Hunter* and *Provost* fighters and two *Wessex* helicopter squadrons; and Lebanon boasted 50 *Centurions* (one half of its entire tank strength) and 12 *Hunter* jets and 6 *Vampire* bombers (100 percent of its combat air force).[16]

Perhaps Britain's most sustained arms sales have come in the field of naval warships. Between the years 1945 and 1955, Britain sold 47 ships, mostly destroyers, to 13 countries. These deliveries represented 52 percent of all naval ships delivered throughout the world in that period. Britain's greatest markets were her former colonies: mainly Egypt, India, Pakistan, Australia, New Zealand and South Africa. In the period 1955–65 Britain's share of overall deliveries fell to 34 percent, primarily because of the entrance of the Soviet Union into the arms sales field. The pre-1955 volume, however, was maintained, and particularly successful inroads were made in Latin America.[17]

British warship sales to Latin America led to three of the more notorious postwar arms sales fiascoes. In 1956 Brazil paid $35 million for a secondhand British aircraft carrier that was reconditioned in a Dutch shipyard. No sooner had the ship been delivered than a civil war broke out between Brazilian Navy and Air Force brass over the question of which service was to operate the vessel. In time the argument triggered major crises for four Brazilian presidents and the resignation of ten admirals and ministers. On several occasions the two services actually fought pitched battles. The differences were not resolved until 1965 when a compromise was reached: the Navy was to run the carrier and the Air Force the planes.

Within weeks of this sale, Argentina, too, bought a reconditioned aircraft carrier from Great Britain. The only trouble was that the ship was still so obsolete that it could not accommodate modern jet aircraft.

Finally, in this same period, Britain sold two old cruisers to Peru for $5 million each. Because its navy had insufficient technicians, Peru was forced to operate one ship at a time.[18]

Undoubtedly Great Britain will never recapture the preeminent position it enjoyed prior to World War II, but the current level of activity would indicate that the country is capable of making significant inroads into the market now dominated by the United States. How great an inroad it will be in the years ahead is difficult to predict, given Britain's special financial and economic problems. What is clear, however, is Britain's increasing willingness to sell arms without giving due consideration to all the possible consequences. As with the United States, selling arms has become so built into the fabric of Britain's foreign and domestic policies that it will in time become exceedingly difficult to eliminate. The current mood of Britain is perhaps best summed up by a remark attributed to a British military attaché in Latin America: when chided for having sold such outdated and useless equipment to the Brazilians, Argentineans and Peruvians, he is reported to have replied, "When it comes down to that, old boy, our whole fleet is up for sale."

2

France re-established herself as a major arms supplier relatively late in the postwar era. In the years immediately following World War II, it was preoccupied with rebuilding its entire economic base. Whatever equipment its renascent armaments industry could produce was absorbed by the government itself. Slowly over the years, however, as France gained in military and economic strength, and as it began to cut back in its colonial responsibilities, the burgeoning arms industry shifted its focus from sales to its own government to export sales. By the mid-1950's France was once again a major exporter of arms. The process was hastened in large measure by the United States. The massive economic aid given under the Marshall Plan, for instance, allowed France to divert a part of her resources to rebuilding her arms industry. Furthermore, the $4.2 billion worth of military grant aid given between the years 1950 and 1964 relieved the pressure on the French arms industry to supply its own government, thus permitting it to concentrate much of its energies on developing the export market.[19]

Military exports have increased particularly since Charles de Gaulle came to power. There are no official overall figures for French military exports, but from what reliable sources are available it appears that approximately $100 million worth of arms were exported in 1958 and that by 1968 the yearly volume had increased to nearly $400 million.[20]

Unlike the United States and Great Britain, France sells weapons primarily for political reasons. While it is true that exports help its arms industry and bring back gold, sales are made essentially to broaden French influence, to increase the country's political leverage, and to diminish American and British influence wherever it can. Sales, therefore, are tightly controlled by the government. A decision to sell comes from the Elysée Palace, the Ministry of Defense, or the Foreign Ministry, though it may be carried out by other government departments. Very little surplus is sold on the open market to traders like Samuel Cummings because little political influence would be realized from such a transaction.

France has no "supersalesman" of arms as has the United States and Great Britain. There is no need for one, since both the French bureaucracy and the domestic arms industry are geared to exporting military hardware. The French aerospace industry exports—including aircraft, missiles and space products—amount to 15 percent of *all* French exports. Roughly 60 percent of French aircraft products alone are exported, 70 percent of which represent military orders. France is also the free-world's largest exporter of military helicopters.

The office most closely concerned with the day-to-day sales of weapons is the Délégation Ministerielle pour l'Armement, or DMA. This office reports directly to the Minister of Defense. Under DMA is an office called Direction des Affairs Internationales, or DAI. These two bureaus, DMA/DAI as they are usually designated, determine whether a proposed export sale falls within France's *armaments* policy. If they find that it does and they approve of the transaction, the request is passed on to the Commission Interministerielle d'Etudes des Exportations de Materielle de Guerre. This body, made up of various deputy ministers and sometimes the Defense Minister himself, determines whether the proposed sale fits into France's *political* policy. If the sale is a particularly delicate one, the request will end up at the Elysée Palace for a decision.

France's arms industry is largely government-owned, far more than Britain's. Under the control of DMA are eight departments charged with governing various aspects of the nationalized segments of the industry, including the sale of its products. Specifically, they concern themselves with developments in land vehicles and armaments, aircraft, warships, missiles, laboratory field testing, explosives, scientific research and data communications.

The best known of these departments is the Direction Technique des Armements Terrestres, which concentrates on the research, development and production of armored vehicles, artillery and small arms. Its most famous arsenals are located in St. Étienne, Tulle, Châtellerault and Bayonne (whence the word bayonet).

Obsolete equipment is sold through the Service de Domaine, a semiautonomous agency (much like the Crown Agents) in the Treasury. Most of its sales are to other governments.

On the surface these organizations appear to be quite similar to the British Royal Ordnance Factories and Research & Development Establishments. They differ from their British counterparts, however, in a number of ways. First of all, these organizations and the factories they control operate on commercial principles, all profits going into the Treasury. Second, because so much of the French arms industry is nationalized and because the private sector is geared both to working strictly within the government's foreign policy and to pushing export sales, there exists less antagonism between the private arms makers and government factories. French arms sales bureaucrats assist in the export effort by providing technical expertise to the deputy ministers in the Ministry of Defense. They also work very closely with private arms manufacturers who wish to sell their wares abroad, often opening doors in countries that would otherwise be closed.

The French are very secretive when it comes to discussing arms sales. No figures are released, no agreements are officially announced, no policy objectives are published. In fact, were it not for all those French jets and tanks one can see in foreign arsenals, or all the latest French aeronautical equipment at such exhibitions as the Paris Air Show, it would be very difficult to prove from public documents issued by the government that France was in the arms export business at all.

Recently, however, the French government has taken to printing books describing all the military material available for export.*

* This is not the first time that the French arms industry has advertised its wares. Prior to World War II several nationalized small arms factories published catalogues which experienced wide distribution in the colonies.

These books are restricted in their circulation to a very select group of foreign military men. The idea that these publications should ever fall into the hands of the general public is considered with horror by French bureaucrats. When I suggested to an official of DMA that I be given (or be allowed to buy) a set of these books, I was told that no such item existed. His voice and eyes, however, plainly expressed concern for the fact that I had heard of them.

The books of which I had heard, and the only ones I eventually got to see (from another source), were called "Exposition de Matériel d'Armement Terrestre" and concerned themselves with three types of weapons: small arms and crew-served weapons, fighting vehicles and electronic equipment. These books were secretly distributed to a select audience at the 1967 Paris Air Show.

The books contained pictures of each weapon and a wealth of technical information. Illustrated, for example, were 90 mm, 105 mm and 155 mm cannons; a model 1958 light flamethrower was shown as was a model 1954 portable flamethrower. Also illustrated were seven different types of mortars, several different varieties of grenades and antipersonnel mines, six tank models, at least a dozen different types of other combat vehicles, ten different types of rockets and missiles, and a wide range of munitions—from .22 caliber ammunition to high-explosive shells. All of this material was, and presumably still is, available for sale. The books also showed who made the weapons, models available, the possible uses and many otherwise unavailable technical details. Virtually everything was included except the price (which is subject to negotiation).

To the French mind, selling jet fighters, bombers and transports can be acknowledged and promoted openly, as is done at the Paris Air Show, because it is easy for the public to overlook the fact that such aircraft—as sleek, powerful and rather romantic items—are instruments of destruction. But with hard-core ordnance such as antipersonnel mines, flamethrowers and high-explosive shells, it cannot be admitted publicly that such items are available for sale. While the general public is treated to a lavish display of acrobatics and flyovers at the show, what is never demonstrated is what these aircraft can do. There are no pinpoint bombing displays, no firing of missiles, not even any mock aerial dogfights. Such activities would destroy the effect and drive home the point that these aircraft can be just as dangerous and unromantic as hard-core ordnance.

The French export arms sales policy, it is clear, is currently being pushed heavily. In order to undercut the United States and Great Britain and to increase its own influence, France is currently willing to sell any weapon, except its atomic arsenal, anywhere there is a market. Its arms salesmen have the least scruples of any Western ally, and there is some indication that, could it get away with it, France would sell arms to Eastern bloc nations.

France sold its *Entac* antitank missile to Indonesia during the Sukarno regime as a direct slap at the Dutch and Americans who had withdrawn their aid. It so happens that there were, and are today, very few armored divisions in Indonesia, since the terrain is not suited to tank warfare; nor do any of Indonesia's immediate neighbors maintain any rival tank units. There was some speculation that these *Entacs* were used by Indonesian-backed rebels against British armored cars in North Borneo.[21]

In order to undercut the United States in its particular sphere of influence, the French have been selling jets aggressively to South American nations despite the fact that none of the countries need them. To keep France out, the United States has been forced to step in and offer its own brand of needless weapons. Thus part of the blame for the 1965–67 arms race in the area rests with France.

France, as noted previously, tried to destroy British influence in Nigeria by selling weapons covertly either to the Portuguese or to independent operators, both of which were supporting the Biafrans. To be on the safe side, France also sold military material directly to the Federals. French authorities no doubt felt confident that their country would gain by the exercise.

France has also shown increasing willingness to subsidize the sales price of a weapon with Treasury funds in order to win orders. Its sale of ninety *Mirage V* fighter-bombers to Belgium in 1968 is a good example of this. The battle for this order was joined in 1966 between Lockheed offering F-104's, Northrop offering F-5's, and Dassault offering the *Mirage V*. For a year and a half the competition was fierce and sustained, the gap among all three offers never widening more than 1 percent of the whole contract. The three firms had the full backing of their respective governments. Eventually Dassault dropped its price. It is widely acknowledged that Dassault's final and winning bid was lower than its own production cost figures and that the reduction was made possible through direct government financial aid. France, unlike Great Britain, obviously has taken a page from American arms sales techniques and, in this instance, beat ILN at its own game.[22]

Until the 1967 Sinai war, France was a major supplier of arms to Israel. It secured this market partly through the efforts of French banker Edmond de Rothschild, who had persuaded the French to sell to the Israelis, and partly as a result of Washington's reluctance in earlier years to become too deeply involved. At the outbreak of war virtually the entire Israeli Air Force was equipped with French aircraft. (Their superiority in battle, incidentally, was one of the points pressed by the French in their successful sale of the ninety *Mirage V*'s to Belgium. This is not an uncommon sales tactic: Kuss, for instance, seldom failed to mention that all the weapons he was selling had been combat-tested in Vietnam.)

There is one aspect of French arms sales to the Israelis that serves more as an historical footnote but nevertheless deserves mention here. In 1942 Egypt came into possession of a number of U.S. *Sherman* tanks left over from the North African campaign. They were later incorporated into the Egyptian Army. Some of these *Shermans* mounted 75 mm guns; others mounted 76 mm guns (known as the "Easy Eight" after the designation M-4A3E8). In 1956 the Israelis captured a number of *Shermans* mounting the old 75 mm cannons. They knew that these 75's would never stand up in battle against the 76's still in Egyptian hands, so they set about seeking more modern tanks with higher firepower. The Israelis approached the French with the idea of buying complete AMX-13 tanks, but the demand for these particular vehicles was so great throughout the world in the late 1950's and early 1960's that no orders could be filled immediately. Nevertheless Israel and France did strike a bargain: if the Israelis were willing to wait several years for complete AMX-13's, the French in the meantime would sell them AMX-13 turrets mounting 105 mm guns. Israel bought a quantity of these items and fitted them onto the old *Sherman* chassis. These hybrids subsequently went to war in 1967 and proved their superiority in every tank battle in which they took part.

Immediately after the 1967 war, France abruptly changed its arms sales tactics. It announced that the fifty *Mirages* ordered and two-thirds paid for by the Israelis before the war would not be delivered and that a partial arms embargo would be maintained indefinitely on the country. The reasoning behind this move is still not clear, although many observers believe that a possible revival of the arms race was only incidental to the decision. No doubt France chafed under the restrictions of serving as Israel's major supplier; it obviously saw that more political and diplomatic mileage could be gained by siding with the more than 200 million Arabs than with the 2.7 million Jews and that the war presented her with a good opportunity to change sides. France also saw a good opportunity to undercut the United States, Great Britain and the Soviet Union in the area. For instance, six months after the war Paris had lifted its arms embargo against the Arab states and was deeply involved with Syria, Iraq and Libya in negotiations over mineral rights. As bait to the Iraqis, the French promised to sell them fifty-four of its latest *Mirages* for the sum of $70 million. *The New York Times* stated editorially that De Gaulle was "gleefully playing the role of arsonist in the explosive Middle East," in a cynical attempt to win concessions from the country.

In December 1969, France agreed to sell Libya 100 advanced supersonic jet fighter-bombers, mostly *Mirage V*'s, and 200 combat tanks, for an estimated $500 million (which, incidentally, is approximately 36 times Libya's entire 1966 defense budget). In the same month, five French-built gunboats were smuggled by Israeli agents from Cherbourg to Haifa. Many knowledgeable sources claim that Paris was aware of the plot from the beginning.

France can act this way because of the manner in which it chooses to conduct its foreign policy. Unlike the United States and Great Britain, Paris gives no overt sign of reacting to public opinion until there is disaster at its doorstep (i.e., the 1968 riots and strikes). France does what it pleases and tells the rest of the world that it cares very little for the fact that it might disagree. Most nations realize that objecting to French actions since 1958 has had about as much effect as shouting in a well. Washington and London, on the other hand, are very sensitive to public opinion, and everyone is aware of it. It is interesting to note, for instance, that while it was French aircraft and tanks that wreaked such destruction on the Arabs, it was the United States and Great Britain who were blamed for it.

France has also made great inroads into South Africa, traditionally a British market. It has never gone along with the 1963 arms embargo. It has supplied a score of *Mirage III* fighter-bombers equipped with AS-30 air-to-surface missiles, an unspecified number of *Alouette* helicopters and Panhard armored cars. The Panhards were and continue to be manufactured under license in South Africa. France claims that its policy is not to supply arms that can be used in the defense of apartheid, but the sale of helicopters and armored cars does not lend credence to the claim.

In August 1966 the United States attempted to thwart Paris' policy of breaking the embargo by blocking a sale to the Pretoria government of several *Mystere 20* executive jets equipped with General Electric engines. The French government retaliated four months later by blocking any new military contracts with the United States in order to avoid any "complicity" in the Vietnam War. The weapons it refused to sell in particular were Nord Aviation AS-12 missiles, designed for air attack against surface vessels, which the Pentagon had bought in the past but which were not intended to be deployed in Vietnam.[23]

By stepping into the vacuum created by the U.N. embargo, France has reaped many rewards beyond mere profits from arms sales. Its commercial exports to South Africa rose from $33 million in 1961 to $100 million in 1968. French investment in the country is exceeded only by American and British investments. Paris' rapprochement with Pretoria has also extended French influence into white-run Rhodesia. Among other things, France surreptitiously helps to keep Ian Smith's government supplied with oil.[24]

Among the Western nations, France best understands the influence arms sales can command. There is a minimum amount of ideology (as opposed to politics) attached to any French arms sale; it is done primarily to enhance the country's prestige and influence, and there are very few indications that this course will be modified in the foreseeable future.

3

The remaining free-world arms suppliers of any note—Belgium, Canada, Israel, Italy, Sweden, Switzerland and West Germany—warrant special comment because, while their total sales are relatively small, they are not without influence. Their products—such as Belgian FN rifles, Italian jet aircraft, Israeli submachine guns and Swedish missiles and cannons—appeal to nations that prefer not to be aligned with major powers. Even those countries aligned with a Western power find it to their advantage to cultivate lesser sources of supply, despite the loss in standardization of equipment and a waste of financial resources. Most of these countries, whether aligned or nonaligned, have learned the lessons of recent history: that it does not pay to rely on only one or two suppliers, since any cutoff of material inhibits their ability to act independently.

The United States, Great Britain and France are primarily responsible for the influence these small countries have had in the arms trade. Since the mid-1950's many hundreds of research, development and licensed production agreements have been arranged between Western arms-producing nations, both large and small. The smaller nations seem to have benefited more from these partnerships than the big three suppliers. The reasons why are not difficult to understand. An American license to produce F-104's in Belgium or M-113's in Italy would have a proportionately more favorable impact on the Belgian and Italian economies than on the U.S. economy (had the equipment been produced there) or on the larger British and French economies (had they the benefit of the licenses). These small countries reap a harvest of technological experience that is far out of proportion to what might be expected for their size. Both these benefits increase a small country's ability to compete in the world's arms markets. Behind all of this is the knowledge that without such agreements few of the small countries would be as deeply involved in the arms trade as they are, and that one of them, West Germany, would probably not be in the arms business at all today.

The mechanical procedures for selling arms abroad generally follow the French model. The departments have different names, the duties and responsibilities are slightly different, but the objective is the same: to maximize arms sales with a minimum of bureaucratic delay. None of these countries have "supersalesmen" for the same reason that France does not—both the bureaucracy and the arms industry have long been geared to the export market. Only in Israel, Italy and Sweden is there a substantial government investment in the arms industry; in the others, the arms industry is quite free of government financial control. All of them, no matter what their financial status, operate along commercial lines.

With the exception of Belgium, which has a reputation for laxity (particularly with arms in transit), all of them maintain tight controls over their arms exports. This does not mean, however, that these countries do not wish to have their domestic arms sold abroad; rather, the emphasis is on trying to maintain as much control as possible over the ultimate destination of the material. Sweden and Switzerland, for instance, lay down general guidelines on areas where arms cannot be sold, and their salesmen are free to sell whatever they can elsewhere. Canadian arms salesmen, whether governmental or private, are limited by the same strictures applicable to U.S. arms salesmen. They operate, in effect, as an arm of the ILN office (although they do not like to be told that) because virtually all the weapons exported from the Dominion are U.S. products manufactured under license. The West German government in the last decade has increasingly liberalized its arms export policy because of the financial strain imposed upon its resources by heavy offset purchases of U.S. arms and Treasury notes. Italy also seems to be liberalizing its arms sales policy for the same reasons, but with the added desire to cash in on sales to nonaligned and embargoed nations. Israel, too, is liberalizing its policy because of balance of payments problems. And Belgium, complementing its lax control procedures, will allow its arms salesmen to sell their products virtually to anyone this side of the Iron Curtain. It is said that every Belgian ambassador is a "salesman" for Fabrique Nationale d'Armes de Guerre.

What important sales have these countries made in recent years?

Italy's two largest sales in recent years were six new destroyers to Venezuela and four to Indonesia.[25] It has also sold a large quantity of Macchi jets to nonaligned countries, specifically Ghana, Singapore and Somalia.[26] Italy has also been a major arms supplier to South Africa since the imposition of the 1963 embargo. Light jet aircraft, air-to-surface missiles, helicopters, armored cars and transport planes have all been delivered. In fact the Macchi firm has been instrumental in helping the South Africans develop their own aircraft industry; Italy granted the South Africans a production license in 1964 for the MB-326 jet trainer-attack aircraft, the first one coming off the assembly line at Ysterplaat in 1966.[27]

Israel has exported the Uzi submachine gun, considered the best weapon of its kind in the world today. It was developed by Israeli Military Industries, a government-owned enterprise, and was named after its developer, Army Major Uziel Gal. This weapon has been widely bought throughout the world and is standard equipment for the West German and Dutch armies. Some Uzi's showed up in Cuba after Castro came to power and were later re-exported to procommunist guerrillas in Venezuela.

Belgian FN rifles have also been widely distributed around the world. They have been purchased by, among other countries, Great Britain, the Netherlands, Canada, Australia, Luxembourg, New Zealand, India, Argentina, Chile, Venezuela, Peru, Ecuador, Austria, Israel, Ireland and South Africa. The first weapons bought by Castro after coming to power were three shiploads of FN arms and ammunition. Congo mercenaries and Nigerian rebels have also used these rifles. So great has been the demand for them that they have been produced under license in Great Britain, Canada, Australia, the United States, Israel, Austria and Argentina.[28]

Canada has been a major exporter of *Sabrejets* and *Starfighters*. Its *Sabrejets* have been sold to the British, Italians, West Germans, Swedes, Turks, South Africans and Colombians. Its *Starfighters* have been sold to West Germany, Denmark, Greece, Turkey and Norway. It is current American policy to grant production licenses to Canadian firms for this type of equipment, since it both allows Canada to arm itself more cheaply and provides a second-nation source of arms for the ILN office for sale elsewhere.

West Germany's arms export program is currently comparatively small, but there are signs that it is growing in size and influence. In 1965 Bonn exported to Pakistan *Cobra* antitank missiles which were reportedly used against India in the war of that year.[29] This was at the same time that West Germany tried to sell $80 million worth of secondhand equipment to Israel. In 1966 it sold forty Fiat G-91 jet fighters to Portugal, which planned to use them in Angola. These G-91's were originally built by German companies under Italian license for the United States to provide to Greece and Turkey.[30]

More important than these sales, however, has been Bonn's budding arms aid program. By 1965 Germany was giving military aid to Greece, Turkey, Nigeria, Sudan, Guinea, Somalia, Malagasy Republic and Portugal. Only Nigeria, which acquired surplus aircraft, paid for any of this material. Germany has since extended its program to include Israel, Ethiopia, India, Libya and Tanzania.[31] Apparently its attempt to send 20,000 gas masks to the Israelis immediately following the 1967 war was a part of this effort. Much of what it has given away or sold in these past few years has been U.S. equipment that was being replaced by newer equipment.

West Germany's greatest arms exports, however, have been less in weapons than in weapons technicians. With no armaments industry to employ them after World War II, many weapons innovators and manufacturers sold their talents to the highest bidders. Rocket experts, such as Wernher von Braun and his team, went to the United States; others were pressed into service by the Soviets.

Willi Messerschmitt transferred his aircraft development activities to Spain after the war. Ferdinand Brandner, an Austrian aeronautical engineer who designed planes for the Nazis, went to Egypt and, in cooperation with Messerschmitt and the Spanish firm of Hispano-Aviacion, took over the development of the HA-300 jet fighter. (The European engineers recruited for this work at the Helwan plant outside Cairo actually signed contracts with two obscure Swiss firms, one called MECO and the other called MTB.[32]) Some German engineers went to work for Israeli Aircraft Industries; others followed Kurt Tank, a former chief designer for Focke-Wulf, to India where they helped design and develop the HF-24, a supersonic fighter plane.

As late as 1960 West Germany was still exporting its missile talent, despite the fact that it was producing missiles domestically. In that year, Eugen Saenger, head of the Stuttgart Institute of Jet Propulsion, went to Egypt to help develop an indigenous rocket industry. With him went a clutch of other missile specialists, one of whom was Wolfgang Pilz, mentioned previously, who eventually succeeded Saenger as head of the program.

Pilz is a rocket-design and propulsion expert who helped Nazi Germany to develop its V-1 rockets in World War II. He was an associate of Von Braun's at Peenemünde. After the war he helped France develop the *Véronique* rocket in Normandy. In 1965, as a result of Germany's abortive attempt to sell arms to Israel, Pilz and eighty of his associates in Egypt resigned and left the country. Before they left, Pilz and his team had succeeded in developing three rockets: the *Al Zafir* (Victory) with a 230-mile range, the *Al Khir* (Conqueror) with a 370-mile range, and the *Al Ared* (Vanguard) with a 590-mile range. None of them had been developed sufficiently to be of any use to Egypt in the 1967 war.

It has often been said that one of the reasons Nasser did not recognize East Germany in 1965 following the West-German-aid-to-Israel imbroglio, was his desire to keep these experts working in the country. He was unsuccessful but has since recruited a smaller, less competent team, two members of which are reported to be Americans.[33]

Now that West Germany has once again become an arms manufacturer, it appears that the high-water mark has been reached in the export of its aircraft and missile talent. Many are now returning home to work on domestic programs.

Switzerland and Sweden, two longtime neutrals, have also been two longtime arms exporters. Since World War II Switzerland has concentrated on selling its Oerlikon antiaircraft guns, its MP-48 submachine guns, MG-50 machine guns and its Model 57 assault rifles in such diverse nations as Chile, Denmark and the Congo.

In November 1963 a Swiss manufacturer tried to sell seven batteries of antiaircraft guns and ammunition to South Africa. The Berne government at first allowed the sale to be made, stating somewhat disingenuously that its policy was to limit sales only to areas of international tension or open conflict. But in the following month it reversed itself, its Foreign Minister noting that, while his country was not bound by U.N. actions (because it does not belong to the organization), it nevertheless felt that apartheid was incompatible with Swiss principles.[34] No doubt pressure had been applied. Had that pressure not been applied, Switzerland doubtless would have never questioned the sale and would have allowed many more sales to South Africa without second thoughts.

Sweden claims that its arms policy is to sell weapons only where there is a slight chance that they will ever be used. History has not substantiated this policy. In the 1956 Suez Crisis, the Israelis were armed with twenty-five P-51 *Mustangs* that had been sold to them by the Swedes. The Egyptians in the same war were armed in part with a 40 mm Bofors antiaircraft gun and large quantities of M-45 *Carl Gustav* submachine guns and 7.92 mm Model 42 *Ljungman* rifles. Sweden had sold Egypt a license to manufacture the latter two items only a year before the war broke out. Sweden also has sold the Dominican Republic P-51's and (through Cummings) *Vampires* that were to see action a short time after being delivered.

Sweden has sold a large quantity of its SAAB *Safir* SK-50 piston-engined attack planes to at least twenty countries, the largest buyer being Ethiopia. It has sold its T-28 *Trojan* attack aircraft to, among other countries, Ethiopia, Laos, Cambodia, the Congo, Argentina, Brazil, Haiti and Mexico. It is a large exporter of airborne missiles, military electronics (particularly to France, Spain and South Africa), and bomb-tossing and rocket-firing computers (particularly to Denmark, Switzerland and France). Recently Sweden has been under increasing pressure to sell its Mach 2 *Draken* (Dragon) and its Mach 2 plus *Viggen* (Thunderbolt) jet interceptors, two of the most advanced supersonic aircraft in the world. There is some indication that the *Drakens* will be on the market by 1970 and the *Viggens* several years later.[35] Sweden has also developed a revolutionary turretless tank, called the "Strv-S," which has evoked considerable interest in military circles throughout the world. Undoubtedly it, too, will soon be available for sale.

One noticeable trend is the increasing willingness of Sweden and Switzerland to pool their military technology. Both countries, like Britain and France, are feeling the pinch of high development costs, and they hope to offset them somewhat by working together. Switzerland was particularly shaken by the high costs of producing *Mirages* under license from Dassault. (This development brought a parliamentary inquiry and caused the resignation of the Swiss Air Force Commander-in-Chief in 1966.) As the result of any merger of technologies both countries hope to sell their products not only to each other but also to the "neutralized" countries of Austria and Finland.[36]

One thing that can be said of all the smaller arms suppliers today is that none of them lack the willingness to compete with the United States, Great Britain and France. None of these smaller suppliers have as wide a range of weapons available, but what they do have is no less salable than the products of the big three. Much like any small firm trying to compete with the giants, these countries have tried to corner a small part of the entire market—Belgium with its rifles, Israel with its submachine gun, etc.—and have tried to maintain their grip by offering quicker delivery, more personal service, better performance and cheaper prices.

While there are only seven minor Western arms suppliers, it should be noted that there are a number of other countries struggling to get into the market. Holland, for instance, will soon emerge as another arms supplier of note. One of its firms, Artillerie Inrichtingen, manufactured AR-10 rifles under license from 1957 to 1961; all of the production was exported. Several other companies manufacture under license—and export—*Hawk* missiles, F-104G *Starfighters,* Gloster *Meteor* and Hawker *Hunter* fighters.[37]

Japan, too, is just beginning to enter the arms export market. In 1965 it delivered five fully fueled *Kappa-8* research rockets to Indonesia. Previously Japan had sold *Kappa-6* rockets to Yugoslavia, and it was reported in 1963 that Pakistan had expressed interest in acquiring several of these rockets.[38] This is not much, considering that Japan is the fourth largest industrial nation in the world, but it is a beginning.

Spain and Denmark both export small quantities of pistols, rifles and submachine guns. The high-quality products of Compagnie Madsen, A-S, Copenhagen, are in particular demand by weapons specialists around the world today. Egypt, India and South Africa are all struggling to develop their own arms industries. Egypt already makes rifles and munitions and is working on its own aircraft and missiles. India manufactures its own small arms and ammunition (one cartridge plant courtesy of the U.S. government) and is currently developing its own tank (called the *Vijayanta*) and supersonic all-weather fighter plane (the HF-24).[39] South Africa is virtually self-sufficient in all manner of arms except atomic weapons. There is little doubt that once these countries satisfy their own domestic demand for arms that they, like the others before them, will attempt to sell them abroad.

Thus the decades ahead promise to be lively ones in the field of arms sales.

VII

What Ever Happened to Krupp? . . .

"The seed ye sow, another reaps;
The wealth ye find, another keeps;
The robes ye weave, another wears;
The arms ye forge, another bears."

—PERCY BYSSHE SHELLEY,
Song to the Men of England

1

The decline of the Zaharoffs of this world—that is to say, entrepreneurs selling the products of private arms manufacturers with impunity—has been dramatic. The reasons warrant examination.

Prior to World War II, the fortunes of arms manufacturers fluctuated wildly. In wartime arms industries operated at full capacity, their governments eagerly taking everything they could produce. In peacetime they were plagued by underproduction, their governments showing a distinct lack of interest in their products. It was a feast or famine business, and the rise of the Zaharoff type of salesman was a direct response to the threat of financial hunger. Furthermore, arms manufacturers generally developed their own weapons independently of state financial help. These projects were and still are known as private ventures, or PV's. The Maxim, Nordenfeldt, Hotchkiss, Krupp and Browning products, for instance, were all developed privately. With their own money at stake it was necessary for these arms companies in times of peace to mount intensive sales drives—directed toward both their own governments and foreign markets—in order to recoup their investments. During wartime, of course, they had no problem selling their wares. Their zeal to sell their weapons in peacetime was heightened by the realization that the specialized nature of arms development and production, particularly after World War I (as compared to the state of the art in the mid-nineteenth century), precluded them from switching easily in slack times into the production of commercial goods.

After World War II, however, the situation changed. In a word, it has been feast years for over two decades for arms manufacturers. Beginning in 1947 and continuing to the present, the U.S. government (to be followed later by Great Britain, France and other countries) each year has bought huge quantities of arms from its own industry. To give some idea of the increase, in 1939 the total expenditure for all items by the U.S. military establishment was $1.4 billion; in 1949 it was $14.0 billion; in 1960 it was $41.0 billion and in 1968 it was approximately $72 billion. While it is not clear exactly how much of this money in these years was spent on arms purchases, a conservative average would be no less than 30 percent of the yearly totals. In FY 1969, for instance, $21.6 billion was appropriated for weapons purchases, or nearly 30 percent of the $72 billion defense budget. Procurement as a percentage of defense expenditures appears to be of a higher order in European countries. Between the years 1955 and 1964, for instance, Britain averaged 43 percent and Sweden 53 percent.[1]

What all this means is that instead of operating at 10 to 20 percent of capacity, as they had done in their prewar years of famine, the free-world's arms industries have been operating since the late 1940's at 80 to 90 percent of capacity. With governments ensuring high production levels and buying nearly the entire output, arms industries have had no need of Zaharoff-type salesmen who roam the world in search of sales. In other words, prior to World War II, peacetime demand never satisfied production, but after World War II production has hardly been able to keep up with demand.

The demise of these independents has been hastened by other factors. The research and development costs of PV's, for instance, have become so high that industries can no longer finance them without government help. In fact, today industry rarely spends any of its own money on the development of a new weapon without some guarantees from its own government that it will be assured of at least a minimum sale to its own military. Thus with little or none of its own money at stake and a minimum market assured, industry feels no urgency to mount a large-scale sales campaign. Furthermore, governments so control export sales of arms through licensing that, were a company to undertake a PV, there would be no guarantee that it could recoup its investment by selling to foreign customers. One British arms manufacturer put it to me this way: "If your own money is in it," he said, "you hustle and cannot afford to wait; if government is paying and controlling you, and profits are assured, you say, 'Well, what the hell, why bother?' " Often, he added, it is more profitable to sell the machines that make weapons rather than sell the weapons themselves.

Another factor inhibiting arms manufacturers has been the poor publicity that has come from selling weapons, no matter how honestly or openly it might be done. In the public's mind, particularly in America, it is not so bad that the Pentagon sells arms, but it is considered unethical for Colt, Remington, General Electric, Chrysler or some other weapons company to have an army of salesmen roaming the world flogging their wares. There is little logic to this, but it is a fact and every company is aware of it. Executives are so sensitive to the charge of selling arms that they often do not even admit in print that they are in the business. Perusing annual reports for information on military products, arms sales figures or arms customers is an exercise in frustration and is reminiscent of Eximbank reports. General Electric, for instance, barely admits to manufacturing the 20 mm M-61 *Vulcan* cannon, a hopped up Gatling-type gun that can fire 6,000 shots a minute, or 100 a second. One has to dig deeply to find that Vickers admits to making tanks and naval guns. One would not know from reading Avco's annual report that it is the world's largest manufacturer of military fuses.

This reluctance to admit to manufacturing arms is often so profound that manufacturers scatter their arms production among various subsidiaries. In other words, it is better to make less profit by scattering production than to make more profits and to increase efficiency by consolidating the military products into an ordnance division. General Motors is the best example of this. Some estimate that its annual arms sales (mostly to the U.S. government) run to $2.5 billion, yet it is nowhere reflected in its annual report. The Allison Division makes jet engines; the Hydramatic Division, whose ostensible purpose is to make automatic transmissions for cars, makes M-16A rifles (a variation of the Colt product); and in another division it manufactures the MBT-70 tank.

"We want to be known as a car and appliance manufacturer, not a merchant of war," said one GM official. "But we also want to be ready to profit from the apparently endless series of brushfire wars in which the U.S. seems to involve itself. We don't start the wars, and we don't want them to start, but war seems to be here to stay just as much as peace."[2]

Stockbrokers' attitude to shares of arms companies provides some insight into the change in the fortunes of the private entrepreneurs. In the late 1930's any hint of rearmament would push such stocks up dramatically. That war was good for business, especially the arms business, was a byword of the times. After World War II, however, this attitude changed. From 1947 to the middle of the 1950's, it is true, shares of arms companies again increased substantially, paralleling the return to a high level of defense spending. But from then on any hint of war has depressed the market for these shares. There are a number of reasons for this. First, many arms companies have become large conglomerates where the actual production of military goods is a relatively small percentage of their overall output. Second, because heavy government demands for weapons in peacetime has ensured a continuously high production rate, any increase due to limited war has been relatively small. The shares of a company such as General Electric, whose military business today makes up 20 percent of the whole, are not more attractive if its military business increased by, say, one-quarter (to meet the demands of limited war), because such a growth still represents only a small overall increase in its total business. Even a company that sells all its products to the U.S. military establishment is not a more attractive investment if its production advances from 80 percent of capacity to 90 percent. In the late 1930's, in comparison, an arms company operating at 20 percent of capacity with prospects of immediately jumping to 90 percent *was* an attractive company in which to invest.

Today war acts as a depressant on arms company shares because other factors become more important. As long as there is relative stability and a continuously high demand for arms from the U.S. government (without those arms actually being used), the prices of such shares remain firm. But when there is a war, such as in Vietnam, the advantages of a 10 or 20 percent increase in arms production are offset by greater threats of inflation, by balance of payments problems and by a feeling of uncertainty about future trends. It is interesting to note, for instance, that from mid-1961 to the spring of 1968 arms shares went into a slow decline (with a few exceptions) along with the rest of the stock market. But the moment there was a hint of peace in Vietnam, the market—arms shares included—rebounded vigorously. To brokers, a return to peace meant a return to stability—but a stability still coupled with a high level of peacetime government arms purchases. In the 1930's or before, the market would have retreated at the first sign of peace, with arms shares leading the way, because peace meant a general slowing down of the overall economy and a drastic diminution of arms production. If the U.S. government after the Vietnam War were to cut back its year-to-year high spending on arms to the pre-World War II production level of 20 percent, only then would the shares of armaments companies plummet. But there is little hope that this will happen.

The change in the old-style arms and munitions merchants themselves has been no less dramatic. Du Pont, for instance, no longer makes any special effort to sell military munitions abroad. It has become such a huge, diversified company—in chemicals, resins, plastics, films, fibers and allied products—that its powder products, once making up 100 percent of its business, now account for less than 1 percent of the whole. What munitions it does produce are either bought by the U.S. government or sold on the domestic market as explosives to industry or as cartridges to sportsmen. It does own explosive factories in Chile, Mexico, Brazil and Canada, but its products there are mostly for use in the commercial markets.[3]

American rifle manufacturers—Remington (60.58 percent owned by Du Pont) and Winchester (owned by Olin Mathieson), to name two of the most famous merchants in times past—have also abandoned the military export trade. They and others have found that the domestic sporting-goods market is far more lucrative. In the process, they have lost the art of making military weapons. It used to be that U.S. military rifles, like the Springfield .30-06 and the M-1 Garand, were precision-made products. Military rifles are today made with stampings, plastic moldings and castings (as opposed to hardwoods and forgings). Such companies as TRW, Inc., and Cadillac Gage (no relation to General Motors), it has been found, are far better qualified to make these new types of weapons. Colt Industries in Hartford is about the only old-time small arms manufacturer that has been able to make this transition with any success.

American cartridge makers like Remington and Winchester-Western, who boasted of large and continuing foreign sales from the Civil War to the outbreak of World War II, now no longer sell their products abroad in any quantity. Most countries with any industrial capacity have their own cartridge factories and, because of cheaper labor, can produce the material far less expensively than the American firms. The U.S. government has also hindered any postwar export sales by its own cartridge makers. In 1963, for example, it shipped to India a complete ammunition factory consisting of two high-speed assembly lines capable of producing several million rounds of ammunition daily in sizes ranging from 7.62 mm to 20 mm. Britain has done much the same thing. It has encouraged its own large chemical firm, Imperial Chemical Industries, to set up munitions factories around the world. Through one of its subsidiaries, it has set up several ammunition factories in South Africa.[4]

In Europe, many of the old names have disappeared from the

ranks of aggressive arms exporters. Vickers, for instance, is still the largest private armaments manufacturer in Great Britain; but with a few minor exceptions, its only customer for military products is Whitehall. Since the end of World War II it has not, with the exception of the *Vigilant* antitank missile, undertaken any private ventures. It still makes naval guns, warships, tanks and, most recently, nuclear submarines. It no longer makes any small arms; the Vickers and Maxim machine guns are now history. While gone, however, they are not forgotten: in January 1968, in a tearful ceremony, a highly polished Vickers machine gun that had seen fifty-five years of service was presented by the British Army to the members of Vickers' board of directors; it now sits in a walnut case in the boardroom behind electrically operated curtains.

Of all the arms companies that I visited, Vickers was by far the least cooperative in supplying information. They treated my inquiries for an interview with deep suspicion and eventually denied me an opportunity to talk with anyone employed in their London headquarters. In the United States, on the other hand, representatives of arms companies elbowed each other aside for an opportunity to explain the "true" nature of their business.

Birmingham Small Arms, another famous weapons manufacturer and exporter of old, no longer makes any military arms at all. It has switched to manufacturing motorcycles and inexpensive sporting rifles. Both BSA and Vickers were offered the Mauser Works after World War II; but when they inquired what assurances they would have that they could sell in foreign markets and were told that there would be none, they declined to take up the challenge.

In France, the Société des Forges et Ateliers du Creusot is still part of the Schneider empire and still makes military equipment. It has lost its financial interest in Skoda and has tended to move out of the arms manufacturing field into military motors and heavy transport vehicles. It manufactures the hulls for the AMX-13 tank but plays no part in the sale of this vehicle to foreign customers. Like Vickers and other companies of this nature, Schneider has expanded its interests from mining, iron and steel manufacturing, and naval construction into other fields such as electrical equipment construction (in partnership with Westinghouse), automation equipment, oil exploration and research, nuclear research, general public works construction, banking and credit. In 1966 Schneider reported that the Société des Forges et Ateliers du Creusot, the subsidiary in which most of its military equipment is manufactured, increased its deliveries over the previous year by 4 percent. While M. Eugene Schneider, the famous arms merchant in the Zaharoff era, would no doubt have been dismayed by such a small growth rate, today's management of the company can announce that such a rate reflects "satisfactory progress."[5]

Hotchkiss guns are still being made. Today, after a series of mergers, the work is done under the corporate name of Thomson-Houston–Hotchkiss-Brandt. This company, which employs 35,000 people, has one of the highest growth rates in its field. It manufactures a wide range of commercial equipment: x-ray machines, television sets, refrigerators, electronic equipment, trucks, buses and scientific equipment. In the military field, TH-HB is France's largest manufacturer of mortars, ranging in size from a 60 mm "commando" type to a 120 mm mortar mounted on wheels. It also manufactures mortar ammunition, 30 mm and 90 mm tank-mounted light combat guns, walkie-talkies, at least three different types of airborne rockets, and the French jeep.

Hotchkiss-Brandt, before it merged with Thomson-Houston in 1966, was very successful selling its wares to the French government during the wars in Indochina and Algeria. But with the ending of these conflicts and the government's subsequent concentration on its Force de Dissuasion, orders for rockets, mortars and ammunition were drastically reduced. The company was thus forced to seek new markets overseas. Of all the private French arms makers, it is the most aggressive in seeking foreign sales independent of government encouragement. Undoubtedly it cooperates closely with the government, but the impetus to sell abroad rests primarily with the company itself rather than the government. Exactly which countries have bought TH-HB military equipment is not clear; neither DMA/DAI nor the company publishes such information. But most authorities believe that it goes to former French colonies. Hotchkiss-Brandt's turnover doubled between 1960 and 1965 and it boasted that 25 percent of its business came from foreign trade.[6]

Not far behind in aggressiveness is the firm of Hispano-Suiza, a manufacturer of cannons, munitions, heavy industrial equipment, aircraft engines and Bugatti cars. It has plants throughout Europe and is perhaps the world's foremost developer of 20 mm cannons. In the 1950's Hispano-Suiza was involved in supplying armored personnel carriers of its own design to the West German Army. The transaction contained so many hints of scandal and mismanagement that it has since been termed the "HS-30 Affair."

The HS-30 was a tracked vehicle similar to the M-113 of U.S. design. It was lightly armored and carried a 30 mm flak cannon. In 1954, the Federal Republic, as part of its rearmament program, expressed interest in purchasing a troop carrier. The existing HS-30 at the time did not meet the German requirements, so it was hastily redesigned. In the summer of 1955 Hispano-Suiza representatives showed the Germans photographic slides of their remodeled carrier; later in the year a chassis with no turret was unveiled for inspection in Paris; and in May 1956 a wooden mock-up was produced for scrutiny by West German engineers. However, two months previously, in March, before any working model had been built and before any tests had been carried out and even before final drawings had been approved, the contract was let to Hispano-Suiza. It called for the production of 10,680 vehicles at a total cost of $625 million. The German Defense Ministry did not bother to wait for the experts' written opinion on this new version of the HS-30 because, it was claimed, all four experts were representatives of two of the firms that were to manufacture it, and it was assumed that they would approve.

The three main contractors were Hanomag in Hanover, Henschel (which since has gone bankrupt) in Kassel, and the Leyland Bus Company in England. Other subcontractors included Hispano-Suiza in Geneva, Rolls Royce, the Allison Division of General Motors and Rheinmetall in Germany. It was subsequently learned that the Bonn government was so anxious to have production start that it paid many of the manufacturers in advance. Some $3 million was also deposited in advance in a special closed account in the Oppenheim Bank in Cologne to be paid later as license royalties to Hispano-Suiza once deliveries began.

The contract called for first deliveries to be made in October 1957, but it was apparent from the start that the schedule would never be met. So many modifications were made because the original design was so poor that various superstructures would not fit and in themselves had to be redesigned. The engine, it was found, was so placed as to be impossible to service quickly. The tracks were too weak; the steering, braking and springs never worked properly; and it was discovered that it was dangerous for troops to climb in and out of the vehicle because the tracks were improperly protected. During all of this, the modifications increased the weight of the vehicle from 10 to 14.6 tons, which had the effect of lowering its overall performance capabilities.

Nearly two years later, in September 1959, the first deliveries were made, just at the time when the Germans were deciding to build their own tank (the *Leopard*), which would render the HS-30's obsolete. The last HS-30's were delivered in early 1962, but only 1,000 of the last batch of 2,800 were accepted. The Germans had become displeased with this personnel carrier because of its very high rate of breakdowns. In order to keep its army mobile, the Defense Ministry was forced to order 2,800 M-113's which, despite weaker armor and lighter firepower, had one advantage: they ran.

Two men connected with this deal were Hans "China" Klein, a German with a Chinese passport who made a reputation for himself in years past as an arms salesman to both Chiang Kai-shek and Mao Tse-tung, and Robert Pferdmenges, the late head of the Oppenheim Bank and the man who supposedly convinced Chancellor Adenauer to purchase the F-104G *Starfighter.* Also involved were Bonn ministers and generals and a Liechtenstein firm.

So many rumors of scandal began circulating in Switzerland, Germany and France that a special parliamentary committee was set up by the Bonn government in 1967 to investigate them. One charge, as yet unproven, is that the entire transaction was designed to enrich the Christian Democratic party's election fund. Another, also unproven, is that bribes were accepted by a Bonn lawyer, now dead, in order to ensure that the contract was let to Hispano-Suiza. Many others involved are also now dead. As of this writing the parliamentary committee has not published its report. It seems apparent at this juncture that Klein and Pferdmenges were only middlemen in the operation who profited handsomely (but legally) from the deal. Whether the ministers and generals either gave or accepted bribes has not been established.[7]

The current aggressiveness of Thompson-Houston–Hotchkiss-Brandt and Hispano-Suiza is matched by several other European arms firms of note. The most famous, of course, is Fabrique Nationale d'Armes de Guerre of Liège, Belgium. FN manufactures sporting pistols, rifles and shotguns. One of its best-selling products is the Browning over-and-under shotgun; 75 percent of all those it makes are exported to the United States. FN also manufactures under license the General Electric J-79 jet engine for the F-104G *Starfighter* and the Rolls Royce *Tyne, Avon* and *Derwent* military jet engines. It has also developed a light armored vehicle complete with FN-manufactured cannon and machine gun, and is currently working with Boeing on the development of a turbine engine for the European market.

The bulk of FN's revenues comes from the sale of military small arms and ammunition. Approximately 98 percent of this material is exported each year to eighty or ninety countries. In other words, there is virtually no country in the free world without a stock of FN arms and ammunition on hand. Most in demand are its 7.62 mm NATO Light Automatic Rifle, the older 7.62 mm NATO SAFN rifle, ammunition to go with these two weapons, and the 9 mm Uzi submachine gun, which is manufactured under license from Israel. All this material is turned out on perhaps the world's most modern and efficient armaments assembly line.

FN is so aggressive in its export sales that it is one of the few companies in the world that can make a good living selling ammunition to foreign customers. Its success in this field, however, is not due solely to its own efforts; in part it hinges on the volume of military activity throughout the world. The *Financial Times* of London reported in 1967 that FN experienced a certain drop in orders in the cartridges division not only because of increased competition but because of "a relative lack of disturbance in the world, together with a fall in military budgets."[8]

The greatest market for FN's military weapons and ammunition, the United States, was lost when the Pentagon chose to switch from the 7.62 mm NATO cartridge to the .223 caliber cartridge. Realizing that the United States might one day begin to export this new ammunition in quantity, along with the M-16 rifle in which it is used, FN developed its own automatic rifle using the same .223 caliber ammunition. It was such a success in trials that it went into production in 1968. FN has also set up a .223 caliber cartridge production line in anticipation of future sales; it knows that it can produce this material far more cheaply than U.S. manufacturers. By this move, FN officials are confident that their company will maintain its dominant position in the decades ahead.[9]

The Swedish firms of Bofors and SAAB and the Swiss firms of Werkzeugmaschinenfabrik Oerlikon Buhrle and Schweizerische Industrie-Gesellschaft (or SIG for short) also display an aggressiveness that stems more from self-interest than from government policy. These four companies are the only ones in the world in which a major proportion of their weapons development programs still are underwritten privately. Almost no government money is involved, and it is of interest that all four are located in neutral countries. The impetus for foreign sales rests squarely with the company rather than with the government. The difference between, say, the British system and the Swedish and Swiss systems is that the British arms makers would first seek Foreign Office permission for a sale, then would go out and make the sale; the Swedes and Swiss, on the other hand, first make the sale and only at the last moment seek official government sanction for it.

The vice-chairman of the board of SAAB is Dr. Marcus Wallenberg, one of Sweden's wealthiest men, the owner of the Stockholms Enskilda Bank, and a board member of sixty to seventy other companies. His son, Marc Wallenberg, Jr., is also on the board of SAAB. The eight-man board of directors of Bofors includes Sven Hammarskjold, a judge of appeals from Malmo and a second cousin to the late U.N. Secretary General.[10] Very little is known about the two Swiss firms. It is known, however, that Oerlikon Buhrle manufactures aircraft guns, artillery, aircraft rockets, ammunition and what most armament experts consider to be the finest antiaircraft guns in the world, some of which have seen service on U.S. warships. In its annual report, SIG limits its remarks on the manufacture of weapons to a few sentences.[11]

2

The demise of two old armaments firms once renowned for the zeal with which they sold their wares around the world, namely Mauser and Krupp, should be noted.

The Mauser company, like other German firms, ceased operations at the close of World War II. Most of the undamaged precision machine tools at its main plant in Oberndorf were carted away as war booty by the Soviet Union. Its highly skilled technical teams were broken up, some members being pressed into service by the Soviets, others seeking employment elsewhere. Eventually, after several unsuccessful attempts to sell the firm to British arms manufacturers, the company came into the possession of the Quandt family. The Quandts revived the firm but in the process sacrificed the reputation it held for nearly eighty years as a manufacturer of high-quality rifles and pistols. Today, Mauser limits its product line to small-caliber sporting weapons, which virtually everyone with whom I talked in the arms business described as "cheap" and "second-rate."

The Quandts of Mauser were very successful in the ordnance field during the Hitler regime. After the war they rebuilt their empire, which today includes large, and in some cases controlling, interests in Industrialwerke Karlesruhe, or IWK; Deutsche Waggon und Maschinenfabriken, or DWM; Nederlandsche Wapenen Munitiefabriek, or NWM, of Holland; and the Mauserwerke of Oberndorf. The first three all make small-caliber military weapons; NWM in particular is a large exporter of ammunition and is one of FN's major competitors. The Quandt family also has large holdings in the textile machine industry and, with Friedrich Flick (a convicted German war criminal and one of West Germany's wealthiest industrialists), a controlling interest in the Daimler-Benz firm which manufactures Mercedes.[12]

Until his death in 1967, the head of the family was Harald Quandt. His mother, Magda, eloped with and married Joseph Goebbels, Hitler's Propaganda Minister. She committed suicide with her husband and six children at the Fuehrer bunker in Berlin in the last days of World War II. Harald Quandt was a friend of Gerhard Mertins of Merex. They served together in the same parachute regiment during the war. Before he set up his own company, Mertins worked for the Quandts as a Mercedes-Benz salesman in the Middle East. Mertins' man in Washington, Gerhard Bauch, it should be recalled, also maintained ties with the Quandts; he once worked as an agent in the Middle East for Harald's brother, Herbert Quandt, a banker and also a director of the family empire. Exactly what other ties existed between the Quandts and Merex is unclear, but it appears that there are none at this writing.

The most famous—and most feared—name in arms for over a century was the giant manufacturing firm of Fried. Krupp of Essen, the firm that supplied heavy armaments to three generations of German warmakers—Otto von Bismarck, Kaiser Wilhelm II and Adolph Hitler. History will note that Krupp cannon were in such demand between 1870 and 1945 that there were few wars in that period in which identical Krupp guns were not facing each other in battle. It was Krupp that added to the lexicon of war such names as "Long Max," the monster rifle that shelled Paris in 1918; "Fat Gustav," the largest gun ever made, which took part in the siege of Sebastopol in 1942; and "Big Bertha," the giant mortar of World War I fame. It was Krupp who made the *Tiger* tanks; it was Krupp who built many of the dreaded U-boats; it was Krupp steel that shattered the cities of Rotterdam, Stalingrad, London and Coventry. "Krupp! Krupp! Krupp!" cried Berthold Beitz, until recently the firm's general manager. "It sounds like a cannon going off." And for many generations of Europeans it was all too true.

But times change. After World War II the Allies confiscated the Krupp properties and destroyed the U-boat pens at Kiel and dismantled the cannon shops at Essen. An American tribunal convicted the fifth and last family head of the vast industrial empire, Alfried Alwyn Felix Krupp von Bohlen und Halbach, of war crimes and sentenced him to twelve years in prison.

In 1951 John J. McCloy, the U.S. High Commissioner for Germany, commuted the sentence and ordered Krupp released. He also reversed the confiscation mandate and ruled that the bulk of the Krupp properties be restored to the family. This ruling, which brought cries of dismay from the British and French, was hastened by the exigencies of the Cold War.

The Allies, however, still demanded that Krupp dispose of his coal and steelmaking facilities. While this demand was accepted, it was never carried out. Alfried Krupp, with his brilliant manager, Beitz, began in 1953 to move out of the old, declining and high-employment industries of coal and steelmaking and into more lucrative fields of endeavor such as construction, electrical and mechanical engineering, retailing and wholesaling. Eventually Krupp was to move back into the steelmaking business (using the most modern equipment in the world) because it complemented his other worldwide interests.

In 1953 the Krupp empire employed 16,000 workers and was grossing approximately $230 million. Twelve years later, in 1965, the company was employing 112,000 workers and was grossing $1.3 billion in sales. It was manufacturing over 3,000 different items, ranging from specialty steels to lemonade. Its current steelmaking capacity is larger than it has ever been in the company's history.

The Krupp empire, since its founding in 1811, was 100 percent owned by the head of the family. In April 1967 this came to an end when Alfried Krupp found himself in a credit squeeze. He asked the Bonn government for guarantees to tide him over, in return for which he agreed to relinquish sole control and to set up a public stock company. Alfried himself died three months later, in July, and his personal fortune, including the assets of his empire, was willed to a foundation to perpetuate the firm.[13]

Alfried Krupp, upon his release from prison in 1951, vowed that his company would never again make armaments. There are some indications, however, that the company is slowly creeping back into the field, albeit not into cannon making. During Berthold Beitz's tenure as general manager, from 1953 to 1968, Krupp supplied NATO with mobile bridges, radar equipment and military trucks. It supplied equipment for the production of tank armor to India. Perhaps most significant, Krupp purchased a 29 percent interest in Vereinigte Flugtechnische Werke, or VFW, West Germany's largest military aircraft manufacturer. The VFW firm, an amalgamation of the old Wesserflug, Focke-Wulf and Heinkel aircraft companies, manufactures under license F-104 *Starfighters,* Fiat G-91's, Fouga *Magisters* and several other military aircraft.[14]

This trend will no doubt continue. There is some evidence that the directors of the newly reorganized firm, now known as Fried. Krupp GmbH, are anxious to intensify their arms making activities. In October 1968, a company spokesman announced that Krupp was seeking more armaments orders in such military items as armored vehicles and warship hulls. He was quick to point out that the firm would still refuse to make cannons. "Our policy is more armament industry—no items that go bang," he declared. Whether Krupp will in fact avoid a return to cannon making is difficult to predict at the moment. But already the company has reneged on Alfried Krupp's pledge of 1951; it may be only a matter of time before it reneges on its own self-imposed ban on cannon making.

But the future role of Fried. Krupp GmbH does not in the last analysis rest with Alfried Krupp's heirs. The last head of the family himself went to the heart of the matter when he said, "I hope that it will never again be necessary for a Krupp to produce arms, but what a factory makes depends after all not only on the decision of its owners but also on the politics of its government."[15]

3

Despite the decline of many of the large, old-time arms manufacturers, there exist several firms whose current vigor matches that of FN, TH-HB, Hispano-Suiza and the four armsmakers from Sweden and Switzerland. By and large they are small firms doing a relatively small volume of business, particularly when compared to the companies above.

For example, the old Dusseldorf firm of Rheinische Metallwaren und Maschinenfabrik, more commonly known as Rheinmetall, is an exporter of military small arms, most notably 20 mm cannons. Recently it was involved in the sale of $75 million worth of Hispano-Suiza cannon (called the HS-820) to the Defense Department in Washington. This transaction subsequently caused a considerable stir in the United States because the weapon did not function properly and the sale came at a time when the Pentagon was closing down some of its own arsenals. It also created a stir within Jewish communities because it was learned that Rheinmetall had been a major employer of slave labor during World War II and that the company's U.S. representative at the time of the sale was Julius Klein, an ex-national commander of the Jewish War Veterans organization.

A firm called Heckler & Koch of Oberndorf, West Germany, exports a variety of small arms, in particular the Spanish CETME assault rifle which it manufactures under license. Both Rheinmetall and Heckler & Koch sell their own brands of .223 caliber military rifle, their greatest market for these items being the Middle East.

The Italian firm of Beretta exports its pistols with considerable vigor. It set up a pistol factory—complete with Italian dies, tools and technicians—in Santo Domingo during the Trujillo dictatorship and has supplied special small arms to Egypt, Argentina and the United States. Another Italian firm, OTO Melara, sells naval, antiaircraft and field artillery pieces, missile installations, tanks, M-113's (built under license) and ammunition. Like many of its competitors, it often runs full-page advertisements of its military wares in U.S. trade publications.

The small Swedish firm of Fortsvarets Fabriksverk sells the *Carl Gustav* antitank gun and a wide variety of ammunition. Although owned by the government, it operates along commercial lines and is so aggressive that it can sell 7.62 mm cartridges $5 to $10 cheaper per hundred (complete with the store's name on the box) in the United States than domestic producers. Another firm, Bombrini Parodi Delfino of Italy, is a competitive explosives exporter; the French firm of Engins Matra, owned by millionaire racing-car enthusiast Sylvain Floirat, exports missiles, jet engines and munitions; and the Belgian firm of Energa is an exporter of ceramic-jacketed grenades.

The exceptions to the rule that these exporters are small are the engine manufacturers. Such firms as Rolls Royce, Hispano-Suiza, Fiat, Sud Aviation, Nord Aviation, SNECMA, Allison Division of General Motors, General Electric, Pratt & Whitney Division of United Aircraft, MAN Turbo and Turbomeca, all export military engines. But the bulk of their export business is to the larger and faster growing commercial jet engine market. The sale of engines has always been export-oriented, and there is considerable overlap in military and civil aviation requirements. Therefore, unlike other military equipment manufacturers, it has been relatively easy for them to break into this export market.

With the millions of ordnance items that have been distributed throughout the world since 1945, it is inevitable that someone would come along specializing in spare parts to keep this equipment operating. There are many such companies in the world today, all of them feeding off the arms trade, all of them tending to limit themselves to certain types of equipment. For the purposes of illustration, two of the best known, NAPCO Industries and Astra Aircraft Corporation, deserve brief examination.

NAPCO is a diversified auto parts manufacturer located in Minneapolis. One quarter of its business is supplying parts for military vehicles not in current production. Some of its sales are to the U.S. military, but the bulk are to foreign countries where resistance to scrapping is greater. NAPCO will guarantee to deliver any mechanical, electrical or hydraulic part for any combat or tactical vehicle made in the United States since 1940. To back up its guarantee, NAPCO has assembled, in 300,000 square feet of warehouse in a fifty-acre complex, the free world's largest non-governmental inventory of military vehicle spare parts. Most of its inventory was purchased either as "scrap" or as production overruns. What it does not stock, NAPCO will gladly reproduce faithfully from government blueprint specifications.

Like Bannerman, Cummings and the French government, NAPCO publishes a catalogue that is required reading by military purchasing agents in at least fifty-five countries. If a new cylinder block for an old Willys jeep is needed, NAPCO will be happy to sell you one. If your *Sherman* tanks need new treads, NAPCO has them in stock. If your M-8 armored car of 1942 vintage needs new blackout lights, NAPCO will quote you a price. In short, if your army is still equipped with *Stuart, Chaffie* or *Patton* tanks, half-tracks, "Weazles," "Ducks," scout cars, command cars and transport trucks of any size from World War II and Korean War years, NAPCO will sell you parts to ensure that they continue to run.[16]

Astra Aircraft specializes in aircraft and electronic replacement parts. It is located in New York City and is run by Moses D. Acosta, a dapper, erudite individual who affects Continental mannerisms. Unlike NAPCO, Astra stocks no large inventory of spare equipment. Instead, it maintains a very large reference library, not only of what the United States military has bought and sold, but of stock numbers of every piece of aircraft and electronic gear made since the end of World War II. Many customers, Acosta told me, come to Astra seeking equipment already in their military inventories but ignorant of who made the item and when it was made. Astra, through its reference library, can trace down the parts in minutes, find the manufacturer and have the item made for the customer. Ninety-nine percent of Astra's business, Acosta said, is with foreign customers who have been recipients of U.S. military equipment.

In order to stay on top of the business, he added, it is also necessary to keep records of what each country in the free world maintains in the way of military hardware. These records, said Acosta, are by far the most complete in the world, better he claims than the Defense Department's or even the CIA's. The difference, he said, is that "we have to *sell* from our records," while other organizations do not, "so our information *has* to be more accurate."

Astra does not limit itself to aircraft and electronic replacement parts. Part of the "fall-out" from the business, said Acosta, is inquiries for other equipment, and he mentioned military vehicles, riot equipment, arms and ammunition as typical. Astra also represents several foreign armament manufacturers in other parts of the world like the British company of Short Bros. & Harland of Belfast, Northern Ireland. Astra has recently been pushing the sale of Short's *Seacat* ship-to-air missile and its *Skyvan* military transport in the Far East.

In addition to these replacement-part companies, there are four firms that manufacture M-1 and M-2 carbines primarily for the export market. What makes these companies unique is that they began manufacturing carbines in 1960, three years after these weapons had been declared obsolete by the Pentagon and fifteen years after the original U.S. government procurement had ended. Approximately six million U.S. caliber .30 carbines of all models were manufactured between 1942 and 1945 for the U.S. government. They were used throughout most of World War II and in the Korean War. Until 1957, when the Pentagon converted to the 7.62 mm NATO cartridge (and subsequently to the .223 caliber cartridge), they were standard equipment in most branches of the U.S. military. Millions of these carbines were either given away or sold by the Pentagon between the years 1950 and 1965. Yet the demand for these weapons has been and continues to be so great that the government could not keep up with it. These four companies thus stepped in to fill the void.

The most successful of them all is Plainfield Machine Company of Dunellen, New Jersey. It is a ten-man firm with annual sales nearing the one-million-dollar mark. Three quarters of its output of approximately 15,000 carbines is exported; the rest (limited to semiautomatic M-1's only) are sold on the domestic market to sportsmen.* The carbines in question—and Plainfield sales brochures show eight different models—are exact reproductions of the

* Other less sporting customers have evinced an interest in these weapons as well. During the 1967 Newark riots, forty-six carbines were stolen from the company. This theft was one of the factors that prompted the New Jersey National Guard to invade a number of private houses in the riot areas in search of them. From what reports are available, not all of the carbines have been recovered.

earlier GI issue except that some of the parts are castings rather than forgings. They sell from $60 to $100 each.

According to Harold Richmond, Plainfield's sales manager, sales are mostly to "poor nations" in the Middle East and South America. When I was in his office, Richmond spent some time on the telephone haggling over prices with a Peruvian attaché. Large sales have been made to Lebanon and the Nationalist Chinese. All exports, no matter what their destination, are first cleared with the Office of Munitions Control. Rather than get involved with government credit schemes, said Richmond, all sales are "cash on the barrelhead."

4

The most common method all arms manufacturers use to sell military equipment abroad is, like Interarms, through the use of agents. By and large agents are citizens of the country to which they sell arms; they are generally technically trained and, most important of all, they are ex-military men of high rank who have access to the pertinent government politicians and bureaucrats. Ordinarily, above and beyond their salaries, they are paid a percentage, usually no more than 5 percent, of all sales secured.

Many large arms firms—Lockheed, Boeing, United Aircraft, Northrop, Rolls Royce, etc.—maintain branch offices in certain key cities around the world. These offices are used for the purpose of lobbying, collecting technical data, entertaining, financing, and sales coordination with the agents. The firms staff these offices with ex-military men from their own services rather than with local ex-military officers. The man who runs Lockheed's Paris office, for example, is retired Vice Admiral Aurelius Bartlett Vosseller, a specialist in naval aviation since 1930 and a former commander of the USS *Coral Sea.* Vosseller was on the staff of the Supreme Commander Allied Powers Europe in the 1950's and obviously made many good contacts within NATO. Upon his retirement from active duty in 1956, he was hired by Lockheed and is now a vice president for the European area.

Hiring ex-military men is nothing new in the arms business.

There exists an Old Boys' Network in the arms sales field—a relatively small fraternity of like-minded men that over the years has been drawn together by wars, aid programs and educational exchanges. A retired officer, even at a $50,000-a-year salary, is a bargain to industry if he can gain access to his old friends still in power in a foreign military establishment. This friendship often means the difference between winning and losing a large arms order. Lockheed, for instance, appointed a General Steinbach as its chief European representative for the *Starfighter* sale to Germany. Before coming to work for Lockheed, Steinbach was head of the U.S. MAAG in Bonn. There are no major arms producing companies in the free world that do not have a number of high-ranking ex-military officers in their employ.* Even Cummings of Interarms used to have a retired military officer of high rank on his payroll.

Another method of selling arms independent of government encouragement is through licensing arrangements. They are welcomed by all parties: to the licenser they mean extra income and to the licensee they mean steadier employment, higher income and the acquisition of new management and scientific techniques. Governments welcome them because they appear to cut down both in the brain-drain and losses in foreign exchange.

The greatest number of licenses placed since World War II has come from U.S. manufacturers. Most have been placed with European firms and, in their entirety, have created a volume of business that dwarfs the volume created by agreements of this nature between all other countries. Lockheed's license agreements with firms in Belgium, West Germany, Holland, Italy, Canada and Japan for the manufacture of F-104's, and FMC's agreements with three Italian firms for the production of M-113 armored personnel carriers are the best known of all these arrangements. But there have been many others. Hughes Aircraft, for instance, has given a

* In March, 1969, Senator William Proxmire (D.-Wis) revealed that 2,072 retired military officers of the rank of colonel or Navy captain or above were employed by the 100 largest military contractors. Lockheed and General Dynamics, two large firms whose military products are sold widely abroad, alone employed, respectively, 210 and 113 high-ranking officers, nearly an eight-fold increase over the number each employed in 1959.

license to three Swedish firms to produce *Falcon* missiles and to BAC to manufacture space vehicles; Sikorsky has licensed Westland Aircraft and Sud Aviation to manufacture its helicopters, and its parent company, United Aircraft, has agreements with Plessey (U.K.) Limited and Fiat for the production of electronic and engine parts. Fabrique Nationale, Bristol Siddeley, BWM, MAN Turbo and Fiat all have licenses to manufacture General Electric jet engines; SNECMA, Fiat and Svenska Flygmotor have licenses to manufacture the products of Pratt & Whitney; Raytheon *Hawk* missiles are manufactured by Fokker, Phillips Gloeilampenfabrieken and Selenia of Italy; and the German firms of Dornier, Messerschmitt, MAN Turbo and Agusta are licensed to manufacture Bell Aeronautics helicopters. North American Aviation, Fairchild Camera, RCA, Westinghouse, Chrysler and Allison also are a few of the better-known American firms that have licensed their military products to European manufacturers.[17]

There are very few licensing agreements with U.S. firms to manufacture European products. However, the intra-European volume of licensing deals is quite heavy. Rolls Royce, for instance, has licensed its engines to every European engine manufacturer of note. Messerschmitt and VFW manufacture Fouga *Magisters;* the German electronics firm of AEG manufactures the military products of Marconi, EMI, Phillips and Decca under license; the Italian firms of Macchi, Alfa Romeo and Fiat manufacture, respectively, Fokker, Bristol Siddeley and de Havilland products under license; SAAB has a license to manufacture Sud Aviation military helicopters. In the interest of space, this list is only partially complete.[18]

The behavior of arms manufacturers when selling abroad—whether the companies are operating independently or as the result of government prodding—varies widely, from honest to crooked. My impression is that arms salesmen behave little better or worse than their commercial counterparts. Generally they operate in an atmosphere of honesty and mutual trust and whatever business they transact, because it is routine and unflamboyant, receives little or no publicity.

One common trait, particularly with U.S. arms manufacturers, is to send ex-military officer employees on junkets around the world in search of sales. Sometimes they go at the behest of ILN, other times with the blessings of their own head office. These people on occasion can cause a great deal of damage. Ralph Dungan recalls, for instance, that when he was ambassador to Chile he ran across one American ex-military officer—formerly an Air Force G-2 whose last post was with CinCSouth—who did nothing but travel around Latin America as an employee of a large U.S. aircraft manufacturer. He knew every Chief of Staff south of the Rio Grande and, in the course of renewing old acquaintanceships, would attempt to sell his company's products, in this instance a large military transport plane. Dungan found that whenever he questioned the propriety of such a sales technique, the ex-military man would usually respond by saying that he was "only doing a job" and that he had no interest in becoming entangled in the local political situations. "The trouble with this thing," said Dungan, "is that every one of these guys are really decent fellows, doing a job, just as if they were selling [household] hardware . . . absolutely nonideological and, by and large, apolitical. But this is exactly the point: in an intensely political and an intensely ideological business, you've got the wrong guys handling it."

Sometimes companies will send platoons of blue-ribbon executives abroad to ensure that a sale is secured. These men wine and dine their prospective customers, lobby in the corridors, shoulder aside the competition and, if necessary, bribe. Until the mid-1960's this type of behavior was limited to U.S. companies because they were the only ones that could afford to do it. Now, several European companies, facing up to the competition, have adopted these same tactics. The future trend is toward more and more arms companies using these sales techniques in order to survive.

One recent example of how arms manufacturers behave was the case of Lockheed's sale of F-104's to West Germany, the political aspects of which were discussed previously. According to a cover article that appeared in a 1966 issue of *Der Spiegel,* the company took advantage of Bonn's inexperience in the field of defense contract negotiations. The article stated that once Lockheed learned in October 1958 that the F-104 had been chosen over the other two competitors, it took advantage of its monopoly position before pricing and licensing arrangements had been fixed. Lockheed succeeded in having the Bonn government sign a contract that was so loosely worded that the company and its subcontractors were relieved of normal guarantees of an existing-but-modified weapons system such as delivery dates, performance standards and minimum operating life. Nor did the contract specify cost limits to subsequent modifications. As a result Bonn was saddled with heavy extra costs over which it had very little control.[19]

When deliveries of the modified F-104 began in 1961–62, the Luftwaffe found that many of the aircraft were not up to performance requirements. In reply to a number of complaints by the Germans, Lockheed officials pointed out that their contract only called for a fully functional machine, made with the best materials and properly assembled. Bonn also complained that the inertia guidance system, made by Litton Industries, failed to meet specifications. Litton pointed out that nowhere in its contract was there a requirement to meet any specifications; the German standards were described as "design goals" and therefore were not technically binding.[20]

The mistakes of the Bonn government—it employed inexperienced negotiators, it accepted something less than a binding contract, its efforts lacked coordination, and it displayed an unhealthy haste to acquire the aircraft—do not absolve Lockheed of responsibility for its behavior. Lockheed would never have been able to act in this manner with the U.S. government for the modification of an existing aircraft. Had it by chance signed as loose a contract as this with the Defense Department, there would have been a domestic outcry, far more serious than the one that subsequently broke in the German press. Had it loaded on as much excess costs for post-contractual changes as there were on the *Starfighter* contract—an estimated $60 million—renegotiation proceedings would have been initiated, which the Federal Republic is not likely to attempt with Lockheed.

Nor is the U.S. government without blame. It will be recalled that it was Pentagon lobbyists and salesmen, working with a large Lockheed team, that exerted an unprecedented amount of economic and political muscle on the German Defense Ministry to award the contract to Lockheed. This activity on the part of Pentagon bureaucrats helped to create the atmosphere of hysteria, confusion and haste that led Bonn to sign such a contract in the first place.

A less typical example of the way in which companies behave is the case of one U.S. arms manufacturing firm that convinced the Sixth Fleet in the Mediterranean to display its equipment whenever its ships pulled into port. The Fleet at first went along with the idea but it was soon found that the company, and not the Navy, was deciding visits to ports. This practice was stopped when the Fleet Admiral realized that it was getting out of hand.

Occasionally there are scandals. One of the most recent that has not been mentioned previously in this volume took place in Japan. In 1967 the Japanese government voted a $6.5 billion military budget, the purpose of which was to re-equip and to modernize the country's 250,000-man self-defense force by 1971. By ordinary postwar Japanese standards this was a huge military outlay: $2.7 billion was to be spent on domestically produced arms, the remainder on arms purchased abroad. The contracts were so large that few were surprised at the ferociously competitive bidding that took place.

The first hint of a scandal occurred in October 1967 when the civilian head of the Japanese Defense Agency's equipment bureau committed suicide by thrusting his neck under the wheels of an express train. He apparently disapproved of the award of a vital air defense contract. In March 1968 the vice president of the Air Force's Technology & Science School was detained in prison and was questioned on the leakage of state secrets to Hughes Aircraft to help it bid on defense contracts. A $13 million contract was eventually awarded to Hughes, and it is apparent now that considerable effort was made by the company and its agents to win the order.

When the scandal finally broke in the spring of 1968, Major General Jiso Yamaguchi, Chief of the Defense Division's air staff office, expressed shock at the revelations. He tendered his resignation, but it was refused. Shortly thereafter he, too, committed suicide. In his pockets police found a note that said, "I am solely to blame for everything. I will apologize by killing myself."[21]

For years a number of European companies have been trying to break the NATO Strategic Embargo, which is designed to prevent certain free-world goods from reaching communist countries. The embargo embraces weapons, rare metals, the ABC (Atomic, Bacteriological and Chemical) List, and advanced technologies. This ban has been dented repeatedly in recent years by aggressive European firms. The products most often sold to Iron Curtain countries have been computers. Despite objections by the U.S. government—the strongest supporter of the embargo—several firms have succeeded in selling their wares to communist countries. The British firm of International Computers & Tabulators sold $1.4 million worth of its most sophisticated computers to the Peking regime in 1967. Another British firm, English Electric Computers, announced in the same year that it had won orders worth $280,000 from Czechoslovakia and Yugoslavia, and that it was negotiating with Bulgaria, East Germany, the Soviet Union, Poland and Rumania for more sales. The English Electric computers employ many U.S.-designed and -manufactured components. Elliott Automation, a third British firm, also has sold computers to Red China and eastern European countries.* General Electric, the American firm, has sold computers to the Soviet Union, but the equipment was made in France and Italy.[22]

Part of the difficulty in containing this traffic lies in the fact that the word "strategic" has never been given a clear definition. When, for instance, is a computer strategic and when is it not? Those in favor of a sale to communist countries argue one way, and those opposed argue another. The same applies to such items as oil pipeline, heavy-duty trucks and automobile plants. While some items on the embargo list are subject to dispute, there is no evidence to date that any first-rank strategic goods—rare metals,

* These three British firms have since been merged into one company called International Computers Limited. This new company has stepped up its sales effort in eastern Europe.

items on the ABC List and arms—have been sold openly to the communists.

One is tempted to ask why companies bother to venture independently into the foreign arms market when such a large percentage of their output is bought by their own governments, and what is left over is actively sold on foreign markets by the same governments. No doubt part of the reason is that there *are* profits to be made that are greater than what one would expect were the government to handle the sale. Many foreign sales also follow naturally from commercial efforts. But one of the major—and seldom acknowledged—reasons companies sell abroad is to interest their own governments in their products. If a company develops, say, a better ejection seat, and the government expresses no interest, then a brief export drive is initiated; a small quantity of the items is sold, usually at giveaway prices, to select foreign countries. The home government hears of the sale, because of the need for clearances and export licenses, and reasons that if such-and-such a country is interested in the new ejection seat, then perhaps a second look should be taken at it.

There are many variations to this tactic, but they are all designed to force one's own government to act in one manner or another. A typical example is the way Colt Industries forced the Defense Department to buy more of its M-16 rifles.

Beginning in 1960 a series of Defense Department contracts were awarded to Colt for large quantities of the M-16. The contracts stipulated that the Defense Department would take Colt's entire production of the weapon. By mid-1967 the Pentagon was purchasing 25,000 of them per week. But Colt, in the meantime, had slowly increased its output to 32,000 per week. It went to the Defense Department and said, in effect, that if the U.S. government would not take the additional 7,000, as it said it would, the company should be allowed to sell the excess to foreign governments. The Pentagon demurred, eventually agreeing to take all the additional rifles.

But nothing was forthcoming from Washington; the government continued to order only 25,000 per week. Colt then went back to the Pentagon and laid before its officials company figures which showed a 32,000-per-week production rate. This document was promptly classified because it would have embarrassed the government official who previously had stated publicly that the government was taking all of Colt's production.

Colt then went out and sold 20,000 M-16's to Singapore. Kuss was upset with this development. He was unaware that Colt had excess M-16's because the company figures—being classified by some other department in the Pentagon—were not available to him. The demand by Singapore for these rifles was so insistent that Kuss could not stop the sale without causing an embarrassing diplomatic uproar; so he took over responsibility for the sale and delivered the M-16's through the ILN office. "The facts are," Kuss told me, "if Colt hadn't fouled that damn thing up in the first place, we wouldn't have sold [M-16's] to Singapore. If Colt hadn't been out stirring up the thing without our approval to do so, we wouldn't have been in any trouble. This is an example of something that was out of control, but it is damn well *in* control now."

Although Kuss' annoyance is understandable, it is questionable how far Colt allowed the situation to get beyond its control. Shortly after this episode the Pentagon increased its weekly order to 27,500 units.

Yet, as in many other instances, the Defense Department has had the last word. In April 1968 the Pentagon quietly gave a $56 million contract to General Motors to manufacture 240,000 M-16A rifles. (This contract, and a similar one given to the firm of Harrington & Richardson, were awarded without competitive bids being submitted and subsequently were to cause a minor congressional uproar.) The ostensible reasons for switching suppliers were that the rifle, as produced by Colt, was prone to malfunctions and that Colt's profits were running to 19 percent instead of the usual 10 percent on cost-plus work. These seem unlikely reasons, first, because most if not all of the defects had long since been corrected (putting a layer of chrome in the chamber, for instance, so that there would not be a buildup of carbon) and, second, because the award to GM will cost the Pentagon over twice as much per weapon as before. No doubt these had something to do with the switch, but certainly one of the unspoken reasons was bureaucratic pique at Colt's attempt to up the weekly purchase rate and all the embarrassment and muddle that came with it.

Several trends are noticeable among private arms manufacturers. One is the increasing numbers of mergers, undertaken primarily for reasons of efficiency. The process of concentration has been a continuous one since the end of World War II, but in recent years it has increased in tempo. In France, for instance, aircraft companies, both private and government-owned, in the north and center of the country were merged in 1949, resulting eventually in 1954 in the formation of Nord Aviation. Sud Aviation was the result of mergers in 1957 of companies in the southeast and southwest areas. Many other arms companies have merged in France, the Thomson-Houston–Hotchkiss-Brandt case being typical.

The Hawker Siddeley group of aircraft companies is the result of the merger of seven aircraft firms. The British Aircraft Corporation was created in 1960 by amalgamating the airframe divisions of Bristol Aircraft, English Electric Aircraft, Hunting Aircraft and Vickers Armstrong. Rolls Royce and Bristol Siddeley have both absorbed smaller engine companies.[23] The electronic field has produced a giant in the merger of English Electric Computers, Elliott Automation and International Computers & Tabulators, forming International Computers Limited, noted previously.

Germany's largest aircraft firm, VFW, is also the result of a three-way merger. It recently merged again with Fokker, Holland's largest airframe manufacturer. This process is by no means limited to European firms. In the United States, for example, arms producers such as LTV, Inc., Avco, Litton, General Dynamics and McDonnell-Douglas were all the products of mergers, and few of them have lost the acquisitive instinct. The concentration of industry in the United States does not need to be further detailed here. Suffice it to say, arms industries around the world are tending to become fewer in number but bigger in size.

The pressure to merge is still intense and does not always stem from the grand designs of corporate executives. The French government wants Breguet to merge with Avions Marcel Dassault; the British are considering merging Bristol Siddeley into Rolls Royce to form one large national engine maker. It also wants BAC to absorb the Hawker Siddeley airframe group of companies. Both the French and the British shipbuilding industries are being concentrated into fewer yards, and the United States is encouraging the reorganization of its shipyards into economically viable units.

Another trend is the increasing willingness of U.S. firms to take a financial interest in major European defense companies. Pratt & Whitney holds a 10 percent interest in the nationalized French company of SNECMA; its parent company, United Aircraft, holds 26 percent of the shares of VFW (three percent less than Krupp) and 20 percent of the shares in the French electronic firm of Precilec. Boeing owns one quarter of the shares of Bolkow, the large German airframe firm; Northrop controls 20 percent of Fokker (which, since the merger with VFW, means that Northrop now has a toehold in the West German aircraft industry); Lockheed holds 20 percent of Macchi's stock; General Electric controls the French computer firm of Machines Bull; Bendix owns half the shares of Teldix, a German electronics company; and Raytheon owns 45 percent of the shares in Selenia in Italy. There are no American holdings in British or Swedish aerospace industries, although Hughes Aircraft maintains very close links with SAAB, Pratt & Whitney with Svenska Flygmotor, and Allison with Rolls Royce.[24]

Intra-European financial ties are not as extensive. Nord Aviation owns another 25 percent of Bolkow; Fokker owns a half interest in the Belgian airframe maker of SABCA (which in turn profits Northrop); and the British firm of Marconi owns 29 percent of Svenska Radio.[25]

The purpose of the large American holdings in Europe is not to take over the defense production in a country. Rather, the minority shareholdings, in most cases, give the companies an opportunity to keep abreast of technological developments in Europe and to utilize any new scientific breakthroughs that may emerge. They also give the minority shareholders a European base from which they can recruit talented individuals for the parent company in the United States. Much of Europe's brain-drain stems from the activities of these companies.

Where these two trends will lead the private arms manufacturers in the future is difficult to predict with any certainty. Certainly the trend toward concentration will create a situation where governments will be unable to back out of the arms business. If the well-being of a country is tied to the health of a few large armament makers, it will become vital that they continue to increase their sales and profits. A country whose airframe manufacturers, for instance, are scattered among ten or fifteen different enterprises can afford to have one or two of them lose money once in a while as the natural consequence of business cycles; but with *one* national airframe manufacturer, *one* national engine maker, *one* national electronics giant, and so on, a country cannot ever afford to have one of them lose money, because the effects on the entire economy would be unsettling.

In the interim, most arms companies, if the past is any indication, will continue to venture into the foreign market at sporadic intervals, whenever unique or lucrative opportunities arise. However, this would change if governments ever cut back on their own large domestic arms purchasing plans. In such an event, arms makers would be forced to seek other markets, most likely foreign, in order that their production rates and profits be maintained. The day this happens will be a chaotic one for them, and every executive in the business with whom I spoke shuddered at the thought that such a day might possibly arrive within their lifetime. Almost without exception they said that it was mandatory that the arms trade continue on its current course, despite inherent weaknesses and occasional crises, as long as the communists remain a threat.

It is to this specter of communist arms sales, then, that we now turn our attention.

VIII

The Communists as Arms Traders

"Every Communist must grasp the truth, 'Political power grows out of the barrel of a gun.' "

—MAO TSE-TUNG

1

The arms trade has always been a major tool of Soviet foreign policy since the country became a great power after World War II. Even during the early years of the regime, from 1917 to 1930, the arms trade was used to aid those countries opposed at that time to the "main enemy" (Britain and France), to play upon the "contradictions in the capitalist camp" and, above all, to further world revolution. Moscow sent arms to Turkey in the Turko-Greek War of 1921; it secretly helped to rearm Germany during the 1920's and early 1930's; it even tried to foment a revolution in the Yemen in 1928.

From 1930 to 1953 Soviet objectives were modified somewhat. Stalin sought to create "socialism in one country" (i.e., the Soviet Union), but nevertheless he still encouraged the stirring up of trouble abroad, both to weaken capitalism and to insure that he had the last option. Manifestations of these attitudes were expressed before World War II in Soviet military aid to the Loyalists in the Spanish Civil War; during the war in arms aid to many partisan groups, particularly in the Balkans and Far East; and after the war in arms aid (via Czechoslovakia) to the Israelis during the Palestine War in 1948.

Soviet objectives have undergone further modification following the death of Stalin in 1953. Today, worldwide revolution is no longer an acceptable objective to Moscow; wars of liberation, however, are considered justifiable and are given maximum Soviet support. Aid to the anti-Western regime in Syria and the radical regime in Guatemala in 1954 was the first public expression of this attitude. Moscow also seeks, as it always has, to undercut Western influence wherever it can and by whatever means at its disposal. Since the late 1950's a further objective has been to offset Chinese communist influence.

Approximately $8 billion worth of arms has been distributed around the world by communist countries since 1955. The Soviet Union and eastern Europe have accounted for over 95 percent of this trade, the Chinese communists for the remainder. This volume reflects a total average annual outlay of more than $500 million in weapons, which is roughly one-fourth the U.S. outlay.* While the communist arms trade is thus relatively small compared to the U.S. effort, it has had an effect on events, as will be shown, that is far out of proportion to its size.

In 1955, when it agreed to supply Egypt with approximately $200–$225 million worth of arms, the Soviets moved into the postwar arms trade in a significant way. Since that time their overall efforts can be divided into two eras. The first, from 1955 to 1960, was marked by two characteristics: the focus was primarily on Middle Eastern countries—Egypt, Syria and Iraq in particular—and Indonesia. The weapons provided to these countries were surplus items, generally considered obsolete. The second, from 1960 to the present, has been marked by a large increase in the

* These figures, and any components of them, are subject to question. No figures emanating from communist countries reflect accurately the monetary value of military material exported to nonbloc countries. In many cases what figures are given reflect a political price that bears no relationship to true value; in other instances military sales figures are hidden in economic trade statistics. The $8 billion and $500 million figures are the result of judgments made by various Western authorities in the field and are considered at the moment to be the most accurate reflection of true value.

number of recipient countries and by a shift to providing the most modern, up-to-date weapons in the Soviet arsenal.

A number of propitious signs in the early 1950's encouraged the Soviets to move into the field. Chief among them was the decline of Western influence in the old colonial areas. Moscow reasoned correctly that many of the resulting vacuums were ripe for exploitation. Like the United States and its allies, the Soviets fully recognized the impact nationalism had on emerging countries, that it was a far stronger force than any ideology out of the East or West. They also realized that many of these new nations needed military (and economic) support but were not willing to give their loyalty to a major power to get it. They were aware, too, of what seemed to be an insatiable demand for arms—arms that were needed, so the new nations claimed, for reasons of prestige, internal security, national sovereignty and wars of liberation.

Moscow was fortunate at this time in that it was in the throes of changing the nature of its military posture. During Stalin's dictatorship, the emphasis had been on massed land armies rather than on an air force and navy. Following Stalin's death in 1953, Soviet military planners began to place more emphasis on air power. (In the mid-1960's the emphasis was to shift once more to increased naval power.) This process required the replacement of obsolete military equipment with more modern weapons systems. Faced with disposing of large quantities of unwanted arms, Moscow chose to use the material as an instrument of its foreign policy. The recipients of Soviet arms in the 1955–60 era, therefore, received mostly old rifles, tanks, artillery pieces and subsonic MiG-15 jet fighters. Around 1960 the Soviet Union, like the United States, ran out of this surplus material and turned to supplying its customers with its newest equipment. This process has continued to the present.[1]

To Soviet military and political strategists, the world at the death of Stalin was divided in two: the Northern and the Southern Hemispheres. In the Northern Hemisphere there existed a stalemate, a standoff between East and West that for the immediate future seemed to offer no great hopes of diplomatic gains. But in the Southern Hemisphere, in the vast, underdeveloped areas of the world, no standoffs or stalemates between East and West existed. This is the area where the Soviets believe that the most gains can be made and it is where they have concentrated most of their efforts since 1955.[2]

To gain influence, the Soviets realized that a new approach was necessary to make any headway. To be bombastic, as they had been over Berlin, they realized, would swiftly create another area of confrontation which would inevitably result in another standoff. Such a confrontation in the underdeveloped areas of the world, they have since come to believe, would only benefit the revolutionaries of Red China. Thus the Soviets developed a policy of giving just enough military aid to unsettle an area, just enough not to force the West to take a stand. In many instances, as will be demonstrated, Moscow misjudged events to the extent of forcing the West to focus its attention on Soviet activities. The basic assumption of this policy is that the promotion of arms races and wars of liberation, as long as they do not culminate in a major East-West confrontation, benefit the Soviet Union and hinder the West. Thus while the West seeks to discourage such activities, the Soviets continue to encourage them.[3]

This policy required a subtle approach. To implement it Moscow decided to use intermediaries, mainly eastern European countries: Bulgaria, East Germany, Poland and Czechoslovakia. This is why the 1955 Egyptian arms deal was actually effected by the Czechs, why the Guatemalan deal of the year before was handled by the Czechs, why the East Germans aided the Zanzibari rebels, why the Poles are so deeply involved in supplying the Vietcong, and why the Bulgarians have aided the Yemeni and Eritrean rebels. By using intermediaries, Moscow could disown them in the event they provoked a confrontation with the West.[4]

When the occasion has called for it, the Soviets have used nonbloc customers as intermediaries. These countries are usually willing tools who export—or more likely re-export—Soviet arms to various trouble spots at Moscow's behest. Egypt, Algeria, Guinea and Ghana (during the Nkrumah regime) have been the most active in this area.

It would be a mistake to believe, however, that all Soviet arms are transferred via intermediaries. This is done only when Moscow believes that a direct sale will provoke the West. Nor is this game limited to the Soviets: the United States has tried its hand at it on several occasions—the 1965 attempt to supply Israel with tanks via West Germany is one example—and has shown no notable finesse. It is apparent that the Soviets have developed this method of transfer to a higher degree of subtlety.

Of all the intermediaries, Czechoslovakia is by far the most active. There is a reason for this. Historically, Czechoslovakia has always been a large producer of arms. Some of the oldest factories in Europe were located in Bohemia, Moravia and Slovakia. By the nineteenth century such firms as Skoda (now known as the Lenin Works) at Pilsen and the Czechoslovak Armaments Works at Brno and Prague had become the major armorers for the Austro-Hungarian Empire. In 1938 Czech arms exports accounted for 15 percent of the total world volume, second only to Great Britain's 17 percent. After the communist coup in 1948, these factories shifted to producing Soviet-type armaments.

Moscow, in its attempts to solidify its hold over eastern Europe, worked out a plan whereby each Comecon* nation was to produce a narrow range of goods to the exclusion of other items. Thus Poland was instructed to concentrate on such things as transport equipment, livestock and coal; Hungary was to concentrate on bauxite mining, textiles, agricultural products and light industrial machinery; and Czechoslovakia was to concentrate on glassware, toys, shoes and armaments. What each country could not absorb of its own production the Soviets guaranteed to take for themselves or for distribution to other satellites. By denying to each country an opportunity to create a balanced economy, Moscow hoped to make each country economically dependent upon the Soviet Union.

The plan worked only so long as the Comecon nations operated as a monolithic bloc and traded only among themselves. By the late 1950's, however, the process of decentralization had taken hold. The satellites acquired more and more freedom of action,

* An acronym for Council for Mutual Economic Aid, the eastern European equivalent of the Common Market.

and the Soviet Union itself began to expand its trade with the West. Faced with slackening demand from Moscow and no guarantee that the goods it lacked would be supplied by its allies, each country was forced to export its excess production to nonbloc countries in order to acquire adequate foreign exchange to pay for the imports it needed.

Czechoslovakia, the country that concerns us here, was one of the first Comecon nations to push the sale of its specialties outside of the communist bloc. Its glassware, toys and shoes soon were being shipped to the far corners of the earth. More than anything it began to push the sale of its weapons. The Soviets had succeeded in the first decade after World War II in rebuilding their own arms industry (some of the tools coming from the Mauser factories) to the point where they had less need for Czech-made arms. Likewise, other eastern European countries were able to acquire their arms directly from Moscow and were thus less dependent on the Czechs as a source. The Prague government decided that it was far wiser to continue its high production of arms and to sell them abroad for the foreign exchange they brought in than to cut back in an effort to balance the economy.

The incessant demand for foreign currency is one reason why Omnipol has developed into one of the most aggressive and independent arms trading firms in the world. Its policy is to sell weapons for the highest possible price to anyone willing to buy. It has become so nonideological, for instance, that while it ships arms to the Vietcong it still advertises its wares in Western trade journals. It has also maintained for years a booth at the annual convention of the U.S. National Sporting Goods Association (usually held in Chicago), even during the height of the Vietnam War. The agency is so aggressive that it does not hesitate to stoop to Zaharoff-like tactics to make a sale. It once told India that it had an agent in Pakistan pushing Czech arms and that if India wished to retain its military supremacy it should increase its orders with the Prague-based firm.

Today Czechoslovakia finds itself still the largest producer among eastern bloc nations. But only a small part of its output is absorbed internally or by its allies; and it not only still acts as the major intermediary for the Soviet Union but is a willing accomplice in the export of arms to nonbloc countries.

To gain a certain measure of influence with the underdeveloped or nonaligned nations of the world, the Soviet Union has been willing to support right wing and even reactionary regimes as in Afghanistan and the Sudan. Occasionally it cooperates with existing or potential rulers rather than with the local communist parties. It has sold arms to Nasser, for example, even though the Egyptian Communist Party was and still is outlawed. It has provided arms to the anticommunist Indonesian Army rather than to the once-legal Indonesian Communist Party. Furthermore, the Soviet Union has sometimes sold its most modern military equipment to its nonbloc customers before it has provided such equipment to its own eastern European allies. Today, Egypt, Algeria, Syria and several other nations have more modern Soviet equipment than any eastern European country except Czechoslovakia.*

Most important of all, however, the Soviets realize that despite the poverty of most of the recipient countries, it is better to sell the arms than to give them away. The Soviets usually sell weapons at low (by western commercial standards) interest rates—from 2 to 2.5 percent payable over a ten- to twelve-year period. Often they barter arms in exchange for a local commodity. With the exception of its aid to the North Vietnamese, which is a special case, there are no instances on record where the Soviets have ever given anything of significant value away. There are two basic reasons why the Soviets only sell or barter arms: it satisfies the pride of the recipients, and it ties up a country's exports in repayment which has the effect of reducing its economic and political relations with the West.[5]

Moscow doubtless hoped that these tactics would lead to a measure of control over arms recipients. But, like its adversaries in the West, it too has found that it is not always able to keep recipient countries from doing what they please with the weapons supplied to them. It too has found that the more radical a leader,

* One of the reasons the Soviets invaded Czechoslovakia in August 1968 was the knowledge that the independent-minded country was the best armed militarily in all of Central Europe.

the less control it has over him. The Soviets have also come to realize that once an investment has been made in a country their options are reduced, which has the effect of inhibiting their actions. For instance, Moscow could not cut its huge investment in Egypt in 1967, despite Nasser's follies, without great loss of face and the dissipation of Soviet momentum in other areas of the Middle East. The Soviet Union would rather cut off military aid (which it actually has done) to Albania and Red China than to Egypt.

To its chagrin, Moscow has found that accepting commodities in return for arms, or forcing its intermediaries to accept them, angers the very parties it hoped to please. For instance, Czechoslovakia may spend many months manufacturing arms for, or forwarding Soviet arms to, a recipient country; yet all it receives in return are such things as copra, dried fruit, camel skins and watermelon seeds, which have only a limited market in Europe. Since the arms seller has no use for them, they are more often than not "dumped" on the market for a nominal sum. Thereupon the original arms buyer may well complain to his benefactor that the market for the rest of his copra, dried fruit, camel skins and watermelon seeds has been destroyed.[6]

From what few sources are available it appears that from the very beginning all Soviet arms aid policies have been formulated within the Politburo. Once they are set, the operational control of the policies has been passed on to the political intelligence organization to operate. This agency is now called the KGB (*Komitet Gosudarstvennoy Bezopasnosti,* or "Committee for State Security"). It was previously known as the Cheka, GPU, OGPU, NKVD or MGB. For a while during the 1930's it appears that the Soviet arms aid program was a monopoly of the GRU (*Glavnoye Razvedovatelnoye Upravleniye,* or "Chief Intelligence Directorate"), still today the name for the military intelligence service. The GRU's current role in the Soviet arms aid program is not clear. Nor is it clear precisely what organizations handle the financing and technical details of Soviet arms transactions, although no doubt all operations of this sort are closely supervised by both the Politburo and the KGB.

2

Underlying every Soviet arms sale has been the desire to destroy Western influence, particularly in the underdeveloped areas of the world. With nonaligned countries, Moscow will attempt to increase their dependence on Soviet arms; with pro-West nations, Moscow will first try to neutralize them with a shipment of arms, and once it believes the recipients are nonaligned, it will move to bring them under its domination with even more arms. Whatever economic and political leverage Moscow can bring to bear is used to augment these efforts. There are a number of examples worth citing. For instance, the sale of MiG-15 jets and T-34 tanks to Morocco in 1961 (followed by a shipload of spares in 1967) was designed partly to undercut U.S. influence and to hasten the closing down of SAC bases in the kingdom. Soviet aid to Kwame Nkrumah was designed in part to diminish British influence in Ghana. The sale of military equipment to the Algerian FLN (with Czechoslovakia acting as the intermediary) was designed in part to destroy French influence in North Africa. One of the many objectives of selling approximately $100 million worth of arms to Iran in January 1967 (to be followed shortly thereafter by a large economic development program) was to encourage this pro-Western nation, and a member of CENTO, to become nonaligned. The aid to rebels in the Congo, Angola and Mozambique was designed in large measure to bring down pro-Western governments. The sale of $14 million worth of arms in 1964 to the government of Prime Minister Makarios was partly intended to isolate Cyprus from Western influence.[7]

Attempts to undercut Western influence find no better example than the case of Soviet arms aid to Egypt. To Moscow, Egypt was an inviting target. The British were in the process of withdrawing from their Egyptian bases, thus leaving a vacuum to be exploited. Egypt also controlled the vital bottleneck at Suez. Nasser himself was sufficiently charismatic that he held a large percentage of Arabs in thrall. Controlling Egypt, the Soviets knew, would give them considerable leverage in controlling other Arab states.

Egypt, at this juncture, was susceptible to Soviet overtures. Nasser was not prepared to accept the arms which both the United States and Great Britain were prepared to give him. He also felt threatened by the formation of CENTO. Furthermore, Nasser favored a show of independence from all forms of Western influence. He had been impressed by the potential strength of the nonaligned countries that had attended the April 1955 Bandung Conference. He believed that, by accepting arms aid from both power blocs, he could provide the leadership for this third world.

In September 1955 Nasser announced that his government had signed a military assistance agreement with the USSR whereby Egypt would receive \$200–\$225 million worth of arms over a two-year period. Repayment was not to be made in cash (in this instance) but in basic commodities and foodstuffs.

Beginning two months earlier, in July, an extremely rapid transfer of arms took place. Egypt received 150 MiG-15's and MiG-17's, 40 I1-28 bombers, 300 T-34 heavy tanks, 2 destroyers, 6 submarines and a large quantity of infantry weapons. This equipment severely upset the Middle Eastern balance in arms. Within a year, in November 1956, war had broken out and the Israelis captured or destroyed approximately one half of the equipment supplied by the USSR.[8]

It should be noted that it was not the *use* of Soviet arms that led Israel into the war but their presence. While Great Britain and France had other primary motives for invading Egypt, Israel took part because she was frightened by the large buildup of Egyptian arms. It should also be noted that, while the Soviet Union welcomed a destabilization in the Middle Eastern arms balance, it did not welcome the war (except insofar as it accidentally helped to obscure Soviet brutality in suppressing the Hungarian Revolution which took place at the same time). The moment the war broke out, the Soviets withdrew their 40 I1-28 bombers from Egypt lest they be used.

Following the Suez crisis, the USSR once again replenished the Egyptian arsenal. The quality of arms was also upgraded. Now Nasser was sold MiG-17's and MiG-19's, W-class submarines, better destroyers and more modern small arms.* By 1963 the quality was upgraded one more notch. Egypt received MiG-21 fighters, the best operational jet in the Soviet inventory at the time, TU-16 medium bombers and SA-2 and SA-3 surface-to-air missiles.[9] The Soviets had also participated earlier in establishing in Egypt an experimental nuclear reactor and in the financing of a munitions factory. By June 1967 the value of all arms sold to Egypt by the Soviets was estimated to be approximately one billion dollars.

Soviet arms aid to Egypt was so heavy between the years 1957 and 1967 that it turned Egypt into an arms exporter in its own right. To pay for the MiG-19's and MiG-21's, for instance, Nasser was forced to sell his MiG-17's on the world market.[10] Egyptian aid to various African rebel movements was prompted in many cases less by the USSR's desire to have Cairo act as an intermediary than by Egypt's need to sell its old equipment to pay for the newer arms. Algeria, also a large recipient of Soviet arms, has found itself in a similar position.

The buildup in tensions that eventually exploded in the Six-Day War in June 1967 stemmed largely from Nasser's confidence in his Soviet equipment. Plagued by economic difficulties at home (due in large measure to the heavy cost of weapons), bogged down in a war in the Yemen, and increasingly criticized by his Arab followers for hiding behind the U.N. truce-keeping force in Gaza, Nasser was eager to reassert himself by leading another attempt at destroying Israel with his Soviet ordnance. With all those arms and the moral backing of Moscow, Nasser saw no need to settle his differences with the Israelis through peaceful negotiations. In mid-

* Apparently the Soviets insisted on as much control over this equipment as the United States and Britain demanded during arms negotiations prior to 1955. Nasser obviously chafed under such restrictions; he not only was unsatisfied with Soviet technical support and his dependence on another country for spares but between 1959 and 1961 he was embroiled in a quarrel with Moscow. Thus by 1960 Nasser had turned back to the West for personnel and training that would support an indigenous weapons program. Out of this came the development of the HA-300 jet fighter and the three tactical missile programs under the direction of German technicians mentioned previously.

May the Egyptian President demanded that the 3,400-man U.N. force be withdrawn from the Gaza Strip and the Gulf of Aqaba and U.N. Secretary General U Thant reluctantly complied. Egyptian, Jordanian and Syrian forces (the last armed with 400 Soviet tanks and 100 MiG's) were mobilized, the Gulf of Aqaba was blockaded, whereupon Israel attacked.

The events during those six days in June need not be commented upon here. Suffice it to say it was no "small" war. Roughly 3,000 tanks saw action on both sides—a third more than saw action in the twelve-day battle of El Alamein in October-November 1942.

If responsibility for this war must be apportioned, part of it would fall on the U.N. Secretary General, whose inscrutable actions have yet to be fully explained; part would rest with the major Western powers who steadfastly refused to act in a forthright manner; and part would rest with Nasser and his limited vision. But the bulk of the blame rests with the Soviet Union.* Undeniably this war would never have occurred had there not been a massive infusion of arms into the area. Nasser, without such equipment, would have been reluctant to act in such an arrogant and cock-sure manner. Jordan, a relatively conservative Arab state armed with Western equipment, would not have been forced into a shotgun alliance with its antagonist Egypt† had not Nasser called for Arab solidarity in his showdown with Israel. Syria, as radical an Arab state as Egypt, and also armed by the Soviets, would have

* One influential organ which conspicuously refused to condemn the Soviets was *La Stampa,* Italy's second largest newspaper. Not a word of criticism was to be found among its pages during or following the crisis. One of the reasons put forward was that the paper is owned by Giovanni Agnelli, an extremely wealthy Italian businessman who runs and controls the Fiat company. It so happens that at the time of the war Fiat was in the process of building a large auto plant in Russia and, according to several sources, did not want to risk losing this business with any unseemly criticism. Fiat was also negotiating at the time for a $50 million loan from the Eximbank to finance equipping this plant with U.S. machinery, but its request was turned down.

† A week before the war Radio Cairo called King Hussein, among other things, "the Hashemite Harlot."

hesitated to go to war alone, but it was caught up in the passions inflamed by Nasser.

The Soviets were reportedly displeased with the Egyptian President. Of the 716 aircraft and 1,200 tanks sold to Egypt, the Soviets had seen 356 of the former and approximately 700 of the latter destroyed or captured within a period of 144 hours. All of the Soviet SA-2 *Guideline* missile batteries located in the Sinai peninsula were lost, and infantry equipment for 15,000 men was either destroyed or captured. Nor was Moscow too pleased with Syria, which lost over half of its Soviet-built tanks and jet aircraft.[11]

Within a month after the cessation of hostilities the USSR, repeating its actions following the 1956 debacle, began to replenish the depleted stocks of both Egypt and Syria. The value of this equipment has been estimated to be nearly one billion dollars.* As of this writing Egypt has more and better arms than before the 1967 war. The percentage of MiG-21's in the Egyptian Air Force, for instance, is 45 percent of the whole, which is a higher proportion than in any eastern European country except the Soviet Union itself. In return for all this material it is understood that the Soviets demanded and received even more control over its use. How effective this will prove to be is, at the moment, debatable.

The 1967 Egyptian disaster unquestionably damaged the Soviets' Middle Eastern policy. But it is also clear that Moscow's influence in Cairo has subsequently become stronger and more dominating than ever. Far from souring Soviet-Egyptian relations, the defeat propelled Cairo into a full embrace with Moscow. To salvage its prestige, Egypt could not turn to the Western powers—who, if they did not overtly provide arms to the Israelis as most did, clearly expressed sympathy for their cause—but was forced to turn back to its old benefactor, the Soviet Union.

If destroying Western influence is a major Soviet objective, so too is its desire to undercut Red China. Usually the two objectives

* Total Soviet military aid to Egypt, Syria and Iraq from 1955 to the present is estimated to be in excess of $2.5 billion, or over one-third the entire value of Moscow's postwar arms aid program.

overlap. For instance, the arms sold to the Congo Simbas were intended to offset Chinese influence as much as to destroy the Tshombe government; the arming and training of Nkrumah's private praetorian guard was undertaken in order to neutralize the influence of the Chinese, who were training foreign saboteurs in the country; and the Algerian FLN was also provided with arms to counter a drive by Peking to bring the rebel group under its influence.

Soviet arms aid to Indonesia and India, designed in large measure to thwart Chinese influence, deserves more than passing mention.

Between the years 1958 and 1964 the Soviet Union sold one billion dollars' worth of equipment—one seventh of its total postwar sales to date—to the Sukarno government. Moscow provided arms for many of the same reasons it sent military equipment to Egypt: to ensure Indonesia's neutrality; to strengthen its own image as an anticolonialist; to undercut Dutch, British and American influence in the area; to control the Straits of Malacca; and to tie Indonesia to the USSR through debts incurred and dependence on spares.[12]

Above all, Moscow wished to stop Indonesia's drift toward Peking. There were three major political forces in the country in these years: the Sukarno clique and its followers, the anticommunist army, and the Indonesian Communist Party, or PKI. The PKI, at that time the largest Communist Party in the nonaligned world, was becoming increasingly more sympathetic to the Peking line. Moscow hoped that by giving arms to the anticommunist military it would effect two results: the power of the PKI would be neutralized and the military's hostility to communism would be softened.[13]

Indonesian motives for buying Soviet arms were based on other considerations. A number of anti-Sukarno revolts in the late 1950's and early 1960's had to be suppressed. One major rebel group had the sympathy of the U.S. government and the covert backing of the CIA, which angered the Jakarta government. Washington, while it had delivered some arms in August 1958, hesitated to supply Jakarta during these years of civil turmoil, so Sukarno turned to Moscow in an attempt to coerce the United

States into resuming its aid. The rebellions were put down by 1961, but still Washington demurred because Sukarno seemed procommunist.

Moscow saw its opportunity and opted to send as much arms as necessary to bring the Jakarta regime into the Soviet orbit. Between 1961 and 1963 the bulk of the one billion dollars worth of arms was shipped to Indonesia—MiG-21's, TU-16 bombers, a heavy cruiser, eight destroyers, a dozen submarines, at least a hundred other naval craft, helicopters, tanks, antiaircraft guns, field artillery, surface-to-air missiles and small arms.

The Indonesians used their Soviet arms to embark on two foreign adventures. One was a campaign to force the Dutch to turn over their holdings on New Guinea to the control of Jakarta. A number of armed bands were sent into the area by Sukarno to harass the Dutch, and while they were singularly unsuccessful in their military venture, success was achieved in May 1963 when West Irian, as the area was called, was turned over to Indonesia. No sooner had this adventure ended than Sukarno launched his "crush Malaysia" campaign, which lasted until 1965. It was unsuccessful and was one of the factors that led to the attempted Sukarno-PKI coup against the army in September 1965.

The downfall of Sukarno and the destruction of the pro-Peking PKI in 1965 was accomplished, as history has recorded, by an anticommunist army equipped with Soviet weapons. What is generally overlooked, however, is that most of the Soviet arms went into the creation of a navy and air force, two services of which Indonesia had no tradition prior to the arrival of Soviet equipment. It would be a mistake to think that Moscow simply gave weapons to an anticommunist army with the vague hope that somehow such a gesture would soften its hostility and, in turn, neutralize the PKI's pro-Peking sentiments. It is clear now that Moscow created two new services hoping they would be more sympathetic to the Soviet line. They, it reasoned, would force the army to soften its stand and, taken all together, would act as a pro-Moscow counterforce to the PKI.

In the last analysis, Moscow lost in Indonesia. While the 1965 army counteroffensive destroyed the pro-Peking PKI as a political force, the massive arms aid program failed to persuade any of the three services to voice any lasting sympathy for Moscow in particular or communism in general.

Soviet aid to India has been prompted in large measure by its desire to offset the Chinese military threat to the country. The first transaction involving military equipment took place in 1960. In an arms deal valued at $31.5 million, India received a small quantity of Soviet transport planes, helicopters and communications equipment. At this point it appeared that the Soviets were more interested in countering U.S. aid to Pakistan and in converting India to a more pro-Moscow stance.

But after October 1962, as the result of Chinese attacks on the Indian border, Moscow supplied India with additional equipment, mostly helicopters and jet fighters. This aid was a warning to the Red Chinese to cease their aggression on the border or else the Soviet Union would come to the aid of India. By 1964 Soviet aid had been increased to include such items as a $42 million SA-2 missile complex, more jet aircraft and tanks, and the construction of a factory to produce MiG-21's.

Indian motives for buying Soviet equipment varied. Chiefly, the New Delhi government wished to improve its defenses against Red China; it also wished to remain neutral and to broaden its military supply base; further, India was angered by U.S. aid to Pakistan and hoped to give pause to Washington by purchasing Soviet arms. (The United States also sent arms to India in 1962 following the Chinese attacks on condition they be used only against the communists; noted before, most of them were used against Pakistan in 1965.) India also sought Soviet arms because it wished eventually to create a self-sufficient military establishment, and Moscow was the only one sympathetic to the idea. In exchange for its arms, Moscow agreed to take rupees and local commodities.[14]

The Vietnam War is the best illustration of the manner in which the Soviet Union supports wars of liberation. The Moscow-Peking rivalry has also played a part in the Soviet military aid effort to Hanoi.

To conquer South Vietnam and to unify all of Vietnam, North

Vietnam has relied on both Moscow and Peking for arms. At the same time, Hanoi has been concerned that its close proximity to Red China would lead to eventual domination by its northern neighbor. Thus it has always encouraged Moscow to continue its involvement.

Prior to 1961 the Soviets were prepared to concede primary influence over the area to Peking, but the Sino-Soviet split, which was beginning to turn bitter in 1961, changed all that. The Soviets decided that they should do all they could to keep North Vietnam from falling by default into the Peking sphere of influence. They also realized that it was a relatively inexpensive way of undercutting U.S. influence throughout all of southeast Asia.

Reliable source material is scarce on the Soviet and Chinese aid efforts to the Hanoi regime. However, certain facts are known and deserve comment.

In the spring of 1961, the Soviets began airlifting military equipment from various points in the USSR to Hanoi and Tchepone, the latter a southern Laotian town which was (and presumably still is) a major Vietcong base of operations. Heavy equipment came via two routes: over the Trans-Siberian railroad to Harbin and Mukden in Manchuria, then to Peking and Hanoi and finally to the Vietcong via various trails and roads; or by ship from Odessa in the Black Sea or from Stettin in the Baltic.

The Red Chinese supplied a small quantity of obsolete MiG's and small arms; these jets were transported directly over the border, and the small arms, during this early phase of the war, were mainly run via junks into various Vietcong strongholds along the South Vietnam coast. From 1961 to 1964 this trade was relatively small in volume, designed only to match the slow buildup of allied forces. The quality of these arms was generally poor but, even so, it was better than that of the homemade and captured French and Japanese weapons which for so long had been the mainstays of the rebels' arsenal.

In 1965, to match the large U.S. buildup in South Vietnam, there was a quantum jump in the volume of Soviet arms aid. The number of SA-2 and SA-3 missile batteries increased sevenfold in the course of a year; the most modern Soviet and Czech weapons

—antiaircraft guns, AK-47 assault rifles, and especially lightweight mortars and bazookas—were shipped to the Hanoi government. East Germany, no doubt on Moscow's urging, supplied small arms (mostly Czech), electronic equipment, medical supplies and bicycles and motorcycles to transport the material from supply depots to the front. Red China stepped up its supply of rice, medical supplies, bicycles, small arms and ammunition. The Soviets claim that they supplied $555 million worth of military goods in 1965 alone and along with its eastern European allies would provide one billion dollars worth in 1966, but these figures are suspect, since they are not only meant to mislead the United States but to impress Red China.

The Sino-Soviet split by 1965 was nearly total. In January of that year Moscow turned down a Chinese request for arms, and six months later Peking retaliated by denying the Soviets the opportunity of building air bases in northwest and south China for the purposes of facilitating its airlift to the North Vietnamese. Nevertheless, China did allow Soviet goods to pass across its territory, although it reserved the right of inspection.

By the middle of 1965 Moscow was complaining that, while its technicians were transported from border to border with all possible dispatch, its arms shipments—consisting mostly of antiaircraft guns, surface-to-air missiles and electronic gear—were subject to unnecessary delays. One reason given was the general difficulty in operating the rail route: besides two gauge changes enroute, the Chinese rolling stock and railbeds were considered inadequate to the task. The other reason given by the Soviets was that the Chinese were purposely slowing down the traffic to embarrass Moscow.

It was not too long before Moscow was accusing Peking of hijacking some of the material and replacing it with inferior goods. The Soviets also accused the Chinese of relabeling some of the crates to make it appear as if the contents were of Chinese origin. While Peking denies these accusations, it is generally understood that the delays in Soviet shipments were also due to the Chinese practice of copying material. In many instances the weapons appeared to have been damaged in transit, but this was due less to maliciousness and carelessness than to the inability of the Red Chinese to reassemble properly the material they had taken apart to copy.

The argument raged throughout 1965 and 1966 and appeared to have been resolved in April 1967 when the two countries reached an accord whereby the North Vietnamese would take title to the arms at the Sino-Soviet border and be responsible for their transit through China to Hanoi and beyond. In June 1968 there occurred sporadic delays to further Soviet shipments crossing China. The reasons were not clear, although several authorities have suggested that the delays were due either to disruptions caused by warring Red Guard factions or to Peking's displeasure over the Paris peace negotiations.[15]

This running argument with Peking encouraged the Soviets to ship most of their material by sea. Toward the end of 1966 an average of thirty communist ships—at least two thirds of which came from the Soviet Union and eastern Europe—per month were bringing supplies to Haiphong. It has been estimated that by 1968 approximately 80 percent of all Soviet military goods for the Hanoi government were being delivered by ship. Earlier, probably in 1965, the Soviets had developed a third route: by rail to Vladivostok and from there by sea to Haiphong.

Peking did little to dissuade the Soviets from sending most of its supplies by sea. Apparently it believed that increased traffic into Haiphong would lead to an American blockade and to raids on the port itself. This, the Chinese hoped, would lead to a break between Washington and Moscow and encourage Hanoi to increase its reliance on the Peking regime for supplies.

While little authoritative information is available, it appears that Allied bombing raids on North Vietnam were sufficiently effective by early 1967 that the communists were forced to decentralize their supply routes. Haiphong harbor, by Allied decision, was still an untouchable target, but this did not apply to supplies once they were moved out of town. The rail journey from the Chinese border south was hazardous at best. No matter from where the arms originated, it appeared that a smaller and smaller percentage of them were reaching their destinations undamaged. The North

Vietnamese and the Vietcong, therefore, sought additional avenues of supply other than their traditional routes. One which they chose ran eastward across southern Laos to the so-called Ho Chi Minh Trail. It was and still is used to move rice, fuel and small arms and ammunition to the Vietcong. This route begins at the port of Sihanoukville in Cambodia on the Gulf of Siam and is reportedly serviced by approximately 40 riverboats, 60 trucks, 2,000 bicycles and thousands of coolie porters. Both the Soviets and Red Chinese have used this supply route; it is considered far safer than a trip to Haiphong.[16]

Despite Red Chinese claims, the majority of military supplies to the North Vietnamese since 1965 have come from the Soviet Union and eastern Europe. Preliminary evidence would seem to indicate that this aid has helped Moscow to keep the Hanoi government from falling under the domination of Peking. But, in truth, Moscow's success here has been relatively easily gained. The Red Chinese were not, and still are not, able to supply Hanoi with any large volume of material. Had it been left to them alone to support North Vietnam, the war effort would probably have collapsed in 1966, and the Hanoi government would have been drawn into Peking's sphere of influence. The Soviet Union, mindful of its own interests, could not let this happen.

There are other objectives to the Soviet Union's arms aid policy. One is to preserve a series of buffer states between itself and the outside world. The Soviet Union sees itself protected to the west by eastern Europe, to the north by the Arctic wastes, to the east by the sea, and to the southeast by Outer Mongolia and the Pamir and Altai Mountains. The frontiers of the Soviet Union running from the Black Sea to Tibet, however, are seen by Moscow as particularly vulnerable to Western incursions. Thus considerable economic, political and military pressure has been brought to bear on three countries bordering the Soviet Union in this area: Turkey, Afghanistan and Iran. Much of this pressure has been expressed in military aid.

The Soviets have had very little success in converting Turkey into a buffer state. Turkey is a loyal member of both NATO and

CENTO and is armed with U.S. weapons. Historically the Turks have mistrusted Moscow because of the Russian desire to wrest control of the Bosporus away from them. The only recent "victory" Moscow can claim was the removal of *Jupiter* missiles from Turkey (and Italy) in 1962—not, as many people believe, in trade for the removal of Soviet missiles in Cuba, but because the *Jupiter* missile had been rendered obsolete by the *Polaris*.[17]

With Afghanistan it is another story; historically this country was a buffer between Czarist interests in the north and British interests to the south and east. It was one of the first nations to receive military equipment from the Soviet Union after World War II. The Soviets originally gave arms to Afghanistan in order to counter Western aid to Pakistan, a CENTO and SEATO member; they also supported Kabul's claim to Pushtoonistan, a disputed province in Pakistan. Today Moscow sees Afghanistan primarily as a buffer against all Western interests.

Between 1955 and 1960 approximately $100 million worth of military aid was furnished to the Kabul government, including MiG-15's and MiG-17's and Ilyushin jet bombers. A large economic aid program was initiated at the same time and has concentrated on heavy construction—roads, airports and river port facilities. While it has accepted U.S. aid and remains on friendly terms with Western nations, Afghanistan seems to prefer the role of buffer state to any other role. Thus it can be said that Moscow, by ensuring that things remain as they have in the past, has succeeded in its goal.

With Iran it is yet another story. Iran has long mistrusted its northern neighbor. Both Czarist and Soviet governments have coveted some of Iran's provinces, particularly those west of the Caspian Sea. Between 1941 and 1946 the Soviets occupied all of Iran north of Tehran and tried to take over the entire country during the last two years of its occupation. From 1951 to 1953 it supported the unstable procommunist regime of Mohammed Mossadegh. In each instance Moscow was unsuccessful; it appeared in the mid-1950's that Soviet fortunes in Iran were most unpromising.

Furthermore, the Shah, following his return to power in 1953, aligned his country with the West. Iran became a member of CENTO in 1955, and it profited handsomely from large military and economic aid programs from the United States. This assistance was accelerated after the 1958 coup in Iraq. By 1962 the United States had entered into a long-range military agreement with Iran whereby in return for grant aid *and* sales aid, Tehran would undertake certain civil and military reforms. By 1966 total U.S. military aid, both grant and sales, amounted to approximately $1.4 billion since the end of World War II. Iran was and still is considered one of the eleven "Forward Defense" countries* whose stability, anticommunism and fighting ability the United States believes are vital to its own security.

Despite all this largesse from the United States, Iran signed an arms agreement with the Soviet Union in early 1967 for the purchase of $110 million worth of military equipment. The Shah had decided to turn to Moscow apparently because he wished to erase the "U.S. client only" tag, because he was irritated by the Pentagon's insistence that he *pay* for arms on relatively stiff credit terms, and because he was not able to convince the United States to sell him the modern jets and missiles he wanted. Later on in the year, Iran signed a $700 million trade agreement with Moscow which included plans to build steel mills, pipelines and a subway, and to develop natural gas and oil fields.[18]

These developments unnerved Washington, since Iran was the first Western pact nation to have signed a military agreement with the Soviet Union. (Pakistan has subsequently bought Soviet arms, and is the only other Western pact nation to do so as of this writing.) The Pentagon offered to augment a previous sale of F-4 *Phantoms* with an additional squadron (even though F-4's were still in short supply in Vietnam). Iran agreed to buy. But then in March 1968 Tehran broadened still further its economic and military ties with the USSR. Three months later, in June, the Shah was back in Washington asking for an additional $600 million in arms.[19]

While there is little evidence to believe that Iran was swung over to a pro-Moscow or even a neutralist position, there is no denying the effectiveness of the Soviets' military aid. If Iran's military

* The other ten: Greece, India, Laos, Nationalist China, Pakistan, the Philippines, South Korea, South Vietnam, Thailand and Turkey.

forces become sufficiently dependent on Soviet equipment, then Moscow will have effectively destroyed whatever military value there is to CENTO. If that happens, it will be one small step toward Iran's becoming a buffer state.

A lesser Soviet goal is to maintain "forward facilities." These facilities are usually airfields or ports where Soviet aircraft or naval ships can stop for repairs and fuel. Moscow views such facilities as potential strategic bases, as stopover points for long journeys, as bases for the re-export of arms and as points from which aerial spying flights can be inaugurated. Landing rights at Conakry Airport in Guinea, for example, are considered a vital link for flights between Moscow and Havana, as a point from which Soviet and Czech arms can be re-exported and where aerial photographic reconnaissance missions can begin or end. Landing rights at Khartoum in the Sudan, and at Sa'ana in the Yemen; docking rights at Alexandria and Port Said in Egypt and Mers el Kebir in Algeria; and flyover rights with at least two dozen African and Near Eastern countries have all been acquired by the Soviet Union and are all considered potential strategic assets.[20]

The Soviet Union is also in the arms trade for the money. This is one reason why Moscow, while claiming to champion the equality of all peoples, sells arms to South Africa. They have been just as contemptuous of the embargo as have France and Italy. Most of the sales to the Pretoria government have occurred since the 1963 U.N. embargo was imposed. Exactly what the Soviets have sold is not clear, but most sources claim that the material is support equipment such as tools, electronic testing equipment, replacement parts, explosives and fuel. None of the major attention-gathering ordnance in the South African armory—jets, missiles, tanks, armored cars, warships—carry the Soviet label; such a situation would bring too much unfavorable publicity. As of this writing, the Soviets show no signs of slackening their sales of military equipment to South Africa.

The following exchange took place between Samuel Cummings and Senator Symington during the Senate arms aid hearings in March 1967:[21]

Mr. Cummings. Russia is also supplying South Africa, and Russia claims that they, of course, only want to support the blacks. The Russians like the money.

Senator Symington. More than they do the black people?

Mr. Cummings. Yes. There are wonderful regulations and pronouncements of policy, and White Papers, but the plainest print cannot be read through a gold eagle.

On occasion Moscow will use military aid to disrupt the internal politics of a nation. For sheer mischievousness, its attempt to stir up trouble in Kenya in 1964 and 1965 has no equal. In early 1964 Kenya had approached the Soviet Union with the hope of acquiring arms. An agreement was reached later in the year whereby the Soviet Union promised to supply certain unspecified arms virtually free of charge. It was common knowledge in late 1964 that there also existed a rift between Prime Minister Kenyatta and his gifted, wealthy and procommunist Minister of Home Affairs, Oginga Odinga. In late November of that year, it was reported that mysterious crates had arrived at Nairobi Airport aboard a Czech plane and had been trucked away by Odinga's men without being subjected to customs inspection. In April 1965, police raided Odinga's office building and confiscated several dozen crates of small arms, including grenades and machine guns. Two other caches were also seized, one of them located in the basement of an east European embassy. A week later, a Soviet freighter, the *Fizik Lebedev,* arrived in Mombasa with a cargo of heavy weapons. The Kenya government was taken by surprise; while it had an agreement with Moscow for the "free" delivery of unspecified arms, no one was sure who had ordered the weapons, although suspicion fell heavily on Odinga. Along with the cargo came a seventeen-man team of "advisers" whom no Kenyan would admit having invited. Kenyatta realized that the Soviets, under the vague terms of the agreement, were trying to infiltrate the Kenya military with a "gift" of old World War II tanks and howitzers. Apparently Moscow felt confident that a shipload of arms, like beads and trinkets, would blind the Kenya government to the fact that the shipment had nothing to do with the original agreement. Refusing to be taken in, the Prime Minister ordered the boat and its cargo out of the harbor, told the seventeen advisers to pack up and leave, and abrogated the agreement.[22]

Next to the United States, the Soviet Union is the world's largest gunrunner. The Soviets can take credit for the greatest gunrunning venture—if the definition is stretched a bit—of all times: namely, the attempt to smuggle offensive missiles into Cuba in 1962. This particular event has been commented upon on numerous occasions, and little need to be added here except to say that it reflects not only the fact that the Soviets place no restrictions on the scale of their smuggling but that they are willing to carry on such activities up to the point of possibly provoking nuclear warfare.

It is estimated that less than 8 percent of the entire Soviet gunrunning traffic is ever revealed. Nevertheless, the number of actual postwar instances discovered is impressive, attesting to the high total volume of all Soviet gunrunning ventures. Some cases are worthy of comment to illustrate the scope and range of these illegal operations.

In 1961 Soviet gunrunners engineered a plot to smuggle small arms and ammunition from the Middle East to the Cameroons. The items were packed in crates marked "almond nuts" and shipped by British and American commercial carriers first to Zurich, then to Gibraltar and then to Las Palmas in the Canary Islands. The plot was discovered when two pilots noticed the difficulty the loaders had in transporting the "nuts" from hangar to plane.[23]

Bulgaria was caught in August 1966 sending arms to the opponents of a government with which officially it had friendly relations. A crate of "duty-free" goods, addressed to a Bulgarian firm in Ethiopia ostensibly dealing in foodstuffs, was found by customs officials to contain machine guns. These weapons were destined for Eritrean rebels. Nine months previously, a Bulgarian freighter was unloading in Beirut when a crate marked "sewing machines" broke open to reveal arms. Other crates, some marked "mechanical spare parts," were found to contain 1,500 automatic weapons.[24] Exactly to whom these arms were directed has not been made public.

In the early 1960's many Soviet intermediaries were active much in the manner of Bulgaria. Czechs ran guns to the Algerian FLN; Cuban Reds have smuggled both Soviet and Western arms to insurgent guerrillas in many Latin American countries, the most notable examples being Venezuela, Bolivia and Guatemala; and pro-Moscow smugglers have carried on a brisk trade supplying small arms to dissident factions and warlike tribes in Burma, Thailand and Laos.

The Soviets have also been engaged in what might be called "reverse smuggling"—the illegal running of military equipment from the West into eastern European bloc countries. Berne, Switzerland is a center for many of these smuggling rings. One case involved $80,000 worth of C-47 parts that ended up in Poland. This material was allowed to be exported from the United States because ostensibly it was to go to a Paris firm. But enroute the parts were reloaded onto a Polish freighter and delivered behind the Iron Curtain before Western authorities realized what had happened. In another case, Rolls Royce jet engines, sold by the Royal Navy in 1962 to independent dealers as "damaged beyond repair," supposedly found their way to Czechoslovakia where they were rebuilt. The Soviets have also been involved in smuggling technical manuals and American Sidewinder missiles from the West into their own sphere of control.[25]

The best-known case of smuggling in which the Soviets were involved was in the Congo from 1960 to 1965. In the early days of the Congo's independence, from June to September 1960, the USSR openly supported with arms the government of left-wing Prime Minister Lumumba. President Kasavubu dismissed Lumumba in early September because of the latter's preference for Soviet aid over U.N. assistance. He also closed down the Soviet and Czech embassies whose staffs were swollen with "technicians." Moscow was unhappy with this development, since it apparently believed that it was on the verge of precipitating a communist takeover. From that moment on, particularly after Lumumba's murder in early 1961, the Soviet Union turned its ire on both the U.N. and the legitimate Congo governments.

In the chaos that followed the Congolese Army mutiny, the

Katanga secession, the Lumumba murder, and the lack of any government to speak of from September 1960 to August 1961, the Soviets chose to roil the waters still further by supporting with arms the Gizenga rebels in Stanleyville. The 512-man UAR contingent, when it was withdrawn from the U.N. Congo Force in February 1961, was supposed to have left behind at Soviet suggestion some 67 tons of arms for the antigovernment rebels. By 1963, the Soviet Union, once more with a diplomatic base in the country, was supplying the exiled left-wing Congo leader, Christophe Gbenye, with financial aid to buy weapons and with a printing press to turn out forged Congolese franc notes.[26]

Soviet aid to Congolese rebels in the first three years of independence was small in volume compared to its aid to the Simbas between July 1964, when the revolt first broke out, and late spring 1965, when the revolt was finally crushed by Congolese and white mercenary troops. No one knows the entire story, either how the rebels acquired their arms or the full motives behind why the Soviets and their allies supplied the weapons in the first place. According to several sources, one of them a former high-ranking Simba, the few who do know are reluctant to say anything: there are still too many people jockeying for power in the Congo who were once involved in the smuggling whose careers would be compromised were the full facts to be known.

Moscow's motives for giving arms aid to the Simbas was based above all on its desire to oppose the pro-West government of Moise Tshombe, who became Prime Minister at the same time that the revolt broke out. Tshombe was then the most hated politician in Africa; he was widely regarded as a Belgian stooge, and he committed the unpardonable sin of admitting that he had hired white mercenaries because his troops would not fight without white officers. Above all, Tshombe was a realist, which was a political asset in the Congo in 1964. What better way to win the allegiance of the world's dark-skinned peoples, reasoned Moscow, than to give aid to those who were fighting white mercenary racist neo-colonialists? The Soviets realized that the Western powers had staked their reputations on the stability and pro-West bias of the unhappy country; and a direct challenge of that status, they knew, would provoke a confrontation. Thus they decided to use the services of intermediaries. From a technical point of view the Soviets were never directly involved.

Spurring Moscow on was the competition from Peking. The Red Chinese maintained embassies in the Congo-Brazzaville, a former French colony, and in Burundi, on the Congo's eastern flank. Each embassy was bloated with "diplomats" whose real job was to subvert the legitimate government of Leopoldville. In April 1965, for instance, China's Brazzaville embassy employed 30 "officers" and 180 other Chinese whose diplomatic duties were obscure.[27] There was one Chinese attached to the embassy for every 3,800 citizens of the Congo-Brazzaville. (At that rate, a Red Chinese embassy in Washington—were that day ever to arrive—would number 52,631 people.) These individuals ran guns to the rebels of "General" Nicolas Olenga and Gaston Soumialot; they set up camps to train the youthful followers of Pierre Mulele; and occasionally they fought in the field as Simba commanders.

Soviet weapons were smuggled to the Simbas from Kiev, via air to Cairo, and from there to Khartoum, and finally to Juba near the Congo border. The arms were then carried both by hand and by Soviet truck to Aba, a rebel supply depot. An alternate route ran from Algiers into the Khartoum-Juba-Aba pipeline. (Some of the Algerians who helped load the arms onto the planes received part of their pay in U.S. surplus food.)

In order to preserve the fiction that it was not involved, the Soviet Union smuggled these arms in planes carrying the markings of Algeria, Egypt, Guinea, Ghana and Mali. The planes themselves were of Soviet origin, mostly AN-12 transports, and were manned by Soviet crews. The weapons came either from Czechoslovakia and the Soviet Union or from the intermediary countries whose stocks were replenished later by Moscow. Some Algerian equipment came from Castro's Cuba.*

* Castro's African aid effort was quite ambitious until domestic crises forced the Cuban dictator to rearrange his sense of reality. Castroite Cubans acted as military advisers to the Simbas; Cuban arms have been sent to Eritrean rebels; and a contingent of Cuban Negroes still form the backbone of the Presidential Guard in the Congo-Brazzaville.

The other route was by sea to Dar-es-Salaam. The material was either trucked across Tanzania and Uganda to the Congo border or was flown from Dar to Khartoum and then down to Juba. Uganda was a focal point for large quantities of arms being smuggled to the Simbas. Occasionally Uganda gave the rebels arms from its own arsenals.[28]

Like all other arms transactions, these weapons were not given away free of charge by the Soviets. What exactly were the terms of trade is not known, but it is known that the Simbas paid in gold bullion, stolen from the Moto mining complex in the northeast Congo. Estimates of the amount of ore removed by the rebels by March 1965, when the rebellion was in its last stages, range from one to two metric tons, or approximately $1.2 million to $2.4 million worth.[29]

By April 1965 it became clear to the Soviet Union and its intermediaries that further aid to the rebels was fruitless. Both Nasser and Ben Bella, who three months earlier boasted of the aid they were giving to the Simbas, now rejected pleas for aid on the grounds that most of the arms were straightaway falling into the possession of the Congolese and mercenary troops. With Nasser, however, it was not simply a question of recognizing the facts of life; he halted his arms aid only after the U.S. government temporarily suspended wheat deliveries to his famine-stricken country.[30]

When it comes to fiascoes in military aid programs, the Soviets make some American and British mistakes seem like triumphs in comparison. Most Soviet mistakes stem from neglecting a country's basic needs in favor of selling it politically motivated products and projects. In 1963, for instance, Moscow sold some MiG jet fighters to Somalia, a country of two million people that had a per capita income of less than $50, a literacy rate of 10 percent, a college graduate population of roughly 100 (in 1962), and no technicians or pilots even remotely capable of operating the equipment. The Soviets once sold Guinea mobile antitank guns, complete with white sidewall tires; none of Guinea's neighbors nor any of its known enemies maintain tank units against which these guns might be used. The Soviets have sold tanks to the Yemenis which have proved worthless in Yemen's rugged terrain. They also sold to the Sukarno regime tanks which were and continue to be useless in a land that is covered mostly with steaming jungles. Moscow also provided Indonesia with the largest navy in southeast Asia—a navy that to date has shown no talent for the craft nor any inclination to leave port. (In both the West Irian and "crush Malaysia" affairs, for instance, the navy played no significant role.) in the Six-Day War of 1967 many Soviet tanks were disabled, destroyed and/or captured because their air filters, designed for temperate climates, were unable to strain out fine grain sand.

The Soviets have had the habit, furthermore, of taking a commodity they accepted in payment for arms and passing it on to another country as "economic aid," at a higher price. In the early 1960's, for instance, Moscow sent Guinea marked-up Egyptian textiles that it had obtained in exchange for arms delivered to Cairo. Cases such as this can be found in virtually every underdeveloped country that receives Soviet arms. All of this comes on top of the Soviet propensity for dumping unwanted commodities on the world market. For instance, while Guinea is going deeper into debt buying marked-up Egyptian textiles, the Soviets are busily destroying Guinea's bauxite market by dumping on the market the bauxite they took in exchange for arms. If they are not dumping the bauxite they are selling it competitively wherever they can. Either way, Guinea loses.

Moscow has sent arms to Somalia at a time when the Soviets were wooing Ethiopia—a country with a border dispute with Somalia. Thus in the course of one transaction it managed to irritate two parties. Two of the reasons it sold arms to Morocco were to support Rabat's claims to Mauritania and to help it defend its border against Algeria; but then Moscow turned around and voted for Mauritania's admission into the United Nations, and gave aid to Algeria ostensibly to bolster the Algiers government in its border dispute with Morocco.[31]

Some of Moscow's most promising ventures have been destroyed by the very arms meant to preserve them. Pro-Soviet leaders such as Sukarno of Indonesia, Ben Bella of Algeria and Nkrumah of Ghana all were toppled by troops armed with Soviet weapons. Tanks crashing through the gates of the Presidential Palace, Moscow has learned to its chagrin, are now not always old *Shermans* and *Pattons*. Ex-ambassador to India John Kenneth Galbraith, testifying in 1966 before the Senate Committee on Foreign Relations, noted that too many Americans argue that if the United States does not provide arms to a country the business will fall by default to the Soviets, with dire results for other free-world nations. Citing numerous Soviet arms aid disasters, he said, "One can only conclude that those who worry about Soviet arms wish to keep the Russians out of trouble. This could be carrying friendship too far."[32]

3

Red Chinese arms aid, while small in volume compared to the Soviet program, nevertheless still has an impact on world affairs. Peking's foreign policy objectives—anti-imperialism, antirevisionism, Afro-Asian-Latin solidarity, and the creation of an "arms struggle" to overthrow the capitalists—are tied very closely to its arms aid policy. In fact, the two policies are difficult to separate. The essential difference between Moscow's and Peking's arms policy is that Moscow provides arms in support of wars of liberation and to undercut Western and Chinese influence, while Peking provides arms to promote domestic conflict, worldwide revolution and war.

This frankly revolutionary policy appeals to the more radical political leaders in the world, those who are most dissatisfied with the divisions of world power. Sheik Abdul Rahman Mohamed, or "Babu," once Zanzibar's Foreign Minister and now a Tanzanian minister, is a typical example: his political career has been based on both spiritual and physical support from the Red Chinese. Another is Alphonse Massamba-Debat, once President of the Congo-Brazzaville. And yet another is Oginga Odinga of Kenya, now out of power. One can find politicians in Mali, Burundi, Uganda, Guinea and Algeria who pay obeisance to the communist leaders in Peking.

The fact that all these countries are located in Africa is no coincidence. It is on that continent where Mao Tse-tung believes that his revolutionary goals will next be achieved. Chou En-lai's much publicized tour of Africa in 1964 is one manifestation of the importance Peking places on dominating this area. To the Red Chinese, the entire world is a great guerrilla battlefield where the principles of Mao are just as valid as in the mountains of China.

To hasten "the inevitable outcome of the historical development of China," Peking's preferred tactics have been gunrunning and interfering in the internal affairs of nations it wishes to dominate.

The most noted case of Chinese gunrunning in recent times took place in May 1965. A convoy of 40 trucks loaded with Chinese weapons was intercepted by Kenyan police after it had crashed through a roadblock on the Tanzania border near Lake Victoria. The arms were supposedly destined for Congolese Simbas and were to be delivered via Uganda. Rather than go the long way around Lake Victoria, the convoy leaders decided to cut into Uganda through Kenya. They believed that there would be no trouble because the sliver of Kenya that separates Tanzania and Uganda in the east is inhabited by Luo tribesmen, of which Odinga is an important chief. But it was only a month previously that Odinga was caught with a cache of communist arms, and neither Kenyatta nor his border guards were inclined to pass off the existence of forty truckloads of Chinese arms in Odinga's home territory as merely a coincidence. The arms were released only after Prime Minister Milton Obote of Uganda came to Nairobi to explain and apologize to Kenyatta.[33] The same type of incident has occurred in Mozambique, Angola, Burundi and the Congo-Brazzaville.

Interference in the internal affairs of others has been so heavy-handed that it suggests that Peking is its own worst enemy. Hardly had Zambia achieved its independence in 1961 than a Chinese-backed plot to overthrow the government was discovered. In Malawi the Chinese, through their embassy in Dar-es-Salaam, reportedly offered a bribe for diplomatic recognition which precipitated a major political crisis in the country. Peking gave military aid to a group of Cameroonians that led to an unsuccessful and near-communist revolt in the years 1960–62. The Red Chinese were so disruptive in Burundi—stockpiling arms and ammunition, plotting the assassination of leaders, arming Tutsi tribesmen refugees, training Congolese rebels—that diplomatic relations were broken in 1965. Peking's meddling in the affairs of the Central African Republic—including a scheme to create a secret "popular army" that would take its orders from Chinese officers—led in 1966 to the downfall of the country's president and the expulsion of all Red Chinese citizens.[34]

Besides heavy-handedness, other drawbacks impede the growth of Chinese influence in underdeveloped areas in general and in Black Africa in particular. The Red Chinese insist, for example, that their ideology is superior to all other ideologies, including nationalism. They push this message to the point where it irritates and angers Africans. Moscow is less hidebound and can operate with more flexibility. It has never made the mistake of underestimating nationalism as a force.

China also advocates warfare as a solution to problems. The Soviets, conversely, appeal to a nation's desire for economic improvement. Furthermore, the Chinese urge a frankly racist line, which offends Africans just as much as their warlike approach to problems. Nor are the Chinese very convivial guests to have in a country: usually they cannot speak either the native or old colonial languages. Lastly, Chinese Reds have the habit of promising large amounts of aid but actually delivering very little. What they do deliver is usually of inferior quality and purposely designed so that it cannot be used in conjunction with Western-designed equipment.[35]

In spite of these drawbacks Peking still appeals to a number of countries in the market for arms. It is the only communist country, for instance, that gives interest-free loans for arms purchases. Another advantage Peking offers is the prospect of immediate Soviet counteroffers of military aid. Wise political leaders know that Soviet arms are of better quality, more dependable and more versatile than Chinese arms; but to get Soviet arms, it is often necessary first to succumb temporarily to Peking's blandishments.

The future of both the Soviet and Chinese arms aid programs appears at this point to be promising. The lack of any East-West conventional arms agreement affords the communists many opportunities at present. As long as there remains a heavy demand for arms from underdeveloped and nonaligned countries, as long as gains can be realized in areas of the world that are convulsed by economic, social and political upheavals, as long as the communists believe that they can undercut Western influence through the distribution of arms, and as long as there remains competition for ideological supremacy, there will be little incentive for either Moscow or Peking to seek any compact with the West on the control of conventional arms.

But there are several clouds on the communist horizon. If, for instance, the Sino-Soviet rivalry becomes more bitter, it will tend to discredit communism in general, since there is so much disagreement even today on what Marxism means. A long, drawn-out family fight will tend to throw the entire ideology into disrepute, and the consequences will be seen in the declining demand for communist arms. Furthermore, if Peking ever decides to move into the arms aid field in a big way, it may frighten Moscow sufficiently into seeking some form of arms accommodation with the West. If Moscow believes that the actions of Peking can provoke an East-West confrontation or a large-scale war, then it may be forced to temper its current activities with more discretion.

But the largest cloud on the communist horizon is a dilemma that neither Moscow nor Peking has been able to solve: namely, by giving arms to a country it builds up a military caste that by its very nature is anticommunist. Thus the more arms they give to nations around the world, the more they tend to impede the advance of communism.

PART FOUR

CONCLUSION

IX

New Eras, New Policies

"How are the mighty fallen, and the weapons of war perished!"

—2 SAMUEL 1:27

1

Certainly the gun is the bride of war. Without the large quantities of modern weapons available to him in both 1956 and 1967, Nasser would never have provoked the two wars with Israel. If Sukarno had had no arms, he would never have undertaken the Malaysian and West Irian ventures. Had there been no large volume of arms available to the Federals and Biafrans, the Nigerian Civil War would never have taken place. Nor would the Pakistan-India War over Kashmir in 1965 have taken place; nor would have the Yemeni Civil War, nor the Congo Crisis, nor the Korean and Vietnam Wars, nor nearly all the other wars that have occurred since 1945.

The trade in arms encourages arms races and transforms political conflicts into war. It has happened twice in the Middle East within the last fourteen years, and the world is now witnessing a third arms race in the area that will inevitably culminate in yet another round of violent conflict. Hardy perennials such as Cyprus and Kashmir are still with us largely as a result of arms races. The Latin American arms race, while it has not yet led to any interstate wars, has already provoked some interservice wars and has encouraged governments to consider the use of force as a means of solving their international problems.

In the absence of arms and arms races, most of these postwar conflicts would have been channeled into diplomatic and political avenues for negotiation and solution.

Ninety-five percent of all the post-World War II conflicts have been fought in the underdeveloped areas of the world, and all have been fought with imported weapons. For any country that wants arms, it is still not difficult today to acquire them. The easiest weapons to buy are small arms and crew-served weapons. There are literally scores of suppliers eager to make a sale, not only producer countries and private entrepreneurs, but those nations that are upgrading their arsenals with newer equipment. Armored cars and secondhand jet aircraft are almost as easy to acquire, but in this case it is usually more difficult to keep the transaction a secret. The latest tanks, combat aircraft, warships and missiles are the most difficult items to buy because the transaction is usually limited to a producer country and an approved recipient. What controls are exercised are virtually limited to these weapons. Nevertheless, an "unapproved" customer, if he shops around sufficiently, can buy even these items from some source that is not concerned about the consequences. To all intents and purposes, restrictions on the resale and end-use of weapons have proved ineffectual, and most embargoes have been practically worthless.

The buying habits of recipient nations fall into a general pattern, particularly with those countries that gained their independence after 1945. The first stage consists of buying small lots of old weapons from one source, usually the former colonial ruler. The second stage occurs several years later after power has been consolidated and a national police force or military service has been established. At this point, fancy, new and expensive weapons are sought, mostly for reasons of prestige, occasionally for *bona fide* needs. This equipment is usually acquired from one major source as part of a long-range aid program. The third stage occurs years later when the recipient becomes disenchanted with the major supplier, and a program to increase the number of sources is initiated.

It is at the end of the second stage that hostilities are most likely to break out. The infusion of large quantities of arms into a country precipitates an arms race with its enemies. Large weapons purchases change the political and military perceptions of both recipients and adversaries and stimulate the outbreak of armed conflict. Often the mere presence of arms in an area is enough to provoke a war. Since most arms deliveries are made by governments, more and more wars, no matter how small, involve great power prestige and thus carry the seeds of a major East-West confrontation. The level of conflict in small wars escalates in proportion to the amount of great power prestige at stake.

Usually at the end of hostilities the recipient country, whether winner or loser, decides to increase the number of his suppliers. The broadening of the purchasing base invariably leads to an intensification of an arms race. Thus, the antagonists, better armed and little wiser, plunge ahead toward an inevitably higher level of conflict; until that day arrives, they live in an atmosphere of increasing hostility, where differences become more polarized and where peace is at best fragile, at worst illusory.

Examples of this buying cycle are legion, including the continuing Pakistan-India and Arab-Israeli conflicts. With slight variations the cycle is applicable to Indonesia, Iran, Morocco, Israel, Saudi Arabia, Iraq, West Germany, Spain and half a dozen South American countries.

This distressing state of affairs is largely the fault of the United States' arms aid program. The policy on which it is based has become obsolescent, almost an anachronism. The United States conceived its arms aid policy at a time when communist expansion efforts had to be contained. Large quantities of weapons were subsequently given to anyone who would help in this task. But following the death of Stalin in 1953, those who ran our arms aid program began to lose touch with changing world realities. They failed to grasp the fact that the Soviets had modified their belief in all-out war as a means of spreading their creed to relatively limited goals of supporting wars of liberation and undercutting the West at every opportunity. But while this was going on Washington did not modify its arms aid program in the light of these new realities. It has continued to pump large quantities of arms into the world markets as if we still lived in the Cold War years of 1947–53.

Although obsolescent by 1955 and clearly obsolete by the time the ILN office was created in 1961, the U.S. arms aid program had created sufficient momentum on its own by the mid-1950's that it soon became an end in itself. Before long Washington felt the need to justify the program: it devised three reasons why the program should continue, reasons that have little or nothing to do with the original concept behind the aid effort. Outside of several congressional heretics, few government officials since 1961 have questioned this change of emphasis.

The rest of the world's leading arms suppliers—Great Britain, France and the Soviet Union—are partially to blame for the proliferation in the conventional weapons of war. They have shown no inclination to restrain the hectic pace of the trade; few critical voices are heard in the capitals of Europe and Asia. But with this said, one cannot escape the fact that it was the United States which was responsible for these other nations becoming such large and active arms traders. It was the United States that both directly and indirectly brought these suppliers into the market, whetted their appetites, taught them the tricks of the trade and encouraged them to remain active. It has created not only its own competition and a market that is dangerously uncontrolled, but the seeds of its own destruction.

2

It is a fact of life today that no one wants to control the trade in conventional arms—rifles, pistols, machine guns, tanks, artillery, fighter planes and bombers, warships, tactical missiles and conventional explosives.

No organization, either national or international, has created any machinery to cope specifically with this problem. There are no agreements among nations to control the proliferation of these arms. There are no conferences or discussions under way, or even planned, to bring some order to this field. There is not even much demand for action; few people discuss the subject. Everyone has been talking about atomic warfare and how to avoid it, when all the killing is being done by these "mundane" weapons.

Very little literature exists on the subject. One would think, for instance, that the United Nations would be fertile ground for information. But not at all. The U.N. library carries no literature on conventional arms traffic, its statistical section makes no effort to compile data on arms, and the disarmament section maintains a library that, were it open to public scrutiny, would subject the entire organization to considerable derision.

One U.N. official, high in the organization's hierarchy, told me in 1967 that he wrote a twenty-page report on the post-World War II international trade in arms "so that, if the question came up in the Security Council or during a disarmament discussion, *we'd have something in our files*" (italics added). I was not allowed to have a copy of this report because the author said that it was "restricted"; but he did note proudly that it had two pages of bibliography in the back. "Of course," he added, "I didn't read any of it; I just took it from another [independent] report."

Other members of the U.N., when I interviewed them, seemed more interested in historical precedents than in coping with the problem at hand. One man went into a long dissertation over some of the more obscure aspects of the arms trade prior to World War I and during the days of the League of Nations. When I asked what was being done today, he seemed annoyed that I had brought up such a question.

The number of independent academic authorities on the subject in the free world today totals no more than 150 individuals. Of these, only a few in the Arms Control and Disarmament Agency in Washington, the Center for International Studies and the Browne & Shaw Research Corporation in the Boston area, and the Institute for Strategic Studies in London feel that the public or even government officials should be made aware of the situation. By and large the remaining experts are apathetic toward bringing the subject to the public's attention. Many write learned papers that circulate only among their peers. They have invented an arcane argot—worse in many respects than that used by sociologists—which ensures that few outsiders understand what they are talking about.

Official secrecy is also a part of today's reality. Few government officials will talk—and then only privately and in confidence. The rate is slightly higher among those no longer in office. Most of those in office will claim that the material desired is classified, whether it is or not. European bureaucrats are especially prone to rely on this excuse. My experience indicates that the Czechs and Soviets are not used to having such questions put to them at all, and their reaction is generally stunned incredulity.

The reaction in the United States differs from all the rest. Military and civilian intelligence officers whom I interviewed, flanked by pin-studded maps and fireproof, top-secret, combination-lock safes, would shrug their shoulders and say to me, deadpan, "I'm sorry, I don't know anything," and then suggest that I see so-and-so down the hall. For reasons that are not entirely clear, few of them are capable of admitting that they *do* know something on the subject but that it is classified. Most of them are not willing to talk even in the most general terms about unclassified aspects of the trade or even admit that there are unclassified aspects. This type of behavior is not limited to rank-and-file bureaucrats. Former CIA Chief Allen Dulles in an interview a year before his death told me that he knew nothing about the arms trade and that the last time he had anything to do with armaments was 1925.

Potentially the most serious danger in the arms trade lies in the fact that it is concentrated in the hands of very few government officials. It used to be said in the 1930's that if only the trade were nationalized, if only the responsibility were divided among many sober and enlightened public servants, then some semblance of order and reason would return to the field. But what has happened? The trade in effect *has* been nationalized. The trade is in the hands of sober and, generally speaking, intelligent and well-meaning government officials.

But the shift from the private to the public sector in the past quarter-century has not improved matters. In fact, it has made matters worse for obvious reasons. By and large the very few government officials who control the trade in Western nations are subject to no specific recall. They are not elected to their posts. They control budgets that would stagger the imagination of a

Zaharoff, and they operate in bureaucracies that are so large, so Byzantine, so powerful that effectively they are beyond the control of elected representatives. However disruptive a Zaharoff in the past, he was in the last analysis subject to review by law: he could be subpoenaed, his records could be scrutinized, and he could be prosecuted.

Today's bureaucrats are immune to this type of treatment. Technically they can be subpoenaed and prosecuted, but in effect they seldom are because their behavior, if exposed, would reflect on the entire operations of government and not just one segment of it. Technically government records are available to certain elected representatives, but as has been pointed out, this is not so in practice. The government officials who sell arms today have power that Zaharoff never dreamed of, they are protected to a degree that no private entrepreneur of old ever enjoyed, and they operate with less restraints upon them than even those few imposed on the master arms merchant himself two score years ago.

The effective control and direction of the entire world's arms trade lies in the hands of perhaps 200 people (not to be confused with the hundreds of thousands who implement the policies). They are for all practical purposes beyond anyone's control. The power these men possess, given the very large volume of traffic they direct and the extraordinary killing capacity of modern weapons, is frightening in its implications. The consequences of one misjudgment are chilling to contemplate. One misstep by these individuals could result in a holocaust from which there would be no return. On occasion these men have stumbled—in the Middle East, in Cuba twice, in the Congo, and in numerous other places. One day they may stumble irrevocably.

It used to be said in the 1930's that one of the more unattractive features of the private arms merchants was the selfish manner in which they went about their business. Arms, it was said, were purposely sold to start wars, and wars created a demand for more arms and, throughout it all, large profits were to be made. What was needed, went the argument, was the detached, cold-blooded approach of government officials, since this would lead to fewer mistakes being made. This has not happened. Instead of selfish mistakes being made by private arms salesmen, we now have detached, cold-blooded mistakes made by bureaucrats.

Another feature of the pre-World War II era was the relative ease with which a critic could identify the protagonist. The Zaharoffs of this world were easily recognizable—flesh-and-blood humans who often looked the part they played—and it took no special effort to assign blame to them. Today, however, the protagonist is not easy to identify. One can point to Kuss or to Raymond Brown, or to the Secretary of some Department, or to a President or Prime Minister and say, "This man or these men are to blame." But in truth none of them individually deserves full blame: they are bound by the limitations of their office and they are restricted by events. The real culprit today has become diffuse, an abstraction, a zephyr that often defies precise identification. In a way the villain is an attitude that has run unchecked for decades, and with particular intensity since the end of World War II.

This attitude, harbored by millions of people around the world, is one which assumes that many problems can be solved only by the use of force. This assumption has been built into the fabric of virtually every government in the world and consciously or unconsciously has encouraged over the years the increasing militarization of many policies. This is reflected, for example, in the policies the United States pursued in Vietnam and the Bay of Pigs, in the policies Britain, France and Israel applied at Suez in 1956, in the line Egypt has followed time and again against Israel, in the course Moscow took over Hungary, Berlin, and Czechoslovakia, and in the line Red China took over Tibet and India. It is not limited to right-wing militarists who talk of "bombing Hanoi" or to communist fanatics who seek to destroy Western culture through war. It can be found among left-wing British Labour MP's who believe, as several have told me, that the only solution to the South African problem is an invasion of the country. It can even be found among U.N. officials who talk of a huge world military force that will be used to "keep the peace." Kuss, Raymond Brown, the French, the Soviets and others involved in the arms trade are simply manifestations of this attitude.

Ex-ambassador Dungan, speaking in this instance of the United

States alone, put the point best when he said, "The basic thing that bothers me is that we have in our government these days a large group of people who, by profession and by oath of office, are committed to this particular line: *to solving problems by the use of arms. That's the really gut issue!*"

Most alarming perhaps is that the arms trade today is justified not simply in terms of military security alone but in terms of other national considerations. Selling arms, one is told, helps to balance the budget, reduces trade deficits, ensures full employment, raises income, creates friends, strengthens alliances. Every government department—and not just in the United States, but in every country engaged in the trade—has a stake in the venture. Many special interest groups—unions, businessmen, scientists, academic institutions, etc.—depend upon it. Millions of individuals earn their living either directly or indirectly from it. No aspect of human endeavor is entirely free of its influence. Thus the policy of selling arms is no longer just an extension of a nation's military policy, but an integral part of its total policy. The trade is such a dominant factor today that in most countries the maintenance of a healthy economic, fiscal and social climate is dependent upon its continuance.

3

If the arms trade is to continue along its current course without any major change in direction, what may mankind expect to witness in the foreseeable future?

At the moment new hostilities continue to break out on an average of one every five months. This trend is increasing and is not too difficult to understand when one considers that there are nearly twice as many armies in the world today than there were in 1945.

While most wars in the past two decades have been "small" in the sense of the Six-Day War, there is reason to believe that future wars will progressively increase in intensity. The world may have been split up into smaller political entities but that does not mean that the wars they fight will be correspondingly small. On the contrary, the more powerful weapons available today make it likely that the conflicts of tomorrow will be larger and more brutal than ever. Most of these new wars will break out in the underdeveloped areas and will be fought with increasingly sophisticated conventional arms distributed by foreign powers. At what level of intensity will the two great world powers become so involved that neither can back down? Suffice it to say, the upper levels have been probed on at least one major occasion (Cuba, 1962) and on many other relatively minor occasions.

Every sign points to a continued growth in arms sales. Between 1950 and 1968 the international trade in arms grew from $2.4 billion to $5 billion. The trade in the West alone will reach an estimated $10 billion per year in the early 1970's—double the 1968 figure. ILN officials believe that the United States will supply 25 percent of that market.[1] Great Britain, France and other European countries will continue to be active; so, too, will the Soviet Union, Czechoslovakia and Red China. The longer they stay in, the more their arms industries become concentrated, the more they come to depend on the trade and the more difficult it will be to slow down or redirect their efforts. The arms trade has its own logic that sweeps along all those who accept it in a millrace of circumstances and events; once involved, it is no easy task to opt out; in many instances it is impossible. If that were not disturbing enough, there are at least a score of countries, many of them highly unstable, who are struggling to join the fray.

The resale of equipment to third parties will become a cause for primary concern in the years ahead. The process will find fresh impetus with the periodic re-equipping of both NATO and Warsaw Pact nations. Prior to the years 1963–65, there existed no great resale problem because prime client countries absorbed all the arms passed down to them by the major powers; in other words, the recipients were filling actual military hardware voids with the tanks, jets, missiles and warships given or sold them. Sometime during the years 1963–65, a basic saturation of arms was reached by many prime client states. All the sheds were filled with tanks, all the hangars with planes, and all the armories with guns. So by the mid-1960's, when the great powers began once more to upgrade their own arsenals, a new type of disposal problem was created. The prime client states could not absorb the arms cast off by the major powers without, in turn, casting off their own, even older equipment to third parties. Now the half-empty sheds, hangars and armories of third parties are filled with obsolescent equipment received from the prime client states; the prime client states have refilled their sheds, hangars and armories with less obsolescent equipment bought from the major arms suppliers; and the major arms suppliers themselves have filled their own sheds, hangars and armories with the latest item their own technologists can design.

While a basic saturation in arms has been reached in many countries, there seems to be no letup in the demand for more and better arms. A saturation point is reached as the result of financial, technological and military limitations: there are only so many dollars in a country's treasury, and the arms they buy with them are essentially limited to the number of technicians available to service them and crews to operate them. But the *demand* for more knows no such bounds, particularly in countries that are poor and can least afford arms. There exists a constant pressure to increase and upgrade a country's arsenal, and it stems from a desire for "prestige," a real or imagined threat from abroad, the desire to consolidate one's power, a wish to embark on some foreign adventure, or from a number of other motives. Often these demands are successful and result in a country becoming *over*saturated in arms. In some instances this situation has bankrupted nations, in many other instances it has ensured that the countries remain backward and poor.

In the following decades this process will be repeated until third parties will be glutted with the latest weapons. And each time the leaders of one succumb to the temptation of using these fascinating new toys, the level of violence will rise.

In the next decades the world will also witness an increase in the indigenous production of weapons. India will be producing its own tanks and supersonic fighters; Egypt will be manufacturing jets and tactical missiles; Israel's arms capacity will increase to include armored vehicles and missiles; and South Africa, now virtually self-sufficient, will increase its production in the years ahead.

However, the bulk of production will continue to take place in the 34 countries of the world with a Gross National Product of $3 billion or more, an industrial work force of 200,000 or more, and an annual military budget of $200 million or larger.[2] There is no indication that any of these countries plan to cut back their rate of arms production. In fact, production is increasing in all categories of weapons in all of these countries. Canada, Italy, Red China, Sweden and West Germany, for example, are producing jet aircraft so fast that they will soon emerge as major manufacturers and suppliers of this weapons system.

Many of the countries embarking on a program of either establishing or augmenting their arms production capacities will undoubtedly, like the major powers before them, soon shift the emphasis from purely military or ideological considerations to economic considerations. More and more in the future the world will witness the likes of India, Egypt, Italy, Israel and Red China selling weapons to acquire foreign exchange. The same old reasons will be cited: it keeps production levels high, and it offsets trade deficits. The prospect of military considerations becoming a minor, if not a forgotten, factor in the international arms trade is not too remote.

Another trend worth noting is the increasing cost of weapons. The financial burden on major powers is currently so large that in the United States, for instance, it is creating a disjointed economy and a misdirection of priorities. But with less-wealthy countries, the burden of buying arms may become intolerable. It is one thing to buy 200,000 rifles and another to buy six jet fighters, and there are very few countries in the world today that are satisfied with the possession of small arms alone. A nation that finds itself in hock to its arms suppliers, knee-deep in a keep-up-with-the-Joneses arms race, and in increasing fiscal and economic difficulties because of the rising costs of weapons, may well turn to violent solutions as a way out of the impasse. Sometimes it is expressed in *coup d'etats,* other times in foreign military adventures designed to divert attention from domestic difficulties. Indonesia, Egypt, Ghana, Mali, Algeria, Red China, India, Pakistan and many other nations have chosen these avenues of escape at one time or another. As the burdens become heavier in the future, an increasing number of countries will follow suit.

Even when nations can avoid such courses of action, the problem of potential conflict is in no way lessened. One of the basic traits of a military establishment is that it inevitably feels itself compelled to justify its existence. An army, navy and air force is like a late-model car: one does not buy it to store away in the garage, to be polished occasionally for the benefit of visitors; it is bought to be used. Perhaps it is first bought for reasons of "prestige," but after that euphoria wears off and as each model is replaced year after year by newer, more expensive models, pressures mount to justify such costs. These pressures are particularly intense among the underdeveloped nations—those that can least afford such a luxury, those that are the least politically and militarily mature and those that have the least to lose by embarking on a venture whose sole purpose is to justify the existence of its military establishment.

The trend to increase the sophistication of weapons has its own pitfalls. The belief that more complicated and more versatile weapons are somehow better than simple and inexpensive armaments is most entrenched in the West, particularly in the United States. Americans tend to "puff up the cushion on which we sit," Colonel Jarrett, one of the world's leading authorities on armaments, told me—to make things easier for the soldier through a complex array of sophisticated military hardware. The cost of such equipment is astronomical, as any U.S. Defense Budget will show. The Soviets, on the other hand, while they are dedicated to technological improvements, have never lost sight of the fact that the best weapons are those that are inexpensive, dependable, light of weight and capable of being operated under a variety of adverse conditions by the ordinary soldier.

Tank development is a case in point. The future NATO tank, the MBT-70, will be an extremely complicated piece of machinery, complete with pushbutton controls, laser-beam fire-control gear and other sophisticated equipment. It will be capable of operating fully submerged, and the crew will be shielded from atomic radiation. The cost of each tank may run as high as $600,000. The latest Soviet tanks are less sophisticated but they have a greater operating range, as high a firepower, and cost an estimated one-third as much as the MBT-70. Maintenance of a Soviet tank is relatively uncomplicated and the responsibility of its crew. This capability alone gives it a great advantage over an MBT-70, which will be so complicated that it will have to be followed into battle by a small army of highly trained technicians, for all but the smallest breakdowns will be beyond the capability of the crew to repair. Puffing up the cushion, says Jarrett, is not only an expensive pastime but ultimately misguided. "A Cadillac," he said, "will give you a *better* ride, but it won't give you any *more* of a ride." Furthermore, Jarrett told me, "I have yet to see a tank that could stand up to a twelve-inch antitank mine over an eight-inch shell."

If the trend to sophistication continues, the United States and its Western allies may lose their competitive position to the Soviet Union and other eastern European bloc suppliers, not only because of the staggering costs but because the weapons themselves will be beyond the capabilities of most underdeveloped nations to maintain. Some American weapons are now so complicated that they require scientists rather than soldiers to operate them. Soviet weapons, by no means inferior in effectiveness and in many instances superior, are still capable of being operated by moderately trained soldiers. Most of the countries in the market for arms, because they have few scientists and plenty of soldiers, may tend to view Soviet equipment with increasing favor. This loss of competitiveness, as long as there is no abatement in arms sales and as long as the economic and political well-being of Western nations is tied so closely to arms sales, may force the Western allies into some rash act in the future.

To whose advantage do these trends work? Probably only the most revolutionary such as Red China, the most repressive and despotic such as South Africa and Haiti, and those with the most irresponsible leaders such as Egypt.

It is ironic to think that while the two major powers, whose arms race revived in part the trade, have spent billions of dollars and rubles respectively stabilizing the balance of power, they have also risked destroying this precarious relationship by pumping large quantities of weapons into unstable areas. Furthermore, the arms competition that exists among the Western allies themselves, coupled with the increasing willingness of the Soviet Union and its eastern European neighbors to compete in the world's arms markets, has worked to unhinge the respective military alliances to which those arms-producing nations belong. While this may lead to the easing of some tensions, to some realignment of political, economic, social and military forces, to some actual improvements, it does not guarantee any net decrease in tensions or any realignments and improvements that are truly more beneficial and lasting. Given no change in direction, the international trade in arms in future years may well create situations that are potentially so explosive and dangerous to the continued existence of mankind that they will make today's difficulties seem mild in comparison.

4

What are the chances of controlling this trade in arms?

In a power-oriented world, arms mean power; and to most nations, especially the newer ones, arms are vital to the maintenance of the regime, sometimes vital to the existence of the state itself. Countries without any industrial base are usually the first to insist that there be no restrictions on the arms trade because they are dependent upon outsiders for their military supplies. Thus the thought of any limitations is abhorrent to most of the world's leaders. A vote in the United Nations limiting the trade in even the slightest degree would probably show no more than ten nations in favor, at least half of which would be arms-producing nations. Member countries of the U.N. will gladly vote for "disarmament" and nuclear restrictions because it is good public relations, but few would be affected by the decisions. They may vote for an arms embargo against South Africa, but only because it is a specific restriction against an unpopular and vulnerable nation and because few will be affected. But any across-the-board vote to restrict their own lifeblood—arms—would be dismissed as inappropriate.

Many well-intentioned people hold that somehow everything would be much better if the great powers replaced arms sales with economic aid. This, they say, would cut down the size of the military and build up the economic sector and, in turn, give greater leverage to the nonmilitary and presumably more enlightened voices in the country. It is not good enough, however, just to switch the emphasis because, as long as countries demand arms, any economic aid relieves the pressure on local budgets for economic needs, thus freeing that amount of money to buy arms. Economic aid from the great powers, if it is to be substituted for arms, must be tied to a country's economic spending. But even this expedient does not solve the problem because the *desire* for arms is still there. The problem is one of creating a situation where governments—particularly the poor, backward ones—do not feel the need to buy arms, where it is to their advantage to spend their money in more productive fields.

With these built-in difficulties in mind, what then can be done to bring some order to this field? It is not my purpose here to discuss all the ramifications involved in establishing and fortifying procedures to control the international arms trade. But perhaps a few suggestions might one day lead to some measure of control, considering that virtually *nothing* is being done now to restrict this trade.

One of the first things that can be done—indeed, it must be done—is for the United States, its allies and the USSR to begin talks on ways and means of controlling the trade. The talks should follow the pattern undertaken by the great powers at Geneva to limit the spread and use of nuclear weapons. What is important is that conversations begin *now,* because nothing substantial will change until millions of words have gone into the record. No amount of U.N. debate will resolve the matter; nor will unilateral action by the United States. Perhaps these talks can take place in conjunction with the current interest in limiting the development of offensive and defensive nuclear missile systems. Perhaps the major Western powers should first come to an agreement among themselves, then turn their attention to dealing with the Soviets.

It behooves the United States, as the world's largest arms dealer, to take the initiative in these conversations. There is some evidence that such talks would be welcome in the West, because it is beginning to dawn on some responsible individuals that the long-term effects of the trade outweigh any short-term advantages. How to bring the Soviet Union to the bargaining table would be an especially difficult question to resolve. But, again, there is some indication that its leaders are not entirely adverse to the idea of limiting the trade. The Soviets will come to the bargaining table the day they realize that the trade is ultimately detrimental even to their own interests. Hopefully it will not take another Six-Day War or Cuban Missile Crisis to drive the point home.

An East-West conventional arms agreement, to be effective, should include regional arms freezes. The major arms freeze should be applied first and foremost to the Middle East, the most explosive area in the world today and in all probability the area where the next large-scale round of hostilities will begin. Other arms freezes should be placed on Pakistan and India, Cyprus and certain Latin American and African countries. These arms freezes should be coupled with nonacquisition and nonproliferation agreements, and selective arms and technological embargoes that are backed up with conviction and determination. Above all, the United States and the Soviet Union should consider seriously the idea of destroying on an equal basis certain types of their obsolescent equipment rather than selling them. This would amount to a partial disarmament.

Whatever agreements are reached between the United States, its allies and the USSR would inevitably have an inhibitive effect on other nations participating in the trade. Arms sales prosper in large measure from the free-wheeling nature of the East-West competition, and if there were some agreement limiting this competition, many other nations would hesitate to expand their arms trade if they knew that they would incur the displeasure of the signatories to the pact. Furthermore, the very act of discussing the subject at a conference not only will bring the topic to general public attention but will tend to diminish the actual number of transactions themselves through unfavorable publicity.

Until the day that such agreements are signed, there are a number of activities the United Nations and the free world's arms purveyors can undertake unilaterally to set their own houses in order. By so doing none of them will be put at a disadvantage.

The United Nations, for instance, should begin to keep records of arms transactions, much like those records kept by the League of Nations. While such records in themselves would not halt the reckless course of the trade, they would serve to alert responsible officials around the world to dangerous trends and, like an East-West conference, would tend to keep the trade before the public eye.

The U.N. should also undertake research into all aspects of conventional arms control. It should build up a first-class source of information on the subject and be prepared to disseminate all of it to interested parties. In short, the United Nations should become *the* focal point for information, research material and general public enlightenment—something it is obviously not today.

A specific study the U.N. could begin immediately is one concerned with comparing the worldwide financial return on arms sales with the cost of putting down the violence the same arms provoke. If a study showed that the U.S. government was spending two or three times more on putting down violence caused by the arms it sold than it was getting back from the sale of those arms themselves, it would inhibit someone such as Henry Kuss boasting how much his efforts had "enriched" the U.S. Treasury. No one knows the true "cost" of arms sales, and if it were proved that everyone—the United States, Britain, France, the Soviet Union and others—lost money, then considerable steam would be taken out of the trade.

There are a number of things that the United States, as the world's leading purveyor of arms, can do to set its house in order. The first thing that should be done is to review the entire arms sales policy. This policy has led to the creation of many competing arms industries where none existed before; it has tended to set ally against ally, neutral against neutral; it has polarized the world into many armed camps and has inevitably heightened world tensions. It has led to an increase in anti-Americanism, a dissipation of U.S. influence, a worldwide glut of arms. It has led to the bankruptcy of nations, the downfall of friendly governments, a collapse in the mechanisms of control and, ever more frequently, to war.

Most urgently in need of review is the policy of selling arms to offset the U.S. balance of payments deficit. There is no justification for countering the gold drain by selling weapons of destruction. This is particularly true in the case of poverty-stricken countries. For the Defense Department to say that "only" 6 percent (discounting the fact that a more accurate figure would be between 25 and 30 percent) of U.S. arms is sold to underdeveloped nations reflects a basic moral bankruptcy of the policy. It suggests that the United States is "only slightly" immoral, "only occasionally" crooked and "only incidentally" greedy, none of which it should be. It must be recalled that it has been "only" these arms sales that have provided the weapons used in nearly all the wars since the program began.

A thorough review of "balancing" an area with arms is called for. While balancing may keep antagonists temporarily at bay, it also creates at least three unhealthy effects: it tends to increase the level of the balance, thus making any conflict that much more violent; it tends to make a war that much more difficult to stop, since both sides are militarily each other's equal; and, above all, it tends—in most cases by the mere presence of arms—to provoke war itself, the one act such a policy is designed to prevent.

There is also a need to review the existing control measures with a view to tightening them. Some steps have been taken following the revelations brought out by the congressional inquiries and debates of 1967: Congress has demanded more information and control; some of the Defense Department's and Eximbank's authority has been cut back; and certain regional ceilings on foreign military sales have been imposed. But these are only timid, first steps. Much more needs to be done. What are necessary are bold strokes that will fundamentally change the present course of the U.S. foreign military sales program.

First of all, the decision-making process needs to be changed. It should be broadened as much as possible at the higher levels of government and drastically reduced at the lower levels. All sales decisions—*all of them*—should be made by the President or the National Security Council. General authority for the arms sales program should be vested in the State Department; the decisions should be implemented by the Pentagon, and coordination should be effected through the Senior Interdepartmental Group (SIG). In other words, the ILN office should have no power of decision; its sole function should be to carry out the orders of the President or National Security Council. The fact that a relatively minor civil servant such as Henry Kuss has the authority to decide whether or not a country can afford arms without damaging other segments of its economy suggests how far out of control the decision-making process has strayed.

Office of Munitions Control officials should also be given the authority to enforce end-use agreements. The office should be given the authority and personnel to enforce the growing volume of resales to third parties. It should be required to maintain complete records of all transactions, and it should take part in all sales decisions. The OMC should have a veto power if it feels that the ultimate use of U.S. arms would be beyond Washington's capacity to control. Military advisers in the field should be required to report all violations of control procedures to the OMC.

MAAG's that still operate in countries where no Military Aid Programs exist should be abolished; the authority of Military Missions and military attachés to peddle arms should be eliminated; military co-production and offset arrangements should be phased out and eventually abolished, since they encourage other nations to remain active in the arms trade; the Defense Department should not be allowed to be in the banking business, and its authority to subsidize arms sales loans should be abolished; no government agency should be allowed either directly or indirectly to advertise American weapons; and there should be an interval of time—say, two years—during which a military officer upon retirement could not work for a major U.S. military contractor.

The Arms Control and Disarmament Agency should be given more authority; its voice should be heard more clearly in the National Security Council. The U.S. government must enforce embargoes it chooses to impose on an area or country; these arms bans should not be, as most of them have been, exercises in public relations. More information on the arms trade must be made available; it need not all be made available to the general public, but far more must be available to members of Congress. The opportunities of bureaucracy to shield its policies and operations behind the cloak of secrecy called "security" should also be curtailed.

There is, furthermore, a need to reappraise the government's propensity for succumbing to blackmail. Washington is too concerned with the possibility that if it withholds arms from a country it may turn to the Soviet Union and that the market will thus be forever lost. It might be to the United States' advantage every once in a while not only to say "No" to a blackmailer but to encourage him to buy Soviet. The effect might be traumatic, since, as all arms recipients have discovered, not all Soviet aid is a blessing. It does not bring any financial relief, and in many instances it does not even result in the upgrading of a country's arsenal. In fact, it usually brings more problems than it solves. It might be beneficial for all concerned that these blackmailers taste some bitter fruit.

The United States should also consider further penalizing underdeveloped nations that spend their money on advanced weaponry. The penalties should augment the current government policy that reduces the amount of economic aid in relation to the amount of money wasted on useless military hardware. Such penalties, imposed fairly and uniformly, would serve notice on the world that the United States will no longer tolerate the currently unchecked military spending habits of the underdeveloped countries. At the same time, Washington should provide economic incentives to poor nations to switch their financial resources away from the military sector.

The U.S. government should also begin to encourage all arms-producing nations to work toward the abolition of the private trade in arms. Although private entrepreneurs sell weapons in relatively small volume, they can still sell them in sufficient quantities to provoke a fair-sized war. In the years ahead increasing firepower will allow these entrepreneurs to equip armies to the point where very large wars can be fought. There is no estimating where this may lead if nothing is done. The private trade in arms is an anachronism that is of no benefit to mankind. What little necessary business it performs can be better carried out and better controlled by governments themselves. Unless abolished, this trade will be a source of considerable mischief in the future. Indeed, it will become a positive danger.

Above all, the United States arms policy must return to basic principles, for if it does not, none of the above changes will have any meaning. The United States must stop providing arms in bulk quantities to over half of the world's nations. It must cease providing arms that serve only momentary financial, commercial or private industrial interests. Arms must be furnished only on a highly selective basis, to meet a specific threat with specific weapons. When the threat has passed, these same arms should be either returned to the United States or destroyed. Under no other circumstances should U.S. arms be provided to another country.

This means that countries that are not directly threatened by communist aggression or anarchy or fascism should receive no sophisticated arms at all. It means, for instance, that there should be no supersonic jet aircraft sales or missile sales to Latin America, Africa, the Middle East and southeast Asia. It means that the entire U.S. arms aid program should be cut back drastically and in certain areas eliminated completely. The attitude that the United States is the free world's armorer—and by implication its policeman and peacemaker—will not be changed until this is done.

The United States is not solely responsible for the world's arms trade and its grave threats to peace. The Soviet Union, by encouraging arms races and supporting "wars of liberation," is at least equally to blame. But other countries too must share in the responsibility. Great Britain deliberately fosters the export of arms, mostly for financial gain. France, Italy, West Germany and Belgium also export arms with little regard for the consequences. Sweden and Switzerland, playing the pious, peace-loving neutrals at the front door, sell arms vigorously out the back. Most of these countries refuse to bear the responsibility for controlling the violence that their own arms provoke.

Still, today's arms trade is essentially an American problem. No nation talks more loudly about peace, yet no nation distributes as many weapons of war. No nation has spoken so passionately in favor of nuclear controls, yet no nation has been so silent on the subject of conventional arms controls. Nor has any nation been as vocal in its desire to eradicate hunger, poverty and disease, yet no nation has so obstructed the fight against these ills through its insistence that poor countries waste their money on expensive and useless arms.

It is time that the actions of the United States match its words. To achieve this will require a fundamental reversal of this iniquitous trade in arms. America's arms policy must be subordinate to its overall, long-term foreign policy objectives; it must be tightly policed and, above all, it must be flexible, reasonable and minimal. Today it is none of these. It is truly "a monster fearful and hideous, vast and eyeless"; it is overblown, overstaffed, misguided and almost out of control. If America seeks a more peaceful world, it must first set its own house in order. If it does not, there is little hope that others will. Indeed, if America does not do it soon, it may be too late for everyone.

Notes

Rather than clutter the text with footnote numbers, I have grouped references under one number wherever appropriate at the end of paragraphs.

PART ONE: PROLOGUE

CHAPTER I

1. Bloomfield, Lincoln P., and Leiss, Amelia C., *et al. The Control of Local Conflict. A Design Study on Arms Control and Limited Wars in the Developing Areas* (Center for International Studies, Cambridge, Massachusetts, June 30, 1967), Vol. III, p. 9. Four wars have been added to the authors' list of 52: Hungary 1956, the Six-Day War of 1967, the Nigerian Civil War 1967-70, and the El Salvador-Honduras War of 1969. The authors give no definition of war. They admit that there is no objective way to measure violence and that any such list is somewhat arbitrary. Nevertheless, their list appears to be the most complete of major conflicts since 1945.
2. *Ibid.*
3. *National Observer,* Dec. 11, 1967.
4. Kemp, Geoffrey. "Arms Sales and Arms Control in the Developing Countries," *World Today,* September 1966. Sutton, John L., and Kemp, Geoffrey. *Arms to Developing Countries, 1945–65,* Adelphi Paper No. 28 (Institute for Strategic Studies, London, October 1966). *Military Assistance Facts* (Defense Department pamphlet, May 1, 1966). Since none of the five countries mentioned have published figures continuously since 1945, these figures were arrived at by taking reliable data for certain years and estimating from it military aid for the remaining years on the basis of each country's activity at that particular time. Generally the figures conform to judgments made by authorities in the field.
5. Kemp, *ibid.*

6. Engelbrecht, H. C., and Hanighen, F. C. *Merchants of Death* (Dodd, Mead & Co., New York, 1934), pp. 13–14.
7. Millis, Walter. *Arms and Men* (G. P. Putnam's Sons, New York, 1956), Chapter 1.
8. Engelbrecht and Hanighen, *op. cit.*, pp. 59–61.
9. *Ibid.*, pp. 43–44.
10. *Ibid.*, pp. 45–47.
11. *Ibid.*, p. 30.
12. *Ibid.*, Chapter VIII. McCormick, Donald. *Pedlar of Death* (Macdonald, London, 1965), p. 124.
13. McCormick, *ibid.*, p. 77.
14. *Ibid.*, pp. 104–5.
15. *Ibid.*, p. 67.
16. Engelbrecht and Hanighen, *op. cit.*, Chapter XII.
17. *Ibid.*, pp. 61–69.
18. *Catalogue of Military Goods* (Francis Bannerman, 1903; reprint, 1960), p. 2.
19. Engelbrecht and Hanighen, *op. cit.*, pp. 62, 64–65.
20. *Ibid.*, pp. 63–64.
21. *Ibid.*, p. 63.
22. Wiltz, John Edward. *In Search of Peace, The Senate Munitions Inquiry, 1934–36* (Louisiana State University Press, Baton Rouge, 1963), p. 130.
23. McCormick, *op. cit.*, pp. 221–22.
24. *Ibid.*, pp. 120–21.
25. *Wiltz, op. cit.*, p. 160.
26. *Ibid.*, p. 76. Engelbrecht and Hanighen, *op. cit.*, pp. 200, 229–34, 240–46.
27. *Military Assistance Facts,* May 1, 1966.
28. Sutton and Kemp, *op. cit.*, p. 31.
29. *Foreign Military Sales Program* (Defense Department pamphlet, undated, probably 1967).
30. *Military Assistance Facts,* May 1, 1966. (Figures added through FY 1968.)
31. *Ibid.*

PART TWO: FREE ENTERPRISE ARMED

CHAPTER II

1. Kobler, John. "The Man with the Crocodile Briefcase," *Saturday Evening Post,* March 24, 1962.
2. *Ibid.* Adler, Dick. "Arms and the Man Called Sam," *Town* (London), July 1965.
3. *Ibid.*
4. *Sunday Times* (London), January 2, 1966.
5. de Gramont, Sanche. "Arms Merchant to the World," *New York Times Magazine,* September 24, 1967.
6. Kobler, *op. cit.*
7. Wheeler, Keith. " 'Cursed Gun' —The Track of C2766," *Life,* August 27, 1965. See also *The President's Commission on the Assassination of President Kennedy* (Warren Report), (Government Printing Office, 1964), pp. 118 ff.
8. *The Times* (London), November 26, 1965. Washington *Post,* October 29, 1966.
9. de Gramont, *op. cit.*
10. *Ibid.*
11. *Ibid.*
12. *Ibid.*
13. *Ibid.*
14. Confidential Memo from the House Committee on Un-American Activities, dated February 2, 1960.
15. Brownsville (Texas) *Herald,* January 10, 1962.

CHAPTER III

1. *Hearings before the Subcommittee on Near Eastern and South Asian Affairs of the Committee on Foreign Relations,* U.S. Senate, 90th Congress, First Session, March 14, April 13, 20, 25, June 22, 1967, "Arms Sales to Near East and South Asian Countries," pp. 10–11. (Hereafter referred to as *"Near Eastern and South Asian Hearings."*)
2. *World Trade Directory Report,* U.S. Department of Commerce, 1968.
3. *New York Times,* March 5–7, May 11, August 3, 22, 1965.
4. *Near Eastern and South Asian Hearings,* pp. 30–31; this part of transcript heavily censored. *Der Spiegel* (Hamburg), No. 35, 1967.
5. *Der Spiegel, ibid.*
6. *World Trade Directory Report,* 1967.
7. *Near Eastern and South Asian Hearings,* p. 63.
8. (Toronto) *Financial Post Survey of Industrials,* 1967.
9. *Near Eastern and South Asian Hearings,* pp. 31, 60–61, 80–81.
10. *Hearings before the Subcommittee to Investigate Juvenile Delinquency of the Committee on the Judiciary,* U.S. Senate, 88th Congress, First Session, January 29, 30, March 7, May 1, 2, 1963. Part 14, "Interstate Traffic in Mail-Order Firearms," pp. 3348–49, including photograph of arrest report.
11. *Ibid.,* 88th Congress, Second Session, March 26, April 24, 25, 1964. Part 15, "Interstate Traffic in Mail-Order Firearms," pp. 3553–54.
12. *Ibid.,* pp. 3664, 3678, 3713.
13. *Ibid.,* pp. 3547–48, 3550, 3553, 3580.
14. *Ibid.,* pp. 3661–70.
15. *Ibid.,* pp. 3670–71, 3676, 3680, 3697–98, and elsewhere.
16. *Ibid.,* p. 3715.
17. *Ibid.,* pp. 3546–77.
18. *Ibid.,* p. 3576.
19. *Ibid.,* p. 3543.
20. *Ibid.,* p. 3581.
21. *Ibid.,* pp. 3545–49.
22. St. George, Andrew. "The Arms Merchants," *Daily Telegraph Magazine* (London), July 28, 1967.
23. *Ibid.*
24. *Ibid.*
25. *Ibid.*
26. *Hansard,* February 18, 1964, col. 1023–25. *The People* (London), February 2, 1964.
27. *Ibid.,* April 8, 1964, col. 1014–15.
28. *Ibid.*
29. *New Yorker,* July 11, 18, 1931.
30. *Newsweek,* November 3, 1952.
31. *New York Times,* August 24, 1962.
32. *New Yorker,* July 18, 1931.
33. *Sunday Times,* August 29, 1965. *The Times,* January 24, 1966.
34. *Le Figaro,* February 8, 1961.
35. *Der Spiegel,* No. 44, 1960.
36. *Ibid.,* No. 52, 1963.
37. *Ibid.,* No. 13, 1959.
38. *Ibid.,* No. 44, 1960. *Newsweek,* September 4, 1961.
39. *Der Spiegel,* No. 10, 1960.
40. *New York Times,* September 28, 1961.
41. *Sunday Times,* August 29, 1965.
42. *Ibid.,* August 1, 1965.
43. Washington *Post,* February 18, 1965. *Sunday Times,* August 1, 1965.
44. *The Guardian* (London), August 17, 1967.
45. *Der Spiegel,* No. 45, 1966.

46. *Daily Telegraph,* November 6, 1962, December 20, 1965. *The Times,* January 26, December 22, 1966. *New York Times,* March 24, 1967. *World Journal Tribune,* February 19, 1967.
47. *New York Times,* September 12, 1963. *New York Herald Tribune,* August 5, 1964. "The War in the Yemen," reprint of speech given by Lt. Col. Neil McLean, DSO, October 20, 1965.
48. *Daily Telegraph,* April 12, 1966.
49. *Sunday Times,* July 5, 1964. *Daily Express* (London), November 11, 1965.
50. *Sunday Telegraph* (London), June 4, 1967.
51. *The Times,* January 4, 1964. *New York Times,* April 17, 1967, March 18, 1968.
52. *New York Times,* February 11, 1957.
53. Wise, David, and Ross, Thomas B. *The Invisible Government* (Random House, New York, 1964), *passim.* Tully, Andrew. *CIA, The Inside Story* (William Morrow, New York, 1962), *passim.* Blackstock, Paul W. *The Strategy of Subversion* (Quadrangle, Chicago, 1964), *passim.* Meyer, Karl E. and Szulc, Tad. *The Cuban Invasion* (Praeger, New York, 1962), *passim.*
54. Meyer and Szulc, *op. cit.,* p. 109.
55. Washington *Post,* September 29, 1964, January 11, 1965. *New York Times,* May 27, 1965.
56. Washington *Post,* November 25, 1966. *New York Times,* January 4, 6, 1967. *Newsweek,* January 16, 1967.
57. Smith, Sandy. "The Mob," *Life,* September 1, 8, 1967.
58. *Hearings before a Subcommittee of the Committee on Government Operations,* House of Representatives, 90th Congress, First Session, Part 1: April 5, 13, May 16, 1967, pp. 98–99.
59. Tully, *op. cit.,* pp. 32, 196–99, 201–2. Wise and Ross, *op. cit.,* pp. 106–9, 129–46.
60. *Sunday Telegraph,* November 25, 1962. Washington *Post,* January 31, February 12, March 29, 1964. *The Guardian,* February 15, 1965.
61. *Sunday Telegraph,* March 11, 18, 1962, January 27, 1963.
62. "Nkrumah's Subversion in Africa" (Ghana Ministry of Information, Accra-Tema, 1966), *passim.*
63. Collier, Bernard Law. "The Whacky Spy Caper," *Saturday Evening Post,* July 2, 1966. *New York Times,* September 21, October 7, 8, 14, 1966.
64. Washington *Post,* July 19, 1963, March 29, December 17, 1964. *New York Times,* November 21, 1966.
65. *Sunday Times,* October 23, 1966. *The Times,* January 6, 1967.
66. *New York Times,* August 11, 13, 20, 22, 1967. *Sunday Times,* August 20, 1967.
67. *New York Times,* July 29, August 11, 15, October 27, November 5, 1967, June 14, 1968. *Sunday Times,* August 20, 1967, July 14, 1968.
68. *New York Times,* July 29, October 31, November 5, 1967, February 2, 1968. *Sunday Times,* August 20, 1967.
69. *Sunday Times, ibid.,* and elsewhere.
70. *Ibid.*
71. Hoare, Mike. *Congo Mercenary* (Robert Hale, London, 1967), *passim. Sunday Times,* December 24, 1967.
72. *Newsweek,* August 12, 1968. *New York Times,* June 28, Au-

gust 16, 1968. *Sunday Times,* July 14, 1968.
73. *Sunday Times,* October 8, 1967.
74. "Report of the Officer-in-Charge of the U.N. Operation in the Congo," *U.N. Review,* November 1962, pp. 61–62.
75. *New York Times,* December 12, 1961.

PART THREE: BUREAUCRACY ARMED

CHAPTER IV

1. Hovey, Harold A. *United States Military Assistance* (Praeger, New York, 1966), Chapter 10.
2. *Ibid.*
3. Green, William. *The World's Fighting Planes* (Doubleday, Garden City, 1964), pp. 7, 202, 205. Johnson, George B., and Lockhoven, Hans Bert. *International Armament* (International Small Arms Publishers, Cologne, West Germany, 1964), Vol. II, p. 161. Calmann, John. *European Co-operation in Defense Technology: The Political Aspect,* No. 1 of *Defense Technology and the Western Alliance* study series (Institute for Strategic Studies, London, 1967), pp. 2 ff. Harlow, C. J. E., *ibid.* No. 2, Part 2, *The European Armaments Base: A Survey,* p. 50. James, Robert Rhodes, *ibid.* No. 3, *Standardization and Common Production of Weapons in NATO,* pp. 18–19.
4. *Armed Forces Management,* January 1965, pp. 27 ff.
5. *Ibid.,* January 1967. Updated as necessary.
6. "World-Wide Military Expenditures and Related Data," Arms Control and Disarmament Agency research report 67–6, calendar year 1965, p. 6. *Hearings before the Committee on Foreign Relations,* House of Representatives, 90th Congress, 2nd Session, June 26, 27, 1968. "The Foreign Military Sales Act," pp. 23–24.
7. List attached to memo dated October 2, 1964, signed by Deputy Secretary of Defense Cyrus Vance.
8. The *Guide* was discontinued in January 1967 and replaced by the weekly *Military Export Reporter.*
9. *Military Assistance Facts,* May 1, 1966.
10. *Near Eastern and South Asian Hearings,* p. 58.
11. Minifie, J. M. "The Good and the Bad Merchants of Death," *Commentator,* October 1966, p. 10.
12. McCarthy, Senator Eugene J. "Arms and the Man Who Sells Them," *Atlantic Monthly,* October 1967.
13. *Ibid.*
14. *New York Times,* February 8, 1968.
15. *Congressional Record,* August 14, 1967, p. S11491.
16. *Near Eastern and South Asian Hearings,* p. 17.
17. *Congressional Record,* August 15, 1967, p. S11583.
18. Committee on Foreign Relations, U.S. Senate, Staff Study, "Arms Sales and Foreign Policy" (1967), p. 8.

19. Washington *Star*, April 20, 1967. *Near Eastern and South Asian Hearings*, p. 9. *Der Spiegel*, No. 35, 1967.
20. *Near Eastern and South Asian Hearings*, p. 70.
21. *Ibid.*, pp. 9, 28, 33, 43, 70.
22. Sutton and Kemp, *op. cit.*, p. 36.
23. *Der Spiegel*, *op. cit.*
24. *Near Eastern and South Asian Hearings*, p. 70.
25. *Congressional Record*, August 14, 1967, p. S11490.
26. *Ibid.*, p. S11492.
27. *Hearings before the Subcommittee to Investigate Juvenile Delinquency of the Committee on the Judiciary*, U.S. Senate, 90th Congress, First Session, July 10–12, 18–20, 25, 28, 31, August 1, 1967, pp. 219–34.
28. *Near Eastern and South Asian Hearings*, pp. 13–14, 79.
29. Hovey, *op. cit.*, pp. 186 ff. Staff Study, pp. 5–7. *Military Export Guide*, chapter on "Sources of Financing Military Exports."
30. *Military Export Guide*, Staff Study, *ibid.*
31. *Ibid.* Also *New York Times*, July 19–21, 1967. St. Louis *Post-Dispatch*, July 23, 1967.
32. *New York Times*, July 20, 1967.
33. *Ibid.*, July 19–21, 26, 28, 30, 1967.
34. St. Louis *Post-Dispatch*, *op. cit.*
35. *Ibid.*
36. *New York Times*, July 21, 1967.
37. *Ibid.*, July 24, 1967.
38. *Ibid.*, July 31, 1967.
39. *Ibid.*, July 26, 1967. Chicago *Daily News*, August 5, 1967.
40. *New York Times*, August 10, 11, 15, 16, 1967.
41. *Military Export Reporter*, July 27, 1967, p. 290.

CHAPTER V

1. These three objectives are prominently displayed on most ILN literature.
2. *Der Spiegel*, No. 5, 1966. *New York Times*, August 30, 1966, December 13, 1968.
3. *The Observer* (London), February 21, 1965.
4. *New York Times*, February 18, 1965.
5. *The Observer*, February 21, 1965.
6. *The Guardian*, February 11, 1965. *New York Herald Tribune*, February 25, 1965. *The Times*, February 16, 1965. *Financial Times* (London), May 18, 1965.
7. *The Times*, February 7, 1966. *New York Times*, May 20, December 23, 1966.
8. *New York Times*, June 6, 1966.
9. *Die Welt*, June 24, 1966.
10. Schlesinger, Arthur M., Jr. *A Thousand Days* (Houghton Mifflin, Boston, 1965), pp. 856–66. Sheehan, Neil. "You Don't Know Where Johnson Ends and McNamara Begins," *New York Times Magazine*, October 22, 1967.
11. *The Times*, September 14, 1967.
12. *Ibid.*
13. McArdle, Catherine. *The Role of Military Assistance in the Problem of Arms Control: The Middle East, Latin America and Africa* (Center for International Studies, Cambridge, Massachusetts, August 10, 1964), pp. 22–23. *Near Eastern and South Asian Hearings*, p. 50. *The Military Balance 1964–65* (Institute for Strategic Studies, London), p. 26.
14. *Near Eastern and South Asian Hearings*, p. 50. Mydans, Carl

and Shelley. *The Violent Peace* (Atheneum, New York, 1968), pp. 366 ff.

15. *Sunday Telegraph*, September 12, 1965.
16. *Near Eastern and South Asian Hearings*, p. 51.
17. *New York Times*, March 29, 1968. *Hearings before the Committee on Foreign Relations*, U.S. Senate, 90th Congress, 2nd Session, June 20, 1968. "Foreign Military Sales," pp. 34–37.
18. *Hearings before the Committee on Foreign Relations*, U.S. Senate, 89th Congress, 2nd Session. April 6, 18, 20, 25, 27, 29, May 2, 9, 11, 1966, p. 234.
19. *New York Times*, July 14, September 19, December 14, 1966, February 8, 20, 1967.
20. *Ibid.*, February 10, May 6, 7, 1967.
21. *Ibid.*, October 6, 1967, March 31, 1968.
22. See Laqueur, Walter. "The Middle East Is Potentially More Dangerous than Vietnam," *New York Times Magazine*, May 5, 1968.
23. *New York Times*, October 18, 1967.
24. McArdle, *op. cit.*, pp. 44–59. Lieuwen, Edwin. *Arms and Politics in Latin America* (Praeger, New York, 1960; paperback, revised, 4th printing 1967), p. 208.
25. "World-Wide Military Expenditures and Related Data," *op. cit.*, 1965, p. 9.
26. See Lieuwen, *op. cit.*, for best and most thorough critique of the United States' Latin American arms policy, Chapters 8 and 9.
27. *New York Times*, July 21, 1967.
28. *Time*, November 11, 1966.
29. *New York Times*, May 17, 24, 1968.
30. *Armed Forces Management*, January 1967, p. 46. *Military Assistance and Foreign Military Sales Facts* (Defense Department pamphlet), May 1967, p. 35.
31. Green, *op. cit.*, p. 209.

CHAPTER VI

1. Sutton and Kemp, *op. cit.*, p. 28.
2. *Ibid.*, pp. 9, 36–37.
3. *Sale of Military Equipment Abroad*. Second Report from the Select Committee on Estimates, Session 1958–59. London, HMSO.
4. Kemp, *op. cit.*
5. *The Times*, May 6, 1966.
6. *Hansard*, April 8, 1964, col. 1013.
7. *The Statist* (London), October 15, 1965. *Daily Telegraph*, December 5, 1962. Personnel figures quoted at 300 in Saudi Arabia and 200 in Bonn which appear high. *Military Assistance Facts*, May 1, 1966, lists 222 in Saudi Arabia; Hovey, *op. cit.*, p. 79, lists 118 in Bonn in 1966. These latter figures appear to be more accurate.
8. *Interavia* (Geneva), September 1966.
9. Buchan, Alastair. "Arms Nobody Wants to Control," *New Republic*, November 6, 1965.
10. *The Times*, March 22, 1966. *Daily Telegraph*, June 9, 1967.
11. Kuebler, Jeanne. "Traffic in Arms," *Editorial Research Reports*, April 28, 1965, pp. 310–11.

12. *Sunday Times,* January 21, 1968.
13. *Daily Telegraph,* May 13, 1965, February 22, 1966.
14. Tompkins, John S. *The Weapons of World War III* (Doubleday, Garden City, 1966), p. 307.
15. *The Military Balance 1965–66. The Guardian,* September 7, 1965. Sutton and Kemp, *op. cit.,* pp. 40–41.
16. Mimeograph pamphlets distributed by the Institute for Strategic Studies at the outset of the war.
17. Sutton and Kemp, *op. cit.*
18. Washington *Post,* October 1, 1965. *Time,* November 11, 1966.
19. Hovey, *op. cit.,* p. 81. Grant aid actually ceased in 1961, but future commitments carried over into 1964.
20. Kuebler, *op. cit.,* p. 315. Sutton and Kemp, *op. cit.,* p. 28. Hoagland, John H., Jr., and Teeple, John B. "Regional Stability and Weapons Transfer: The Middle Eastern Case," *Orbis,* Fall 1965, pp. 721–23. *Revue Militaire d'Information* (Paris), June 1963.
21. Sutton and Kemp, *op. cit.,* p. 18.
22. *New York Times,* January 14, 1968. *Sunday Times,* February 18, 1968.
23. Washington *Post,* September 1, 1966. *New York Herald Tribune,* January 14, 15, 1967.
24. *Newsweek,* April 1, 1968.
25. Sutton and Kemp, *op. cit.,* pp. 40–41.
26. Hoagland, John H., Jr., and Corning, Erastus, III, *et. al. The Diffusion of Combat Aircraft, Missiles and Their Supporting Technologies.* Report prepared for the Office of the Assistant Secretary of Defense (International Security Affairs), (Browne & Shaw Research Corporation, Waltham, Massachusetts, 1966), p. A16.
27. *Ibid.*
28. Johnson and Lockhoven, *op. cit.,* Vol. II, pp. 203–17.
29. Sutton and Kemp, *op. cit.,* p. 38.
30. *Flying Review* (London), March 1966, p. 402. *Wehr und Wirtschaft* (Munich), April 1966, p. 210. *Air Progress* (New York), May–June 1966, p. 47.
31. *The Economist,* February 20, 1965. *New York Times,* February 21, 1965.
32. *New York Times,* April 5, 1963.
33. Hoagland and Teeple, *op. cit.,* pp. 717–19. Hoagland and Corning, *op. cit.,* pp. E6–E11.
34. *The Guardian,* November 13, December 7, 1963.
35. *Flying Review,* July 1965, pp. 17–26. *Military Review,* February 1967. *New York Times,* November 22, 1967.
36. *Military Review,* February 1967. *Sunday Times,* December 18, 1966.
37. Harlow, *op. cit.,* No. 2, Part 2, p. 56.
38. Hoagland and Corning, *op. cit.,* p. D31.
39. Bloomfield and Leiss, *op. cit.,* Vol. III, pp. 322, 326.

CHAPTER VII

1. Harlow, C. J. E. *Economic Aspects of Defense Procurement,* No. 2, Part 1 of *Defense Technology and the Western Alli-*

ance study series, p. 8. *New York Times,* September 6, 8, 1968.
2. *Sunday Times,* April 21, 1968.
3. E. I. Du Pont de Nemours & Co. Annual Report 1967, p. 52.
4. *Africa Today,* No. 5, 1962, pp. 11–12. *The Observer,* March 28, 1965. *New York Times,* September 2, 1963.
5. Schneider S. A. Annual Report 1966.
6. *Group Panorama,* TH–HB publication (undated, probably 1967).
7. *Der Spiegel,* No. 47, 1967.
8. *Financial Times,* July 12, 1967.
9. Various FN publications.
10. Bofors Annual Report 1966. Swedish Information Service, New York.
11. Directory of Swiss Manufacturers and Producers (Swiss Office for the Development of Trade, 1965). Various company publications.
12. IWK Annual Report 1966, and elsewhere.
13. Batty, Peter. *The House of Krupp* (Stein & Day, New York, 1967), *passim.*
14. Harlow, *op. cit.,* No. 2, Part 2, p. 50.
15. Batty, *op. cit.*, p. 235. *New York Times,* October 8, 1968.
16. NAPCO Master Parts Catalogue, 1960.
17. Harlow, *op. cit., passim.*
18. *Ibid.*
19. *Der Spiegel,* No. 5, 1966.
20. *Ibid.*
21. *Sunday Times,* March 10, 1968. *Time,* March 15, 1968.
22. *Financial Times,* April 19, 1967. *The Guardian,* April 20, 1967.
23. Harlow, *op. cit.,* No. 2, Part 2, p. 18. *Sunday Times,* September 8, 15, 1968. *Time,* September 20, 1968.
24. Harlow, *op. cit.,* No. 2, Part 1, p. 17.
25. *Ibid.*

CHAPTER VIII

1. Georgetown Research Project. *The Soviet Military Aid Program as a Reflection of Soviet Objectives* (Atlantic Research Corporation, Washington, June 24, 1965), pp. 7–8.
2. Ra'anan, Uri. "Tactics in the Third World," *Survey,* October 1965.
3. *Ibid.*
4. *Ibid.*
5. Georgetown Research Project report, p. 5. McArdle, *op. cit.,* p. 29, states 2–3 percent.
6. Hinterhoff, Eugene. "The Pattern of Soviet Military Aid," *The Tablet,* November 24, 1962, p. 1126.
7. Georgetown Research Project report, pp. 18–19.
8. McArdle, *op. cit.,* p. 32.
9. Hoagland, John H., Jr., and Teeple, John B. *Arms Control and Weapons Transfer* (Bendix Corporation, Ann Arbor, August 1965), Section 2, p. 3.
10. Bloomfield and Leiss, *op. cit.,* Vol. III, p. 713.
11. *Time,* June 30, 1967. *Sunday Times,* June 11, 1967. *New York Times,* June 17, 1967.
12. Georgetown Research Project report, pp. 73–74.
13. *Ibid.*
14. *Ibid.*, pp. 61–65.
15. *Christian Science Monitor,* January 14, 1966. *Sunday Telegraph,* January 8, 1967. Parry, Albert. "Soviet Aid to Vietnam," *The*

Reporter, January 12, 1967. *Congressional Record,* January 17, 1967, pp. H256–62. *New York Times,* March 20, 1966, *January* 18, April 12, 1967. *Hearings of the Committee on Foreign Relations,* U.S. Senate, 90th Congress, First Session, February 2, 1967. Testimony of Harrison E. Salisbury, Assistant Managing Editor of the *New York Times,* pp. 8–11, 16, 24.

16. *New York Times,* April 28, November 24, December 1, 1967.
17. Schlesinger, *op. cit.,* pp. 807–8, 903.
18. *New York Times,* July 14, September 19, December 14, 1966, February 8, 13, 20, August 24, 1967. *Milwaukee Journal,* March 5, 1967. *The Times,* September 26, 1967.
19. *New York Times,* March 15, May 22, 1968.
20. Georgetown Research Project report, p. 9.
21. *Near Eastern and South Asian Hearings,* p. 36.
22. Attwood, William. *The Reds and the Blacks* (Harper & Row, New York, 1967), pp. 244–47. Whaley, Barton. *Soviet and Chinese Clandestine Arms Aid,* working draft (Center for International Studies, November 1965).
23. *Daily Telegraph, Daily Express,* August 5, 1961.
24. "Bulgarian Arms Duplicity," Notes of the Month, *African Review,* August 1966.
25. Hutton, J. Bernard. *The Traitor Trade* (Obolensky, New York, 1963), p. 45 ff. Frank, Lewis A. *The Arms Trade in International Relations* (Praeger, 1969), p. 181.
26. Schlesinger, *op. cit.,* pp. 574–75. Lefever, Ernest W. *Crisis in the Congo* (Brookings Institution, Washington, 1965), *passim. Sunday Telegraph,* February 19, 1961, November 24, 1963.
27. *Daily Telegraph,* April 27, 1965.
28. *New York Times,* December 13, 1964, April 13, 1965. *The Times,* December 15, 1964. *Sunday Telegraph,* January 24, 1965.
29. *New York Times,* March 2, 1965.
30. *New York Herald Tribune,* April 24, 25, July 12, 1965.
31. Attwood, *op. cit.,* p. 69. *New York Times,* November 11, 1963. *Observer,* July 24, 1966.
32. *Hearings of the Committee on Foreign Relations,* U.S. Senate, 89th Congress, 2nd Session, April 25, 1966, p. 234.
33. Attwood, *op. cit.,* p. 248.
34. *New York Herald Tribune,* April 19, 1966. *The Times,* November 12, 1964. Warner, Denis. "China Fans the Fires," *The Reporter,* January 14, 1965.
35. Yu, George T. "China's Failure in Africa," *Asian Survey,* August 1966. Author's views applicable to other areas of the world besides Africa.

PART FOUR: CONCLUSION

CHAPTER IX

1. *Armed Forces Management,* January 1967, p. 40. Henry Kuss speech to American Ordnance Association, October 20, 1966.
2. Bloomfield and Leiss, *op. cit.,* Vol. II, pp. 111–13.

Bibliography

Arms Control and Disarmament Agency. *World-Wide Defense Expenditures and Selected Economic Data,* 1964, 1965. ACDA Research Reports.

Bakal, Carl. *The Right to Bear Arms,* McGraw-Hill, New York, 1966.

Batty, Peter. *The House of Krupp,* Stein & Day, New York, 1967.

Bell, M. J. V. *Army and Nation in Sub-Saharan Africa,* Adelphi Paper No. 21, Institute for Strategic Studies, London, August 1965.

———. *Military Assistance to Independent African States,* Adelphi Paper No. 15, Institute for Strategic Studies, London, December 1964.

Blackstock, Paul W. *The Strategy of Subversion,* Quadrangle, Chicago, 1964.

Bloomfield, Lincoln P., and Leiss, Amelia C., *et al. The Control of Local Conflict* (A Design Study on Arms Control and Limited War in the Developing Areas). 3 vols. Center for International Studies, Massachusetts Institute of Technology, Cambridge, June 30, 1967. Prepared for ACDA.

Buchan, Alastair. *The Implications of a European System for Defense Technology.* No. 6 (of 6) of *Defense Technology and the Western Alliance* study series, Institute for Strategic Studies, London, 1967.

Calmann, John. *European Co-operation in Defense Technology: The Political Aspect.* Number 1 of *Defense Technology and the Western Alliance* study series, Institute for Strategic Studies, London, 1967.

Center for International Studies. *Regional Arms Control Arrangements for Developing Countries,* Cambridge, Massachusetts, 1964. Report prepared for ACDA.

Committee on Foreign Relations, U.S. Senate. *Arms Sales and Foreign Policy.* Staff Study pamphlet, 1967.

Dallin, Alexander, *et. al.* *The Soviet Union, Arms Control and Disarmament: A Study of Soviet Attitudes,* School of International Affairs, Columbia University, New York, 1964.

Department of Defense. *Military Assistance and Foreign Military Sales Facts,* pamphlet, May 1967.

———. *Foreign Military Sales Facts,* pamphlet, May 1967.

———. *Military Assistance Facts,* pamphlets, March 1, 1966, May 1, 1966.

Department of State. *International Traffic in Arms.* Federal Register, Vol. 31, No. 233, December 2, 1966, Part II (Revisions of Rules and Regulations).

Dinerstein, H. S. *War and the Soviet Union,* Praeger, New York, 1962.

Engelbrecht, H. C., and Hanighen, F. C. *Merchants of Death,* Dodd, Mead, New York, 1934.

Ewing, Laurence L., and Sellers, Robert C. *1966 Reference Handbook of the Armed Forces of the World,* Robert C. Sellers and Associates, Washington, 1966.

Frank, Lewis A. *The Arms Trade in International Relations,* Praeger, New York, 1969.

Garthoff, Raymond L. *Soviet Military Policy,* Praeger, New York, 1966.

Georgetown Research Project. *The Soviet Military Aid Program as a Reflection of Soviet Objectives.* Atlantic Research Corporation, Washington, D.C., 1965.

Green, William. *The World's Fighting Planes,* Doubleday, Garden City, 1965 (revised edition).

Gutteridge, William. *Armed Forces in New States,* Oxford University Press, London, 1962.

Harlow, C. J. E. *The European Armaments Base: A Survey: Part 1: Economic Aspects of Defense Procurement, Part 2: National Procurement Policies.* No. 2 of *Defense Technology and the Western Alliance* study series, Institute for Strategic Studies, London, 1967.

Hatch, Alden. *Remington Arms in American History,* Rinehart, New York, 1956.

Hoagland, John H., Jr., and Corning, Erastus III, *et. al.* *The Diffusion of Combat Aircraft, Missiles and Their Supporting Technologies,* Browne & Shaw Research Corporation, Waltham, Massachusetts, 1966. Report prepared for the Office of the Assistant Secretary of Defense (International Security Affairs).

Hoagland, John H., Jr., and Teeple, John B. *Arms Control and Weapons Transfer: The Middle Eastern Case,* Bendix Systems Division, Bendix Corporation, Ann Arbor, August 1965.

Hovey, Harold A. *United States Military Assistance,* Praeger, New York, 1965.

Hunt, Kenneth. *The Requirements of Military Technology in the 1970's.* No. 5 of *Defense Technology and the Western Alliance* study series, Institute for Strategic Studies, London, 1967.

Hutton, J. Bernard. *The Traitor Trade,* Obolensky, New York, 1963.

Institute for Strategic Studies. *Strategic Survey 1966.* London, 1967.

———. *The Military Balance 1962–* . Yearly publication; earliest titles vary slightly.

Institute of International Education. *Military Assistance Training Programs of the U.S. Government.* Institute of International Education, New York, 1964.

James, Robert Rhodes. *Standardization and Common Production of Weapons in NATO.* No. 3 of *Defense Technology and the Western Alliance* study series, Institute for Strategic Studies, London, 1967.

Jane's All the World's Aircraft. Yearly publication, Sampson Low, Marston & Co., London.

Jane's Fighting Ships. Yearly publication. Sampson Low, Marston & Co., London.

Janowitz, Morris. *The Military in the Political Development of New Nations,* University of Chicago Press, Chicago, 1964.

Johnson, George B., and Lockhoven, Hans Bert. *International Armament,* 2 vols. International Small Arms Publishers, Cologne, Germany, 1965.

Johnson, John J. (ed.) *The Role of the Military in Underdeveloped Countries,* Princeton University Press, Princeton, 1962.

Kramish, Arnold. *Atlantic Technological Imbalance: An American Perspective.* No. 4 of *Defense Technology and the Western Alliance* study series, Institute for Strategic Studies, London, 1967.

Lieuwen, Edwin. *Arms and Politics in Latin America,* Praeger, New York, 1961.

McArdle, Catherine. *The Role of Military Assistance in the Problem of Arms Control: The Middle East, Latin America and Africa.* Center for International Studies, Cambridge, Massachusetts, 1964. Report prepared for ACDA.

McCormick, Donald. *Pedlar of Death,* Macdonald, London, 1965.

Meyer, Karl E., and Szulc, Tad. *The Cuban Invasion,* Praeger, New York, 1962.

Millis, Walter. *Arms and Men.* Putnam's, New York, 1956.

———. *Road to War.* Houghton Mifflin, Boston, 1935.

Report of the Committee of Inquiry into the Aircraft Industry 1964–65 (Plowden Report), London, HMSO, Cmnd. 2853, December 1965.

Sale of Military Equipment Abroad. Second Report from the Select Committee on Estimates, Session 1958–59, London, HMSO.

Smith, W. H. B. *Small Arms of the World.* Stackpole, Harrisburg, Pennsylvania, 1943 (revised periodically).

Sutton, John L., and Kemp, Geoffrey. *Arms to Developing Countries 1945–65,* Adelphi Paper No. 28, Institute for Strategic Studies, London, October 1966.

Washburn, Alan V. *Compendium of U.S. Laws on Controlling Arms Exports,* ACDA Research Report, May 1966.

Whaley, Barton. *Soviet and Chinese Clandestine Arms Aid,* working draft. Center for International Studies, Cambridge, Massachusetts, 1965. As yet unpublished.

Wiltz, John Edward. *In Search of Peace: The Senate Munitions Inquiry, 1934–36.* Louisiana State University Press, Baton Rouge, 1963.

Wood, David. *Armed Forces in Central and South America,* Adelphi Paper No. 34, Institute for Strategic Studies, London, April 1967.

———. *The Armed Forces of African States,* Adelphi Paper No. 27, Institute for Strategic Studies, London, April 1966.

———. *The Middle East and the Arab World: The Military Context,* Adelphi Paper No. 20, Institute for Strategic Studies, London, July 1965.

Wright, Quincy. *A Study of War.* University of Chicago Press, 1965.

Other valuable sources of information are the *Christian Science Monitor, Daily* and *Sunday Telegraph, Der Spiegel, New York Times,* the London *Sunday Times* and *The Times,* and the Washington *Post;* also *Africa Confidential* (London), *Air et Cosmos* (Paris), *Air Pictorial* (London), *Air Progress* (New York), *Alata Internazionale* (Milan), *Armed Forces Management* (Washington), *Avia* (Rotterdam), *Aviation Magazine International* (Paris), *Aviation Week and Space Technology* (New York), *Flight International* (London), *Flugwelt-Flug Revue* (Stuttgart), *Flying Review International* (London), *Interavia* (Geneva), *Military Export Reporter* (Washington), *Military Review* (Ft. Leavenworth, Kansas), *Missiles and Rockets* (Washington), *Ordnance* (Washington), and *Wehr und Wirtschaft* (Munich).

The *Congressional Record* and *Hansard* are good sources of information; so too are published transcripts of hearings before the Senate Committee on Foreign Relations (and its various subcommittees), the Senate Subcommittee to Investigate Juvenile Delinquency of the Committee on the Judiciary, and the House and Senate Appropriations Committees.

Index

About the Author

George Thayer was born in 1933 in Philadelphia, Pa., and educated at St. Paul's School, the University of Pennsylvania and the London School of Economics.

Since 1963 he has devoted himself to writing and political research. He worked for a year as a research assistant to the late Randolph Churchill on the biography of Sir Winston Churchill, and his first book, *The British Political Fringe,* was published in England in 1965. His second book, *The Farther Shores of Politics,* was published in 1967 and won immediate acclaim.

Mr. Thayer now lives in Washington, D.C.